Our
Daily
Bread
Favorites

Our
Daily
Bread
Favorites

Discovery House

Our Daily Bread Favorites

Editors:
RICHARD W. DEHAAN and HENRY G. BOSCH

Additional Contributors:
HERBERT VANDER LUGT and PAUL VAN GORDER

Daybreak Books
Zondervan Publishing House
Grand Rapids, Michigan

OUR DAILY BREAD FAVORITES

Copyright © 1967, 1968, 1969, 1970, 1971
by Radio Bible Class

Daybreak Books are published by Zondervan
Publishing House, 1415 Lake Drive, S.E.,
Grand Rapids, Michigan 49506

ISBN 0-310-23590-1

Library of Congress Catalog Card Number 73-156257

Printed in the United States of America

88 — 20

FOREWORD

The *Our Daily Bread* devotional guide, first published in 1956, has grown to be one of the leading ministries of Radio Bible Class.

The original format, with its goal of presenting the practical truths of God's Word in a palatable way and replete with true-to-life illustrations, soon caught the public fancy. Carefully honed literarily, each meditation from its title to its closing "thought for the day" is designed to exhibit unswerving continuity. Its pointedness is intended to produce a pleasing and unified spiritual impact.

With millions now reading the monthly editions, this cloth-bound volume, compiled by popular request, gathers together in permanent form the "cream selections" from the last five years of publication.

We send it forth with the prayer that fresh blessings will be generated for you from the Word of God on which its messages are firmly based.

If your heart is warmed and your soul is drawn closer to the Savior through these meditations, our highest goal will have been attained.

Joyfully in His Service,
The Editors
RICHARD W. DEHAAN
HENRY G. BOSCH

Our
Daily
Bread
Favorites

HAPPY NEW YEAR

*Happy is he that hath . . . God . . . for his help, whose
hope is in the Lord, his God.*   Psalm 146:5

The wish for happiness repeated by countless millions today is
often just a formality. For some it's another way of saying, "Good
luck!" For others it's a genuine heartfelt expression of their desire for God's blessing upon their friends. In this spirit we say
"Happy New Year" to you.

The Bible tells us how we can be sure of a year filled with
366 days of gladness and blessing. Psalm 146:5 declares, "Happy
is he that hath . . . God . . . for his help, whose hope is in the
Lord." This is the formula for true and lasting joy. An aware-
ness of God as our Heavenly Father, Sustainer, and Protector,
combined with a wholehearted and deep-seated trust and confidence in His Word, produces a tranquillity and brightness of spirit
which even the most severe testings of life cannot destroy. Notice
the words of the Psalmist: *"Blessed* are all they who put their
trust in him" (Ps. 2:12); "Thou hast put *gladness* in my heart
. . ." (Ps. 4:7); "O God . . . the children of men put their trust
under the shadow of thy wings. They shall be abundantly *satisfied* . . . and thou shalt make them drink of the river of thy
pleasures" (Ps. 36:7, 8); "For he satisfieth the longing soul, and
filleth the hungry soul with *goodness"* (Ps. 107:9).

Blessedness, gladness, satisfaction, pleasures, and goodness — all
of this and much more is reserved for the one "whose hope is
in the Lord."

If you place your trust in God through faith in His Son, this
will be the happiest year you have ever known!

> *I know the year I now begin*
> *A happy year will be,*
> *If Thou dost guide, and I but do*
> *The thing that pleaseth Thee.* —Anon.

**The Christian's future is always as bright as the promises of
God!**

"TIME" AND "ETERNITY"

*See, then, that ye walk circumspectly, not as fools but
as wise, Redeeming the time, because the days are evil.*
Ephesians 5:15, 16

Recently, at a conference of magazine publishers in the United
States, the respresentatives were requested to stand and give the
name of their publication. Inevitably it seemed that a delegate
from the Christian magazine, *Eternity*, always followed one from
the secular periodical, *Time*. A burst of laughter among the delegates resulted when TIME and ETERNITY were thus linked together. Yet there is food for thought here, for indeed the two are
vitally related and closely interlocked. The final rewards and
position of the saved will be governed by their faithfulness, after
their conversion, in filling the hours here with loving service,
holy adoration, and diligent study. The lost too will be beaten
with "few" or "many stripes" in relation to their deeds and attitudes while here on earth. Therefore, someone has wisely written:
"Use well opportunity, drift not with the tide; killing time is not
murder, it's *suicide!*" Indeed, eternity will *magnify* that which
we have done in *time*.

May I make a practical suggestion for the new year? Always
carry something with you to fill the moments that would otherwise be spent in idleness. For instance, take with you a little New
Testament which you can study and mark up as you wait your
turn in the doctor's office; or a text — printed on a card — which
you can memorize while you ride the bus to work; or a notebook
in which you jot down helpful suggestions or prayer requests.
These are all good ways to "redeem the time" and make golden
investments in eternity.

Too busy to read the Bible, too busy to wait and pray!
Too busy to speak out kindly to someone by the way!
Too busy to care and struggle, to think of the life to come,
Too busy building mansions to plan for the heavenly Home.
Too busy for all that is holy on earth beneath the sky,
Too busy to serve the Master, but — not too busy to die!
—Anon.

**ETERNITY will be appreciated only in the measure that we
have rightly handled TIME!**   —F. King

GOD LOVES NAUGHTY BOYS

*But God commendeth his love toward us in that, while
we were yet sinners, Christ died for us.*   Romans 5:8

The love of God goes beyond all human comprehension. With
our finite minds we cannot fully grasp the significance of this
truth. It is impossible to fathom how a holy God should so love
sinners that He would actually give His very own Son to die that
they might be saved. Who of us would ever give one of our
precious children to die that the world's worst criminal might be
spared from paying his just debt to society?

God's love for sinners is beautifully emphasized in a story told
by the late Dr. H. A. Ironside. When he was a lad he attended
a missionary meeting where the speaker displayed many interesting curios which he had brought back from the field. Right in
the middle of his talk, however, he stopped abruptly, and said,
"Boys, I'd like to tell you what kind of Gospel we preach to the
people in Africa. But, first of all, this one question: How many
good boys do we have in the room today?" All of those present
wanted to raise their hands, but not a one dared — their mothers
were there and they knew better! Since not a hand was lifted,
the missionary continued, "If that's the case, then the message I
have for you is exactly the same that we give to the heathen in
Africa, for God loves *naughty* boys!" Dr. Ironside says that as a
lad he first rebelled against that statement, since he had always
heard that the Lord loved you if you were *good.* But then, as the
speaker continued, he discovered that the missionary was right
after all. God did not wait for people to become good before He
decided to save them. Rather, "God commendeth his love toward
us, in that, while we were *yet sinners,* Christ died for us."

Yes, God *hates* sin, but He loves the *sinner.* Have you taken
time to thank Him for His love today?

> The love of God is greater far
>   Than tongue or pen can ever tell;
> It goes beyond the highest star,
>   And reaches to the lowest Hell. —F. M. Lehman

God loves us out of His own nature, and not on conditions.
                                                        —Beecher

A BLESSED, TRANSFORMING BOOK

*The law [the revealed truth] of the Lord is perfect,
converting the soul.*   Psalm 19:7

When Columbus sailed into the mouth of the Orinoco River,
he said in substance, "Gentlemen, this is not an island but a con-
tinent; for there is no such river in a small body of land." The
great volume of water in that mighty stream was absolute proof
to him of the vastness of the area it drained. Commenting on
this, David L. Cooper says, "Thus, as I stand before the Word
of God, I behold such a flood of marvelous truths regarding every
phase of life . . . that I am led to exclaim, 'Scripture, like a
fathomless river of perfection, flows from the boundless source
of the infinite wisdom of God.'" Yes, the Lord's written revelation is a reservoir of knowledge and blessing which when appro-
priated "converts the soul."

A man selling individual books of the Bible was stopped and
robbed one night as he passed through a forest in Sicily, and was
ordered to burn his wares. After lighting a fire, he asked if he
might read aloud a brief porition from each before surrendering
them to the flames. Given permission, he read from one the
twenty-third Psalm, from another the Sermon on the Mount,
from another the parable of the Good Samaritan, and from another Paul's hymn of love in 1 Corinthians 13. After each ex-
cerpt the outlaw exclaimed, *"That's a good book!* We won't burn
that, give it to me." Consequently, none were destroyed but all
were taken by the thief. Some years later the robber appeared
again, but now as *an ordained minister!* Reading the Bible had
accomplished the miracle.

How much do you know of this blessed, instructive and transforming Book?

> *Thy Word's a land of wealth unknown*
> *Where springs of life arise;*
> *There seeds of holy bliss are sown,*
> *And hidden glories rise.*   —Watts

The Bible is an inexhaustible mine of knowledge and virtue!
                                                     —Adams

"SOUL MUSIC"

> *And he hath put a new song in my mouth, even praise*
> *unto our God.*   Psalm 40:3

In an article dealing with "soul music," *Time Magazine* carried the following comment: "Has it got soul? Man, that's the question of the hour. If it has, then it's tough, beautiful, out of sight. It passes the test of with-it-ness . . . . But what is soul? It is a way of life—yet it is always the hard way. Its essence is ingrained in those who suffer and endure only to laugh about it later."

I don't know what you think about today's so-called "soul music," but I came across something the other day which I feel is *real "soul music."* The world might not call it such; but to the trusting child of God, it reaches down into the innermost depths of one's being and lifts the heart until it renders enthusiastic and fervent praise to God. I found a song on the time-yellowed pages of a Methodist hymnbook which, while it is ancient, has real "soul." Listen to it: "Let not the wise their wisdom boast, the mighty glory in their might; the rich in flattering riches trust, which take their everlasting flight. The rush of numerous years bears down the most gigantic strength of man; and where is all his wisdom gone, when dust, he turns to dust again? One gift alone can justify the boasting soul that knows his God; when Jesus doth His blood apply, I glory in His sprinkled blood. The Lord my righteousness I praise; I triumph in the love divine: the wisdom, wealth, and strength of grace, in Christ to endless ages mine."

This is the *real* "soul music" — that "new song" which the Lord gives us, "even praise unto our God."

> *Awake, my soul, to joyful lays,*
> *And sing thy great Redeemer's praise;*
> *He justly claims a song from me,*
> *His loving-kindness, oh, how free!* — Medley

Only those whose souls have struck the deepest notes of penitence can reach the highest notes of praise!

PRECIOUS IN HIS SIGHT

*Take heed that ye despise not one of these little
ones . . . .*   Matthew 18:10

Some Christians need to be humbled because they have too
exalted an opinion of themselves; others stand in constant need
of encouragement because they have a tendency to dwell too much
upon their own inadequacies. One of the problems a minister
faces is that of preaching messages which will convict the proud
without utterly discouraging those who have a difficult time believing they could possibly be precious in the sight of God.

Our Savior, using a little child as an object lesson, very effectively humbled the self-seeking disciples; yet, at the same time,
He showed lowly believers that they were important in God's
sight. He told the Twelve they needed to become like that little
one, ever realizing their personal inadequacy and their complete
dependency upon Him. If they failed to do so, they would not
be fit to take their places in His kingdom. Our Lord then pointed
out that every Christian, however obscure and unimportant in
the eyes of man, is still precious to God. To fellowship with
these lowly ones is to honor the Savior (v. 5), but should unbelievers seek to harm them, Jesus warns that such persecutors
will be severely judged (vv. 6, 7). Moreover, to despise any of
those who come to Christ in a childlike spirit is to take a position
which is completely contrary to God's attitude toward them. He
has, in fact, appointed holy angels as their representatives in the
court of Heaven. As the shepherd is concerned about one stray-
ing sheep, so the Lord Jesus places great value upon even the
lowliest believer.

Christian, you are important to God! He will judge all who
seek to harm you and has provided you with angelic guardians.
You need not fear that He will ever let you perish!

> *The humble, God will keep and bless;*
> *They are the objects of His grace.*
> *To such, His promises are sure;*
> *Their angels e'er shall see His face!* — Bosch

**To have the comforts of grace and God's full blessing, humble
yourself; for the holy place is ever the lowly place!**

"TOGETHER FOREVER"

. . . so shall we ever be with the Lord.
1 Thessalonians 4:17

My wife Margaret and I have found it very interesting to walk through cemeteries. Our children cannot understand, thinking it rather morbid and gruesome. We don't see it that way — death is a reality, and we might as well face it. The believer, especially, should be able to look it "straight in the eye," since Christ has removed its "sting." The real reason for our strolls, however, is to read the various epitaphs on the markers. They tell a great deal about a person's past life and his future hope. We have had many good sermons from the "messages" engraved on tablets of marble. For instance, First Thessalonians 4:16 is inscribed on my father's gravestone as a testimony. It speaks of "That Blessed Hope" which pervaded and influenced his entire ministry and life.

Just a few days ago, we saw a number of markers in a St. Petersburg cemetery, all bearing the message "Together Forever." The thought struck me with real force — these words can either express a tremendous blessing or a terrible fate. I don't know anything about the people buried there; but if they truly knew the Lord Jesus Christ as Savior, the fact that they — husband and wife — were "together forever" with the Lord was a most comforting thought. However, if they were not saved, they were "together forever" all right, but in the place of suffering and separation from God. This is almost unbearable to contemplate.

First Thessalonians 4:17 tells of the coming of the Lord Jesus Christ when we who know Him will be caught up *together* with our loved ones in Christ, and then "shall we *ever be with the Lord.*" That thought, "together forever" with Him, certainly brings comfort and joyous anticipation to the heart of every believer. We would cry out with John in Revelation, "Even so, come, Lord Jesus" (Rev. 22:20).

> *When we all get to Heaven,*
> *What a day of rejoicing that will be!*
> *When we all see Jesus,*
> *We'll sing and shout the victory.*—Eliza E. Hewitt

He who is on the road to Heaven should not be content to go alone!

KNOWING HEREAFTER

*What I do thou knowest not now, but thou shalt
know hereafter.*   John 13:7

The disciples did not always understand what Jesus said and
did. Like the blind man of Bethsaida in our Scripture reading
for today, their prophetic insight was as distorted as one who
sees "men as trees walking." In John 13:7 Jesus tells them not
to become confused or bewildered by the heartbreaking events
that were to transpire. They were to proceed by faith, resting on
the precious promise that "hereafter" they would comprehend His
wise purposes.

There is an old Hebrew legend that tells of a rabbi journeying
on a mule through a wild country. His only companion was a
rooster whose shrill crowing at sunrise awoke him to his devotions.
He came to a small town at nightfall and sought shelter, but the
inhabitants turned him away. Outside the village he found a cave
in which to sleep. He lit his lamp before retiring, but a gust of
wind blew out the light. During the night a wolf killed his
rooster and a lion devoured his mule. Early in the morning he
went to the town to see if he could buy some food. To his surprise he found no one alive. A band of robbers during the night
had plundered the settlement and killed all the inhabitants. "Now
I understand my troubles," said the rabbi. "If the townspeople
had received me, I would now be dead. Had not my rooster and
mule been killed their noise or the light of my lamp would have
revealed my hiding place. God has been good to me."

Christian, trust the Lord's wise leading. You may not understand it all now, but you shall know *"hereafter."*

> *I know not now why schemes were spoiled
> And lofty aspirations foiled;
> I know not now why briars and thorn
> Should mar ambitions nobly born.
> Hereafter I shall know, shall see
> These very things were best for me!* —A.G.

We must TRUST God even when we cannot TRACE Him!

REMEMBRANCE

. . . he remembereth the obedience of you all. . . .
                                        2 Corinthians 7:15

Two preachers, who for some reason never got along very well, met on the street one day. The one said, "I heard you speak the other night, and recognized that sermon as one you preached fourteen years ago." The other, somewhat chagrined by this intended dig, retaliated, "I heard you speak just three weeks ago, and *I can't remember a word you said!*" There's a lesson which can be drawn from this incident: our lives should be like *good* sermons, conveying a "message" *worth remembering,* that we in turn may motivate others to godly living. When your life's course has been run, what will folks recall about you? Will your influence have been good or bad?

I read recently about a woman who, when she was dying, complained, "I'm just afraid that when I'm gone nobody will remember me." Her devoted husband took steps at once to have a horticulturist develop a flower to be named for her. As lovely as that bloom might be, the "fragrance of remembrance" produced by the beautiful flower of a godly life is much more to be desired! It not only blesses others, but its sweet perfume ascends to the very throne of Heaven itself. It's all right to have a flower named for you, but how much better a tribute it is if you are remembered as a devoted Christian — a person who loved the Lord and His Word, and who exemplified the Savior in every action.

For what will you be remembered? How tragic to be a Diotrephes, of whom John wrote: "I will remember his deeds which he doeth, prating against us with malicious word" (3 John 10). How much more blessed the memories Paul had concerning Timothy, for in writing to him he said, "I am . . . *mindful* of thy tears" and "call to remembrance the unfeigned faith that is in thee . . ." (2 Tim. 1:5).

Is your life "preaching" the kind of a "sermon" which will long be remembered? Or will folks say, "I can't recall a word he 'said'!"

So live that when you come to die even the undertaker will be sorry!
                                                      —S. C.

THE "LAMB-LIFE"

> . . . *accused . . . he answered nothing.* Mark 15:3
> . . . *as a sheep . . . dumb, so he openeth not his*
> *mouth.*   Isaiah 53:7

Recently I was blessed and convicted in my own soul by the penetrating comments of Mrs. Penn-Lewis, on these and other verses dealing with the amazing silences of Jesus. She began by calling attention to the fact that *the "lamb-life" is characterized by silence!* That is, the sanctified Christian who is living close to his God will manifest humility and supreme self-control under the most adverse and trying circumstances. Says Mrs. Lewis: "We will be *silent* in our lowly service among others, not seeking to be 'seen of men.' *Silent* over the glory of the hours on the mount lest others think of us above that which they ought. *Silent* while we stoop to serve the very ones who betrayed us. *Silent* when forced by others to some position where apparent rivalry with another much-used servant of God seems imminent, only to be hushed by utter self-effacement in our silent withdrawal without explanation, irrespective of our 'rights.' *Silent* when our words are misquoted."

After additional suggestions on the silences of consecration and humility, Mrs. Lewis concludes her article with this impassioned prayer: "O Thou anointed Christ, the Lamb of God, Thou alone canst live this life of silent self-effacement in a world of self-assertion and self-love. *Live Thou this life in me!*"

Are you set on always "getting your rights"? Will you argue for hours to make others understand your "reasonable position"? Then you still have much to learn from *the silences of Jesus!* Oh, may it be said of us as it is of that blessed company in Revelation 14: "These are they *who follow the Lamb* wherever he goeth" (Rev. 14:4)!

> *"Hold Thou my tongue" — for oh, I cannot guard it,*
>   *Unless Thou teach me to control each word.*
> *Guard Thou my thoughts, lest haply I should whisper*
>   *Something to grieve my Savior and my Lord!*
>   — Gladys Roberts

Though the human tongue weighs practically nothing, it is surprising how few persons are able to hold it!—Wm. A. Ward

APPROVED!

Study to show thyself approved unto God, a workman that needeth not to be ashamed.   2 Timothy 2:15

In Paul's exhortation, "Study to show thyself approved unto God," he encourages us to avoid the very thing he feared might happen to him personally; namely, that he might be set aside and no longer used in the Lord's service. He says in 1 Corinthians 9:27, "I keep under my body, and bring it into subjection, lest that by any means, when I have preached to others, I myself should be a *castaway.*" This word is a translation of the same Greek root rendered *"approved"* in 2 Timothy 2:15, only in 1 Corinthians 9:27 it appears in a negative form and means *"disapproved."* When the apostle speaks of his dread of being a "castaway," he is really thinking of the shame of being a "disapproved" one, not of being lost again. His fear is that he might not receive approval as a workman. He has *service* in mind, not salvation!

I have been told that a huge block of stone lies in a Syrian quarry near Baalbek. It has been carefully cut, hewed, and squared. Sixty-eight feet long, fourteen feet high, and fourteen feet wide, its size is overwhelming. And yet, in spite of all the labor and effort which went into this gigantic piece of rock, there it stands. *It was never fitted into that place in the temple for which it was intended!* This massive stone seems to lift a voice of warning, repeating the words of the apostle, "lest that by any means, when I have preached to others, I myself should be a *castaway.*"

May we be faithful in our devotional life, obedient to the will of God, and zealous in our service for Him. In so doing, we will stand *"approved"!*

> *I want among the victor throng*
>   *Someday to have my name confessed;*
> *And hear my Master say at last,*
>   *"You stand approved, you did your best!"*—Simpson

Serving the Lord is much like riding a bicycle—either you keep moving forward, or you fall down.

PLANNED NEGLECT

*But seek ye first the kingdom of God . . . and all these
things shall be added unto you.*   Matthew 6:33

Have you ever noticed how the saints in the Bible were eager
to let God have His way in their lives? They bestirred themselves
as soon as dawn touched the sky in order to worship Him and
seek His leading. For example, Abraham got up very early to
stand before the Lord (Gen. 19:27). Jacob in like manner arose
from his stony pillows to worship God after having seen a vision
of angels in the night (Gen. 28:18). Moses went early to meet
the Lord at Sinai (Ex. 34:4). Joshua did the same when he prepared to capture Jericho (Josh. 6:12), and Gideon followed their
example when he made his way at dawn to examine the fleece
that he had cast upon the ground to discern Jehovah's will (Judg.
6:38). Hannah and Elkanah arose early to worship God (1 Sam.
1:19), as did Samuel when he went to meet Saul (1 Sam. 15:
12). Job left his warm bed to offer sacrifices for his children
(Job 1:5), and the faithful women who had followed the Savior
arose at daybreak that they might go to the sepulcher on the first
Easter morn (Mark 16:2). Say, have you ever gotten up early
to study God's Word, to pray, and to seek His will? Does He
have priority in all you do?

A noted young concert artist was asked the secret of her success
with the violin. *"Planned neglect!"* she replied, and then explained. "Years ago I discovered that there were many things
which demanded my time. After washing breakfast dishes, I made
my bed, straightened my room, dusted the furniture, and did a
host of other things. I then turned my attention to violin practice.
That system, however, failed to accomplish the desired results.
So I realized I had to reverse things. I deliberately set aside everything else until my practice period was ended. That program of
planned neglect accounts for my success!"

Christian, put priority on daily Bible study and prayer, even
if you must neglect some secondary things. "Seek ye *first* the
kingdom of God!"

He who puts God first will find God with him at the last!

USE THE "STRAIGHT RULER"

*Thy word have I hidden in mine heart, that I
might not sin against thee.*   Psalm 119:11

The new morality really isn't new. When you analyze it, you
discover at its core *the old immorality!* It stems from man's desire to cast off the restraints which absolute moral standards
place upon his conduct. One who doubts God's Word and follows instead the dictates of his own reason invites trouble. Mother
Eve took this ill-considered course and lost true righteousness.
In like manner, the *new* morality as well as the *old* immorality
are both deviations from the *true* morality.

The importance of following the unchanging and perfect guide-
lines established by God Himself can be seen in the following
story: "The Bible is too strict and old-fashioned," said a young
man to a gray-haired friend who had been advising him to study
God's Word if he would learn how to live. "There are plenty
of books written today that are moral enough in their teaching
which don't bind me down as the Scriptures do." Without saying a word, the old merchant turned to his desk and picked up
a couple of rulers, one of which was slightly bent. With each of
these, he drew a line and silently handed the paper to his young
friend. "Well," said the lad, "what are you trying to say?" "Just
this," he replied, "notice that one line is straight; the other is
crooked. When you mark your path in life, *be sure to use the
straight ruler!*"

The pathway of true morality leads us through the pages of
God's Holy Word, the Bible. "Wherewithal shall a young man
cleanse his way?" asks the Psalmist; to which he supplies the answer: *"By taking heed thereto according to thy word"* (Ps. 119:9).

> *Thy Word is a lamp to my feet,*
> *A light to my path alway,*
> *To guide and to save me from sin,*
> *And show me the heavenly way.* — E.O.S.

**The Bible will keep you from sin — or sin will keep you from
the Bible!**

THE GREAT DISCOVERY

. . . We have found the Messiah . . . . John 1:41

The renowned physician Sir James Simpson was the first to employ ether in obstetrics and to discover the important qualities and proper use of chloroform. A group of young scientists who highly respected Dr. Simpson asked him, "What do you count as the most outstanding discovery you have ever made?" With tears welling up in his eyes he lifted his head and said, "Young men, the greatest discovery I have ever made is that Jesus Christ is my Savior; that is by far the most important thing a person can ever come to know!" Yes, one can make no greater discovery than this. Whenever men have "found" Jesus Christ they have learned that He makes good on His promises and by His transforming power does something wonderful for them, in them, and through them.

While it is true that for Andrew, Philip, John, Peter, and the rest of the Twelve, "finding Christ" meant poverty, hardship, suffering, persecution, and, in fact, death by execution for most; yet they also discovered in Him a Savior, Lord, Companion and Friend. Those who come to know the Lord today find Him equally precious. As a pastor I have spoken to parents a few moments after a child was suddenly snatched from them by an automobile accident, a drowning, or a brief illness. I have been present as a husband or wife passed from time into eternity, thus disrupting the closest of all human ties; and yet the surviving loved ones experienced God's peace and comfort. I have stood at the bedside of men who had suffered a severe coronary attack — when their life was still in jeopardy — who have calmly testified to our Lord's keeping and sustaining power. Several have exclaimed, "God's way is best. If He wishes to take me, I am ready." Yes, I have seen Christians experience all kinds of sorrow, heartache, and disappointment; but in every case when they were in fellowship with Jesus Christ, I have witnessed in their lives God's strengthening power. The Lord has never failed those who have put their trust in Him. Have you discovered Jesus Christ?

Christ is not valued at all, until He is valued above all!
—Augustine

NOT LIKE THE MULE

Be ye not like the horse, or like the mule . . . . Psalm 32:9

A certain man, prominent in society, asked a church dignitary whether it was according to the rules of etiquette to "say grace" at a banquet table. The preacher replied, "I do not know much about etiquette, but I remember seeing on the wall of a farmer's home a picture showing mules and oxen at a crib. They were devouring the fodder and scattering some of it beneath their feet, and over the picture was this inscription:

> "Who, without prayer, sits down to eat,
> And, without thanks, then leaves the table,
> Tramples the gift of God with feet,
> And is like mule and ox in stable."

My wife Margaret tells about an experience in her childhood that made a deep impression on her. One day when she was at a friend's home for dinner and everyone had assembled around the table, someone suggested they should "give thanks." Evidently it wasn't their custom. After a moment of rather awkward silence, the mother of the house blurted out, "We don't have to give thanks. After all, Daddy worked awfully hard to provide this food!" What a tragedy that people who should know better fail to recognize that "Every good gift and every perfect gift is from above, and cometh down from the Father of lights, with whom is no variableness, neither shadow of turning" (Jas. 1:17).

On the other hand, just going through the motions of "saying grace" at the table can be almost as bad as not praying at all. How easy it is to become mechanical, even in our religious exercises, and to pray just because it is customary or seems to be "the right thing to do." Whenever we bow our heads together, may our expression of thanksgiving always well up from the depths of a grateful heart. Let's not be "like the mule"!

Now thank we all our God with hearts and hands and voices,
Who wondrous things hath done, in whom His world rejoices;
Who, from our mothers' arms, hath blessed us on our way
With countless gifts of love, and still is ours today.
— Martin Rinkhart

Giving thanks is a course from which we never graduate.

AN ELM OR AN EVERGREEN?

. . . I am like a green fir tree . . . .   Hosea 14:8

Some years ago the "Wall Street Journal" carried this story about a youngster named Sally who was so conscientious that she made herself miserable over minor tragedies. Early one Fall, when there was an exceptionally heavy snowstorm, her grandfather took her for a drive. "Notice those elms," he said, "the branches are so badly broken that the trees may die. But just look at those pines and evergreens — they are completely undamaged by the storm. My child, there are only two kinds of trees in the world: the stubborn and the wise. An elm holds its branches rigid, and troubles pile on until its limbs finally break — disfiguring or killing it. But when an evergreen is loaded with more weight than it can hold, it simply relaxes, lowers its branches, and lets the burden slip away — and so remains unharmed. Be a pine tree, granddaughter. Bear what you can, then let the rest of the load slide off."

That story set me to thinking. Checking my concordance, I found that the first mention of a pine tree in the Bible is in 2 Samuel 6:5, where we read: "And David and all the house of Israel played before the Lord on all manner of *instruments made of fir wood."* Turning to other early mentions of this tree in the Bible, I discovered that it is associated *with the building of the temple of the Lord* (1 Kings 5:5-10; Isa. 60:13). Now among the rules of Bible interpretation we have one called, "The Law of First Mention." Simply stated, it means: *"The first time a thing is dealt with in the Bible it displays certain characteristics or qualities which cling to it throughout the Word!* This frequently aids us in understanding other passages in which that subject is once again raised." By this rule then the fir tree (Hos. 14:8) is associated with *praise, worship, and sanctification!*

Are you like the elm tree that tries to bear all its own burdens, only to be broken in the process? Or, remembering the "Law of First Mention," are you like the "green fir tree" praising God, glorifying Him in your trials, and letting the burdens roll on Him (Ps. 55:22)?

God tells us to burden Him with that which burdens us!

WEAK THROUGH THE FLESH

For what the law could not do, in that it was weak
through the flesh . . . .   Romans 8:3

These words of Paul are not a criticism of God's law, but rather emphasize the inability of sinful man to keep its perfect commands.

It was the beloved Bible teacher Dr. William Pettingill who so vividly illustrated the truth of this verse by telling of a personal experience. He had been invited to the home of close friends for dinner. Wandering into the kitchen, Dr Pettingill entered just as the hostess took a large fork and thrust it into a beautifully browned roast, and tried to lift it from the pan. So tender, however, was the meat, and so well done, that the fork could not support it. It just went right through. Finally, after several such attempts, she gave up, and taking a large spatula placed it under the roast and removed it easily. Dr. Pettingill went on to say that the fork reminded him of the law and the roast portrayed man's sinful nature. Although the fork failed to lift the roast out of the kettle, *it was not the fault of the fork!* There was nothing wrong with it at all. It was a good strong one. The problem was in the meat. The fork was "weak through the flesh." That's exactly what Paul was trying to say in Romans 8:3 when he spoke of "what the law could not do." God's law was perfect and good, but it could never save anyone, simply because of the depravity of the human heart and the inability of sinful man to support it. For that very reason, "God sending his own Son in the likeness of sinful flesh, and for sin, condemned sin in the flesh: That the righteousness of the law might be fulfilled in us . . ." (Rom. 8:3, 4).

Salvation is not obtained by keeping the Ten Commandments, for "they that are in the flesh cannot please God." It is received by trusting Christ who alone fulfilled God's perfect law. Through His death at Calvary He paid the penalty for the world of sinners who continually break the law.

> *Free from the law, O happy condition,*
> *Jesus hath bled, and there is remission;*
> *"Come unto me," O hear His sweet call.*
> *Come, and He saves us once for all.* —P. P. Bliss

Over against a demanding Sinai stands a redeeming Calvary!
                                        —G.W.

WHEN THE MASTER PLUCKS A ROSE

*We are . . . willing rather to be absent from the body,
and to be present with the Lord.*   2 Corinthians 5:8

Jesus is the joy and glory of Heaven; therefore we long to
reach that blissful abode only in proportion to our deep, heartfelt
love for Him. Paul, who had been caught up to the paradise of
God for special revelations (2 Cor. 12:1-7), knew the joy and
rapture of that happy place. Therefore, he speaks with eagerness
of his longing to depart and to be with Christ, "which is *far
better.*" Oh, that we might grow in grace so that our earnest
desires, too, would coincide with that of the apostle. If we but
understood a little of the wonderful "pleasures" of the Father's
right hand (Ps. 16:11), we would more readily rejoice through
our tears at the passing of our saved loved ones.

A certain nobleman had a spacious garden which he left to
the care of a faithful servant, whose delight it was to water the
seeds, support the stalks of tender plants, and to do everything
he could to make the estate a veritable paradise of flowers. One
morning the gardener rose expecting to find his favorite blooms
increased in loveliness. To his surprise and grief, he discovered
that one of his choicest beauties had been rent from its stem.
Looking around he missed from every bed the most beautiful of
his flowers. Full of anxiety and anger, he hurried to his fellow
servants and demanded who had thus robbed him of his treasures.
He found no solace from his grief until someone told him, "The
lord of the manor was walking in his garden this morning, and
I saw him pluck them, and carry them away with a smile of joy."
He realized then that he had no cause for sorrow. It was well
that his master had been pleased to take "his own."

Has the Savior plucked some favorite "rosebud" or lovely
"bloom" from your "garden" and transported it to His Home
above? Rejoice that your dear one is now so radiantly happy.
The Master has but taken His own which in grace He lent to
you for a few fleeting hours.

**Death to the Christian is "gain" because it means Heaven, holi-
ness, happiness, and Him — Hallelujah!**   —Hertel

FLEAS AND SINS

. . . if we walk in the light . . . the blood of Jesus
Christ, his Son, cleanseth us from all sin. 1 John 1:7

The much maligned skunk is really an intelligent creature. Note, for instance, the ingenious way he rids himself of fleas. First he gathers a mouthful of grass or straw and then slowly wades into a stream until only his muzzle is visible. At this time the straw gives him the appearance of having a large, bushy mustache. As the skunk submerges, the fleas are kept busy moving upward to get out of the water until finally the dry stalks he holds in his mouth are black with hundreds of the tiny insects. Our striped friend then opens his mouth, releasing the grass, and his unwelcome guests go floating down the stream. He has freed himself of the itch-producing pests by placing them in an environment which is unfavorable to them.

The believer — who though saved still has to contend with his "old nature" — should hate his sins and desire freedom from them as much as the skunk wants to be rid of his pesky fleas. He must remember too that he will never overcome the besetting sins of his life in his own strength. New evils will crop up as fast as the old ones are defeated. However, even as the fleas were out of their element when under water, so evil thoughts, words, and deeds are incompatible with *"walking in the light."* Communion with God by means of Bible study and prayer, accompanied with *humble confession of sins,* will give the believer freedom from the accusations of a guilty conscience and provide the daily cleansing he needs.

Christian friend, only as you "walk in the light," that is, in conscious fellowship with the Father and the Son, can you enjoy a life of spiritual victory.

Search me, O God, and know my heart today;
Try me, O Savior, know my thoughts, I pray.
See if there be some wicked way in me;
Cleanse me from every sin and set me free. — Orr

Use sin as it will use you: spare it not, for it will not spare you!

THE PEACE OF GOD
And let the peace of God rule in your hearts . . .
Colossians 3:15

The story is told about a wounded soldier who was being taken to a hospital tent by some of his comrades. After they had carried him but a short distance, he urged them to put him down and go back to rescue someone else. As he was mortally wounded, he knew there was no hope for him anyway. Granting his request, they left him and returned to the combat area. In a few minutes, however, an officer stopped to ask him whether he could assist him in any way. The wounded soldier weakly replied, "No, thank you, sir. There's nothing at all you can do." "But can't I at least get some water to quench your thirst?" the officer inquired. The dying man again shook his head saying, "No, thank you, sir. There is one thing, however, you could do for me. In my knapsack you will find a New Testament. Please open it to John 14. Near the end of the chapter you will find a text beginning with the word 'Peace.' I would appreciate it if you would read just that one verse to me." The officer found the passage and read these words, "Peace I leave with you, my peace I give unto you; not as the world giveth, give I unto you. Let not your heart be troubled, neither let it be afraid" (John 14:27). "Thank you, sir," said the dying soldier. "I have that peace and I am going to the Savior who made that promise. God is with me, I want no more." Shortly after that, the wounded man entered into the presence of his Lord. Because he had Christ, he had peace *with* God, and since he had learned to commit everything to His care, he also had the peace *of* God. How important for all of us to remember that the Bible admonishes, "Be anxious for nothing, but in everything by prayer and supplication with thanksgiving, let your requests be made known unto God. *And the peace* OF *God . . . shall keep your hearts and minds through Christ Jesus!*" (Phil. 4:6, 7). Yes, in our joys and in our sorrows, in life's sunshine, or in the "valley of the shadow," we who are at peace *with* God can also know the peace *of* God which passeth all understanding.

> *Peace, perfect peace, in this dark world of sin?*
> *The blood of Jesus whispers peace within.*
> *Peace, perfect peace, with sorrows surging 'round?*
> *On Jesus' bosom naught but calm is found.*
> —E. H. Bickersteth

Peace rules the day when Christ rules the heart!

"HIS EYE IS ON THE SPARROW!"
*Are not two sparrows sold for a farthing? And one
of them shall not fall on the ground without your
Father.*   Matthew 10:29

These words of Jesus are a rebuke to faltering faith, and an exhortation to put our trust in God. A sparrow in Jesus' day was worth about one-eighth of a cent, and yet He who controls the universe is interested in each one of these insignificant little birds. If His eye notes the sparrow's fall, will He not also enter into every pang that rends the heart of His children?

C. F. Bundy has an interesting commentary on this passage. He writes: "This precious verse is usually misquoted. Note that it does not say 'to the ground' but 'on the ground.' Picture in your mind an active little sparrow, and the significance of the difference will become clear. The sparrow does not have to fall from a height, or die, but *merely stumble as it hops along 'on the ground,'* and God knows and cares! How much more is He concerned when one of His children stumbles and falls or is tried in the way of life! Not only so, but He is ever ready to help, strengthen, and restore such a fallen one. Don't wait for an emergency or a great tragedy before you call upon the Lord; rather, present to Him the problems, perplexities, and the little needs of everyday living!"

An anonymous poet exclaims: "When the birds begin to worry, and the lilies toil and spin, and God's creatures all are anxious, then I also may begin; for my Father sets their table, decks them out in garments fine, and if He supplies their living, will He not provide for mine? Just as noisy, common sparrows can be found most anywhere — unto some a worthless creature, if it perish who would care? Yet our Heavenly Father numbers every creature great and small, caring even for the sparrows, marking when each one doth fall. If His children's hairs are numbered, why should we be filled with fear? He has promised all that's needful, and in trouble to be near!"

> *If God sees the sparrow's fall,*
> *Paints the lily, short and tall,*
> *Gives the skies their azure hue,*
> *Will He not then care for you?* — Anon.

**With God's strength behind you, His love within you, and His
arms underneath you, you are more than sufficient for the job
ahead of you!**   —Wm. A. Ward

KEEPING OUR VOWS

I will pay my vows unto the Lord now in the
presence of all his people.   Psalm 116:14

The night before a scheduled attack, many soldiers wrote letters to their parents. The chaplain who censored the mail was
unable to read them until after the battle had taken place. When
he did, he found two were in the same handwriting—one penned
before and one after the brief but intense engagement. In the
first, the young soldier wrote his mother, ". . . I vow to God
that if I come through tomorrow, I am going to be a better man."
The second letter, written after the danger was over, was addressed to a friend in another regiment. ". . . I've just come
through a scorcher up front. . . . If you can get leave and meet
me in Paris, boy, we'll go out on the town!" The vow made in
the face of great danger had been quickly forgotten.

The writer of Psalm 116 had already experienced deliverance
when he wrote his song of praise. He had been in deep distress
because he had stood at the very door of death. Rejecting the
counsel of men that no help was available, he had cried out to
God in faith and hope, pledging allegiance and worship to Him.
The Lord had restored him to health, and now he was determined
to fulfill the vows he had made. First, he would go to the house
of God; and in the presence of the worshipers pour out the drink
offering, the "cup of salvation," as a testimonial of his full surrender. Secondly, standing in awe at the thought that a simple
person such as he, was precious to God, he would publicly acknowledge Jehovah's mercy (vv. 14-16). Thirdly, he would present an offering of thanksgiving to the Lord, something of worth
to display his love and gratitude. Unlike the fickle soldier, the
Psalmist did not forget the vows he had made while in distress.

Are you keeping your vows to God?

Salvation's cup of blessing now
I take, and call upon God's name;
Before His saints I pay my vow,
And here my gratitude proclaim. — Psalter

Better is it that thou shouldest not vow, than that thou should-
est vow and not pay.   —Ecclesiastes 5:5

WINDS OF LOVE

. . . God is love.   1 John 4:8

A certain man had a weather vane erected on his barn, on which appeared the text, "God is love." A friend passing by, thinking that it was a rather strange place for such a Scripture, asked about it. The farmer informed him, "This is just to remind me that no matter which way the wind blows, God is love." Yes, trusting child of God, it's true — no matter what your circumstance, how difficult the road, or how dark the hour of trial — whichever way the winds of life may be blowing, *God is love!*

When the warm "south wind" with its soothing and balmy breezes brings showers of blessing, "God is love." For "every good gift and every perfect gift is from above, and cometh down from the Father of lights, with whom is no variableness, neither shadow of turning" (James 1:17).

When the cold "north wind" of trial and testing sweeps down upon you, "God is love." We know that "all things work together for good to them that love God, to them who are the called according to his purpose" (Rom. 8:28).

When the "west wind" breathes hard upon you with its punishing intent, "God is love." For "whom the Lord loveth he chasteneth" (Heb. 12:6).

When the "east wind" threatens to sweep away all that you have, "God is love." For despite appearances, He "shall supply all your need according to his riches in glory by Christ Jesus" (Phil. 4:19). He knows when some things should be taken away, and *in grace* He removes them. Yes, "no matter which way the wind blows," God is love!

Perhaps, Christian friend, you are discouraged and downhearted; if so, remember, God still cares for you. That which you are experiencing has either been sent or allowed by Him for your own good. (See Hebrews 12:11.)

> God is love; His mercy brightens
>   All the path in which we rove;
> Bliss He wakens, and woe He lightens,
>   God is wisdom, God is love.   — J. Bowring

No affliction would trouble the child of God if he knew the Lord's blessed reason for sending it.

PRAYER AND PRETZELS
. . . making mention of you in our prayers.
1 Thessalonians 1:2

I can imagine some of you are surprised by the title of this devotional — and I will freely admit that I used it to get your attention. However, there is a very real relationship between prayer and pretzels! The twisted bits of salted, baked dough that go by that name were first made in northern Italy about A.D. 610. A monk who had been baking bread found he had some dough left over, so he formed it into thin, pencil-like rolls, and then twisted them into *little figures representing children with their arms folded in prayer!* Coating them with syrup and salt he put them in the oven. Finding them very palatable, he gave them as rewards to the youngsters who learned their catechism lessons. He called these tasty morsels *"pretiola"* which in Latin means "little reward." This monk who invented pretzels, and gave them to the children for knowing answers to Bible questions, was using good psychology. Explaining that the twisted dough represented them in an attitude of devotion, perhaps he hoped thereby also to remind them to *"pray in"* the truths of the Word they had only mentally digested. Can we not all learn a lesson from this? Let us also add much prayer to our study of the Bible, beseeching God to give us a deeper "heart understanding" of its precepts, and a greater wisdom in applying its purifying lessons to our daily lives.

From now on, every time you see pretzels, I hope you are reminded that they represent *"children at prayer."* Incidentally, if more people thought of their youngsters praying for them when they ate those salted goodies, they would not drink along with those snacks some of the things they do! (Enough said?)

> *Someone prayed as I met the test*
> *Of temptation fierce and strong;*
> *I felt God near, He gave me rest;*
> *Somebody prayed, I know.*
>
> *Someone prayed when my faith was dim*
> *And when Satan pressed me sore,*
> *God answered them, gave strength within;*
> *Somebody prayed, I know.*   —Mrs. M. Spittal, alt.

Prayer will drive sin out of your life; or sin will drive prayer out!

WITNESS!

And ye also shall bear witness . . . . John 15:27

The other evening I heard a man on the radio emphatically state that he did not believe in the resurrection of Jesus Christ. I could sense that he had a real feeling of scorn for those who do. Prominent men in public places have also expressed their contempt for "born-againers." This is typical of the general attitude toward orthodox Christians and the truths they confess. Although the worldling may not show personal animosity toward a believer, yet he looks upon him as "narrow" or "bigoted." While he may treat Christians in a rather cordial manner, the fact remains that the worldly man is against us. We can never know when this secret hostility will flame out into violent persecution.

In the face of the world's hatred what are we to do? The answer is: *witness!* We are not to return "evil for evil," or retort in scorn to their words of contempt. As graciously and as sweetly as God enables us, we are to give to them a message of life. We will be greatly helped if we bear in mind the words of the Lord Jesus: "If the world hate you, ye know that it hated me before it hated you" (John 15:18). The world rejected Jesus Christ. Few homes opened their doors to Him and His small band of followers. The multitude enjoyed the scene as the Roman soldiers mocked Him, spit upon Him, and pressed the crown of thorns upon His head. They cried out for His death, and taunted Him as He hung in agony on the cross. Let us never forget this, for *"the servant is not greater than his Lord!"*

By God's grace, let us then be patient with men as they sometimes mistreat us. Let us be careful too not to bring down violence upon ourselves by antagonizing the world needlessly through words or actions that do not reflect the spirit of our Lord. Faithfully, graciously, and tactfully let us witness concerning the transforming grace of God which is available through Jesus Christ.

> *Though the world may scorn and hate us,*
> *And the devil strong oppose,*
> *We must tell the lost of Jesus —*
> *That He died, and for them 'rose! —* Anon.

Every Christian must witness, for there is an impelling GO in the GOspel!

AN ACCEPTABLE SACRIFICE

*I beseech you therefore, brethren . . . that ye present
your bodies a living sacrifice, holy, acceptable unto
God . . . .*   Romans 12:1

The admonition of the apostle Paul in this verse is not at all
unreasonable; in fact, it is a most logical request. In consideration of the mercies of God and all that He has done for us, and
in contemplation of Christ's work of redemption at Calvary and
the great sacrifice He made there, it is only reasonable that believers give their bodies back to Him as living sacrifices for service. Nothing less than a *complete* presentation of our bodies,
however, will ever be *acceptable* to God. Our "sacrifice" must
involve an entire and full surrender.

It was Dr. Arthur T. Pierson who gave a most striking illustration of the need to give our "all," with nothing held back.
He said, "Supposing you had one thousand acres of land and
someone approached you and made an offer to buy your farm.
You agree to sell the land, except for one acre right in the very
center, with provisions for a right of way. Do you know," he
continued, "that the law would allow you to have access to that
one, lone spot in the middle of that thousand acres? You could
build a road all across the remainder of that farm to get to that
small plot of ground. And so it is with the Christian who makes
less than a one-hundred-percent surrender to God. You can be
sure that the devil will make an inroad across that person's life
to reach the unsurrendered portion and, as a result, his testimony
and service will be marred and have little effect upon others."

Christian, does the Lord have your body? Have you ever by
a very definite act of the will presented it to Him for His control,
His use, and His glory? If not, why don't you do so right now?
Just say, "Lord, I've already given You my heart, but now here
is my *body!* Help me to keep it clean, pure, and undefiled. Use
me for Your glory in any way You see fit. I'm Yours to command!"

> Poor is my best and small;
>   How could I dare divide?
> Surely the Lord shall have my all,
>   He shall not be denied!   —Anon.

**There is no risk, only blessing, when we surrender ourselves
to God!**

POOR RICH PEOPLE

. . . the rich he hath sent empty away. Luke 1:53

Martin Luther once observed, "Riches are the least worthy gifts which God can give a man. What are they to God's Word, to bodily gifts: such as beauty and health; or to the gifts of the mind, such as understanding, skill, and wisdom? Or what are they compared to spiritual treasures? Yet men toil for wealth day and night, and take no rest. Therefore *God commonly gives riches to foolish people, to whom He gives nothing else!*"

The children of a certain family, during a period of prosperity, were constantly left in the nursery in the care of servants. At length a depression came, the servants had to be discharged, and the parents once again cared for their little ones. One evening when the father returned home after a day filled with business worries, his little girl climbed up on his lap and, twining her soft, childish arms around his neck, said, "Papa, don't get rich again. You didn't come into the nursery when you were rich; but now we can be around you and get on your knee and kiss you. *Please, please, don't get rich again, Papa!*" The father suddenly realized how empty his life had been when he was busy making money but neglecting his family. He saw how he had actually been squandering his God-given time which should have been devoted to higher goals, and abiding values.

Some years ago in Bogota, Colombia, a tame pigeon swallowed a diamond and several emeralds worth $40,000 and flew away. The news item stated that the children of a millionaire had been playing with the stones when the bird snatched them. What a parable on wealth that is amassed at the expense of spiritual, moral, and personal values. Such riches soon "take wings and fly away." Jesus says that few rich men reach the kingdom. Completely occupied with the affairs of this world, neglecting the things of the soul, they are "sent empty away" when their time to leave this earth arrives.

> *Carve your name high above shifting sands,*
>   *On rocks that defy decay;*
> *All that you'll hold in your poor, dead hand*
>   *Is that which you've given away!*   —Anon.

The real measure of our wealth is how much we would be worth if we lost our money!

PROFITABLE READING

> . . . *and he shall read therein all the days of his*
> *life . . . .*   Deuteronomy 17:19

Some of the greatest scholars in the world have stated without apology that no man's education can be complete without an acquaintance with the Bible. Not only are its contents of inestimable value, but its very literary perfection and beauty are also worthy of our special attention and admiration. If we are to know this Book, it goes without saying that we must be willing to read and study it faithfully. No man can master any subject without diligent effort, concentration, and application. Much of the criticism laid against the Scriptures has come from those who have never studied it, much less even read it through.

A certain Bible teacher, boarding a train, found a seat next to a man who was diligently reading his newspaper. Opening his briefcase the preacher took out his Bible and began to read. The gentleman with the newspaper, glancing out of the corner of his eye, saw this unusual sight and his curiosity was aroused. Finally he said, "Pardon me, Sir, are you a minister?" "Yes, I am," said the man, and began talking to his questioner about the Bible. He explained some of the mysteries of that wonderful Book and its marvelous doctrines and revelations until the other exclaimed in amazement, "How in the world did you ever learn so much about that Book?" The Bible teacher simply replied, "I certainly did not get it by reading the daily newspaper!" Now, we should know what's going on in the world today. But I am concerned over the amount of time that is taken up in reading our newspapers, magazines, and periodicals as compared with the Bible.

By the way, how much time do you spend in spiritual meditation each day? How diligently do you study God's Word? Upon your answer will depend your knowledge of the Scriptures and the Man of the Book, the Lord Jesus Christ.

> *In my soul, in my soul,*
> *Send a great revival;*
> *Teach me how to watch and pray,*
> *And to read my Bible!*   —Anon.

There are multitudes whose Bibles are "read" only on the edges!

"WHERE THE FIRE HAS BEEN"

*But he was wounded for our transgressions . . . and
with his stripes we are healed.*   Isaiah 53:5

The great Bible teacher H. A. Ironside often told the story of
a group of pioneers who were traveling westward by covered
wagon. One day they were horrified to see in the distance a long
line of smoke and flame stretching for miles across the prairie.
The dry grass was on fire, and the inferno was advancing upon
them rapidly. The river they had crossed the day before would
be of no help as they would not be able to return to it in time.
One man, however, knew what to do. He gave the command
to set fire to the grass behind them. Then, when the ground
had cooled, the whole company moved back upon it. The people
watched apprehensively as the blaze roared toward them. A little
girl cried out in terror, "Are you sure we won't be burned up?"
The leader replied, "My child, we are absolutely safe, nothing
can harm us here, for we are standing on the scorched area
where the flames have already done their work."

The fire of God's holy wrath against sin came down upon
Jesus Christ the day He died on the cross. His own words "It
is finished" and His resurrection from the tomb furnish us with
infallible proof that He paid the price for our sin in full.

Christian friend, do not be afraid of death and the judgment
that will follow. Positionally you are now safely seated "in heavenly places in Christ Jesus" (Eph. 2:6), because by faith you
have taken refuge in the "burned-over place" of Calvary. The
fire of God's wrath cannot touch you there for He will not demand payment for your sins twice. Let this be your comfort:
you are standing in safety "where the fire has been."

> *On Him almighty vengeance fell,*
> *Which would have sunk a world to Hell.*
> *He bore it for a chosen race,*
> *And thus becomes our Hiding Place.* —Anon.

To escape God's justice, flee to His love!

WISDOM FROM ABOVE

Wisdom is the principal thing; therefore, get wisdom;
. . . get understanding.   Proverbs 4:7

A series of cartoons in a New York newspaper depicted a young woman, garbed in cap and gown, holding a diploma with much pride. With her head held high she is looking down her nose at "Mr. World," while that cold, cruel cynic is saying, "Well, who do we have here?" Next, with shoulders thrown back, the young lady replies, "Certainly you know who I am. I'm Cecelia Shakespeare Doaks, a graduate of Prestige College. I have my A.B." "My dear child," Mr. World says in reply, "come with me, and *I'll teach you the rest of the alphabet!*"

Now, we certainly would not discourage the quest for learning, nor the desire to pursue an education to meet the demands and opportunities of life — we would encourage it! But it's important to remember that there is more involved in a well-rounded education than the completion of some college courses. Four years of classroom instruction, even under the most competent teachers, doesn't make one all-wise. The "school of hard knocks" often makes a far greater impact than the "university of hard facts." Even with the best education and down-to-earth, practical experience, however, a man or woman really "knows" nothing apart from God. "The fear of the Lord is the *beginning* of wisdom" (Prov. 9:10). Knowledge is the acquisition of facts. Wisdom is the ability to use this knowledge rightly. A person may acquire much knowledge, but without wisdom his acquired storehouse of facts will do him little good; in fact, it may even be spiritually harmful to him. Get an education? Yes, but also seek for that wisdom which is from above. James tells us, "If any of you lack wisdom, let him ask of God . . . and it shall be given him" (James 1:5).

"Who is a *wise man* and endued with knowledge among you? Let him show out of a good life [behavior] his works with meekness of wisdom" (James 3:13).

> *A man may store his mind with facts,*
> *Till knowledge from it overflows,*
> *But lacking wisdom from Above,*
> *He's still a "fool" till Christ he knows.*—Bosch

True wisdom consists principally of two parts: the knowledge of God, and the knowledge of ourselves!   **—John Calvin**

A CALENDAR AND A WASTEBASKET

. . . brethren, the time is short . . . . 1 Corinthians 7:29

It was the last day of the month. Taking my desk calendar and reviewing the engagements fulfilled, the projects accomplished, and the obligations met, I tore it from the pad, rolled it up into a wad and threw it into the wastebasket. As I did so, however, I was arrested with the thought: that which I'm disposing of represents an entire month of my life. Have I been faithful in accomplishing that which the Lord has given me to do during those days? Were those precious minutes and hours utilized in the very best way? Or could it be that time has been squandered, opportunities disregarded, and the minutes wasted? Could it be possible that the month itself had been spent in such a way that God considered it fit only for the "wastebasket" of broken vows and dead works?

Frequently we categorize our misdemeanors, putting some down as greater than others. If we are at all justified in doing this, I believe one of the worst sins on the list is that of wasting time. Those hours, minutes, and seconds which are given to us must be considered as a treasured trust. They must not be wasted nor put to improper use, for they can never be recalled. On various occasions I have been startled by the sudden realization that the immediate, passing seconds would soon be beyond recall. This particular moment which is mine right now will never come again. Each passing second slips away, never to return. Especially Christians, who believe the coming of the Lord draweth nigh, and that we are living in the midnight hour of this age, should endeavor to spend every day in pursuits which are profitable and which glorify God.

Yes, another month is gone! It's time to tear that current page from the calendar and throw it into the wastebasket. May that act, however, not characterize the quality of its activity. Rather than throwing away the months, let us give them to the Lord.

Don't just count days, make the days count; for "lost time" is never "found" again!

BELIEVING GOD

By faith the walls of Jericho fell down. . . . Hebrews 11:30

In the story about Joshua and the city of Jericho, we have a most vivid illustration of faith. God commanded Joshua to gather all the men of war and have them march around Jericho once a day for six days. Then, on the seventh day, they were to compass the city seven times, after which the priests were to blow with the trumpets and all the people were to shout with a great shout. The Lord promised Joshua that if they did this, the walls of the city would fall down flat.

Have you ever tried to put yourself in Joshua's place, and imagine how you would have reacted to such a command? When the Lord gave him these instructions, do you suppose Joshua responded: "Lord, that's a reasonable thing to do. In fact, I'm rather ashamed of myself that I didn't devise such a brilliant plan in the first place. It really makes a lot of sense." Of course, he said nothing of the kind, simply because God's command was *not* a "reasonable" one to Joshua's mind. That is, he couldn't take out his "slide rule" and calculate scientifically that the predicted results would necessarily follow such actions. And yet, even though some would have ruled it an insane plan thus to attempt the conquest of Jericho, Joshua obeyed God anyway, simply because he had faith! Yes, he was willing to rely on the word of the Lord, despite the fact that it seemed contrary to his own understanding of things. That's what God expects of us today. He wants us to believe His Word — to accept the Bible record in its entirety — whether we can comprehend it or not. There is much in the Book we cannot explain: for example, the Trinity, the virgin birth, Christ's substitutionary death, His resurrection, and His coming again; yet we believe these things with all our heart *just because God says so!* Remember, without such faith it is impossible to please God (Heb. 11:6).

The tow'ring walls of Jericho did seem a barrier strong,
Yet trumpet blasts and shouts of faith did conquer it ere long;
And so today as we go 'round our Jerichos of doubt,
Let's trust the Lord for victory; He knows what He's about!
                                                            —H.G.B.

God said it, I believe it; that settles it!

THE "SOILED RAG" MASTERPIECE

My little children, of whom I travail in birth again
until Christ be formed in you.   Galatians 4:19

As a mother is in pain till the birth of her child occurs, so Paul was also in agony over the condition of the Galatian Christians. Though saved, they were still so confused on law and grace that the Lord Jesus Christ had not been allowed to possess them fully, to impart to their lives all His wondrous power and blessing. Paul wanted them to live nothing but Christ, think nothing but Christ, and *glory in nothing but the Savior and His righteousness!* However, like many lukewarm, mixed-up believers today, the Galatians had missed the full purpose of their calling.

An artist was once falsely accused of a crime and thrown into prison. Although allowed to take his brushes and paints with him, he had no way of obtaining a canvas. One day in desperation he asked a guard for something upon which he might paint. Indifferently the man picked up a dirty old handkerchief and tossed it to him saying, "There, see what you can do with that soiled rag!" The artist, being a Christian, painted upon it his conception of the face of Jesus. Having labored on it long and faithfully, he thought he would show it first of all to the man who had given him the dirty piece of cloth for a canvas. When the official looked upon its marvelous sweetness, his heart was moved, and tears flowed unbidden down his face. The painting later became famous.

If a poor human could take an old soiled rag and make it glow with such loveliness that a careless, indifferent man was touched to tears by it, what might not the Master Artist do with your life and mine if we allowed Him to have His way with us?

In our sinful self we are just old "soiled rags," devoid of spiritual beauty; yet, if unleashed, the power of God's Holy Spirit can change us into a masterpiece of divine grace!

I am the Lord's—yet, teach me all it meaneth,
All it involves of love and loyalty,
Of holy service, absolute surrender,
And unreserved obedience unto Thee! —Anon.

A Christ-filled life is still the best commentary on the Bible!

START THEM YOUNG!

And that from a child thou hast known the holy
scriptures . . . .   2 Timothy 3:15

A United Press International article appearing in one of our local newspapers reads as follows: "The time to start a child on a musical career isn't too far beyond the bootie and bottle age. This is the word from Miss Anastasia Jenpelis who teaches violin at the Eastman School of Music in New York, and is a new member of the National Music Camp faculty here. Miss Jenpelis is the first instructor in Interlochen to employ the increasingly popular Suzuki method of teaching. This approach to the violin was originated by Dr. Shinichi Suzuki of the Matsumoto School of Matsumoto, Japan. It is based, according to Miss Jenpelis, on the idea that the earlier the child is exposed to music, the better a musician he will be. Just, for example, as a child imitates gestures, he can also imitate music. For this reason it is extremely important that a child hear *nothing but good music from a very early age,* she said. While Dr. Suzuki likes to start his students in classes between the ages of 2 and 4, he begins exposing them to music even earlier."

If the value of early training, environment, and example is so vital in music training, how much more is this true in regard to influencing our children for Christ! Dr. Suzuki says it is extremely important that a child hear nothing but good music from a very early age. What do the children hear in your home? I'm not thinking of music alone, but of everything in general. Is it good? What blares from the radio and television? What kind of language do they hear from your lips? Is the emphasis on spiritual things, or only on pleasure, money, and earthly things? How wonderful a testimony Paul gives concerning Timothy. He says, ". . . that *from a child"* he knew *"the holy scriptures."* Could this be said of your children? How important to "start them young!"

> *Begin to train them early*
> *To fear and love the Lord,*
> *To carry on life's pathway*
> *God's lamp — His holy Word!* — Clara Fennema

The flower of youth never appears more beautiful than when it bends toward the Son of Righteousness!   —Matthew Henry

THE TATTERED RUG

> *. . . teach the young women to . . . love their chil-*
> *dren, to be . . . keepers at home . . . that the word*
> *of God be not blasphemed.*   Titus 2:4, 5

A preacher tells how he was once entertained by a teacher and his wife who had two boys in their middle teens. He writes, "Immediately on entering, I felt the home atmosphere. They were evidently a fine Christian family. However, I noticed that the carpet in the living room was tattered, and that there were actually holes in it. Nevertheless, the family was without doubt self-respecting. Before I left, the mother told me a story that helped me to understand about the rug. She said that one day when she was ready to sweep and dust, half a dozen boys were in her home. 'Now,' she had said, 'you fellows will have to go out for a while for I have some things to do in the house this morning.' 'But where shall we go?' they had asked. 'How about your aunt's?' she then suggested to one. 'Do you think she would have us in her place? *Not much!*' the boy had replied. Then she said to another, 'Why don't you go over to your house?' and he had answered quickly, 'Oh, Mother would never allow six of us in her fancy home!' A few more questions and she found that hers was the only place where the boys were allowed to come in at will and have fun. She confided that now they always gathered at her place, and that was why they would soon have to buy a new carpet. After hearing her story, her tattered rug was transformed in my estimation! It became to me the most beautiful one I had ever seen — for it was worn out in keeping and making good boys."

We all like to see a house that is neat and well cared for, but not at the expense of human values. Mothers, if it is not absolutely necessary for you to go out to work, think twice before you do. Your first duty is to be good "keepers at home." Only thus can you honor the great privilege that God has given you of being a companion and friend to your children. If you have a "tattered rug" in your house, it may well be more of a badge of honor than an eyesore!

> *O blest the parents who give heed*
> *Unto their children's foremost need,*
> *And weary not of care or cost;*
> *That they to Heaven be not lost.* — C. Von Pfeil

How much above good housekeeping is good homemaking!

February 5   Read Exodus 17:1-16

HELPING HANDS

. . . and Aaron and Hur held up his hands . . . .
Exodus 17:12

Exodus 17 records a most interesting experience in the life of Moses. As long as his hands, grasping the rod of God, were upheld, Joshua and the Israelites prevailed against the Amalekites. As the battle progressed, however, Moses' hands became so heavy that he could no longer retain his posture. Aaron and Hur then held his hands up for him, and victory was achieved.

Even as Moses needed the assistance of Aaron and Hur, so today those called to spiritual leadership need the undergirding of the people to whom they minister. I am thinking especially of pastors. I don't know of another work so demanding, discouraging, and fraught with potential pitfalls. These men need our support and encouragement. By the way, how long has it been since you took your pastor's hand and verbally expressed your gratitude for his ministry? A word properly timed will be, in effect, "holding up his hands," and will help to assure spiritual victory in your church.

A terrible fire was raging, and many attempts were being made to save a child who stood at a top window frantically waving and calling for help. One man, braver than the rest, put forth a last bold endeavor to rescue the boy. Sensing the almost impossible odds, and fearing he might fail, someone in the crowd cried, "Cheer him, cheer him!" The people caught the words and shouted loudly. Inspired and encouraged by their support, the man doubled his efforts and rescued the child from the flames.

Do you know any Christian worker who is similarly trying by all means in his power to snatch "brands from the burning," and to save immortal souls? *Cheer him,* and then see how your kind sympathy helps him to work on with fresh courage and renewed energy.

Why not make this "appreciation week" for your pastor? Encourage him, "cheer him"!

O *"hold up the hands" of the worker for Christ,*
  Encourage his soul by your prayer;
A handclasp, a smile, or a word of good cheer,
  Will help him life's burdens to bear. — G.W.

Wouldn't it be fine if all those who point a critical finger would hold out a helping hand instead?

GOD NEVER SLEEPS!

Behold, he who keepeth Israel shall neither slumber nor sleep.   Psalm 121:4

This beautiful Psalm was one of the songs sung by the ancient pilgrims as they made their journey to Jerusalem for the great festivals of the Hebrew faith. As Mount Zion and Mount Moriah came into view, one of the singers, alluding to these sacred peaks near Jerusalem where God had often manifested His presence, would begin, "I will lift up mine eyes unto the hills. From whence cometh my help?" Another would immediately respond, "My help cometh from the Lord, who made heaven and earth." This confident affirmation in song would then set the whole company to singing the rest of the Psalm, a moving poem of assurance and trust. They believed the Lord would care for them on their journey, protecting their feet from slipping, preserving them from the heat of daytime and the cold of the night, and preventing any real harm from befalling them. Their faith in the God who never sleeps enabled these pilgrims to retire sweetly under the open sky with complete confidence. Many a soldier has testified that this same faith also made it possible for him to sleep in his "foxhole" on the battlefield.

Two elderly gentlemen lived in a home for senior citizens. One day one of them said to the other, "You know, there is something I can't understand about you. You go to bed at night and sleep until morning as soundly as a baby. I wake up several times and am restless and fitful. How in the world do you do it? I wish I could relax like that." His companion replied, "I'll tell you. Many years ago I used to worry a great deal, and found sleep difficult; then I read that the Lord never slumbers, but constantly cares for His own. I decided that it didn't make much sense for both of us to be up all night; so *I decided to go to sleep and let Him take over!*"

Knowing that God never slumbers but ever watches over His own should help all of us to sleep better tonight.

> *My Father watches o'er me,*
> *His eye is never dim;*
> *At morn, at noon, at twilight,*
> *I safely trust in Him!* —G. B. Adams

Implicit faith in God's provision and watchcare is the best of all tranquilizers!   —Bosch

A DIVIDED WORLD

. . . one on the right hand, and the other on the left.
Luke 23:33

Is there life on other planets? What about flying saucers? Do they come from outer space? I don't know the answer you give to these questions, but of this I am certain: should there be life "out there," and should some space "creature" visit this earth, he would not stay very long. Just a five-minute newscast would tell him that we are living in a world divided into two distinct camps whose ideologies are in such sharp contrast that both sides are "armed to the teeth." Each possesses the potential of destroying life itself upon this earth. This would be enough to make any "visitor" want to hop right back in his spaceship and be gone to wherever he came from. However, today I'm thinking of an even greater division than this: one that has eternal implications. After all, the present differences between nations will not always exist, for when Jesus comes, "nation shall not lift up sword against nation, neither shall they learn war any more." There is a division in the world today, however, that will last for all eternity; it is that which exists between those who are saved and those who are lost. Everyone belongs to one of these two classes. You are either on the devil's side or God's side. You are either traveling the broad way that leads to destruction, or you are on the narrow way that leads to life everlasting. You either believe in Christ or you reject Him. But, I can hear someone say, "You're wrong. I'm neutral." Oh no you aren't! Jesus said: *"He that is not with me is against me"* (Matt. 12:30).

When Jesus hung on the cross, two men were crucified with Him, "one on the right hand, and the other on the left." One rejected Him, and the other received Him by faith. One is in the place of the condemned. The other is in the presence of the Lord. Everyone in the entire world of mankind is represented by one or the other of these men. On which side are you?

> *What will you do with Jesus?*
> *Neutral you cannot be;*
> *Someday your heart will be asking,*
> *"What will He do with me?"* —Simpson

To talk of being neutral in regard to Christ is like a falling man with a parachute saying he can be neutral about pulling the ripcord!   —H.G.B.

SPEAK OF HIM!

Let the redeemed of the Lord say so . . . . Psalm 107:2

A businessman on his way to prayer meeting saw a stranger looking thoughtfully into an open window of the local church. Moved by a strong impulse, he smiled and then tactfully invited the man to attend the service with him. The gentleman consented, and it was the beginning of a Christian life for him and his family, for he was saved before the meeting was dismissed. Afterward he said to the friend who invited him to the service, "Do you know I lived in this city seven years before I met you, and no one ever asked me to go to church. I had not been here three days until deliverymen from the bakery, the dairy, and a local laundry hunted me up and made a contact. Yet, in all those seven years, you are the first person who ever expressed an interest in my soul." The sad part of this story is that it finds its counterpart in the lives of thousands, yea millions of unbelievers that constantly rub elbows with "silent Christians" who never attempt to witness to them concerning the Savior.

A little girl once said to her Christian mother, "Do you love Jesus?" "Why yes, my child, but why do you ask such a strange question?" "Well, Mama, you speak of Papa, of Auntie Mae and Uncle Joe, but I never hear you talk about Jesus. I thought if you loved Him very much, I would sometimes hear you say so." The Holy Spirit gave wings to the words of the child, and like arrows of conviction, they lodged in the heart of her negligent parent. From that day on the mother became a better Christian and a faithful witness for the Lord.

Today, while there is still time and opportunity, will you mention the Savior's name to some weary soul who needs His grace? Remember, the admonition of the writer of Psalm 107 is more than a suggestion, it is a divine command: "Let the redeemed of the Lord *say so!*"

> *How glad you'll be when day is done,*
> *As you breathe your last breath,*
> *To know some word of yours has helped*
> *To save a soul from death!*   —Anon.

Speak out for the Lord; remember, silence isn't always GOLDEN, on occasion it may be just plain YELLOW!

"LED" INTO PRISON

> . . . we endeavored to go . . . assuredly gathering
> that the Lord had called us. . . .   Acts 16:10

In a vision, Paul saw a man of Macedonia who said, "Come over . . . and help us." Assured that the Lord Himself had thus called him to preach the Gospel in that area, he and Silas — and evidently Dr. Luke — set out at once for their new "mission field." But what a reception they received! The record tells us that the "multitude rose up together against them" and "beat them" and "thrust them into the inner prison, and made their feet fast in the stocks." If they would have reacted like many of us today, Paul would probably have complained, "Well, isn't this just fine: *led by God into prison!* Here we were obedient to the heavenly vision, and this is our reward!"

Was this Paul's attitude? I should say not! Listen to the story in Acts 16:25: "And at midnight Paul and Silas prayed, and sang praises unto God." Singing in prison! Paul knew that "all things work together for good to them that love God." With the eye of faith he could see some future good, and in that confidence was happy even while enduring severe trial. When the Lord had accomplished His purpose, demonstrated His power, and saved the jailer and his family, then Paul and Silas were commanded to "depart and go in peace."

Sometimes we find ourselves in troubling situations as the result of our service for the Lord. Doing that which we believe to be right and according to His will, we seem to end up in the "prison" of suffering, hardship, and loss, and are tempted to complain, "Lord, is this what I get for my faithfulness?" Then He comes and assures us that He "doeth all things well," and that Romans 8:28 is still in the Book! When all has been accomplished, we shall be able to look back and clearly see His hand and purpose in it all. "Wherefore let them that suffer according to the will of God commit the keeping of their souls to him in well-doing, as unto a faithful Creator" (1 Pet. 4:19).

> There's One who will journey beside me,
>   In weal, nor in woe, will forsake;
> And this is my solace and comfort,
>   "He knoweth the way that I take!" —Anon.

Every lock of sorrow has a key of promise to fit it!

GOD IS IN THIS PLACE

*. . . Surely the Lord is in this place; and I knew
it not.*   Genesis 28:16

When I was overseas during World War II, a chaplain told me that some officers would use vile and profane language in his presence and then in a humorous manner turn to him and say, "Excuse me, Chaplain!" The others would usually laugh as if this were a wonderful joke. Some time later when this happened again, the Chaplain decided it was time to express himself concerning their flippant attitude in regard to taking God's name in vain. Turning upon the offending one he said, "Do not ask *me* to excuse you! You are displeasing Someone far higher and holier than I. You had better ask Him to forgive you!" Absolute silence reigned in the officers' quarters for a few moments, and from that day forward there was a marked decrease in profane and vulgar language when this Chaplain was near. They respected him and felt it would be wrong to offend this servant of God who took the things of the Lord so seriously.

On several occasions I have walked into a place of business where some men were engaged in conversation, and noticed a strange silence fall upon them. Apparently what they were saying was of such a nature that they didn't want a minister to hear it. How foolish! What about the fact that God hears every word? Have men forgotten about Him?

Dear friend, if what you talk about isn't fit to be said in the presence of a minister, it certainly isn't right to say in God's hearing. Remember, the Lord sees every act, hears every word, and reads every thought that comes into our minds. When the realization of this truth came home to Jacob the morning after he had fled for fear of Esau, and after he had so brazenly and shamelessly deceived his aged father, he felt a deep sense of awe. May the truth that "God is here" also influence our every thought, word, and deed.

> *Lord, put a seal upon my lips,*
> *Help me to guard with care*
> *The things I say, and swift repeat;*
> *O tongue of mine, beware!* — G.W.

Live innocently; God is watching!   —Linnaeus

HOW TO GET RID OF THE PREACHER

And he gave some . . . pastors . . . . Ephesians 4:11

What a blessing it is to have a pastor who loves the Lord, who teaches the Word, and who leads his "flock" aright. I thank God we have a man like that in the church which I attend. In these days of apostasy, when there is such a tragic departure from an emphasis on the Word, how we should praise the Lord for those who are true to the Book, who live the life, and who speak with the fire of conviction. If you have such a pastor, thank God for him, pray for him, and give him a word of encouragement. (By the way, how long has it been since you gave your pastor a good firm handshake and said, "I thank God for you, and all that you have meant in my life. I'm praying for you every day"?)

"Oh," but you say, "that may be all right for your church, but we're trying to figure out how to get rid of the pastor in ours." Is that your problem? Well, then perhaps the following article I found some time ago will be of help to you: "Not long ago, a well-meaning group of laymen came from a neighboring church to see me. They wanted me to advise them on some convenient, painless, yet successful method of getting rid of their pastor. Here's what I told them: 1. Look him straight in the eye while he is preaching and say 'Amen!' once in a while. He'll preach himself to death. 2. Pat him on the back and brag on his good points. He'll soon work himself to death. 3. Re-dedicate your own life to Christ, and ask the preacher for a job to do; or tell him you plan to lead some lost soul to Christ. He'll die of heart failure. 4. Get the church to unite in prayer for the preacher and he'll soon become so effective that some large church will take him off your hands."

> *When your preacher is doing*
> *The best that he can,*
> *Pray for him, help him —*
> *He's only a man!*   — P. Langvand

Prayerless pews make for powerless pulpits!

FISHING IN A TUB

Thou, therefore, endure hardness, as a good soldier of Jesus Christ.   2 Timothy 2:3

The other day I read about a man who decided that his weekly fishing excursion was costing him too much money and causing him too much work. Therefore he purchased a large washtub, filled it with water, placed it under a shade tree in his backyard, pulled up a comfortable lawn chair and started his fishing. It seemed like a great idea. He thought of the money he was saving, and of the fact that he was no longer weary from hooking and unhooking his boat and loading and unloading his motor. He was also avoiding the bother of toting a gasoline can, tackle box, and supply of bait. Often he caught as many fish out of the tub as he did when he worked so hard on the lake or stream! (Exactly nothing!) However, this business of fishing in a tub gradually lost its appeal. He never felt the tingle of excitement that comes when the bobber disappears and a sudden tug is felt on the line. He also missed the fact that he no longer could tell stories to his friends about the large fish he caught, or the larger one that got away. Finally, he decided that although fishing in a tub is cheaper and easier, it is not nearly as rewarding as going to a lake or stream.

Christians who are primarily concerned with relaxation and ease will soon find that life without discipleship and zealous service is not very rewarding. It's like fishing in a tub! Paul knew this, so he exhorted Timothy to endure hardness like a good soldier, to strive to excel like a determined athlete, and to toil patiently like a faithful farmer. This is the kind of Christian life that pays dividends and produces inner joy and satisfaction. Only thus can one know the thrill of being a true "fisher of men" and of bringing a needy soul to Jesus Christ!

> *Fishers would you be of men?*
> *Cut loose every shoreline then;*
> *Listen to the Master speak:*
> *"Launch out! Launch out into the deep!"*
> — J. Oatman, Jr.

If you are not "FISHING," you are not properly FOLLOWING the Lord!

ABOVE REPROACH

. . . neither was there any error or fault found in him.
                                        Daniel 6:4

The kingdom of Babylon had fallen to Darius the Mede. It was placed under the jurisdiction of 120 princes, who in turn were responsible to three presidents, of whom Daniel was number one. He so conducted himself in that high office that Darius "thought to set him over the whole realm." However, the other presidents and princes — apparently jealous of this Hebrew — began to devise means of getting rid of him. In their time there wasn't anything like the FBI, but I'm sure that in some way they had Daniel placed under surveillance day and night with the orders, "Watch that man! Investigate him thoroughly. Report anything which might be used to bring about his demotion." But, hard as they tried, "they could find none occasion nor fault; for . . . he was faithful, neither was there any error or fault in him." What a record! What a testimony! In his secular employment he was loyal to his superior and conscientiously performed his duties, all the while giving God first place. That's why they said, "We shall not find any occasion against this Daniel, *except we find it against him concerning the law of his God.*" So far above reproach was Daniel's life that they had to manipulate things to "create" a situation where his "religion" would come into conflict with his "government job."

I wonder, how would we stand under such an examination? In our places of employment, are we so faithful in fulfilling the obligations of our positions that our fellow workers can "find none occasion nor fault"? It's wonderful to speak about Christ to others, but the influence of a life so lived, a job so faithfully performed that others find "no error or fault" is something that silences the critic, "speaks" with great eloquence, and glorifies God. So live that others may "see your good works, and glorify your Father, who is in heaven" (Matt. 5:16).

> *Give me a faithful heart, likeness to Thee,*
> *That each departing day henceforth may see*
> *Some work of love begun, some deed of kindness done,*
> *Some wanderer sought and won, something for Thee.*
> — S. D. Phelps

The world judges your faithfulness not so much by what you PROFESS, as by what you PRACTICE!

THE CRY FOR LOVE

Beloved, let us love one another; for love is of
God. . . . 1 John 4:7

Someone sent me this clipping — from what source I do not know — which touched me so deeply that I take the liberty of passing it on to you. A father writes: "One year ago today I sat at my desk with a month's bills and accounts before me, when my bright-faced, starry-eyed lad of 12 rushed in and impetuously announced, 'Say, Dad, this is your birthday; you're 55 years old, and I am going to give you 55 kisses, one for each year!' He began to make good on his word, when I exclaimed, 'Oh, Andrew, don't do it now; I am too busy!' His silence attracted my attention, and looking up I saw his big blue eyes fill with tears. Apologetically I said, 'You can finish tomorrow.' He made no reply, but was unable to conceal his disappointment. His face wore a grieved expression as he quietly walked away. That same evening, I said, 'Come and finish the kisses now, Andrew.' But he either did not hear me, or was not in the mood, for he did not respond to my invitation. Two months later, as a result of an accident, the waves of a nearby river closed over his body and we carried him away to 'sleep' near the little village where he loved to spend his vacations. The robin's note was never sweeter than his voice, and the turtle dove that cooed to its nestlings was never so gentle as my little boy, who left unfinished his love-imposed task. If only I could tell him how much I regret those thoughtless words I spoke, and could be assured that he understands and knows how much my heart is aching because of my unkind request, there would be no man in all this wide world so inexpressibly happy as the one who sits today and thinks how he prevented an act that love inspired, and grieved a little heart that was all tenderness and affection."

Such regrets are most painful! Today let us go forth determined to *take time to show love* — especially to our dear ones.

> *Take time to laugh and sing and play*
> *To really cherish and enjoy*
> *A little girl with flaxen curls,*
> *Or the small wonder of a boy.*
> *They ask so little when they're small:*
> *Just love and tenderness — that's all!* —Anon.

The love we give is the only love we keep!

CRAMMING FOR THE FINALS

. . . be ye doers of the word and not hearers only,
deceiving your own selves.   James 1:22

Some time ago *The Grand Rapids Press* carried an article about a man 91 years of age. Introduced as a guest at a luncheon for retired people, he told them he divided his time between reading and attending meetings of the American Association of Retired Persons. Asked what he read, he replied, "The Bible!" His questioner expressed surprise that at 91 he was just now consulting that Book. "Oh, I've read it before," he explained, "but *I'm cramming for the finals!"*

It certainly was commendable for this elderly gentleman to be occupied with the Word of God as he faced up to the brevity of life, but one doesn't "cram for the finals" in that way! While we should study the Scriptures and learn all we can about them, the important thing is to be sure first of all that we know the Christ of the Bible as a personal Savior, for only then through the Holy Spirit's power will we be able to put into practice the teachings of the Scriptures. Just "cramming" and getting a lot of *head knowledge* is not very profitable. Some people can quote the Bible books backward as well as forward, and recite many favorite passages, but have never translated that knowledge into "action." James says, "Be ye *doers* of the word and not hearers only, deceiving your own selves." In Romans 14:10 we are told that "we shall all stand before the judgment seat of Christ" where "every man's *work* shall be made manifest . . . because it shall be revealed by fire; and the fire shall test every man's *work* of what sort it is. If any man's *work* abide which he hath built upon it, he shall receive a reward. If any man's *work* shall be burned, he shall suffer loss; but he himself shall be saved, yet as by fire" (1 Cor. 3:13-15). The best way to prepare "for the finals" is not by "cramming" at the last minute, but starting as early as possible to receive the Word of faith, and then to be *"doers"* of it as well!

> *The Word of God by faith received*
> *Imparts regeneration;*
> *And he who hath in Christ believed,*
> *Lives out a new creation!*   —Whittle

Regarding the Bible, we should know it in our heads, stow it in our hearts, and show it in our lives!

TWO VIEWS OF LIFE

Henceforth there is laid up for me a crown of
righteousness . . . .   2 Timothy 4:8

Every year thousands of people commit suicide; in fact, the number of such deaths has been increasing at an alarming rate. The reason is not difficult to discover. Most educated people who do not know Jesus Christ believe we are the accidental products of evolution. They say there is nothing that has lasting value, and our actions whether good or bad are not of eternal consequence. In other words, they reject the idea of Heaven or Hell after death. As a result, most of these individuals are wretchedly unhappy, even though they may give themselves quite unreservedly to sensual pleasures. Without faith in God, life is absurd, tragic, and meaningless. Although it is popular to think in terms of living without God, it is becoming increasingly evident that human beings, created in the likeness and image of God, cannot live with such a concept

We see evidence of this in modern art. Many of us have laughed as we stood before such so-called "masterpieces." All we could see was an apparently meaningless mixture of lines, blots, and blurs. Yet these works are considered great from the artistic point of view because through them the painter has expressed his utter frustration with life as he sees it. They exhibit the feelings of his tortured soul. Indeed, some artists have committed suicide right after the completion of such a painting. *The world is going mad because men who have been made for God are trying to live without Him!*

How utterly different was Paul's concept. Because of Jesus Christ, life for him had real meaning. He looked forward to Heaven where he would receive a glorious reward for earthly faithfulness (2 Tim. 4:8). If you know Christ, thank God for the difference He makes. Then share this good news with others.

"To live is Christ," and death is "gain,"
If for the Lord we spend each day!
"Redeem the time" — 'tis God's own gift,
Let us not squander it away! —Bosch

Life is the seedtime of eternity!

PRECEPTS FOR PILLOWS

And we know that all things work together for good
to them that love God . . . . Romans 8:28

In prayer meeting at church one night, one of the ladies shared a story she had heard that morning about a woman in the hospital. In the days prior to her operation, the afflicted woman spent much time in prayer and Bible study and found three verses which brought special comfort. They had to do with God's love, His mercy, and His wonderful grace. She thought of these three Scripture passages as "pillows," since she was resting upon them in a very special way in view of the coming surgery.

As she came out of the anesthetic following the operation, she grasped for one of the pillows on her bed. The doctor quickly stopped her and said, "I'm sorry, but you can't use that since it's very important that you lie perfectly still and remain on your back." "Well, doctor," the woman replied, "you may keep *that pillow* from me, but I have three of my own that you can't take away." The doctor assumed she wasn't fully conscious and humored her, saying, "Three pillows of your own? I don't see any!" More alert than the doctor imagined, the patient explained that three Bible verses had become her "pillows of comfort" as she prepared for surgery. "My first pillow is Romans 8:38, 39, 'For I am persuaded that neither death, nor life, nor angels, nor principalities, nor powers, nor things present, nor things to come, nor height, nor depth, nor any other creation, shall be able to separate us from the *love of God* . . . .' My second pillow is Psalm 13:5, 'But I have trusted in thy *mercy* . . . .' And the third is Ephesians 2:8, 'For by *grace* are ye saved through faith . . . .' These are my three pillows that you can't take away, doctor, and I am resting upon them!" Leaving the room, the physician paused a moment in the doorway and whispered to her nurse, "We don't have to worry about her. She'll be well in no time!"

Though I do not know the reason,
I can trust, and so am blest;
God is love, and God is faithful,
So in perfect peace I rest. —Anon.

God's good promises put a rainbow of hope in every cloud and a "pillow of grace" in every bed of affliction! —H.G.B.

DON'T MISS IT!

*Not forsaking the assembling of ourselves together,
as the manner of some is.* Hebrews 10:25

At the time these words were written, Jewish believers were experiencing great persecution. They were being watched, beaten, and some were even killed. Any defection from their profession of faith was a source of great satisfaction to the enemies of Christ. One way which demonstrated to the world that they were holding "fast the profession of . . . [their] faith" (v. 23) was their assembling together. Matthew Henry wrote, "Forced absence from God's ordinances and forced presence with wicked people are great afflictions; *but* when the force ceases and such a situation is continued *of choice,* then it becomes a great sin." Some are unavoidably detained from meeting with other believers. Prolonged illness, an unalterable work schedule, residence in a remote area — these could be legitimate reasons why one could not gather with other Christians, for fellowship and instruction. To such comes the encouragement of His Word, "Where two or three are gathered together in my name, there am I in the midst of them" (Matt. 18:20).

Every Christian should desire to be with God's people when they assemble. The church service is where the power of the Word is brought to bear upon the hearts and lives of those who profess to be children of God. I remember well the little widow in our home church who with her eight children walked nearly two miles summer and winter in order to meet with other Christians. She has seen the influence of that training multiplied in the lives of her son and daughters.

Christ's promise to be "in the midst" should be sufficient incentive for every believer to be present.

I love Thy church, O God!
I prize her heavenly ways;
Her sweet communion, solemn vows,
Her hymns of love and praise. — Dwight

CH - - CH means nothing unless UR in it!

NO COMPLAINING IN OUR STREETS

> *. . . deliver me, . . . that there be no complaining*
> *in our streets.*   Psalm 144:11, 14

In the concluding verses of Psalm 144, David can be heard expressing his desire for the Lord's blessing upon his people. One of the things he requests from God is that there be "no complaining in our streets." One translator renders this phrase, "no outcry in our streets." Another says, "that there be no cry of distress in our city squares." Still another gives it this way, "May there be an end of raids and exile and of panic in our streets."

Any one of these renditions expresses a prayer that is most appropriate for our land today. We have departed from the Word of God and rejected His absolutes — those principles which would unify us and make us strong. As a result, an increasing polarization of divergent views divides us and contributes to the "complaining in our streets."

The only solution to our problem — the only thing that will help "bridge" the great chasm of differences between the various generations, races, and strata in society — is to return to the Bible, the written Word of God, and to the Lord Jesus Christ, the living Word.

How thankful we should be, however, that even though "complaining" and riots may not cease and may even increase for a time, we have the assurance that the Lord Jesus is coming again; and when His kingdom is established, ". . . the earth shall be full of the knowledge of the Lord, as the waters cover the sea" (Isa. 11:9). In that day there will be peace among the nations and "no complaining in our streets."

> *O happy day, when flock and field*
> *Their rich, abundant increase yield,*
> *And blessings multiply;*
> *When plenty all Thy people share,*
> *And no invading foe is there,*
> *And no distressful cry!*   —Anon.

When men forsake GODLY PRINCIPLES, they invite DEVILISH PROBLEMS!

REPRODUCTIONS IN MINIATURE

Looking unto Jesus . . . .   Hebrews 12:2

Many years ago the "High School Christian" related the following pointed incident: A young unknown artist wanted to copy a large beautiful picture that hung in a palace at Rome. While people were permitted to visit this royal gallery, they of course were not allowed to take a chair and easel and sit there and paint for long periods of time. The ambitious young man, however, did make one such attempt, but was told to move. He therefore decided to copy from memory the massive painting, and reproduce it in miniature. Hour after hour he would spend before the masterpiece until he could shut his eyes and see it in all its lovely detail. Then, hurrying home, he would begin to paint. Each day as he gazed on the picture, he saw some new loveliness. At last his small copy of that outstanding canvas was finished. The people who came to see it said, "Oh, this is so beautiful we must go and see the large, original picture," and then they would hurry off to the palace.

Christian, would you like to be like that artist? By grace you can be, for you can give to others a miniature view of the loveliest Person in the universe — the Lord Jesus Christ. To do so, however, you must spend much time with Him each day reading His Word, listening to His voice, and heeding His blessed admonitions. Then, as time passes, you will become more like Him as the Holy Spirit impresses the Savior's graces on your character and life. As a result, others will come to see that the Lord you serve is such a wonderful Person they will want to know Him too.

May the Lord help us to become so conformed to the image of His Son that we will be blessed reproductions in miniature of Him who is altogether lovely!

Oh, to be like Thee, blessed Redeemer,
 This is my constant longing and prayer.
 Gladly I'll forfeit all of earth's treasures,
 Jesus, Thy perfect likeness to wear.
                                        — T. O. Chisholm

Be sure you have the "mind of Christ," for the thoughts you think irradiate you as though you were a transparent vase!
                                        —Maeterlinck

February 21   Read Luke 9:57-62

"ME FIRST!"

> . . . *If any man will come after me, let him deny
> himself* . . . .   Matthew 16:24

The three men described by Luke in chapter 9, who showed
an interest in following the Savior, never really did so because
of "I" trouble. In verse 59 we hear Jesus saying to one of them,
"Follow Me." But notice the man's answer: "Lord, permit *me
first* to go and bury my father." In verse 61 another said, "I
will follow thee; but let *me first* go bid them farewell, who are
at home at my house." And in verse 57 we see that the other
individual must also have had *"me first"* trouble, since, when
faced with the discomforts of the "Jesus way" and the self-sacrifice required of those who would follow after Him, he suddenly
lost all interest. After Jesus' words to him, this one just seems
to disappear from the scene. Yes, all three men in Luke 9 had
"I" trouble. Confronted with the challenge of serving Christ
and the demands He placed upon them, it was their *"me first"*
attitude which robbed them of the joys and rewards of discipleship.

We don't have to go back into ancient history to find *"me
firsters."* One of the greatest drawbacks to the spread of the
Gospel today is that large number of believers who put themselves first and Christ last. For some, the idea of serving Christ
is frightening, the inconvenience involved is repelling, and the
"offense of the cross" embarrassing. There seem to be many who
are willing to come *to* Christ for salvation, for that costs them
nothing as Jesus has paid the complete price of redemption. Few,
however, are ready to follow *after* Christ, simply because this
involves self-sacrifice and saying no to selfish desires. Discipleship is not for the *"me firsters."*

When called upon for service — whether it be on the mission
field, in the pulpit, or just to minister to our nextdoor neighbor—
may we never be guilty of saying *"me first."* *Christ must always
have "first place" in our lives!* "For whosoever will save his life
shall lose it; and whosoever will lose his life for my sake shall
find it" (Matt. 16:25).

The first lesson in the school of Christ is that of SELF-denial!

"TIRED BLOOD"

> *. . . but by his own blood he entered in once into*
> *the holy place.*   Hebrews 9:12

God requires a blood sacrifice. From the time sin entered the world this has been true. He Himself slew the innocent animal, shedding the blood to clothe the sinful pair in the garden of Eden. Abel was accepted because he brought the offering God required: the firstling of the flock, a blood sacrifice. All of these were but promissory notes anticipating the Lamb of God whose blood was to be shed, providing the "one sacrifice for sins forever." Only *His blood* could atone for sin.

A friend facetiously sent us a card reading, "The Blood Donors Association wishes to inform you that no donation will be necessary because you have tired blood." This is true of Adam's family; we have not only tired but tainted blood, for "by one man sin entered into the world, and death by sin, and so death passed upon all men, for all have sinned" (Rom. 5:12).

An unblemished sacrifice was *essential* in paying the price of man's redemption. Only the spotless Lamb, God's well-beloved Son, could atone by shedding *His blood*. The poet expressed it so well: "Not all the blood of beasts on Jewish altars slain could give the guilty conscience peace or wash away the stain. But Christ the Heavenly Lamb takes all our sins away; a sacrifice of nobler name and richer blood than they." Not the "tired blood" of a sinful man or animal, but the precious blood of the Heaven-sent Sacrifice makes possible the removal of our sins.

Let us not forget it: "Without shedding of blood is no remission," and it is *"the blood that maketh atonement for the soul."* God is satisfied with His Son's offering. Nothing more is required.

> *Have you been to Jesus for the cleansing power?*
> *Are you washed in the blood of the Lamb?*
> *Are your garments spotless? Are they white as snow?*
> *Are you washed in the blood of the Lamb?* — Hoffman

God spells salvation with five letters: B-L-O-O-D !

GOD'S LIMITLESS SUPPLY

Blessed is the man whose strength is in thee, . . .
[he goes] from strength to strength. Psalm 84:5, 7

The story is told of a lady who had never seen an ocean. With much enthusiasm, therefore, her grandchildren finally had the opportunity to take her to the seashore. They could hardly wait to get her reaction when she first saw that huge expanse of water. As they drove to the beach, she was perfectly silent. Walking down to the water's edge, she still made no comment of any kind. Finally they could wait no longer and cried out, "Well, Grandma, what do you think of the ocean?" She took one more long, hard look and then said quite abruptly, "I'm disappointed. *I thought it was bigger!*"

We smile at this because such a comment seems ridiculous. To the human eye the ocean stretches out as it were into infinity. Yet, in the spiritual realm, how many Christians limit the boundless ocean of God's mercy, love, and grace because of their small faith. They act as if the provisions of their Heavenly Father will not be sufficient for their particular circumstances. How foolish! For as Annie Johnson Flint expressed it so beautifully,

"His love has no limit, His grace has no measure,
His power has no boundary known unto men,
For out of His infinite riches in Jesus,
He giveth and giveth and giveth again!"

Have you availed yourself of God's gracious offer of salvation? Have you experienced the joy of redeeming love? Is the peace of God flooding in upon your soul? If so, you know by personal experience the joys of God's limitless supply!

Marvelous, infinite, matchless grace,
Freely bestowed on all who believe;
You that are longing to see His face,
Will you this moment His grace receive?
— Johnston

The Lord's super-abundant GRACE to us may be simply defined as God's Riches At Christ's Expense!

FAITH OR FEAR — WHICH?

Be anxious for nothing.   Philippians 4:6

Worry is merely unbelief parading in disguise! The Scriptures repeatedly warn us against this grievous sin. Ian Maclaren exclaims, "What does your anxiety do? It does not empty tomorrow of its sorrow, but it does empty today of its strength. It does not make you escape the evil; it makes you unfit to cope with it when it comes. God gives us the power to bear all the sorrow of *His making,* but He does not guarantee to give us strength to bear the burdens of *our own making* such as worry induces."

An experienced physician decided to analyze the "worriers" who were his patients. He found that 40 percent of them were apprehensive over things that never happened. About 30 percent concerned themselves with past matters now beyond their control. Another 12 percent anxiously feared the loss of their health, although their only illness was in their imagination. And the rest worried about their families, friends, and neighbors, but in most cases he discovered no basis for their fears.

A bassoon player once came to the great conductor Toscanini with furrowed brow and complained that his instrument would not sound the high E flat. Toscanini smiled and replied, "Don't worry. There is no E flat in your music tonight." The musician had been needlessly apprehensive. Many of our worries are like that — unfounded and unnecessary.

Worry is both unprofitable and ungodly. God's grace will be sufficient for each day's need. Take comfort in this thought, and tread the pathway of life with faith, not fear!

> *I walked life's path with "Worry,"*
>   *Disturbed and quite unblessed,*
> *Until I trusted Jesus;*
>   *Now "Faith" has given rest.*   — G.W.

Satan seeks to crush our spirit by getting us to bear tomorrow's burdens with only today's grace!

HEART MUSIC

> . . . *in psalms and hymns and spiritual songs* [*sing*]
> . . . *in your hearts to the Lord.*   Colossians 3:16

We are encouraged in the Scriptures to sing. Whether songs of praise, worship, adoration, or dedication, they should emanate from the heart. They must never be mere hypocritical vocalizations of nice-sounding sentiments.

Some good questions to ask yourself the next time you pick up a hymnbook in church are these: Do I really mean what I'm singing? Is this coming from my heart, or am I just going through the motions?

On Wednesday evening we sing, " 'Tis the Blessed Hour of Prayer" and then allow our thoughts to wander aimlessly while others pray. We plead with enthusiasm, "Bring Them In" and later gripe about the repeated call for Sunday school bus drivers. We sing, "For the Beauty of the Earth" and then litter it with garbage and debris. We raise our voices to ask, "Is it the Crowning Day?" and proceed to live as though we had never heard of the Savior's return. We love the hymn, "Holy Bible, Book Divine" but spend most of our time reading newspapers and periodicals. We declare in song, "I Love to Tell the Story" and can't remember the last time we spoke a word for Christ. We sing, "Just One Step at a Time" and immediately begin to worry about tomorrow! This is not singing *from our hearts*. Someone has observed that "when the heart moves devoutly with the voice, true heart-singing results." I would add that it is whenever "the heart *and hand* move devoutly with the voice." The sincerity of our devotion is demonstrated by what we *sing* and *do*. When our songs are matched by our deeds — this is *heart music!*

> Singing and praying and working,
>   Zealously walking His way;
> Heart and hand active in service,
>   Living for Jesus each day!   —G.W.

A SONG coupled with SERVICE will usually outlive a SER-MON in the memory.   —Giles

TOWARD ETERNITY

> *. . . things . . . seen are temporal, but the things*
> *which are not seen are eternal.* 2 Corinthians 4:18

Men have varying reactions when faced with the possibility of departure from this earthly existence. When quite suddenly confronted with eternity, the soul is stripped of sham and pretense.

John Bacon, eminent English sculptor, said on his deathbed, "What I was as an artist seemed to be of some importance while I lived; but what I really am as a believer in the Lord Jesus Christ is the only thing of importance to me now." Michael Faraday, chemist, electrician, and philosopher, was asked by a distinguished scientist, "Have you ever pondered by yourself what will be your occupation in the next world?" Faraday hesitated awhile and then responded, "I shall be with Christ, and that is enough." The Scottish theologian Samuel Rutherford gave this triumphant testimony before he took the step into eternity, "Mine eye shall see my Redeemer. He has pardoned, loved, and washed me, and given me joy unspeakable and full of glory. Glory shines in Immanuel's land!"

These are the words of men who rested their case in the all-sufficient keeping of a living Lord. Worldly attainment meant nothing to them as they contemplated seeing the Lord Jesus. Theirs had been a life lived in communion with God, and not in slavery to a world that is passing away. Let us say with the poet: "Not life, nor all the toys of art, nor pleasure's flowery road, can to my soul such bliss impart as fellowship with God."

Robert Murray McCheyne said, "Live so near to God that all earthly things will appear to you as little in comparison with eternal verities."

> *The things of sight shall pass away,*
> *But things unseen abide for aye;*
> *O soul, what will thy portion be,*
> *Where will you spend eternity?* —Anon.

Let us never forget that the texture of eternity is woven on the looms of time!
                                                        —Lehman

AUTISTIC LISTENERS

*Hear now this . . . [ye] . . . who have ears, and hear
not: Fear ye not me? saith the Lord.* Jeremiah 5:21, 22

Recently the *London Times* stated that there are about 4,000
autistic children in Britain. These unfortunate youngsters usually
do not react to messages received and transmitted from the eyes
and ears to the brain. Consequently, they live in a world where
words have little or no meaning. This is a terrible physical affliction, but my mind immediately was drawn to the oft-repeated
words of our Lord concerning the listeners in His day who were
thus *spiritually* afflicted. Of them He said, "Hearing, they hear
not, neither do they understand" (Matt. 13:13). The reason for
such "autistic" listeners is clear. Unconverted men are spiritually
"dead in trespasses and sins" (Eph. 2:1). Only as the Holy
Spirit enlightens them and gives them life in Christ can they
"hear his voice" and follow Him.

A certain ungodly tavern keeper who was very fond of music
decided to attend one of John Wesley's Methodist gatherings in
order to hear the singing. He had resolved, however, not to listen
to the sermon, and therefore sat with his head down and his
fingers in his ears. But when God wants to speak to a soul, He
can make His voice heard even if He uses means that may seem
strange to us. As the man stubbornly refused to listen, a fly lit
upon his nose. For a moment he moved his hand to drive it
away, and in so doing, nine words of the sermon were brought
to his attention: *"He that hath ears to hear, let him hear."* From
that moment the man had no rest in his soul. He came to the
next meeting, listened eagerly to the Gospel, and was saved. Have
you heard the Savior's voice? "Hear, and your soul shall live!"

> *I hear Thy welcome voice,*
> *That calls me, Lord, to Thee,*
> *For cleansing in Thy precious blood*
> *That flowed on Calvary.*   — Hartsough

There is no one so deaf as the person who refuses to hear!

DOING GOOD

*Bear ye one another's burdens, and so fulfill the law
of Christ.* Galatians 6:2

A poem by Mrs. Charles points out a real need in Christian
circles today — a duty emphasized in our text:

> Is thy cruse of comfort failing?
> Rise and share it with another,
> And through all the years of famine
> It shall serve thee and thy brother.
>
> Love divine will fill thy storehouse,
> Or thy handful still renew.
> Scanty fare for one will often
> Make a royal feast for two.
>
> Numb and weary on the mountains
> Wouldst thou sleep amidst the snow?
> Chafe that frozen form beside thee,
> And together both shall glow.
>
> Art thou stricken in life's battle?
> Many wounded round thee moan;
> Lavish on their wounds thy balsams
> And that balm shall heal thine own.
>
> For the heart grows rich in giving —
> All its wealth is living grain,
> Seeds which mildew in the garner;
> Scattered, fill with gold the plain.
>
> Is thy burden hard and heavy?
> Do thy steps drag wearily?
> Help to bear thy brother's burden;
> God will bear both it and thee.

A dear old saint of God gave this sound advice to a young
Christian: "Do all the good you can; to all the people you can;
in all the ways you can; and as long as ever you can." Very likely
he had Paul's words in mind, "As we have, therefore, opportunity,
let us do good unto all men . . ." (Gal. 6:10).

**The best exercise for the heart is to reach down and pull other
people up!**

WITHIN CALLING DISTANCE

Speak, Lord; for thy servant heareth. 1 Samuel 3:9

A Bible conference speaker, the father of several boys, told this interesting story which has a precious application. He said that when his sons were small they often played outdoors until mealtime. They had been instructed to remain nearby so that they could come in immediately when called. One day one of the lads did not appear with the others in response to the parental summons. The rest of the family had prayer, ate the meal, held devotions, and the table was cleared. Finally the tardy one arrived and expressed his disappointment. "Why didn't you call me?" he asked. The father gently replied, "I did, son, but you were not within calling distance!"

Have you ever wondered why God spoke to Samuel rather than to Eli? It was because Eli had not been faithful in disciplining his wicked sons. He had been more interested in pleasing his sons than in honoring and properly serving God, and consequently was not living in fellowship with Him. Eli was out of "calling distance."

The Lord speaks to us today through His Word as the blessed Holy Spirit takes its message and makes it real. The Christian who daily reads the Bible, spends time in prayer, submits himself to God, and earnestly strives to live victoriously will experience the truth of Romans 8:16, "The Spirit himself beareth witness with our spirit, that we are the children of God."

The Bible teacher's son we mentioned earlier was deprived of a delightful time of food and fellowship because he was not within the range of his father's voice. So, too, the Lord could not communicate with Eli because he was not "within calling distance." Are you living where God can speak to you?

> *O give me Samuel's ear, the open ear, O Lord,*
> *Alive and quick to hear each whisper of Thy Word;*
> *Like him to answer at Thy call,*
> *And to obey Thee first of all!*—J. Drummond Burns

It is hard to tune in on Heaven's message if our lives are full of earthly static!

LITTLE BIG THINGS

Behold, how great a matter a little fire kindleth!
James 3:5

Recently I came across an article which underscores in a most effective way the value and import of so-called "little things," and I want to share it with you today. J. Ellis tells us: "In the state of Ohio stands a courthouse which is uniquely constructed so that the raindrops which fall on the north side go into Lake Ontario and the Gulf of St. Lawrence, while those falling on the south side go into the Mississippi and the Gulf of Mexico. At that point just a puff of wind can determine the destiny of a rain drop. It will make a difference of over 2,000 miles. What a suggestive thought that you and I may, in certain situations by the smallest deed or choice of words, also set in motion influences that shall not only change lives here and now, but also affect their final Home as well."

A sympathetic glance, a kind word, a helpful deed, a sincere testimony, a solemn warning, an invitation to church, yes, even a "pat on the back" — any one of these "little things" can become a big thing. It could be like that "puff of wind" on the raindrops. It could well help to determine the happiness, the direction, and even the destiny of an eternal soul. It is an old truth, but it still can stand underscoring, that "no one lives to himself, for no man is an island." Either by what he does, or does not do, every person has a positive or negative effect upon his "neighbor." We are either hindering or helping others.

So let us remember the story of "the wind and the raindrops," and that sometimes it doesn't take much to alter the course or affect the destiny of a friend's life. A small bit turns the horse, a little rudder guides the ship on a long journey, and a spark can ignite a great fire. Be careful about those "little big things" in life!

> *No service in itself is small;*
> *None great, though earth it fill;*
> *But that is small that seeks its own,*
> *And great that does God's will.* —Anon.

God hangs the greatest weights upon the smallest wires.—Bacon

March 2 Read Proverbs 11:18-31
THE AMPUTEE SOUL WINNER
He that believeth on me . . . out of his heart shall
flow rivers of living water. John 7:38

We are saved to tell others! When the Lord redeems us, He so fills us with "living water" that, if we are normal Christians, we overflow to others in a witness that produces results for God.

There recently came to my attention the true story of an amputee soul winner in Melbourne, Australia, who has a most remarkable ministry. A pastor who visited this crippled woman writes, "When this girl was 18, she was seized with a dreadful affliction and the doctor said that to save her life he must take off her foot. Next the other foot was removed. The disease continued to spread, and her legs had to be amputated at the hips. Then the malady broke out in her hands. And by the time I saw Miss Higgins, all that remained of her was just the trunk of her body. For 15 years now she has been in this condition. I went to offer comfort, but I did not know how to speak to her or what to say. I found the walls of her room covered with texts, all of them radiating joy, and peace, and power. She explained that one day while lying in bed she inquired of the Lord what a total amputee could possibly do for Him. Then an inspiration came to her. Calling a friend of hers, who was a carpenter, she had him construct a device to fit her shoulder, and attach to it an extension holding a fountain pen. Then she began to write letters witnessing to the grace of God. She had to do it entirely with body movement, yet her penmanship was beautiful. She has now received over 15 hundred replies from individuals who have been brought to Christ through the letters she produced in that way." The preacher said to her; "How do you do it?" and she smilingly replied, "You know Jesus said of His own that out of them 'shall flow rivers of living water.' I believe in Him, and He has helped me to overflow to others."

Does not that amputee soul winner put all of us to shame? Have you tried to bring even one lost sheep into the Savior's fold? If not, *why not?*

We are not storerooms, but channels,
We are not cisterns, but springs;
Passing our benefits onward,
Fitting our blessings with wings. —Anon.

If "he that winneth souls is wise" what is the implication concerning those who don't? **—H.G.B.**

THE "LAUGHTER OF THE HEART"

A merry heart doeth good like a medicine. . . .
Proverbs 17:22

After Rufus Mosley became a Christian, he fairly bubbled with irrepressible joy. A few dour souls even doubted his sanity. However, a man who observed him closely for a week said to his wife, "There may be someone 'crazy' around here, but it isn't Brother Rufus!"

Mirth has become a commercial commodity. Entertainers who can make people hilarious with their humor draw fabulous salaries. Laugh meters register the success of a performer, and millions subscribe to the old axiom, "Laughter is the best medicine." We who know the Lord recognize that the adage just quoted contains a good deal of truth. However, we also realize that the world's gaiety is usually shallow, because it does not come from within, nor arise from true contentment of spirit. What men really need is the "deep-down *laughter of the heart.*" Therefore the writer of Proverbs says, "A *merry heart* doeth good like a medicine." Physicians will confirm that people with *true faith in God* and a real "will to live" have a much better rate of survival than downhearted, depressed individuals. Yes, "laughter of the heart" is a splendid "medicine"!

The words "rejoice" and "joy" appear in the Bible hundreds of times. Think of Paul writing his epistles from *a Roman prison* and saying, "Rejoice, and again I say rejoice!" Yet, when we think it through, this is not so strange, for believers should be the most contented of all people, knowing that their Savior has forgiven their sins, given them peace with God, and that He constantly guides their feet. Then, to crown it all, eternal glory also awaits them at the end of their earthly road. No wonder the Psalmist exclaims, "Rejoice in the Lord, ye righteous" (Ps. 97:12).

Yes, the Christian faith provides God's children with true happiness and the invigorating "laughter of the heart"!

I came to Jesus as I was,
Weary, and worn, and sad;
I found in Him a resting place,
And He has made me glad. — H. Bonar

Some people carry religion on their backs like a burden, while true Christians carry it in their hearts like a song!

UNBELIEVING PRAYER

*. . . when they . . . saw him [Peter], they were
astonished.*   Acts 12:16

The story is told about a church in a small town which seemed
to have everything going its way. There were no gambling ca-
sinos, no liquor stores, and no "beer joints" in the entire area.
After several years, however, a night club was built right on
Main Street. The congregation was very much disturbed and
held several all-night prayer meetings in which some members
specifically asked God to burn the tavern down. Well, a few
days later, during a tremendous thunderstorm, lightning did strike
the drinking establishment and fire completely demolished it. The
owner, knowing how the church had prayed, sued them for dam-
ages. His lawyer claimed that it was their prayers which caused
the loss. The church, however, hired their own lawyer and
fought the charges. After many hearings and much deliberation,
the judge declared: "It is the opinion of this court that wherever
the guilt may lie, *the tavern owner is the one who really believes in prayer, while the church members do not!*" Doesn't this
suggest how faithless we often are? Even those in the early
church were guilty of such unbelieving prayer. Acts 12 tells us
that Peter, having escaped from prison, went to the house of
Mary the mother of John where many Christians were gathered
together praying for his release. He knocked, and Rhoda went
to the door; but, hearing his voice, she was so thrilled that, without opening it, she ran to the "prayer meeting crowd" and told
them that Peter was outside. "Thou art mad!" they said. As she
insisted that it was really Peter, they concluded, "It is his angel."
As the apostle continued knocking, they finally opened the door.
Seeing him, they *"were astonished."* How often we are like
that: surprised at the way God answers prayer.

When we pray, let us be confident that God "is able to do
exceedingly abundantly above all that we ask or think" (Eph. 3:
20).

> *God answers prayer; shouldst thou complain?*
> *Be not afraid, thou canst not ask in vain.*
> *He only waits thy faith in Him to prove,*
> *Doubt not His power e'en mountains to remove!*
>   —Anon.

Have faith to believe that where prayer focuses, power falls!

A YOUNG LAMB IN HIS BOSOM

*He shall feed his flock like a shepherd; he shall
gather the lambs with his arm, and carry them in
his bosom. . . .*   Isaiah 40:11

Young Donnie looked at the beautiful picture of Jesus which
showed a flock of sheep about Him, and one little lamb cradled
in His arms. As he gazed, he declared thoughtfully, *"Mamma,
that little lamb is me!"* Tiny Donald Sundbo, age four, little
knew how soon he would be at Home with God in Jesus' bosom.
Always a sweet and thoughtful child, he had recently said that
he wanted Jesus to be his Savior. On the last Sunday of his life
his parents held the following conversation with him: "Do you
remember, Donnie, when you were saved at home?" "Oh, yes."
"Are you glad that you're saved, so that someday you can go
to be with Jesus?" "Yes, but tell me, what's it like in Heaven,
Mother?" "Oh, it's lovely there, Donnie, it's very, very beautiful.
The angels will greet you along with Jesus; and Mommie, Daddy,
and sister Betty will come soon, too," he was told, while the tears
coursed down their cheeks. "Will all the people in town come?"
asked the little one innocently. "Yes, if they are saved, Donnie."
Twenty-four hours later the little sufferer was much weaker. But
as his parents were leaving the hospital, he said, "Pray with me."
After the prayer, he spoke the last words they were to hear from
him in this life, "Good-by, Daddy!" The next day, having lapsed
into a coma, Donnie was not aware that his parents were with
him. Both testified, however, that the room seemed to be filled
with a holy presence as if the angels were hovering over his little
bed waiting to carry him home to Heaven. At his funeral, the
songs, "Does Jesus Care?" and "Under His Wings" were sung.
The latter was chosen because Donnie loved it so well and had
sung it so heartily in the waiting room of the doctor's office, just
before they received word that his disease was to be fatal. While
parents and friends wept, the angels in Heaven rejoiced as another little lamb found joy and rest in Jesus' bosom!

> *Lord, a little lamb has left our home,*
> *And entered Heav'n today;*
> *For Thou didst stoop and lift him up*
> *To dwell with Thee for aye!*   —Anon.

Death is but the voice of Christ saying, "Come unto Me!"

A BIRD ON A CHIMNEY

. . . how can one be warm alone? Ecclesiastes 4:11

It was a bitterly cold morning. The night before had been one of those quiet ones when not a breeze stirs, and no cloud dims the brilliance of the starry heavens. Driving up the street from my home, with the sound of crunching snow under the tires, I could see trails of vapor ascending straight up from chimneys all over the neighborhood. These smoky columns appeared a frosty white as they glistened in the rays of the morning sun. Suddenly my eyes were arrested by one chimney in particular. There was a dark object on top of it. As I came closer, I recognized that a bird (and a wise old fellow he was) had perched there to soak up some heat. In that "cold, cold world," he had found a place of warmth, while his other feathered friends were no doubt shivering in their frigid sub-zero surroundings. As I saw him there, I was reminded anew that we, as believers, live in a spiritually cold world that is no "friend to grace." Wise is that Christian who avails himself of those warming influences provided by God Himself, such as Bible study, prayer, and the asembling together with those of like precious faith. What a blessing is afforded to those who meet regularly with other believers for fellowship and worship. Much of the spiritual coldness we see today is because folks neglect this sacred duty which has been especially ordained by God Himself for the benefit of those who are chilled in their soul by the adverse winds of this hostile world. The author of Hebrews admonishes us not to forsake "the assembling of ourselves together, as the manner of some is," but rather to exhort one another more and more, as we see the day of Christ's return approaching (Heb. 10:25).

The writer of Ecclesiastes asks, ". . . how can one be warm alone?" I would make an application of this to believers today. If a person refuses to gather regularly with others for the teaching of the Word, the breaking of bread, and the joys of Christian fellowship, ". . . how can [he] be warm alone?"

> *With joy we hail the sacred day*
> *Which God hath called His own;*
> *With joy the summons we obey*
> *To worship at His throne.* — H. Auber

"Floating" church members make for a sinking church!

SEEKING GOD IN NATURE

Who . . . worshiped and served the creature more
than the Creator. . . . For this cause God gave them
up . . . .   Romans 1:25, 26

There are at least two reasons why nature is not sufficient in itself to lead men to a proper understanding of God. First, nature has been twisted and distorted by sin; and secondly, man's perception and reasoning in regard to nature has also become warped since Adam's fall plunged the human race into a state of depravity. Man therefore needs special revelation if he is to know God as he ought. While he may discover something of the Lord's power and wise design in creation, he will never find the "Door" of personal salvation apart from the Bible!

Once when Dan Crawford was speaking in Boston, a fashionable society lady came to him afterward and said, "Why don't the natives just look up through nature to nature's God?" "That's just exactly what they do," replied Crawford. "They know from their observation that there is a God, but oh the thoughts they have of Him! Everywhere the strong devours the weak. They see the lion pull down the antelope; the drought and the locust destroy their crops; and the pestilence kills their children, so when they look up into the calm blue heavens they conclude that God really doesn't care what happens to them."

Only when men see God in the Person of the Lord Jesus Christ as He is revealed in the Scriptures, is the human heart satisfied concerning the Lord's great love for all mankind (John 3:16). To know the Divine will it is necessary to study the Bible. The wonders of creation, when interpreted by the Scriptures, have value; but when viewed only philosophically and without the Word, the outcome is disastrous (Rom. 1:21-25). Men, directed only by the light of nature, end up worshiping and serving the creature more than the Creator. As a result, God has to give them up!

Though much in nature sings God's praise,
And reason's light is well possessed,
Still man needs Revelation's rays
To find in Christ eternal rest. — G.W.

Why is it that so many people who say they want to find God only in nature go looking for Him with a golf club or a gun?

BE NOT DECEIVED

. . . Take heed that ye be not deceived. . . . Luke 21:8

A good friend of mine was "taken in" recently. A man, driving a new, luxurious car, stopped at his place of business with a trunk full of jewelry. He claimed that he had purchased this merchandise at a tremendous discount, and was passing on the savings to those who might be interested in making a few extra dollars. Taking out a box, he displayed some very impressive and expensive-looking watches. Across the face of the dials was written what appeared to be one of the best-known and most trusted names in the watch field. My friend was much impressed, especially so when this "gentleman" (?) informed him that he could buy them for only $10.00 each. What a bargain, he thought; and so he purchased 13 of them. The jewelry salesman having gone, my friend began to examine the merchandise more carefully. What a shock he received! Looking very closely he discovered that the name on the face of the watch was not that of a famous make after all. Two letters had been changed in the word, but the printing was so small that he hadn't noticed it before. The watch strap itself bore the information that it was "Genuine *Lizard*," and on the back of the watch case were imprinted these words: "Swiss *base metal*." The imprint on the face of the dial also seemed to convey the idea that it was an *electric* timepiece. Without careful examination one would be led to believe it was a famous make, had a genuine leather band, and an electric movement.

As I heard about this, I was reminded of the words of the Savior in Luke 21: *"Take heed that ye be not deceived."* Even as in the watch business, so there are those in religious circles who would lead us astray. Using theological terminology, they seek to beguile us into accepting their pernicious doctrines as the truth. Today with so many strange voices abroad in the land, what a need there is for us to be grounded firmly in the Word, lest we be deceived.

> *"Last days" shall bring many deceivers,*
>   *Who'll seek to ensnare foolish men,*
> *But with your eyes focused on Jesus,*
>   *Check up with your Bible again!* —Bosch

The principal method for defeating error and heresy is the establishing of truth!   —J. Newton

"I'M SORRY, LORD, I CAN'T MAKE IT!"

Also I heard the voice of the Lord, saying, Whom shall I send, and who will go for us? Then said I, Here am I; send me.   Isaiah 6:8

On occasion I meet Christians who tell me they once felt definitely called to the Lord's service, but through some changing circumstance, or some obstacle the devil threw in their way, they never said with Isaiah, "Here am I; send me!" Instead, their reply to God's insistent demand was, "I'm sorry, Lord, *I can't make it!*"

Recently someone sent me a clipping from the pen of Everek R. Storms which brings home this thought in a most effective way:

Ten future missionaries heard God's call divine;
  One was married wrongly; that left only nine.
Nine future missionaries — they could hardly wait.
  Mother needed one, though; that left only eight.
Eight future missionaries bound for God and Heaven.
  One got to making money; that left only seven.
Seven future missionaries — if only each one sticks.
  One lost out completely; that left only six.
Six future missionaries for the Lord alive.
  One preferred the homeland; that left only five.
Five future missionaries wait an open door.
  One grew tired of waiting; that left only four.
Four future missionaries bound for eternity.
  One no longer willing! that left only three.
Three future missionaries — for the need, how few.
  One the board rejected; that left only two.
Two future missionaries, a daughter and a son.
  One developed ulcers; that left only one.
One future missionary — thank the Lord for him.
  He refused to ever let the vision dim.
Body, soul, and spirit, he to God did yield.
  Now for years he's labored on the foreign field.
God in Heaven rejoices: "Blessed child of Mine,
  You have done My will — *but what about the nine?*"

Are you among those who have said, "I'm sorry, Lord, I can't make it?" I hope not!

At every breath you draw, four souls perish never having heard of Christ!

"NOBODIES" WHO ARE "SOMEBODIES"

*He raiseth up the poor . . . to set them among
princes. . . .*   1 Samuel 2:8

The Christian experience is one that produces revolutionary changes. The miracle of conversion creates a striking contrast between our past and our present state. We were lost, but now are found (Luke 19:10). We were children of wrath, but are now become children of God (Eph. 2:3). We walked in darkness, but now bask in God's "marvelous light" (1 Pet. 2:9). We were dead in sin, but have now been made spiritually alive (Eph. 2:1). Once we traveled the broad way that leads to destruction, but now our feet have been placed on the narrow path that leads to eternal life (Matt. 7:13, 14). We were under the judgment of God, but now are free from condemnation (John 3:18). We were "strangers . . . and without God in the world . . . But now . . . [are] made nigh by the blood of Christ" (Eph. 2:12, 13). These changes affect our day by day, practical living. While we are given a new nature which cannot sin, we must continue to contend with our old nature which still remains, and which can do nothing but sin (1 John 3:9; Rom. 7:15-24). We are in the world; yet we are not to be of the world. In God's sight we are justified, and thus "saints" positionally; yet in our own experience, we sin daily (Rom. 5:1; 1 John 1:8). The time is coming, however, when these apparently contradicting conditions will be resolved (1 John 3:1, 2). Until then, it is imperative that the Christian constantly remind himself of what he is in himself, and of what he has become in Christ. This keeps him alert to present pitfalls, causes him to give all glory to God for any victories won, and generates true humility and thankfulness.

No one of us has anything of which to boast, for in ourselves we are *"nobodies."* Christ, however, has been made unto us wisdom, righteousness, sanctification, and redemption (1 Cor. 1:30), and therefore we have become *"somebodies"!* We who were once spiritually "poor" have been made fit to "sit among princes."

     * *"In the Beloved" accepted am I,*
       Risen, ascended, and seated on high;
       Saved from all sin through His infinite grace,
       With the redeemed ones accorded a place. — C.D.M.
Every Christian has a "dual" nature, and who wins the "duel" depends on which nature he feeds!
           —G.W.

THE FRUIT OF AFFLICTION
. . . we glory in tribulations also. . . . Romans 5:3

We sometimes say that certain people have "two strikes" against them. By this we mean they start out their lives under the cloud of some difficulty. It may be the character of their parents, their environment, their appearance, or a disability that came upon them while they were still young. One such person was Mercy Goodfaith. She was an orphan, and at the age of ten was unhappy, sickly, ill-tempered, ugly, and hunch-backed. No one seemed to love her, and no one wanted her until one day a woman came to the orphanage looking for a child no one else would take.

Thirty-five years later reports were circulated that one county-appointed home for orphans stood out above all others. A case-worker reported that the children were clean and happy. The matron of this home frequently sang with the children while one of the older girls assisted by playing on a small pump organ. They all seemed to have a deep affection for the housemother and constantly flocked about her. She in turn gave each one the utmost in love and gracious attention. This great and helpful woman was none other than the outwardly ugly hunchback named Mercy Goodfaith. Her affliction had not made her bitter, but had led her into a life of service and devotion to others.

The patriarch Joseph also experienced a great deal of misfortune in his lifetime, first at the hand of his brothers and then in his early days in Egypt. He did not deserve the things he suffered. Yet he never became spiteful, never lost his faith, but was able to give a glowing testimony of his submission to the ways of God. The trials were necessary in order that the Lord's loving purpose for the sons of Jacob might be fulfilled.

Your misfortunes need not be tragedies. They can be stepping-stones to a life of sweet fellowship with God and service to others. *It is your response to affliction that makes the difference!*

> *For every hill I've had to climb,*
> *For every stone that bruised my feet,*
> *For all the blood and tears and grime,*
> *For blinding storms and burning heat,*
> *My heart sings but a grateful song—*
> *These were the things that made me strong!*—Anon.

The difficulties of life are intended by God to make us better—not bitter!

THERE IS NO GOD?

The heavens declare the glory of God . . . . Psalm 19:1

Some time ago Dr. W. T. Chewning of Augusta, Georgia, sent me an article, part of which I quote, as follows: "Some men say . . . 'There is no God.' All the wonders around you are accidental. No Almighty hand made a thousand billion stars. They made themselves. The top few inches of our land just happened to have top soil, without which we would have no vegetables to eat, no grass for the animals whose meat is our food. The inexhaustible envelope of air . . . only 100 miles deep, and of exactly the right density to support human life . . . is just another law of physics. Water expands when it freezes, while other substances contract. This makes ice lighter than water and keeps it floating on the surface. Otherwise lakes would be solid ice down to the bottom all year, and no fish could survive. Who made this arrangement? Why does the earth spin at a given speed without ever slowing up, so that we have day and night? Who tilts it so that we get seasons? The sun stokes a fire just warm enough to sustain us on earth, but not hot enough to fry us or cold enough to kill us. Who keeps the fire constant? The human heart will beat for 70 or 80 years without faltering. How does it get sufficient rest between beats? A kidney will filter poison from the blood and leave the good things alone. How does it know one from the other? Who gave the human tongue flexibility to form words, and a brain to understand them but denied it to all animals? It's all accidental? There is no God? That's what *some* people say . . ." but, the *Bible* says, "In the beginning *God* created the heaven and the earth" (Gen. 1:1); yet "The *fool* hath said in his heart, There is no God" (Ps. 53:1).

"GOD IS DEAD" — so says the would-be sage,
    Who prates his knowledge of the sacred page,
With sneers and egotistical bombast;
    A mind that neither reads the future nor the past;
Whoever scans the sunset and sees not God,
    Is as the beast of field — a simple clod;
Who heareth not a seraph song in birds that sing,
    Is like an eagle struggling to fly without a wing!
                    — Robert L. Conlon

Nothing is so impenetrable as a prejudice that closes its eyes to evidence!

TROUBLE WITH THE DOOR

I am the door; by me if any man enter in, he shall
be saved. . . .   John 10:9

The renowned magician and escape artist, Houdini, could get
out of any set of handcuffs, or any strait jacket that was ever
put on him. In fact, he could release himself from almost any
enclosure in less than one minute. Only once did he fail. That
strange incident occurred when he was touring the British Isles.
Arriving at a small town, he agreed to exhibit his ability by es-
caping from the local jail. The cell door was so ordinary looking
that he smiled at the simplicity of the task. On the given signal
he began to use all the terrific speed and dexterity he possessed
to effect his release. To his great surprise, he was unable to
pick the lock! Frantically he tried every device he knew, but
nothing happened. For two more hours he worked feverishly.
Finally, completely exhausted, he fell against the door and lamented his defeat. Immediately it sprang open. His frustration
had been due to the fact that *it had never been locked at all!*
How frequently, by a similar ruse, Satan has deluded poor sinners who are seeking to find a way to open the door of salvation!
They work, they cry, they fret, they pray — trying in every way
possible to bring release to their captive souls. Yet it is only when
they fall exhausted from their own efforts, and rest their all
against the "Door" — the Lord Jesus Christ — that they find the
immediate release they so desperately seek.

You who today are weeping and straining every nerve to escape the clutches of Satan, just let go, and let God do that which
your feverish trying will never accomplish. For having done all
that is necessary to please God, the Savior now provides the only
way to peace and Heaven. Lovingly He still invites men to stop
struggling and to enter by faith into the liberating joys of His
free salvation!

> *Life's uncertain, death is sure;*
> *Sin's the cause; Christ's the cure!*
> *Man can't do it; Hell's in store;*
> *God says, "Trust"; Christ's the Door!* —Anon.

The "windows" of Heaven's blessing (Mal. 3:10), can only open
to those who have first entered its "Door"!

A BIG CHANGE

. . . if any man be in Christ, he is a new creation;
old things are passed away; behold, all things are
become new.   2 Corinthians 5:17

Two flies landed on a man's head. One said to the other,
"There have been some mighty big changes made around here.
Why, the last time we visited this place, there was just a foot-
path. Now, there's a huge landing strip!" We too see change
all around us. It is characteristic of the very world in which we
live. When visiting a city we have not seen for some time, how
striking to observe the transformation that has taken place. Yes,
there is change all about us, and yet, oftentimes we do not
notice such improvement in that one place where we should most
expect it. I am thinking of the lives of those who profess to
know Christ as Savior. There are many who make an outward
profession, but who give no evidence of an inward possession,
or of spiritual growth. It is well for believers periodically to
take spiritual inventory. Determine how much progress has been
made. Comparing your Christian life as it is now with one
year ago, has there been any change? Was it for the better?
The Bible says, "But grow in grace" (2 Pet. 3:18). We revel
in the truth of salvation by grace through faith apart from human
works. Yet certainly, the very ones who are thus saved by grace
should increasingly show forth its transforming power in their
lives. Ephesians 2:8, 9 tells us: "For by grace are ye saved
through faith; and that not of yourselves, it is the gift of God —
Not of works, lest any man should boast." I am afraid, however,
that many do not realize there is a verse 10 which follows this
thrilling declaration. It reads, "For we are his workmanship,
created in Christ Jesus *unto good works,* which God hath before
ordained that we should walk in them."

When folks who knew you before your conversion see you,
they too should exclaim, "There's been a big change around here!
Let us all therefore *"bring forth fruit unto God"* (Rom. 7:4)!

* *What a wonderful change in my life has been wrought*
    Since Jesus came into my heart!
  I have light in my soul for which long I have sought,
    Since Jesus came into my heart!   —R. H. McDaniel

LIVE for Christ — He DIED and lives for you!

* © 1942 Renewal, Rodeheaver Co., owner. Used by permission.

BENEFICIAL DISCOMFORT

[God] led thee through that great and terrible wilder-
ness . . . that he might humble thee, and that he
might test thee, to do thee good at thy latter end.
                                    Deuteronomy 8:15, 16

I sometimes feel sorry for the boys and girls living in this age of affluence and comfort! Few of them know what it is to swelter under a hot sun as they toil in a field, or to feel the bite of winter's bitterly cold blasts while walking to school, or doing chores. Those who have known the discomfort of blistering heat have also appreciated the welcome coolness of a large shade tree, and those who have endured the stinging pain of frostbite have also known the cozy feeling of entering a warm house. This may sound as if I am saying the discomfort was good because it made us appreciate simple pleasures — much like the boy who said he liked to hit himself with a hammer because it felt so good when he stopped. That is not the point, however. True, those hard experiences did make us appreciate ordinary comforts, but they also taught us valuable lessons in *self-reliance, determination, courage,* and *industry!* We felt challenged to accomplish our tasks even though doing so involved some misery and much weariness. Those difficult lessons of life could not be learned in the way of ease and luxury.

The Israelites too had to endure their forty years of wandering through the wilderness, with its fiery serpents, scorpions, and drought, but the Lord subjected them to these trials to humble them and make them ready for their future role as His chosen people in the land of Canaan (Deut. 8:16).

Christian, you may not find pleasure in some of the disciplines of life, but remember that God in this way is also preparing you for eternity. He wants "to do thee good at thy latter end."

> *When through fiery trials thy pathway shall lie,*
> *My grace, all sufficient shall be thy supply;*
> *The flames shall not hurt thee; I only design*
> *Thy dross to consume, and thy gold to refine.*
>   —"K" in Rippon's selection

Sore trial makes common Christians into uncommon saints, fit for uncommon service!

REMOVE THE "GRAVECLOTHES"!

> *. . . put off . . . the old man, which is corrupt. . . .*
> Ephesians 4:22

The raising of Lazarus from the dead is a most striking portrayal of what occurs when one who is lost and dead in sin is given life everlasting through faith in Christ. We are told that when Jesus cried with a loud voice, "Lazarus, come forth," he who was dead emerged from the tomb "bound hand and foot with graveclothes: and his face was bound about with a napkin" (John 11:44). Here was a wonderful miracle, and yet he who was raised had his hands and feet bound like a mummy, and his face wrapped about with a cloth. What a picture of many who indeed have been brought to life through faith in Christ, but who still are not fit for service because certain hindering remnants of the old life must first be removed. Note that Lazarus' *face was bound,* implying that *his mouth was covered!* This is symbolic of those who, although spiritually alive, still have their mouths gagged by the "graveclothes" of worldly habits. In many ways they may be eloquent, but in spiritual things they are silent. Lazarus' *hands and feet were also bound.* This speaks of restricted service. Many believers do very little for the Lord because they are still inhibited by selfish attitudes and the distracting cares of this life. They are hampered in their Christian walk by those things which characterized their "former conversation." How important it is to get rid of those bindings of the world with their "deceitful lusts" (Eph. 4:22).

Removing the graveclothes means putting off the hindrances to spiritual power such as "anger, wrath, malice, blasphemy, [and] filthy communication out of [our] mouth" (Col. 3:8). Only after we have thus "put off . . . the old man" of sin and carnality will we be "meet for the Master's use" (2 Tim. 2:21).

> Stir me, Lord, I long to serve Thee,
> Know the fullness of Thy power.
> Help me, Lord, to yield completely
> Day by day and hour by hour. — I. G. Hallan

Removing the "bindings of sin" readies one for the "blessings of service"!
—H.G.B.

SHOULD YOU BE "COURT-MARTIALED"?

*Not forsaking the assembling of ourselves together,
as the manner of some is . . . .*   Hebrews 10:25

A minister once asked a G.I. to give a few words of testimony. The congregation had just sung, "Like a mighty army moves the Church of God," so when the young soldier arose he said, "You might have been able to sing that hymn some years ago without anyone challenging you, but now millions of men know exactly how an army does move. And it doesn't operate the way a lot of you do. Suppose the military accepted the lame excuses you present as an alibi for not attending services. Imagine this if you can. Reveille sounds, and the squads form on parade ground. The Sergeant barks out, 'Count off! One, two, three . . . say, number four is missing. Where's Private Smith?' 'Oh,' says a chap nearby, 'Mr. Smith was *too sleepy* to get up this morning. He was out late last night and needed the rest. He said to tell you *he would be with you in spirit.*' 'That's fine,' says the sergeant, 'remember me to him. But where is Brown?' 'Oh, *he's playing golf.* He gets only one day a week for recreation, and you know how important that is.' 'Sure, sure,' says the sergeant cheerfully, 'I hope he has a good game. Where's Robinson?' 'Robinson,' explains the buddy, 'is sorry not to greet you in person but *he is entertaining guests today.* Besides, *he was at drill last week.*' 'Thank you,' says the sergeant smiling. 'Tell him he is welcome any time he finds it convenient to drop in for drill.' Honestly, folks, did a conversation like that ever happen in any army? Why, if any G.I. tried to pull that stuff, he would get *twenty days in the brig!* Yet you hear things like that every week in church. '*Like a mighty army!*' *Why, if this church really moved like a mighty army, a lot of folks would be court-martialed within the hour!*"

Christian, read Hebrews 10:25 again and then ask yourself, "Should I be court-martialed?"

Suppose you had to "run" for church membership each year on the basis of what you had done for Christ during that period, would you be "re-elected"?

March 18   Read Psalm 2; Revelation 2:25-29
"HOLD THE FORT!"
. . . hold fast till I come.   Revelation 2:25

One of my father's favorite hymns was "Hold the Fort." Deeply aware of the spiritual battle in which we as believers are engaged, and eagerly looking for the coming of the Lord, how he loved to sing: "Ho, my comrades, see the signal waving in the sky! Reinforcements now appearing, victory is nigh! See the mighty hosts advancing, Satan leading on; mighty men around us falling, courage almost gone! 'Hold the fort, for I am coming,' Jesus signals still. Wave the answer back to Heaven, 'By Thy grace we will.'"

J. B. McClure in his book *Moody's Anecdotes* relates this story: "When General Sherman went through Atlanta towards the sea in the American Civil War, he left in the fort, back in the Kennesaw Mountains, a little handful of men to guard some rations that he brought there. General Hood, however, attacked the fort, and for a long time the battle raged furiously. Half the defenders were either killed or badly hurt, and the general in command was wounded seven different times. When they were just about ready to run up the white flag and surrender, Sherman got within 15 miles of the besieged camp and, through the signal corps on the nearby mountain, sent the message: *'Hold the fort; I am coming. W. T. Sherman.'* That message fired up their hearts, and they held out till reinforcements came, and so kept the fort from the hands of the enemy."

Even as Sherman signaled, "Hort the fort; I am coming," so our Heavenly Commander has given us the same challenge and charge. One of the first messages sent back from Heaven after the ascension of Christ was the assurance of His return (Acts 1:11). The very last promise in the Bible is from the lips of the Lord Jesus who said, "Surely, I come quickly" (Rev. 22:20). Yes, He is *coming!* So, with patience, courage, and hope, let us "hold the fort." The battle will soon be over and then the victory will be ours!

> *Fierce and long the battle rages,*
> *But our help is near;*
> *Onward comes our great Commander,*
> *Cheer, my comrades, cheer!*   — P. P. Bliss

Those who are FAITHFUL here (Rev. 2:10) will be presented victorious and FAULTLESS over There (Jude 24).

THE MOST PRIVILEGED UNDERTAKER

. . . a rich man of Arimathaea, named Joseph . . .
went to Pilate, and begged the body of Jesus. . . .
And when Joseph had taken the body, he wrapped
it in a clean linen cloth, And laid it in his own new
tomb. . . .   Matthew 27:57-60

Those who were crucified by the Romans were usually left exposed to the elements until eaten by birds of prey — a guard being set around the bodies to prevent friends from burying them. Knowing this, Joseph of Arimathaea, "a good man and a just" who as a member of the Jewish council had not consented to the crucifixion of Jesus, went to Pilate and begged for the body of Jesus. The fact that he was a rich and prominent man, and had a newly hewn tomb in a garden near the place of crucifixion, probably influenced the Roman governor to give his consent. In this way Isaiah 53 was fulfilled. For the Messiah must make His "grave with the wicked, and *with the rich in his death."* Having been accorded the privilege of caring for Jesus' body, *Joseph of Arimathaea became the most privileged undertaker of all ages!* Tenderly he took the Savior's bruised body and shrouded it in a large, clean cloth. However, in the "embalming process" that followed, he had an assistant — none other than Nicodemus who had earlier come to Jesus by night to learn how he might be "born again." This formerly secret follower of the Lord came supplied with about a hundred pounds of myrrh and aloes (John 19:39, 40). Together these men wound Jesus' body in additional "linen clothes *with the spices,* as the manner of the Jews is to bury." Then they placed Him in Joseph's new tomb.

The privilege of caring for the dead body of Jesus was given only to those two; yet we today may do service for the Savior by telling others that He physically arose from the tomb, ascended to the Father in Glory, and now offers eternal life to all who believe.

Three days He lay within that dark domain,
Then with new life, forth from the tomb He came;
Christ has the keys, oh, death, where is thy sting?
Our Lord doth live! oh, let your praises ring! — L.S.

Christ by His death and resurrection has built a bridge across the gulf of death!   —A. Young

GOD SEES

. . . the face of the Lord is against them that do evil.
1 Peter 3:12

Ours is an era of glaring inequities, and the forces of wickedness seem destined to prevail. But let us not forget that "the face
of the Lord is against them that do evil." A time of settlement
is coming. God sees all that rears its head in defiance of Him
and knows those who live unrighteously. However, "He will not
always chide; neither will he keep his anger forever" (Ps. 103:9).
While this is the age of grace in which He still bids the sinner
to repent and accept His offer of pardon, it will not always be
true. Judgment is coming!

You will note in checking our Scripture reading that the major
portion of it is a quotation from Psalm 34. Man's heart does not
change from age to age. The Psalmist had observed in his day
just what the apostle was now seeing. The unbridled rebellion
of the human heart runs wild, and havoc is the result in every
area of conduct. Man is always trying to implement his own
schemes and exclude his Creator. As a result, *failure* will again
be written over the futile efforts of the human race to attain
peace and happiness.

Out of the midst of this corrupt civilization God is calling a
people for His name. And for these regenerated ones there is
the promise, *"The eyes of the Lord are over the righteous, and
his ears are open unto their prayers."* As the old spiritual says,
"He hears all you say; He sees all you do. My Lord is writin'
all the time."

Friend, be certain you are on the Lord's side, and that you
are daily conscious of an all-seeing God.

> Jehovah's eyes are on the just,
>   He hearkens to their cry;
> Against the wicked sets His face,
>   Their very name shall die. — Psalter

**If your spiritual eyes are out of focus, you may not see God,
but remember He always sees you.**

"HE SAID HE WOULD!"

*Let thy mercies come . . . unto me, . . . even thy
salvation, according to thy word.*   Psalm 119:41

A young lad was being examined for church membership. During the course of the interview he was asked, "Have you ever been converted?" "Yes, when I was 8 years old," the boy said. "After Sunday school one morning I asked the Lord to save me." "Did He?" his questioner quickly inquired. "Yes, sir, I'm sure," the boy declared emphatically. "How can you be so positive?" one of the men continued. "Wouldn't it be more honest for you to say that you *hoped* He did?" "Oh no, sir," the lad answered. "I *know* He saved me." "And how do you *know?*" the other asked. *"Because He said He would!"* was the confident reply.

The apostle John tells us in 1 John 5, "These things have I written unto you that believe on the name of the Son of God, that ye may *know* that ye have eternal life." If salvation depended upon what we were able to do to merit it, such a certainty would never be possible. We can have this assurance, however, because of that which Christ has done *for us* on the cross. He paid for our sins by dying in our place. And we are sure that His sacrifice was acceptable to God because He raised Him from the dead. The Bible says, "Believe on the Lord Jesus Christ, and thou *shalt he saved"* (Acts 16:31); and again, ". . . whosoever shall call upon the name of the Lord *shall be saved"* (Rom. 10:13). Do you believe that you are a sinner and the Lord Jesus Christ is the Redeemer? Have you ever received Him as your Savior? If so, then you too can say, "I *know* He saved me because *He said He would!"*

*Yes, I found it written down, whosoever will believe
    In the Son of God is saved from every sin;
And I blessed His holy name, that the promise I receive,
    In that "whosoever" I am counted in!*   —J.W.

Many miss the joy of assurance because they are not willing to take God at His Word!   —Moody

THE LOVE OF RIZPAH

*And Rizpah . . . took sackcloth, and spread it for
her upon the rock . . . [and guarded her sons' bodies].*
2 Samuel 21:10

Rizpah is one of the obscure characters in the Old Testament;
yet her great devotion to her sons is a pious and worthy example
to be followed. According to the Biblical record, they were condemned to death because of Saul's wicked slaying of the Gibeon-
ites. Although they themselves were innocent victims, they were
executed to remove the curse of the Lord from the house of
Israel. Spreading sackcloth near the place where her sons had
been hanged, Rizpah sat for many days on the rock of Gibeah
to guard their bodies. She allowed neither the birds of the air
to assail them by day nor the beasts of the field to devour them
by night. The wayfarers on the northern road from Jerusalem
soon grew accustomed to seeing the strange, sad spectacle of that
heart-broken mother guarding her beloved Mephibosheth and Ar-
moni from vulture and jackal. But at last her devotion attracted
the attention of King David, and the bones of her sons were
taken down and given a decent burial.

If we ask what motivated Rizpah, what enabled her to stand
those many days of severe strain, I believe the answer could be
framed in a single word—*love!*

As we look at the touching scene of that lonely, faithful woman
watching beside the "crosses" of her dead sons, let us think of
an infinitely holier Cross and a divine Sacrifice that also demands
our steadfast loyalty. If a mother's love could endure so much,
will not a ransomed soul be willing to bear much more for the
blessed Redeemer? May we so live for Christ that others passing
along the road of life will see our zealous, undying devotion to
Him!

> *My life, my love I give to Thee;*
> *Thou Lamb of God who died for me;*
> *O may I ever faithful be,*
> *My Savior and my God!*   — Hudson

The test of love is loyalty!

NOTHING LEFT TO DO BUT DIE

*Now, O Lord, take away my life. . . . And the Lord
said unto him, Go . . . anoint Hazael . . . and Jehu
. . . and Elisha . . . .*   1 Kings 19:5, 15, 16

The words, "There's nothing left to do but die," spoken by a
twenty-year-old girl who attempted suicide after a drug-taking
episode, still ring in my ears. She was a picture of abject hope-
lessness and despair as she sat across the desk from me for our
interview. She declared that she had committed every kind of
sin imaginable, and had never done anything commendable that
she could recall. Her moments of exhilaration had come only
while under the influence of forbidden and habit-forming drugs.
Now, confined to prison for her misdeeds, she said she expected
soon to die, but admitted she was desperately afraid. I assured
her that God still loved her, that Jesus died for her sins, and that
the Lord would save her and make the rest of her life worthwhile if only she would receive Christ. I pointed out that if she
came to know the Lord, she would become a new and vibrant
person, full of eager anticipation for the future. After counseling
with her, giving her some additional Scriptures to read, and praying with her, I left. Since then I have been praying that God
will reach her by His grace and claim her for himself. As yet
she has not responded to the Holy Spirit's wooings.

Friend, don't make the mistake of that girl in prison who cannot bring herself to believe that God loves her. It is surprising
that even Christians sometimes doubt the Lord when confronted
by adverse circumstances. Note the case of Elijah mentioned in
our text. Although a child of God, he too was discouraged and
wished to die, but the Lord still had much work for him to do.
God in His own good time will call us Home when our task on
earth is finished, but let us never faithlessly declare, because of
our limited perspective, that we have "nothing left to do but die."
God loves us and has a plan for each of us to follow. *Life with
Christ is always worth living!*

Don't be downhearted, look up, look up,
For Jesus is on the Throne,
And He will supply every need from on High;
Cheer up, cheer up, cheer up!   —Old Chorus

No life is hopeless unless Christ is ruled out!

A LETTER FROM J. EDGAR HOOVER

Meditate upon these things; give thyself wholly to them,
that thy profiting may appear to all.   1 Timothy 4:15

The chief of the Federal Bureau of Investigation has often stressed the importance of family Bible reading. Some years ago in a letter to the American Bible Society he said, "Inspiration has been the keynote of America's phenomenal growth . . . and the backbone of its greatness. . . . This inspiration has been from faith in God . . . and in the belief that the Holy Bible is His inspired Word. Reading the Scriptures within the family circle is more important today than ever before. As a small boy I sat at my mother's knee while she read the Word to me and explained its meanings with stories as we went along. It served to make the bond of faith between us much stronger. Then there were those wonderful nights when my father would gather all the children around him and read aloud verses from the Bible. This led to family discussions which were interesting, lively, and informative. Those wonderful sessions left me with an imprint of the power of faith and . . . prayer which has sustained me in trying moments throughout my life."

Regrettably, family altars are fast disappearing from the American scene. People are too busy. The family is seldom together long enough to enjoy such sweet moments of fellowship — and the world is much the poorer for it! The Word of God constantly admonishes us to meditate upon its contents, for only as we absorb its teachings, believe its promises, and hide its precepts in our hearts can we prosper spiritually and live the "more abundant life."

Take a cue from the letter of J. Edgar Hoover; and if you have not yet established a definite time for Bible study in your home, start now — even if you can devote only five minutes a day to this necessary task. Man cannot live by bread alone. He must find sustenance for his spirit by appropriating the truths of God through the avenue of prayer and careful meditation.

How precious is the Book divine,
By inspiration given!
Bright as a lamp its precepts shine,
To guide our souls to Heaven. — J. Fawcett

A Bible that is falling apart usually belongs to a person who is not!

THE FAILURE OF HUMAN WISDOM

*This wisdom descendeth not from above, but is
earthly, sensual, devilish. For where envying and
strife is, there is confusion and every evil work.*
                                        James 3:15, 16

Human intelligence and inventive genius have enabled mankind to produce marvels of technical and engineering skill, and
have provided many physical benefits to millions. Yet the world
is filled with talented people who are making a mess out of their
own lives. Never has the tension between the nations been as
great as it is today. Racial strife, lawlessness, and much unhap-
piness abounds everywhere. Why? Because we humans have a
sinful nature. Apart from God's grace we have an inclination to
become bitter toward those who wrong us, and to strive for the
fulfillment of our selfish ambitions and desires. James says that
those who live in envy and strife do not possess the kind of wisdom that comes from God.

The world's wisdom is superficial and self-centered. The most
brilliant person, if he doesn't know the Lord, thinks only in terms
of this present life, is motivated by the instincts of his fallen
nature, and may even be influenced by evil spirits who are in
league with Satan. One may have his mind loaded with accurate
statistics and be looked upon as an expert in his field, but if he
fails to acknowledge God and believe the Bible, his wisdom will
not solve man's deepest problems. The person who rejects the
Biblical teaching that man was created in the image of God, and
who denies that redemption has been provided for fallen mankind through Jesus Christ, cannot really understand himself or
others. Real wisdom can only be acquired when one humbly
looks to God in faith. How true the words of Proverbs 1:7, "The
fear of the Lord is the *beginning of knowledge"!*

> *Man's wisdom is vain, for 'tis mired in sin,*
> *It thinks but of self — seeks earth's honors to win;*
> *But wisdom that's pure, and that comes from above,*
> *Is purged of its dross and is filled with God's love.* — I. H.

The knowledge of man is folly unless the grace of God guides it!

SAFE DEPOSIT

And he left all that he had in Joseph's hand. Genesis 39:6

From the moment Potiphar, an officer of Pharaoh, left all in Joseph's care, a blessing came upon everything he had. His home, his business, and even his fields prospered! The Christian today also finds that spiritual prosperity comes when he leaves all in the hand of the "Greater Joseph," the Lord Jesus Christ. As you were reading the Scripture (you didn't omit it, did you?), I hope you noticed the words in verse 4, "all that he had he *put into his hand.*" Potiphar made that decision. Attracted to Joseph and persuaded that he was worthy of his trust, he committed all his possessions, interests, and affairs to this faithful Hebrew. Have you definitely given your home, your business, and all your concerns to Christ?

Having put all that he had into Joseph's keeping, he left it there. This is sometimes the most difficult thing to do. Potiphar had a nature similar to ours, and probably worried at times and removed some of his affairs from Joseph's supervision. Perhaps you have surrendered to the Lord some problem or difficulty that plagued you; but when worry again gripped you, you retrieved the burden and removed it from His care, only to be weighed down once more by the load of anxiety. Now the Savior is saying again, *"Leave the matter in My hand!"*

The Lord Jesus is adequate for every circumstance and problem. He wants us to put all that we have of pain or pleasure, profit or loss, into His keeping. He will forgive the sin, sanctify the life, remove the fear, direct the path, and give assurance.

> O wounded soul, there is heavenly balm,
>   Leaving it all with Jesus;
> Then change thy moan to a joyous psalm,
>   By leaving it all with Jesus.   — Gray

Those who see God's hand in everything can best leave everything in God's hand.

LIVING WITH OTHERS IN VIEW

*Let . . . no man put a stumbling block or an occasion
to fall in his brother's way.*   Romans 14:13

To become a Christian is *easy* — for it is just receiving God's
grace through faith in the Savior. To live the sanctified life,
however, is *extremely difficult*, especially since the pathway to
Glory is narrow, and our instructions for travel include such admonitions as: "pray without ceasing," "be ye perfect," and "love
thy neighbor as thyself." In fact, we are told to curb even legitimate desires, if they tend to offend a weaker brother (Rom. 14:
19-21). Paul warns in our text that we must be doubly careful
not to put a "stumbling block or an occasion to fall" in the way
of a fellow believer.

I am told that tourists in the Alps are cautioned at certain
points by the guides not to speak or sing or even to whisper, as
the faintest breath might start reverberations in the air which
could loosen a delicately poised avalanche from its place on the
mountain, and bring it crashing down upon the villages and fields
in the valley below. J. R. Miller, in commenting on this, wisely
points out, "There are men and women who are walking under
such a stress of burdens, cares, responsibilities, sorrows and temptations, that one whisper of censure, criticism, complaint or unkindness may cause them to fall under their load. Let us beware,
therefore, how we conduct ourselves, for it is a crime thus *to*
imperil another soul."

Recognizing the seriousness of life, every Christian who is consecrated at all must guard against being an offense to others. Let
us walk carefully and prayerfully today lest some thoughtless word
or deed impede the spiritual progress of a fellow believer!

> *Have your feet on errands of love been bent,*
> *Or on selfish deeds has your strength been spent?*
> *Has someone seen Christ in you today;*
> *Or has your life led a soul astray?* — V. B. Hopkins, alt.

Live for thy neighbor, if thou wouldst live for God! —Seneca

WATCH THE "OIL"!

*And seek not what ye shall eat, or what ye shall
drink . . . .*   Luke 12:29

The editor of the *Arkansas Baptist,* Erwin L. McDonald, went
to school during the twenties when most people did not drive an
automobile. He lived eight miles from the high school, and did
not even own a bicycle. However, one of his former school
teachers had a Model-T Ford and a daughter who also wanted
an education. The father told the young man he could have his
transportation free if he would consent to drive the car. The
young man carefully deliberated for half a second and said he
would do it.

It turned out to be a very good arrangement for Erwin Mc-
Donald. He not only obtained his education, but ended up marry-
ing an older sister of the girl he drove to school. In addition to
this he received some excellent advice from his future father-in-
law. The day he turned over the key to the lad he said, "Erwin,
watch the oil. It won't run without gas, but you can be driving
down the road thinking all is well, and you can be burning out
the motor for lack of lubrication."

Mr. McDonald later saw this as a parable on life. As a car will
not run without gasoline, so we cannot function without food,
clothing, rest, and some of the material things in life. However,
it is possible to eke out an existence without giving thought to
spiritual realities. It is a tragedy that a person can go day after
day with his heart set on the things of earth, not realizing that
his life is being destroyed because he is running without *"spiritual
oil."* All the comforts and conveniences this earth can afford will
never satisfy the deepest needs of the soul.

Christian, you may have a lovely home, a new automobile, and
a color TV, but — are you watching the "oil"? Be wise, put the
things of God first!

> *O for a life by God controlled,*
> *A heart to do His will;*
> *With Him put first, no lack we'll know,*
> *Our needs His love will fill!*   —G.W.

**Christians are either Bibles or libels, depending on what they
put first in their lives!**
                                              —F. B. Meyer

THE PARABLE OF THE TOOLS

For we are laborers together with God. . . .

1 Corinthians 3:9

Some years ago R. T. Moore penned an interesting parable based on the words of Paul in 1 Corinthians 3:9. "It seems," he says, "that the Carpenter's tools had a conference. Brother Hammer was in the chair, but the others had just informed him that he must leave because he was too noisy. 'All right, I'll go, but if I leave, Brother Screw must go also. Why, you have to turn him around again and again to get him to go anywhere.' To which Brother Screw replied, 'If you wish, I'll go, but Brother Plane must leave as well. All of his work is on the surface. There is never any depth to it.' To this Brother Plane replied, 'Well, Brother Rule will also have to withdraw if I do, for he is always measuring folks as though he were the only one who is right.' Brother Rule in turn complained about Brother Sandpaper, saying, 'I just don't care, he's rougher than he ought to be, and he's always rubbing people the wrong way.' In the midst of the discussion the Carpenter of Nazareth walked in. He had come to perform His day's work. He went to the bench to make a pulpit from which to preach the Gospel to the poor. He employed the screw, the sandpaper, the saw, the hammer, the plane, and all the other tools. After the day's work was over and the pulpit was finished, Brother Saw arose and said, 'Brethren, I perceive that all of us are laborers *together* with God.' O, how many Christians are just like those tools, fussing at each other because we think someone does not do things just the way he should. There was not an accusation made against any one of the tools but that was absolutely true; yet the Carpenter used every one of them; and there was not a place where He employed them that one of the others could have served as well."

Let us be careful not to find fault with any of God's chosen tools, for all of us are "laborers together" in the holy task He has assigned.

Alone our work is of little worth,
Together we are the "salt of the earth."
So it's all for each and each for all;
United we stand, divided we fall! —Anon.

Remember, the fellow looking down his nose at others usually has the wrong slant!

A CLOSEUP

The heart is deceitful above all things, and desper-
ately wicked.   Jeremiah 17:9

Most of us have had the experience of visiting the photographer
to pose for a portrait. Frequently we were disturbed by those red-
dish-brown proofs when we got to see them, but the photographer
would say, "Don't worry, wait till you see the finished picture.
I will touch up the negative." We were delighted to receive the
final product with wrinkles and blemishes gone. But *God never
touches up* the negative when He shows us our true self (Rom.
1:21-32). "For the Lord seeth not as man seeth; for man looketh
on the outward appearance, but the Lord looketh on the heart"
(1 Sam. 16:7).

Some years ago a young cameraman went to China on business.
There he visited the leading oriental photographer in the area, a
man who was a genuine Christian. Speaking in excellent English, he asked the visiting American, "Have you ever seen a
'closeup' of your own heart?" To the visitor's amazement, he
pulled out a copy of the New Testament and read to him Romans
3:10-18. This true, precise picture of man's heart was used of
God for the conviction and ultimate conversion of the young man.

Our Lord said, "For out of the heart proceed evil thoughts,
murders, adulteries, fornications, thefts, false witness, blasphe-
mies" (Matt. 15:19). It is not a pleasant portrait! But it *is* one
that we must acknowledge. We must admit that God's estimate
is correct and the picture accurate. Coming to Him just as we
are, we do not ask for a "touchup," but rather we cry as did
David, "Create in me a clean heart, O God." Have you done
this? Nothing less will do!

> *Gracious God, my heart renew,*
> *Make my spirit right and true;*
> *Make me pure, Thy grace bestow,*
> *Wash me whiter than the snow.* — Psalter

Men may whitewash sin, but only Jesus' blood can wash it white!

NO GREATER LOVE

. . . God commendeth his love . . . that, while we were yet sinners, Christ died for us. Romans 5:8

A young British soldier, Alexander Russell, was on his way to join his regiment in India when the ship on which he was sailing was torpedoed. Within minutes the lifeboats were crowded to capacity. On the one that Mr. Russell boarded was a young mother with her newborn infant. Anxiously looking for her husband, she suddenly spied him struggling helplessly in the water. Becoming hysterical, she cried out for someone to save him. Exhibiting great courage, Alexander Russell dove overboard, rescued the drowning man, and placed him in the boat. Not one of the frail barks bobbing on the waves could possibly bear the weight of another man, so with strong vigorous strokes the young man swam away to his death.

Alexander Russell died for a fine young husband and father. His heroic act reminds us of what Paul says in Romans 5:7, ". . . yet perhaps for a good man some would even dare to die." We admire such selfless courage. What feelings would we entertain, however, if this promising young man had given his life to save a drunkard, a gangster, or a murderer? We might be inclined to say, "That type of person is not worth such a sacrifice!" Yet that was not the attitude displayed by the Lord Jesus. He died for the very people who mocked Him and nailed Him to the cross!

You and I, like those who hated Christ when He was here on earth, are sinners; but despite our enmity, God loved us so much that He was willing to send His Son to die in ignominy and shame to save us. Such compassion surpasses our limited capacity for heroism. It requires a divine love which goes "beyond all human measure."

> *For the love of God is broader*
> *Than the measure of man's mind,*
> *And the heart of the Eternal*
> *Is most wonderfully kind!* —Faber

The wonder of it all is that God loves us out of His own nature, and not on conditions. —Beecher

NOT A TRAMP BUT A PILGRIM

*. . . if ye call on the Father, . . . pass the time of
your sojourning here in fear.*   1 Peter 1:17

During the depression of the early 1930's, many men became
tramps. They hopped freight trains to travel from place to place,
slept in empty boxcars, and obtained a little money by working
at seasonal jobs. When they could find no employment, they
resorted to begging. My mother was a "soft touch" for any such
drifters who came to our door for food. These men wandered
about aimlessly, depriving themselves of family blessings. They
had lost the comfortable security of a home.

A pilgrim, like the tramp, may be without the comfort and
protection of a home, but he knows where he is going. His hopes
and aspirations are set upon a goal. The Christian is that kind
of wayfarer! Therefore, in today's Scripture reading Peter gives
the exhortation, "Pass the time of your sojourning here in fear"
(1 Pet. 1:17). Why should a believer live in reverential awe?
The answer is clear: *he is a pilgrim on his way to Heaven, not
an aimless wanderer!*

Christian friend, God has purchased you at tremendous cost,
and your life is a sacred trust. The Lord is preparing you and
me for eternity, and everything we do is full of significance.
Therefore, though this earth is not our permanent place of habitation, we do not look upon ourselves as vagabonds, but as so-
journers who live responsibly as we travel to our prepared destination. We have a Heavenly Father who loves us and will soon
welcome us into that Home made ready by our Savior. We are
part of a great spiritual family—a multitude of brothers and sisters
in Christ — who are journeying to the "promised land." Indeed,
we are not tramps but pilgrims!

A few more watches keeping,
A few more foes to down,
As pilgrims brave we journey
To win the victor's crown! — Bosch

**Pilgrims, don't drive your stakes too deep; we're moving in
the morning!**

"CELEBRATING" THE RESURRECTION

If ye, then, be risen with Christ, seek those things
which are above . . . .   Colossians 3:1

One Monday morning, following an Easter Sunday, I picked up a newspaper and saw this headline: *Entire World Celebrates the Risen Christ.* On the same page a number of smaller headlines appeared, and some of them read as follows: "Trouble in Vietnam." "Blacks and Whites Clash in Chicago." "Egypt Issues Ultimatum to Israel." There were also others equally discouraging. As I saw this, I thought, how ironic! The major headline declares: *Entire World Celebrates the Risen Christ,* and then the balance of the page tells how men and nations go on disregarding the blessings and grace which Christ by His death and resurrection provides. *What a way to "celebrate the risen Christ!"* Of course, the headline meant by "celebrate" the fact that millions had flocked to churches all over the world in a ritualistic and traditional manner; yet, that's just what is wrong with the world today. There are great numbers who go through the motions of religion, claiming to honor the risen Christ, and yet they don't really believe in Him, either in the significance of His death or in the literalness of His resurrection. It all becomes a mockery. As a result, the world is slipping even farther on its way to judgment.

But let's make this even more practical. Do *you* really believe that Christ arose from the dead? It will make a difference in how you act, what you say, and where you go. That's why Paul says in Colossians 3:1, 2, "If ye, then, be risen with Christ, . . . *set your affection on things above,* not on things on the earth."

The best way for true believers to "celebrate" the resurrection is to realize that we not only have died with Christ, but also have risen with Him, and that therefore — now that we are living *with* Him — it is only natural that we should live *for* Him.

Yes, I'm saved, but do I know Him
In His resurrection power?
Does some brightness of His glory
Fill me every day and hour? — I. G. Hallan

So let the resurrected Christ live in you that your life will be a rebuke to sin wherever you go!

SAYING PRAYERS

. . . Lord, teach us to pray . . . .   Luke 11:1

For two and one-half years I served as student-pastor in a little church on the outskirts of a small town. None of the businessmen of the village attended, for most of them were members of another very large denomination which claimed the majority of the people in that community. They were friendly to me, however, and gave our church a sizable discount each time we made a purchase. Usually the businessman would say, "I want to give this item to you at my cost; I only ask that you say a prayer for me." I believe they said this sincerely because they truly thought it would help if I would do this for them. I told them frankly that I didn't "say prayers" in the routine, perfunctory way they supposed, but that I would remember them when we brought our petitions before the Lord.

No, prayer is not just repeating some memorized phrases designed to produce magical results. *Prayer is talking to God!* If I am really to communicate with Him who is perfect in holiness, I must search my soul, examine my motives, and confess my sins. In fact, God often permits afflictions and crushing disappointments to enter the lives of His children in order that they might be driven to *real intercession!* By nature we are spiritually lazy; consequently, a life of ease and prosperity has a tendency to draw us away from God so that we begin "saying prayers" rather than really praying.

"Saying prayers" will accomplish very little; but heartfelt petitions will keep you close to the Lord, make your life glow with spiritual splendor, and draw your mind away from all that is wicked and carnal. In fact, you cannot be an effective Christian without real prayer, for God has chosen to do His work in this way. Let us ask the Lord every day to keep us from "saying prayers." With the disciples of old, we must approach Him requesting, *"Lord, teach us to pray!"* It will probably cost us something, but it will be worth it!

> *O Thou by whom we come to God,*
> *The Life, the Truth, the Way,*
> *The path of prayer Thyself hast trod;*
> *Lord, teach us how to pray!* —J. Montgomery

Praying is to the soul what breathing is to the body!

SEEING THE GOSPEL

Let your light so shine before men, that they may see your good works.   Matthew 5:16

A man once asked a new acquaintance in a remote area of the world, "Have you ever heard the Gospel?" "No," the other replied, "I have never *heard* it, but I have *seen* it." "What do you mean by that?" the Christian responded. "Simply this," he said, "there is a man in our village whose life has been greatly influenced by a missionary who passed this way. Never have I seen such a change in a person! Before he met the man of God, alcohol ruled his life. He was lazy, neglected his family, and showed no interest in anyone else. Since then, however, his manner of living is completely different. He is no longer a slave to liquor. He works hard and is a good husband and father. I would be proud to have him as my neighbor. Yes, I have *seen* the Gospel and like it so well I would now like to *hear* it!" Because the Gospel had been lived eloquently, it could be told effectively.

To be faithful in our witness for Christ, it is essential that the message of His saving grace and transforming power be *shown* as well as *told*. If our deeds contradict our words, we might better remain silent. May the example of our lives be so consistent with the testimony of our lips that no one could ever say to us, "Your actions speak so loud that I can't hear what· you say."

The walk of the believer should be a living sermon. The world is watching us with a critical eye. Let us be careful, then, making sure that others are *"seeing the Gospel"* at its very best!

> *Jesus bids us shine with a clear, pure light,*
> *Like a little candle burning in the night,*
> *In this world of darkness we must shine,*
> *You in your small corner, and I in mine.*
>
> *Jesus bids us shine, first of all for Him;*
> *Well He sees and knows it if our light is dim;*
> *He looks down from Heaven, sees us shine,*
> *You in your small corner, and I in mine!* —Warner

The only sermon that never wearies us is that of an eloquent life!

THE GOD OF THE VALLEYS

*. . . the Syrians have said, The Lord is God of the
hills, but he is not God of the valleys . . . .*

1 Kings 20:28

The king of Syria, Ben-hadad, together with his great army,
had suffered a humiliating defeat at the hands of Israel. Since
Palestine is rather mountainous, the king erroneously concluded
that the Israelites had been successful because their deity was a
God of the hills. If he could but engage them again in the valley,
he was sure that he could easily overcome them. However, the
prophet of the Lord spoke to King Ahab assuring him that to
vindicate the Lord's honor, and to show He was God of all places
and circumstances, Israel would again defeat the Syrian hosts.
When the battle came, God's people won an even more impressive victory. They were thus reassured that the Lord was always
at their side — *even in the valley of deepest testing!*

Many people today still think God is with them when they
enjoy prosperity, yet mistakenly feel He has forsaken them when
they are called to suffer affliction.

A merchant was informed by his confidential secretary that his
company was in serious financial difficulty. "It's been a bad year,
sir," said the employee; "there have been vast losses and few
gains." The merchant saw that bankruptcy was imminent. When
at last he spoke, his voice was low and steady. "No, John, it has
been a good year in spite of everything. Every one of those figures 'in the red' represent hours of agonizing prayer on my part —
experiences that have made me so spiritually rich that I cannot
despair over any earthly losses. The future is bright, for the Lord
has promised, 'No good thing will He withhold from them that
walk uprightly.'" The secretary looked at him for a moment, and
then said, "I want to tell you it was your steadiness under the
testings of the past year that has made me long to know Christ
as you do; and so the other night I received Him as my Savior.
I agree, sir; it has indeed been *a good year!*" Both men had come
to realize in a wonderful way that the Lord is also *"the God of
the valleys!"*

God's "green pastures" are often found in the lowlands of trial!
—H.G.B.

Read Psalm 119:89-105

April 6

FLYING BY INSTRUMENT

Thou shalt guide me with thy counsel . . . . Psalm 73:24

A few months ago my nephew Dale received his pilot's license. In order to get it he had to take lessons from a qualified instructor and also to log a specific number of hours in actual flight. When he was asked about his training and any unusual experiences he had, Dale mentioned one thing that especially stood out in his mind: the "attitude test." On one particular training flight, he was "blindfolded" in such a way that he could see nothing but the instruments. The instructor then put the plane through a number of turns, dives, and climbs, in an effort to confuse Dale to the point that he would not know which direction he was going, nor if the plane was upright or upside down. It was Dale's duty to determine his "attitude," *by checking the instruments* and then to correct his situation. This is part of basic training, since it is possible for a pilot when in the clouds to lose all sense of direction. You see, the human senses fail us in certain situations, and for that reason something more reliable must be depended upon to tell us the true facts. When "flying blind," the instruments in a plane, not the fallible judgment of the pilot's senses, must be the governing standard.

In life, especially when it comes to spiritual matters, we need a guide — an "instrument" to stabilize and direct us aright — when man's guesses, speculations, and philosophies would turn us upside down and send us in the wrong direction. Even our conscience, which can be seared, frequently fails us. How thankful we should be then for the Word of God. Believing the Bible, adopting that as our standard of conduct, taking God at His Word, we can maintain the "proper attitude" even in the darkest night and amid the thickest clouds of adversity. Those who read and study the Word, and who really believe it and obey it, know what it is to "fly by instrument."

> *Blest Word of God, send forth Thy light*
> *O'er every land and every sea,*
> *Till all who wander in the night*
> *Are led to God and Heaven by Thee.*—H. M. King

Don't criticize the Bible; let the Bible criticize you!

THE CHRISTIAN'S "CORONATION DAY"!

*. . . And the Lord showed him all the land. . . . So
Moses, the servant of the Lord, died. . . .*
                                        Deuteronomy 34:1, 5

When I was a sixth grader, an elderly lady visited our one-room country schoolhouse to announce a community event. Though energetic and full of zest for life, she was somewhat stooped, her hair was white, and her face was lined with wrinkles. After she left, one of the boys loudly said, "I never want to get old." The teacher, a bitter unbeliever, countered with the words, "Do you want to die young?" "No," the boy replied. "Well," came the sharp retort, "you will either die young or grow old and die. There are no alternatives." These words made a deep impression on me. I was only a boy, but even young children think about death. The tone of utter despair in my teacher's voice sent chills down my spine. Without Christ the future is dismal indeed.

How different the prospect for the believer! For him old age can be a time of fullness and blessing, and death does not hold the same dread and fear. I like to think of Moses as he went calmly and serenely up the mountain where he knew he would die. Before God took him from this life, He graciously gave him a full view of the land his people would soon enter. He passed from this life full of faith and confident that the Lord's promises of a glorious future for both himself and his people would certainly be realized.

Another child of God, Dwight L. Moody, had a glorious and triumphant Homegoing. In his final moments he exclaimed, "Heaven opens before me! If this is death, it is sweet! There is no valley here. God is calling and I must go!" "No," said a loved one, "you are dreaming." Moody answered, "No, I'm not dreaming. I have looked within the gates, and I have seen the children's faces. This is my triumph. *This is my coronation day!*" Like Moses, Moody had seen the Promised Land — and then had peacefully "fallen asleep" in the arms of God!

**Death need not trouble the Christian—his future is as bright
as the promises of God!**

THE "CRUCIFIED" CHRISTIAN

I am crucified with Christ.   Galatians 2:20

To participate in the *life* of Christ, we must first be identified with Him in His *death*. "For if we have been planted together in the likeness of his death, we shall be also in the likeness of his resurrection" (Rom. 6:5). Those of us who now have eternal life have died in the person of our sinless Substitute, Jesus Christ, just as surely as if we had consciously been present at Calvary. While in principle our crucifixion is thus an accomplished fact, in daily practice it should constantly mean "death" to the *self-life!*

A young man once approached an older Christian with the question, "What does it mean as far as this life is concerned to be 'crucified with Christ'?" The believer replied, "It means three things: (1) a man on a cross is facing only one direction; (2) he is not going back; and (3) he has no further plans of his own." T. S. Randall, commenting on these three things, says: "First, a crucified man is facing in only one direction. Too many Christians are trying to face in two directions at the same time. They are divided in heart. They want Heaven, but they also are in love with the world. They are like Lot's wife; they are running one way, but are facing another. Second, a crucified man is not coming back. The cross spells *finis* for him; he is not going to return to his old life. Third, a crucified man has no plans of his own. He is finished with the vainglory of this life. Its chains are all broken, and its charms are all gone." In the light of these three truths, would you say that you are truly "crucified"?

If I would crucify the flesh, that Christ in me might reign,
I must not spare my shrinking flesh, the crucifixion pain;
'Tis either Christ or selfish I — what shall the answer be?
Let self be crucified that Christ, alone, might live in me!

                                           —Reich

When men come to die with Christ on the cross, He comes to live in them by His Spirit!   —MacGregor

WATCHING THE SIGNS

. . . rightly dividing the word of truth. 2 Timothy 2:15

How thankful we should be for the wonderful highways which crisscross our nation. This is truly a far cry from the early days of the automobile when paved roads were a rarity, and when the best of highways could be transformed within minutes from a ribbon of dust into a river of mud. Yet there are times when those primitive roadways seem good to me, especially when I arrive in a strange city on one of our superhighways and find myself surrounded by lanes of "speeding steel" and barraged by numerous signs indicating different routes and directions. It can be confusing! But I've found a way to overcome this frustration: know *where* you are going, and the *number of the route* that will take you there. Then watch for that *alone!* The other signs will tend to mix you up if they are not kept in proper relationship with that which really applies to you.

Many folks today are similarly perplexed and confused in their study of the Scriptures, simply because they don't know how to read the "road signs" of the Bible. They have never appreciated the admonition of Paul to Timothy about "rightly dividing the word of truth." If we would fully understand the Scriptures, we must know which passages are directed primarily to us. It is true that *all* of Scripture is *for* us, for we read: "All scripture is given by inspiration of God, and is profitable for doctrine, for reproof, for correction, for instruction in righteousness" (2 Tim. 3:16); yet every verse was not written specifically *to* us. We have no right to claim for ourselves God's special *promises to Israel,* nor would we foolishly appropriate their *curses.*

Even as in traveling along a freeway we must determine which signs apply to us, so, too, in the study of the Word we must always consider *to whom* it was written and for *what purpose.* As we do this, the *entire* Book will become much more meaningful to us.

> Ever present, truest Friend,
> Ever near Thine aid to lend,
> Guide us as we search the Word,
> Make it both our shield and sword!—M. M. Wells, alt.

When you study the Bible "hit or miss," you MISS more than you HIT!

GOD WILL MOVE THE STONE

. . . Who shall roll away the stone . . . ? Mark 16:3

The women who sought to anoint the dead body of Jesus are to be commended for their tender love and regard for the Savior. Yet as they came near the place of burial, the practical difficulty of moving the heavy stone which sealed His tomb brought them unnecessary anxiety of spirit. Actually it had already been moved, and so their fears were groundless. So, too, we are often needlessly concerned over prospective difficulties which He graciously removes or helps us overcome when we have to meet them. Let us therefore be encouraged to exercise greater faith in facing possible obstructions on the pathway of duty. We may be sure of the Lord's providential assistance in such matters when we advance in His name and for His glory!

An anonymous author has given additional practical admonitions concerning this text in Mark's gospel in the following poetic words: What poor weeping ones were saying nineteen hundred years ago, we, the same weak faith betraying, say in our sad hours of woe; looking at some trouble lying in the dark and dread unknown, we, too, often ask with sighing, "Who shall roll away the stone?" Many a storm-cloud hov'ring o'er us never pours on us its rain; many a grief we see before us never comes to cause us pain. Ofttimes, on the dread tomorrow sunshine comes, the cloud has flown! Why then ask in foolish sorrow, "Who shall roll away the stone?" Burden not thy soul with sadness, make a wiser, better choice; drink the wine of life with gladness, God doth bid thee, saint, rejoice! In today's bright sunlight basking, leave tomorrow's cares alone; spoil not present joys by asking: "Who shall roll away the stone?"

Christian, go forward today on the pathway of service undaunted by possible future obstacles! Let your heart be cheered by the thought that God will somehow "move the stone."

> *Oft, before we've faced the trial,*
> *We have come with joy to own*
> *Angels have from Heav'n descended,*
> *And have rolled away "the stone"!* —Anon.

Take courage: if God doesn't choose to remove an obstacle, He will help you plow around it!

"LOVE IS BLIND!"

And Jacob served seven years for Rachel; and they
seemed unto him but a few days, for the love he
had for her.   Genesis 29:20

One of the most beautiful commentaries on love is found in
this verse. Jacob's deep longing and affection for his promised
bride, Rachel, was so great that the seven years of work required
for her hand seemed but a few days! They say, "Love is blind,"
and in Jacob's case it certainly was blind to time and work. He
wanted Rachel to be "Mrs. Jacob" so badly that the many years
of required toil seemed almost as nothing in comparison with the
reward he would receive for them — they were a genuine labor
of love.

In much the same way we as believers, because of our love for
the Lord Jesus Christ, and in view of the coming Glory, can become "blind" to the present hardships of life. Compared with the
future reward, the difficulties of the pilgrim pathway are really
nothing at all. As the Bride of Christ, we look forward with glad
anticipation to the coming of the Bridegroom himself and the
glory of His presence throughout the endless ages of eternity.
Even though our faith may falter now, we know that the "toils
of the road will seem nothing when we come to the end of the
way." It was this hope that made Paul "blind" to his trials. He
said in 2 Corinthians 5:14 that ". . . the *love* of Christ constraineth us . . . ." In Romans 8:18 he declared, ". . . I reckon
that the sufferings of this present time are not worthy to be compared with the glory which shall be revealed in us." Doesn't that
remind you of Jacob? His seven years of labor for Rachel's hand
seemed as nothing because of the love he had for her.

Does the way seem difficult? Do the trials mount with increasing intensity? Then dwell upon the Savior and your love for
Him. As you do, you will become "blind" to the difficulties of
life and have your eyes opened wide to the joys reserved for those
who labor faithfully and endure all things patiently for His sake!

> *Now service for Christ is a love task for me,*
> *He giveth the strength that is needed, you see;*
> *We count not the cost for the Glory we view,*
> *Where grace will reward us for all that we do!* —Bosch

He who has love in his heart has spurs in his heels!

THE SIX-LEGGED LAMB

For he hath made him, who knew no sin, to be sin for us, that we might be made the righteousness of God in him.   2 Corinthians 5:21

When God saves a man, He does more than pardon that sinner of his guilt; He also completely erases the old offenses from the "books," clears the penitent's name, and bestows upon him the perfect righteousness of the Savior. For that reason believers may justly be called *"saints,"* for *they stand perfect in Christ!*

Dr. Harry A. Ironside used to tell of an experience he had while he was the guest of a western sheep herder. One morning he saw an old ewe lope across the field followed by the strangest looking lamb he had ever seen. It apparently had *six legs!* The last two seemed to be torn from the body and were just dangling there. The shepherd caught the odd lambkin and brought it to Dr. Ironside for examination. Closer inspection showed that the skin from another lamb had been stretched over its body. The shepherd explained that this little one had been orphaned, and none of the ewes would adopt it. However, a day or two later a rattlesnake killed another young lamb. Its bereaved mother could not be consoled. She also stoutly rejected this orphaned animal when it was offered to her as a substitute. However, *when they skinned her own dead lambkin and draped its wooly coat over the orphaned one, she immediately accepted it,* because it smelled right to her. Dr. Ironside was much impressed, and said: "What a beautiful picture of substitutionary atonement. We too were once orphans — spiritual outcasts — without hope of Heaven. We were not acceptable to God because of our sin. However, the lovely Lamb of God took the sting of the 'old serpent' and died upon the cross for a lost world. Now by receiving Him through faith we are redeemed and made ready for Heaven because His righteousness has been applied to our account."

Sinner, have you been made acceptable to God "in the Beloved"?

> * *God sees my Savior, and then He sees me*
> *"In the Beloved," accepted and free!*— C. D. Martin

God formed us, sin deformed us, but Christ alone can transform us!

* © Hope Publishing Co. Used by permission.

LOSING THE WORD

*. . . as he sowed, some [seed] fell by the wayside, and
the fowls of the air came and devoured it.*   Mark 4:4

What a strange sight greeted my gaze as I looked out over the
bay. There was old "Pete the pelican" bobbing around on the
waves, and perched right on top of his head was a sea gull.
Looking more closely I discovered that "Pete" had caught a fish,
but its tail was sticking out one side of his huge beak. What a
dilemma the old pelican was in! He had gotten his fish, but now
to eat it he would have to open his mouth, and sitting right there
ready to snatch it as soon as he did so was Mr. Sea Gull. He
knew he had "Pete" right where he wanted him.

As I saw the wise old sea gull ready to grab the food from the
pelican's mouth, I was reminded of Jesus' parable about the
sower and the fact that as some seed fell by the wayside, "the
fowls of the air came and devoured it." Jesus explained that this
was a picture of Satan's tactics in taking the Word from the
hearts of those who, although receiving the message of grace,
fail to understand and believe it.

How important it is that we not only "receive" the Word, but
also that we study it and meditate upon it. Unless we do so, we
are the losers. It is possible for the "seed" to be sown in our
hearts, and yet not to take root! How many there are who, having
been really blessed by a message, come out of a church service,
only to be met by friends who begin at once to talk about the
weather, the ball game, business, world conditions—anything and
everything but the Word of God which they have heard. And
the first thing you know, that which had been received is snatched
away, and the precious seed fails to bear fruit. The Psalmist declared, "Thy word have I hidden in mine heart . . ." (Ps. 119:
11). Remember, when the Word is sown, receive it gladly, meditate upon it intently, talk about it to others, memorize it, and
then allow it to bring forth fruit in your life!

The seed of the Word falls on many a soil,
The fertile, the thorny, the hard;
Lest haply it fruitless in thy heart be sown,
Blest soul, be thou ever on guard. — H.G.B.

**Take heed to the Word; remember, a man's spirit needs daily
food as well as his body!**   —Edmund Nelson

"WHEN THIS GETS ALL"

But my God shall supply all your need according to his riches in glory by Christ Jesus. Philippians 4:19

We had thoroughly enjoyed the meeting in Altoona, Pennsylvania, and the privilege of greeting many friends of the Radio Bible Class who attended the service that evening. Some dear friends invited us to their home after the meeting for a lunch; but when we got there, it was more like a full-course dinner, and what a feast we had! As we were eating, one of the hostesses came into the living room to see if we had enough. Upon leaving, she turned around and said, "There's more in the kitchen when this gets all!" Since I come from the Midwest, this Pennsylvania Dutch expression really tickled me. "There's more in the kitchen when this gets all!" It was just another way of saying, "When what you have is all gone, there's more where that came from!" That was good to know, but how much more wonderful this is in the spiritual realm. How comforting the assurance that no matter how great our need, no matter how heavily we might have already drawn upon Heaven's resources, *there's more "when this gets all!"*

God's love has no measure; God's grace has no limit; and God's power is supreme. His wisdom is unbounded; and, praise His name, *His provisions are never exhausted!* No wonder the Apostle Paul wrote to the church at Ephesus expressing his desire that they might "know the love of Christ which passeth knowledge" and be conscious of the fact that He "is able to do exceeding abundantly above all that we ask or think, according to the power that worketh in us."

Oh, that we might learn to walk in this confidence each day, and never worry about tomorrow! Thanking God for His present provision, we should go forward a step at a time knowing that *"there's more when this gets all!"*

"There's more, there's more, when this gets all";
Assurance blest: He hears our call,
Though sad our way — filled with regret —
Through His supply we'll conquer yet! —H.G.B.

Our prayer and God's supply are like two buckets in a well; while one ascends, the other descends!

THE MATHEMATICIAN'S CONVERSION

For what is a man profited, if he shall gain the whole world, and lose his own soul?   Matthew 16:26

The most precious possession a man has is his soul! However, sin and Satan have so blinded the eyes of the unsaved that they abuse, degrade, and bargain away this "jewel of God" for a pittance. Unless grace enlightens them, they will carelessly barter away their eternal future for a few fleeting moments of earthly pleasure or transient success; yet Jesus in His Word makes it abundantly clear that *there is no greater tragedy than a lost soul!*

A young man, distinguished for his mathematical attainments, was fond of challenging his fellow students to a trial of skill in solving difficult problems. One day a classmate came into his study and handed him a folded paper, saying, "Here is a problem I wish you would solve." Then he immediately left the room. The paper was eagerly spread out and read, but instead of a question in mathematics, there appeared the solemn words of Jesus: "For what shall it profit a man, if he shall gain the whole world, and lose his own soul? Or what shall a man give in exchange for his soul?" (Mark 8:36, 37). With a gesture of impatience, the mathematician tore the paper to bits and turned again to his books. In vain he tried to shake off the conviction the heart-searching words had produced. The Holy Spirit continued to press home the truth of his guilt and eternal danger so that he could find no peace until he had made sure of his soul's destiny by believing in the Lord Jesus Christ. The story goes that subsequently he became a preacher of the Gospel, and that his first sermon was from the very words that brought him to Christ: "For what shall it profit a man, if he shall gain the whole world, and lose his own soul?"

Have you given your most precious possession to Jesus? Remember, that soul of yours is only safe in His keeping!

> *When thou, in the dust art forgotten,*
> *When pleasure can charm thee no more,*
> *'Twill profit thee nothing, but fearful the cost,*
> *To gain the whole world, if thy soul should be lost!*
>   — F. Crosby

Life with Christ is an endless hope; without Him it is a hopeless end!

"THOU GOD SEEST ME"

For the eyes of the Lord are over the righteous . . . .
1 Peter 3:12

The following comforting comments were found in a clipping sent to us by an interested reader: "A child in Burma was permitted by his parents to go to a mission school in order that he might learn to read. By and by they found he was losing faith in the idols. This made them feel very sad. So the father took the lad to one of the gayest of the temples where the fragrance of incense filled the air. There he showed him the glittering images covered with gold and silver ornaments and surrounded by flowers and candles. 'Here,' said the father, 'is a god you can see! The Christians cannot show you their God.' 'Yes,' said the child, 'we can see your god, but he cannot see us. We cannot see the Christian's God, but *He sees us all the time!*' Was not this child wise in choosing the God from whom even the thoughts of the heart cannot be hidden?"

How reassuring the truth that "the eyes of the Lord are over the righteous" so that we can say with Hagar, "Thou God seest me . . ." (Gen. 16:13). How precious the teaching of the Bible about the eyes of the Lord. Psalm 32:8 tells us, "I will instruct thee and teach thee in the way which thou shalt go; *I will guide thee with mine eye.*" And we read in Psalm 33:18, "Behold, *the eye of the Lord is upon those who fear him,* upon those who hope in his mercy." First Peter 3:12 tells us that ". . . *the eyes of the Lord are over the righteous . . . .*"

Child of God, perhaps unnoticed, or even forgotten and neglected by others, remember, you too can say with assurance, "Thou God seest me!" His eyes are not only upon you, but His ears are open unto your cry.

With the little child in Burma we as Christians can rejoice that although we are not able to see our God, we do know and have this assurance that *He sees us all the time!*

Sweet thought! We have a Friend above,
Our weary, faltering steps to guide,
He follows with His eye of love
The precious ones for whom He died. —Anon.

It is comforting to know that He who "guides us with His eye" sees tomorrow clearer than we see today!   **—Bosch**

WOUNDED AND HEALED

. . . he maketh sore, and bindeth up; he woundeth,
and his hands make whole.   Job 5:18

In times of prosperity, men are apt to indulge erroneous notions, and neglect important truths. God therefore often employs afflictions to correct our mistaken ideas, and rectify our foolish intentions. However, when we have learned the lesson He seeks to teach us, He who maketh sore, "bindeth up," and "His hands make whole." Therefore, "despise not thou the chastening of the Lord, nor faint when thou art rebuked of him: for *whom the Lord loveth he chasteneth,* and scourgeth every son whom he receiveth." When your heart seems to be bleeding its life away, God is already at work beginning His "binding up" and healing. His love is infinite, and He will not suffer those who trust in Him to be desolate!

Speaking of chastening, Spurgeon says: "The egg is white enough, though the hen be black as coal. Out of evil comes blessing, through the great goodness of God. From threatening clouds we get refreshing showers; in dark mines men find bright jewels; and so from our worst troubles come our best blessings."

A minister tells of a member of his congregation who, though she claimed to be a Christian, seemed most unresponsive to the things of the Lord. He was never able to touch a single "string" of sympathy in her cold nature. She found it necessary to leave town for several months, and upon her return, the pastor found her strangely altered. Her face was radiant with God's love. She explained that she had passed through a terrible trial. All her possessions had been swept away, her only close relative had died, and nothing had been left to her but God. "Then," she said, "I truly learned to pray. I laid hold on the Lord with many tears until I actually touched Him! Now, oh, the joy that fills my heart!"

Ah, yes, *that is why God woundeth, that His hands may remold us and make us more truly conformed to His Son.* Let Him have His way with you.

> *Ill that He blesses is our good,*
> *And unblest good is ill;*
> *And all is right that seems most wrong,*
> *If it be His sweet will!*   — J. G. Whittier

One of the greatest evidences of God's love is when He sends His children afflictions with grace to bear them!

CASTLES OF SAND
. . . the world passeth away . . . but he that doeth
the will of God abideth forever.   1 John 2:17

Walking along the shores of the Gulf of Mexico early one morning, I came upon quite an elaborate castle of sand. Evidently some youngster the day before had spent hours scooping out the "moats," heaping up the mounds of earth, forming the castle walls, and placing many beautiful shells on them as an added embellishment. How proud he must have been of his work. I can just imagine hearing him call out, "Mommy, Daddy, look at what I made!" and then how his face must have beamed as he received their enthusiastic praise.

As I came along at sunrise, however, the tide was coming in, and with it the continual action of the breakers. They seemed to move in a little closer with each succeeding crash. As I stopped to examine this child's castle of sand, a huge wave broke at my feet, disintegrating a portion of it. Then came another wave, and yet another, adding to its ruin. Returning some time later I found the castle was completely destroyed. It made me think of the "castles of sand" which men and women erect in real life. They spend not just a few hours, but precious years toiling and laboring, thinking they are really accomplishing something. But then comes the night, and after the "builders" themselves are gone, the tides of time swirl in and soon their cherished "castles" disappear, and they and their works are both forgotten.

There is only one way to build a life that counts, and a "work" that endures. It is to found it upon the Rock, Christ Jesus, and to do so with eternity's values in view. To rear and educate your children to succeed in this life is fine, but what are you doing to help them prepare for that which is to come? To be successful in business and receive the plaudits of men may give temporary pleasure and satisfaction, but what are you doing for eternity? What are you building: a "castle of sand," *or a work that abides?* It was Daniel who said, ". . . they that turn many to righteousness, [shall shine] as the stars forever and ever" (Dan. 12:3).

> *To wealth and fame I would not climb,*
> *But I would know God's peace sublime;*
> *And everywhere, and all the time,*
> *I want my life to tell for Jesus!*   — Mrs. F. Breck

Only one life, 'twill soon be past, only what's done for Christ will last!

PRESSING TOWARD THE PRIZE

> . . . *this one thing I do . . . I press toward the*
> *mark for the prize of the high calling of God in*
> *Christ Jesus.*   Philippians 3:13, 14

Determination and tenacity are requirements for success in almost any worthwhile endeavor. Note how a hungry cheetah displays such single-mindedness when he chooses one specific animal in a herd of deer or antelope and goes after it. Ignoring others less desirable, which might easily be caught, the swift predator has been clocked at nearly seventy miles per hour in his hot and unrelenting pursuit of his intended prey. Think of the many scientists who, in spite of discouraging setbacks and negative attitudes on the part of their fellow workers, have persisted year after year in carrying on research in order to find a vaccine for some specific disease. Such tenacity of purpose is highly commendable. What boy has not thrilled to the popular tale of the western rancher who, having set his mind upon capturing a certain wild stallion, did not give up until he had corralled and trained the creature? To attain success, *both determination and perseverance are necessary!*

In like manner, to live a victorious spiritual life, a steadfast resolve and a constancy of purpose are needed. The apostle Paul declared that a desire to experience the fullness of Christ's resurrection power so gripped him that it became the controlling factor in his life. His words "I press toward the mark" describe a runner racing hard with his head forward, body bent and angled, and eyes on nothing but the final tape. Such was Paul's zealous attitude in reaching out toward the spiritual goals of service and blessing. If we would show the same oneness of purpose, we would likewise be filled with joy, experience victory over sin, and possess a deeper sense of God's constant presence.

Let us press toward "the prize of the high calling of God"!

> *I'm pressing on the upward way,*
> *New heights I'm gaining ev'ry day;*
> *Still praying as I onward bound,*
> *"Lord, plant my feet on higher ground."* —J. Oatman, Jr.

Sanctification is much like riding a bicycle — either you keep moving forward, or you fall down.

RICHES OR BREAD?

Labor not for the food which perisheth, but for that food which endureth unto everlasting life. . . .   John 6:27

In the book, *Illustrations and Incidents for Preachers and Teachers,* the story is told about an Arab who lost his way while traveling across a desert. Toiling for two days without food, he became nearly exhausted. At last he stumbled upon a little oasis where travelers before him had halted. He hoped to find some remnant of food, but only a small bag had been left behind. In eagerness he opened it, but to his disgust and disappointment, he found pearls instead of fruit or dates. *He had riches but not bread!* If all the wealth of the world had been given to him, it would have meant nothing as far as his most urgent need of the moment was concerned. What he required was food that he might be nourished and strengthened. Money and jewels without life were worthless!

So it is with many traveling across the desert of this world. Intent upon the acquisition of silver and gold, they give no thought to their spiritual needs. Even though someday they might find their hands full of riches, they lack that which alone can satisfy their souls. What a tragedy when they stand before God and discover that wealth is no passport to Heaven. Fame and success will not qualify them to enter the Pearly Gates. In fact, all such things will be stripped away and left behind.

There is nothing wrong with riches if properly acquired and rightfully used. But the most important thing is partaking of the "Bread of Heaven" and receiving the eternal blessing God imparts (John 6:35). Accept Christ as your Savior, for *"he that eateth of this bread shall live forever"* (John 6:58).

> *The riches of this world are vain;*
> *They vanish in a day.*
> *But sweet the treasures of God's love —*
> *They never pass away!*   —G.W.

To be rich in God is better than to be rich in goods!

THE PARABLE OF THE BARREL

For everyone that doeth evil hateth the light, neither cometh to the light, lest his deeds should be reproved.
John 3:20

Someone who visited a large barrel factory gave this description of the inspection department: "I noticed that the man who makes the final check of those huge containers whirls them around a few times to inspect the outside. Then, rolling them over, he thrusts a small electric light into the hole in their side and with his eye at the same opening gazes quietly for a moment as if looking for something. 'What do you do that for?' I asked. 'To see if it's charred correctly, if there's enough glue on the joints, and if there are any visible flaws.' He graciously allowed me to put my eye to the hole in one of the barrels, but all within was black as pitch. 'Here,' he said pushing me aside and putting the electric lamp through the opening, 'now look.' I did so and the inside was now as bright as day. Every joint and irregularity was clearly revealed."

Our lives are much like that barrel! Only the entrance of God's Word can remove our spiritual darkness. When by grace the Holy Spirit sheds His beams into the heart of a sinner, great conviction grips the soul for all the hidden evil and glaring imperfections show up. The barrel inspector with his light could only *discover* the flaws, but Christ, the Light of the world, can do far more. He can remedy them and *make us anew!*

There are many who enjoy sin so much they refuse to come to Christ lest their deeds be reproved by the light of His presence. I pray that you are not numbered among such foolish individuals. If you are not regenerated by His grace, at the final "checkout" your soul will be rejected by Him as not fit for Heaven. Remember the parable of the barrel, and let the searchlight of God's Word reveal your sin to you. Then seek the spiritual renewing Christ alone can provide!

> *When the holy light of Jesus*
> *Floods your dark and sinful soul,*
> *You will see how much you're needing*
> *His blest grace to make you whole.* — G.W.

The first step toward salvation is to recognize your sin; for he who makes little of his disease will make little of his doctor.
—T. Goodwin

THE BIG DIFFERENCE

*If in this life only we have hope in Christ, we are
of all men most miserable.*   1 Corinthians 15:19

As I left a funeral home one day after a memorial service for
a dear saint of God, one of the directors of the mortuary remarked, "You know, *there's a big difference between the funerals
of those who are Christians and those who are unsaved!*" I have
never forgotten his words. What a testimony to the reality of the
Christian faith! Here was a man who had witnessed hundreds
of funerals and had been impressed by the striking difference between the behavior of true believers in a time of bereavement
and those who had no faith. Paul tells us in 1 Thessalonians
4:13 that the unsaved should not sorrow like worldly individuals
who have "no hope." The reason for Paul's admonition is found
in the following verses, where the apostle describes the day
when ". . . the Lord himself shall descend from heaven . . . and
the dead in Christ shall rise first . . . [and] we who are alive
and remain shall be caught up together with them in the clouds,
to meet the Lord in the air . . ." (1 Thess. 4:16, 17).

Let it be remembered, however, that even believers grieve
when death separates them from their loved ones. After all,
when human ties are broken, it does hurt and tears are bound
to be shed. But notice Paul does not say that we do not sorrow
at all. Rather he declares that we ". . . sorrow not, even as
others *who have not hope!*" The grief is lessened and the heartache softened in the realization that those who died in Christ
go into the presence of the Lord Jesus Himself, and the day is
coming when with glorified, resurrected bodies all believers shall
in one great, glad, grand reunion rise to meet the Lord in the
air. No wonder Paul concludes this passage by saying, "Wherefore, comfort one another *with these words!*"

Those who are looking for that blessed hope find courage and
comfort in the upward look. The thought of Christ's soon return
and reunion with loved ones makes a big difference!

O how sweet it will be on that wonderful day,
So free from all sorrow and pain;
With songs on our lips and with harps in our hands
To meet one another again!   —E. H. Gates, alt.

**UNION with Christ here, means REUNION with loved ones
over There!**   —G.W.

"THINK ON THESE THINGS"

Finally, brethren, whatever things are true . . . honest . . .
just . . . pure . . . lovely . . . of good report; if there be
any virtue . . . any praise, think on these things.

Philippians 4:8

The best way to keep evil ideas out of our minds is to concentrate on things that are good and pure and beautiful. The
mind cannot be entirely at rest; it is not a blank. Hence the
exhortation is given to think about right things. We are to be
occupied with the Scriptures, with loving attitudes and holy desires. We must look only on worthy things and meditate primarily on that which is of good report. To praise rather than to
criticize is our first duty. As we thus allow the Holy Spirit to
bring every thought into captivity to Christ, we will find that
good deeds will automatically flow from such lofty and spiritual
attitudes. Like our blessed Savior, we too will then go about
"doing good" (Acts 10:38).

A college girl who was a fine scholar and had a noble spirit
volunteered to be a counselor at a girl's camp. Despite her abilities, she was required to peel potatoes in the kitchen. The head
mistress of the camp, realizing that this was quite a menial task
for such a talented and highly intellectual girl, exclaimed, "It's
too bad that a young woman of your education should have to
peel potatoes." The girl who was a splendid Christian looked
up brightly and replied, "But, Miss Baldwin, remember, I don't
have to *think* about potatoes while I'm peeling them." The application is obvious. You can keep your soul out of the dust no
matter what your task, if you center your thoughts on the things
mentioned in our text. Let the Holy Spirit discipline your mind
by dismissing suspicion and replacing it with hope and trust.
Forego grudges. Flout envy. Be appreciative, be kind, be gentle.
Rejoice in the Lord a little more. Take pleasure in beauty and
virtue. Clear away the cobwebs of doubt, frustration, and anger.
Let your mind dwell on Christ and He will beautify your life.

> *Think truly, and thy thoughts*
> *Shall be a fruitful seed;*
> *Live truly, and thy life shall be*
> *A great and noble creed.*   — H. Bonar

You're not what you think you are; but what you THINK—
you are!

AUTO SAFETY

> *. . . Who hath redness of eyes? They that tarry long*
> *at the wine. . . .*   Proverbs 23:29, 30

In recent months, we have heard a great deal about auto safety. Demands have been made that manufacturers provide certain safety features in cars as standard equipment in order to spare passengers serious harm. Although every one of us is in favor of doing everything possible in this way to cut down the tremendous toll on our highways, I cannot help but feel that the blame for many of the deaths and injuries has been wrongly placed. I have just read that 50 percent of our traffic deaths are attributed in part or in whole to drunkenness! This is shocking! Why is it then that while such a hue and cry is raised to incorporate more safety features *in* cars, we hear very little about removing the real killers *from* the cars! Could it be that men are more concerned about the few tax dollars which accrue from liquor sales? Or is it possible that politicians are so fearful of losing a few votes that they refuse to take the necessary steps to stop this terrible slaughter on our highways? Personally, I believe the best way to promote automobile safety would be to get "King Barleycorn" off the road. We can produce cars with every conceivable safety device, but until this "monster" — the drunken driver — is barred from our streets, we will still have a major problem on our hands. Collapsible steering wheels, safety belts, and recessed door handles are all fine, but the most necessary change must be made *at the upper end of the steering column!*

The Bible graphically describes the unstable reactions of one under the influence of liquor as resembling a person who "lieth down in the midst of the sea, or as he that lieth upon the top of a mast" (Prov. 23:34). True auto safety can never be achieved as long as men ignore the Scriptural warnings concerning the dread consequences of alcohol! Every government official who has any regard for human life and safety should take action in this matter!

> *'Tis well to note that few survive,*
> *Who often drink before they drive!* — H.G.B.

A "tight" driver is much more dangerous than a loose wheel!

TASTE AND SEE!

Oh, taste and see that the Lord is good. Psalm 34:8

As an aged Scotsman lay dying, a friend asked him, "Have you received *a glimpse of Christ* now that you are soon going to be with Him?" The godly old man man tried to raise himself up a little as he emphatically replied, "I'll have none o' your *glimpses* now that I am dyin' — seein' that I've had *a full look at Him* these 40 years!" That man had experienced God's presence and tasted and seen that the Lord is good!

David wrote Psalm 34 (our Scripture lesson) as a song of praise. He had cried to God when in deep distress, and his prayer had been answered. The Psalmist had discovered that Christ, called "the angel of the Lord" in the Old Testament, protects and delivers those who fear God, and now He wanted others to perceive this truth as a living reality in their own lives. Therefore he issued the invitation, "Oh, taste and see that the Lord is good."

Have you learned by experience that the Lord is gracious, kind, and compassionate? If you haven't, it is not because of reluctance on the part of God. He takes great pleasure in making Himself real to those who trust Him. He delights in testimonies like that of the dying Scotsman, "I'll have none o' your glimpses . . . seein' I've had a full look at Him these 40 years!" Therefore, be assured that He is ready to give you a wonderful sense of His presence. If you have received Christ, you should daily read His Word and believe it, and then humbly accept His perfect will for your life. Act on this advice, and soon you will be joyously saying to others, "Oh, taste and see that the Lord is good."

> *Oh, taste and see that God is good*
> *To all that seek His face;*
> *Yea, blest the man that trusts in Him,*
> *Confiding in His grace*   —Anon.

If God is your DELIGHT, you'll have songs in the NIGHT!

JUST "TIED ON"

*. . . Except a man be born again, he cannot see the
kingdom of God.*   John 3:3

The story is told of a wealthy man who, although he was outwardly religious, was not a Christian. He had in his employ an
old gardener, a true believer, who tried to show him the emptiness of mere religion without Christ. Now it happened that
there was one tree on the rich man's estate which never bore any
fruit. However, one day as the owner was walking in his orchard,
he saw some beautiful apples hanging on it. Imagine his surprise, especially when he went to pick some and found them to
be *tied on!* The gardener by this simple illustration wanted to
point out to his employer the difference between real Christianity
and pious sham. Religion without Christ is like a barren tree
on which the fruit is merely "tied on"!

Many so-called Christians today make an outward show of
piety but it is only "tied on" religion. Their heart is not in it.
They bring no fruit to perfection because they have never been
born again. *There is no genuine spiritual life within!* They go
through the motions, but their outward profession lacks the reality
of an inner possession. Jesus said, "Except a man be born again,
he cannot see the kingdom of God." John tells us that "He that
hath the Son hath life; and he that hath not the Son of God
hath not life" (1 John 5:12).

As sinners, we are spiritually dead. The only way to experience genuine salvation is through Christ who said, "I am the
way, the truth, and the life. . . ." Personally receiving Him as
Savior and Lord, we are born again and made "new creatures."

Have you ever actually trusted Christ, or are you simply going
through the motions? Are those so-called "good works" of yours
just "tied on," or are they the geninue fruit of a new life? "Believe on the Lord Jesus Christ, and thou shalt be saved . . ."
(Acts 16:31).

**The only "works" of unsaved men that will endure in Heaven
are the nailprints in Christ's hands!**   —W. P. Loveless

THE DESTRUCTION OF DEATH

*The last enemy that shall be destroyed is death. O
death, where is thy sting?*   1 Corinthians 15:26, 55

During the last several weeks I have been receiving telephone
calls from a girl who says she is sixteen years old and claims
that the doctors have told her she has less than six months to
live. She refuses to identify herself, informing me that she used
to go to Sunday school but "didn't care about it very much and
quit." The thought of dying gives her an eerie feeling; yet she
has thus far rejected the Gospel, bitterly blaming God for her
illness. I pray that I may be able to lead her to Christ.

Everything non-Christian thinkers have written about death
is mere speculation, but the Gospel gives hope and certainty because it is based upon things that really happened. The Lord
Jesus died on the cross to pay the price for sin and took away
death's sting. He rose from the grave to destroy its power.
Though Paul still called it man's "last enemy," he assured us that
we shall be victorious over it. True, the process of dying is
neither pleasant to observe nor easy to contemplate. In fact, most
of us shed tears when a loved one dies because death tears apart
tender earthly ties. Yet death is a vanquished foe! Christ took
its sting away when He paid the price for sin, and destroyed
its power when He rose from the grave. It cannot truly harm
the believer. Actually, it becomes a friend for one who knows
the Lord Jesus. It can only close our eyes, kiss away our breath,
and usher us into the presence of Christ. While its "shadow"
is there, its sting is gone and its power is defeated. If you believe this, you are blessed indeed!

"Asleep in Jesus," O how sweet
To be for such a slumber meet!
With holy confidence to sing
That death hath lost its venomed sting! — Macay

**Death for the Christian is not bane but blessing, not tragedy
but triumph!**   —G.W.

THE CAPTIVE FREED

. . . reconciled to God by the death of his Son, . . .
we shall be saved by his life.   Romans 5:10

A letter written by Dr. C. I. Scofield recounts the experience of this Bible teacher who has been so greatly used by the Lord. It reads in part: "The all but universal habit of drink among the men of my time overmastered me. I was not a victor in the battle of life, but a ruined and hopeless man who, despite all my struggles, was fast bound in chains of my own forging. I had no thought of Christ. There was no hope that in a church sometime I might hear and believe the Gospel, for I never attended. But then the Savior took up the case. Men were beginning to turn away from me, but the Lord of Glory sought me. Through Thomas McPheeters, a joyous, hopeful soul, Jesus Christ offered Himself to me, that human wreck. From a worn pocket Testament, McPheeters read to me the great deliverance passages. And when I asked, like the Philippian jailer of old, 'What must I do to be saved?' he just read them again, and we knelt and I received Jesus as my Savior. And — oh! put it into the story, put it big and plain: *Instantly the chains were broken never to be forged again — the passion for drink was taken away!* Put it 'instantly,' dear Editor. Make it plain. Don't say, 'He strove with his sin of drink and came off victor.' He did nothing of the kind. Divine power did it, wholly of grace. To Christ be all the glory!"

The Lord Jesus *died* on the cross that we might be saved from the *guilt* of sin. He *lives* to deliver us from its *power*. There is only One who can thus snap the fetters of sin and give deliverance.

> *He breaks the power of canceled sin,*
> *He sets the prisoner free;*
> *His blood can make the foulest clean,*
> *His blood availed for me.*   — Wesley

When God forgives sin, He purges the RECORD, erases the REMEMBRANCE, and empowers the RECIPIENT! —H.G.B.

"DIRTY WHITE" FLAMINGOS

But solid food belongeth to them that are of full
age. . . .   Hebrews 5:14

The *Paralastic* magazine relates: "A flamingo struts around on long thin legs like a crane, has a lengthy extended neck like a swan, and possesses unique, rosy-red plumage. You might judge it to be a rather funny looking creature, but actually it is very attractive. Well, some years ago the San Antonio zoo managed to get some of those exotic birds. At first the keepers were very fussy about them, serving them fresh shrimp and dried flies imported all the way from Mexico. As a result of this special, carefully controlled diet, the flamingos remained healthy and looked beautiful in their lovely red feathers. Then the zoo became economical. They cut out the regular fare, and instead fed them a mixture of dog meal and vegetables. But that was a mistake. Soon the flamingos's red feathers faded to a sickly pink, and then turned a dirty white. Realizing their mistake, the zoo keepers put the birds back on their shrimp and Mexican fly diet. It is estimated that within six months the birds' feathers will regain their full red color."

Those San Antonio flamingos reminded me of what happens to a Christian who gets on the wrong "diet." Even as those birds, when improperly fed, developed an abnormal condition and presented a very poor appearance, so too a Christian whose diet consists of "the husks" of this world will quickly lose his spiritual vitality. Failing to partake of the "meat" of God's Word, he becomes "emaciated." With his inner resources thus weakened he easily succumbs to the temptations of the devil, and becomes unattractive in his daily walk. The believer's life, however, should ever be "colorful" and appealing.

What kind of diet are you on? Does it call for a change? If so, let it be one of feasting upon the "meat" of God's Word. Remember the dirty white flamingos, and as a Christian avoid an equally "off-color" testimony!

Let your life speak well of Jesus every day;
Own His right to every service you can pay;
Sinners you can help to win if your life is pure and clean,
And you keep the joy-bells ringing in your heart!—J. E. Ruark

So feed on the Word and live Christ that you will be a rebuke to sin wherever you go!

WHAT IS MAN?

What is man, that thou art mindful of him? Psalm 8:4

As I was flying from Newark to Detroit, I was suddenly impressed with the insignificance of man. Winging our way at an altitude of over 30,000 feet, I found it difficult even to discern any cars on the highways below. Everything seemed so very small. In fact, at the height at which we had been traveling, "man" was completely lost to view. I was reminded of the words of the Psalmist: "What is man, that thou art mindful of him?" Yes, at 30,000 feet, man could no longer be seen with the naked eye; and yet the Lord, the Almighty, thought so much of us poor, defiled, insignificant creatures inhabiting this tiny speck of dust— one of the uncounted galaxies of the universe — that He was willing to give His own Son to come and die for us. This is a truth that staggers the imagination!

Since it is true that "God commendeth His love toward us, in that, while we were yet sinners, Christ died for us," how much more then will He now care for His redeemed possession! We who have been saved by His precious blood can certainly depend upon Him fully for every circumstance of life — especially so when even a sparrow does not fall to the ground without His knowledge! How inconsistent it is then, for us who know this God as our Heavenly Father, to become easily disturbed, frustrated, and upset by the trials of the way. He has promised, "I will guide thee with mine eye" (Ps. 32:8), and "I will never leave thee, nor forsake thee" (Heb. 13:5). Graciously He guarantees to supply all our need (Phil. 4:19).

Is the way difficult? Are the problems facing you almost insurmountable? Then take comfort in the assurance that God sees you, will guide you, and will provide you with all things that are truly necessary. The secret of peace and victory even in the deepest sorrow is found in Peter's admonition: "Casting all your care upon him; for he careth for you" (1 Pet. 5:7).

> *Oh, yes, He cares; I know He cares,*
> *His heart is touched with my grief;*
> *When the days are weary, the long nights dreary,*
> *I know my Savior cares!*   —F. E. Graeff

God may not give us an easy journey to the Promised Land, but He'll give us a safe one.   —H. Bonar

"THE ROAD OF THE LOVING HEART"

*Prepare ye the way of the Lord, make straight in the
desert a highway for our God.*   Isaiah 40:3

Many years ago Robert Louis Stevenson was stricken with a
fatal illness. Seeking quiet and rest in a favorable climate, he
chose a faraway island in the Pacific Ocean. He soon found conditions to be less than ideal, however, for the native chiefs were
constantly at war with one another. Quarrels and disputes kept
breaking out among them, but gradually Stevenson was able to
solve these conflicts. By every kind act in his power he won their
friendship, and soon he got them to settle their differences, teaching them how to be happy and at peace. These people had never
had such a friend before. The great novelist became their hero,
and they longed to show him their gratitude. They had no money
to buy gifts, but one of the natives said, "We can make him a
wide, smooth pathway straight through the heart of the jungle
that shall lead to his land, for he has longed to have others come
and visit him." All agreed to start immediately on its construction. Today this inscription appears over the entrance of that
highway: *"The Road of the Loving Heart,"* and just below it a
plaque telling that it was built to please Stevenson because he
had brought them joy and peace.

There is One greater than Stevenson who has also shown us
His love, and through His sacrifice has brought *eternal peace* to
our troubled hearts. In gratitude to Him, let us labor to prepare
"the way of the Lord" for others, that through our consecrated
lives and our words of testimony they may find easy access to
our divine Friend. If we show them His grace, many will want
to walk "The Road of the Loving Heart."

*With the zeal of John the Baptist
Let us still "prepare the way"
For the weary feet of sinners
Who would seek the Lord today.*— I. H.

**When God's work comes to a standstill, you can be sure the
obstacles in the way can be removed by human hands!**

GIVING THANKS ALWAYS

Giving thanks always for all things. . . . Ephesians 5:20

In the autobiography of the late Dr. Clarence E. Macartney, the following story is told: Two men were passing through a field in the country when they were charged by an enraged bull. They started for the nearest fence, but it was soon apparent that they couldn't make it before the animal reached them. One said to the other, "Put up a prayer, John. We're in for it!" But John answered, "I can't. I never made a public prayer in my life." "But you must," said his companion, "the bull will soon be upon us." "All right," panted John, "I'll give you the only prayer I know, the one my father used to repeat at the table: 'O Lord, for what we are about to receive, make us truly thankful!'" We may smile at this story; yet it is true that no matter what trials we may face, or how deep the waters through which we must pass, the true Christian should give thanks "always for all things."

Traveling to Cleveland for meetings, I had a tire blow out at seventy miles an hour. As I pulled the car to a stop without losing control, I breathed a prayer of thanks. But I forgot one thing —I didn't praise God for the blowout! In fact, I must confess that I was rather exasperated. It was dark and I was running a little behind schedule. I was tempted to murmur and complain, whereas I should have been thankful even for that seeming inconvenience. As children of God, it is wonderful to know that we can give thanks "always for all things unto God," because "we know that all things work together for good to them that love God, to them who are the called according to his purpose" (Rom. 8:28).

In a world filled with trials, disappointments, and discouragements, what a joy to realize that things never happen by chance to the true believer. Someone has wisely said, "The experiences of life can either make you bitter or better." *The key to becoming "better" is to give "thanks always for all things!"*

> 'Midst sun or rain, 'midst good or ill,
>   Through all my earthly days,
> May nothing bitter quell, O Lord,
>   My grateful song of praise!   —G. B. Adams

If you find yourself wearing a "spirit of heaviness," try a "garment of praise"!

GODLY CONTENTMENT

> . . . I have learned, in whatsoever state I am, in
> this to be content.   Philippians 4:11

Contentment is never the result of multiplying riches, increasing pleasures, or gaining fame. All these only incite discontent, for when one obtains them, he finds he still is not satisfied. Contentment does not depend upon things on the outside, but results from *conditions on the inside!* Paul had suffered more for the sake of Christ than probably anyone else (2 Cor. 11:23-28); yet this is the man who says, "I am content." The apostle was able to interpret all the experiences of life in terms of God's will for his eternal good (Rom. 8:28). Paul did not come to this happy philosophy of life in a moment. He says, "I have *learned . . .* to be content." Aspiring to be what we are not, or grasping after riches which elude us, is not the way to happiness. We must rather do our very best with God's help to accomplish our life's task with the talents and opportunities He presents.

In his famous lecture on "Clocks and Watches," Dr. Joseph Parker related the following story: A little watch, delicately strung, was dissatisfied with its restricted sphere of influence in a lady's pocket. It envied the position of Big Ben, the great tower clock. One day as it passed with her ladyship over London's Westminster Bridge, the tiny watch exclaimed, "I wish I could go up there! I could then serve multitudes, instead of just one individual." "You shall have your opportunity, small watch," she said. The lecturer then dramatically described how the pocket timepiece was drawn up the side of the mammoth tower by a slender thread. When it reached the top, *it was completely lost to view.* In his dramatic way, Dr. Parker concluded his lecture by exclaiming, *"Its elevation had become its annihilation!"*

Pray that you too may not lose the small influence you now have for Christ by coveting something larger for which you are not equipped, and which God constantly refuses you in His love.

> O for the peace of perfect trust
> My loving God in Thee;
> Unwavering faith that never doubts
> Thou choosest best for me.   —Anon.

Discontent makes rich men poor, while contentment makes poor men rich!

LITTLE "SPONGES"

And ye shall teach them to your children. . . .
Deuteronomy 11:19

Sponges have always intrigued me. There is just something about their appearance, feel, and absorptive qualities that is most fascinating. It was with a great deal of interest, therefore, that my family visited Tarpon Springs, Florida, where we could see how sponges are harvested. Donning their helmets, water-proof suits, and their weighted shoes, the divers descended into the murky depths to gather their crop. Sponges are actually animals, and must be cleaned before they are useful for household purposes. All the living matter must be removed so that the skeleton which remains with its open-celled structure can soak up and absorb other elements.

Sponges remind me of children. They, too, quietly and silently soak up everything with which they come in contact. They are what they are, not only because of the inheritance of certain characteristics and traits received from their parents, but also because of their environment. We must be very careful, therefore, of what is allowed to fill their little hearts and minds. How important it is to govern and control their surroundings.

By the way, what are your children absorbing in your home these days? What are they getting from that television set? What enters those young minds through those magazines on your reading table? In listening to your conversation, what kind of words and attitudes are being impressed upon them? Are good examples being set by your love for the Lord and concern for others? Is there a warm, spiritual emphasis in your home? Are you doing what you can to fill their hearts with God's Word? In years to come those children will "give out" only that which has been absorbed during their formative, impressionable years. Make sure those little "sponges" in your home soak up only that which is pure, wholesome, and uplifting.

> *Early let them seek Thy favor;*
> *Early let them do Thy will;*
> *Blessed Lord and only Savior,*
> *With Thy love their bosoms fill.*
> — W. B. Bradbury, alt.

Children seldom misquote you; they repeat word for word what you SHOULD NOT have said!

"LIFE'S REVERSES"

*When my spirit was overwhelmed within me, then
thou knewest my path.*   Psalm 142:3

Some years ago a tourist was being shown through one of the
oldest castles in England. He was quite impressed with the rich-
ness of the furnishings, the valuable art treasures, and the exquisite carvings. He was puzzled, however, by one strange tapestry which had an unusual design and a wild, irregular pattern.
The knotted threads and odd blobs of color made it seem the
work of one with an uncontrolled, overwrought imagination. The
guide, noticing the man's stunned look, smiled and said, "Sir,
that's actually the most beautiful piece of art in the castle, but
from time to time we find it necessary to turn its face to the
wall to protect its delicate colors from excessive exposure to light!"
Carefully rearranging the curious weaving, the guide showed the
tourist what proved to be the most exquisite tapestry he had ever
seen. The design and colors were breath-taking in their loveliness. It was indeed a masterpiece of symmetry and intricate
needlework.

In this simple story I saw a parable. Frequently God finds it
necessary to "turn the tapestry" of our life's plan so that it
faces the "inscrutable wall of baffling circumstance." For a time
all its joyous colors and obvious patterns are hidden from view.
Only the irregular designs of frustration and the knotty problems
of doubt greet our troubled gaze. When our spirit is thus overwhelmed by the confused nature of life's twisting way, we must
not despair, for God knows what He's doing. He recognizes that
too much of the "sunshine of prosperity" would fade our testimony, and ruin His holy design. In His own good time the
Lord will reverse our course so that the beauty and symmetry
of His all-wise purposes will become abundantly evident. In the
confidence of a faith that fully trusts the Hand that directs our
way, let us face life's "reverses" with courage, and "praise the
Lord anyway"!

> *Take courage then, my soul, wait and be still;*
> *Thy God shall work for thee His perfect will,*
> *If thou wilt take no less, His best shall be*
> *Thy portion now, and through eternity.*—F. Hanbury

There are no accidents in God's purposes: all is wise design!

I WILL NOT DOUBT

. . . O thou of little faith, why didst thou doubt?
                              Matthew 14:31

What a picture we have in this passage of the manner in which we often react when we are "tossed with the waves" of adversity and buffeted by the "contrary winds of human experience." When everything appears to be going against us, and the very foundations seem crumbling, how prone we are to forget that our Savior has promised, "I will never leave thee, nor forsake thee" (Heb. 13:5).

Oh, what peace we forfeit when we refuse to take God at His Word. How much better, keeping our eyes on Him and trusting His promises, to say with the poet:

I will not doubt though all my ships at sea
　Come drifting home with broken masts and sails;
I will believe the Hand which never fails,
From seeming evil, worketh good for me.
　And though I weep because these sails are tattered,
　Still will I cry, while my best hopes lie shattered,
　　　"I trust in Thee!"
I will not doubt though sorrows fall like rain,
　And troubles swarm like bees about a hive,
I will believe the heights for which I strive
Are only reached by anguish and by pain;
　And though I groan and writhe beneath my crosses,
　I yet shall see, through my severest losses,
　　　The greater gain.
I will not doubt, well anchored in the faith,
　Like some staunch ship my soul braves every gale,
So strong its courage that it will not fail
To breast the mighty unknown sea of death.
　Oh may I cry, though body parts with spirit,
　"I do not doubt," so listening worlds may hear it
　　　With my last breath.　　—*Ella Wheeler Wilcox*

May this be our trusting prayer today.

Above the tempest's roar, faith hears His voice;
And with its hand in His, it can rejoice.
It fears no cloud, or wind that it can bring;
Faith looks across the storm, and still can sing! —Anon.

I do not want merely to possess faith; I want a faith that possesses me!
　　　　　　　　　　　　　　—C. Kingsley

STAY IN THE PLACE OF BLESSING

Keep yourselves in the love of God. . . .   Jude 21

A believer may easily lose his testimony, joy, assurance, and the Lord's full blessing, if he doesn't spend time in meditation, prayer, and Christian fellowship (Heb. 10:25). As a result he will find himself growing cold and ineffective in his spiritual service. Therefore Jude admonishes: "Keep yourselves in the love of God."

On returning home from a European journey, a traveler presented his wife with a small, curious stone, purchased in France, which he said would sparkle in the dark. Switching off all the lights that evening, the wife held the stone in her hand to watch it glow. Nothing happened! Disappointed, both the husband and the wife concluded that he had been defrauded. The next day, however, the wife examined the stone more closely under a microscope and discovered some finely printed French words which, when translated, read: "If you would have me shine in the dark, keep me in the light during the day!" Following instructions, the wife exposed the newly acquired treasure to the sun's rays for about twelve hours. That night she surprised her husband by triumphantly displaying the jewel which now glowed brilliantly. So, too, if we would shine for the Lord in earth's dark corners, we must constantly keep ourselves in the sunlight of His radiant love.

I believe it was Spurgeon who said, "When it has been a long, rainy day, and the sun has just popped out so that a gleam of sunshine falls upon the floor, I have seen my dog get up, wag his tail, and shift his position so he could lie down where that shaft of light appeared. It's a fine thing as a Christian to have that state of mind: never to stay sullenly in the shadows, but always to go cheerfully to that patch of sunshine that may be left to us, and to make the most of it. There is always something for which we can be thankful, something in God's Word for which we may praise the Lord. Let us ever search for it, and stay in its warming glow!"

Sun of my soul, Thou Savior dear,
It is not night if Thou be near.   —J. Keble

Remember: "Fruit ripened in the sun is the sweetest," so: "Keep yourselves in the love of God!"

THE GOD OF JACOB

Happy is he that hath the God of Jacob for his help.
Psalm 146:5

Some consider it rather strange that the Lord should say, "I am the God . . . of Jacob" (Ex. 3:6). Originally Jacob was a crafty, grasping, unscrupulous man. We sometimes make allowances for one who falls, due to some quick impulse or because he happens to be weak and unwatchful. In fact, we may even have pity and compassion for him. But there is another kind of man, scheming and unworthy, for whom we hold only contempt. How amazing then that this One of absolute holiness should thus identify himself as "the God of Jacob"! It can only be true because of grace.

You may have seen the painting entitled "The Doctor." Sitting by a poor sick youngster stretched out on a cot in a miserable dwelling is a physician—strong, thoughtful, intelligent. His eyes are fixed earnestly and hopefully upon the child. Certainly there is nothing in that place of poverty he wants. But written deep in the lines of his face is the suffering of that young patient. Does he approve of the pain and disease which he sees? No, he hates it, and it is his business to banish it and bring health. In like manner, when God takes His place beside a scheming man like Jacob and says, "I am his God," He is not condoning that "deceiver's" sin, but He wants to do something in him and for him. Christ said, "I came not to call the righteous, but sinners to repentance." When Jacob was crippled by the Lord and brought to a place of weakness, he learned to trust fully and was named "Israel"—meaning "prince with God." Still today the Lord takes sinners and transforms them. Is He *your* God?

> *Christ receiveth sinful men,*
> *Even me with all my sin;*
> *Purged from every spot and stain,*
> *Heaven with Him I enter in.* —Neumeister

God loves us, not for what we are, but for what He can make of us.

TEARING DOWN THE ENEMY'S BANNER!

. . . that through death he might destroy him that had
the power of death, that is, the devil.   Hebrews 2:14

Even as David in delivering Israel from her enemies cut off
the head of Goliath with that giant's own sword, so Christ, in
redeeming mankind, vanquished the Devil with his own weapon;
namely, "death." By allowing Satan to have Him nailed to the
tree of Calvary, our Lord thereby expiated the sin of the world.
That He triumphed gloriously over all His foes was evidenced by
His bodily resurrection. Thus He set us free from the grim
Satanic taskmaster who otherwise would have dragged every
man's soul down to eternal doom.

Many years ago a Swedish newspaper carried this story: On
his morning ride through Copenhagen, Denmark's king, Christian X, noticed a Swastika waving over a public building in
violation of the agreement Hitler had made with their country.
"Take it down!" the king commanded. The German officer refused. "It's up there by new orders from Berlin," he said tersely.
"That flag must be removed before twelve o'clock, or otherwise I
will send a soldier up to do it," the monarch declared. "Any
soldier who tries that will be shot," warned the Nazi officer. "Ah,
but *I will be that soldier!*" replied the king. The Swastika came
down, for the Nazis at that point dared not shoot Denmark's
king. So, too, when the enemy of our soul put his evil flag over
this rebel world, it was our King from Heaven who came to defy
him. The highest angels could not avail for this task; but the
Lord spoke plainly to the demonic tyrant, went to the very heart
of his citadel, and became "sin for us" that through death He
might "destroy him [the devil] that had the power of death"
(Heb. 2:14). Now God's banner over us is "love" (S. of Sol.
2:4; John 3:16). The sting of the "last enemy" has forever been
removed, and the emblem of his rule ripped from the staff of
dominion. Someday soon Christ will assert His full rights as
"King of kings, and Lord of lords!"

> " 'Tis finished!" — all our souls to win
>   His life the blessed Savior gave;
>   Then rising, left His people's sin
>   Behind Him in His open grave! — E. Denny

**The cross is the place where the sins of the world and the love
of God met in redemptive encounter!**

THE GREATEST DISCOVERY

. . . We have found the Messiah . . . . John 1:41

According to the dictionary, the word "discovery" means, "to bring to light, to learn, to find, or to see for the first time." The desire to discover things seems to be a vital and innate part of man's nature. From the dawn of human history, the challenge of discovering new worlds, new ideas, and new frontiers has captivated every generation. From childhood to adulthood, the thrill of discovery is a compelling drive, spurring men ever onward in their search for the new and the exciting. That boy led by an irresistible urge to discover and explore a cave may in later years be searching the depths of the seas or outer space.

There have been so many thrilling discoveries that it seems almost impossible to label anyone as the greatest of all. And yet, when everything is considered, there is one which stands out above all others. It is best described by Sir James Simpson, who was the originator of the use of chloroform as an anesthesia. When he was asked, "What is your greatest discovery?" he answered, *"That I am a sinner, and that Jesus Christ is my Savior."*

The Rabio Bible Class has a television program called, "Day of Discovery." Our prayer is that this new outreach will become the means of leading men and women, boys and girls to the Lord Jesus Christ so that they can say with the hymnwriter Floyd Hawkins: * "Mankind is searching every day in quest of something new; but I have found the 'living way,' the path of pleasures true. I've discovered the way of gladness, I've discovered the way of joy, I've discovered relief from sadness, 'tis a happiness without alloy; I've discovered the fount of blessing, I've discovered the 'Living Word.' 'Twas the greatest of all discoveries when I found Jesus, my Lord."

> I have found a friend in Jesus,
>   He's ev'rything to me;
> He's the fairest of ten thousand to my soul;
>   The Lily of the Valley, in Him alone I see
>   All I need to cleanse and make me fully whole. —Fry

Wise men still seek Christ!

* © 1937, 1965 Lillenas Publishing Co. Used by permission.

A MAYOR'S TESTIMONY

> *. . . . a day in thy courts is better than a thousand*
> *. . . . For the Lord God is a sun and shield; the*
> *Lord will give grace and glory.*   Psalm 84:10, 11

An American businessman and civic leader, by the name of Lee Baxton, has given the following testimony: "While I served my city as mayor for two years, 1952-53, it was my duty to preside over Mayor's Court, during which time 2,400 cases came before me. I started asking those charged with violations of a criminal nature if they had been regular attendants at church or Sunday school during that year, and I made a standing offer that if any person with such a record were convicted, I would pay the court costs and their fine for them out of my own pocket. Many of those I asked would say with some embarrassment and shame, 'Well, a long time ago I used to go,' or 'I plan to go when I am releaves,' but *not once in the 2,400 cases did I have to pay anyone's fine!* This was proof to me that the influence of church and Sunday school is a great factor in keeping down crime. Though all who worship may not be saved, yet God's house and His people have a mighty influence for good on those who do attend regularly."

Yes, it is blessed to go into the courts of the Lord, for we find that there He gives light, grace, instruction, and eventually "Glory" to all who heed His Word.

How long since you attended church and Sunday school *regularly?*

> A Sunday school teacher, I don't know his name.
> A wonderful preacher who never found fame.
> So faithful, so earnest, when I was a boy—
> He stuck to his task tho' I tried to annoy.
> He never was missing, in cold or in heat,
> A smile his face lighted the moment we'd meet.
> He taught by example as well as by word,
> That splendid old teacher who honored his Lord.
> He helped my young life more than ever he knew.
> Later years I remembered and tried to be true.
> I suppose he has gone now to join Heaven's ranks,
> But I hope up in Glory someday to say, "Thanks!"—Anon.

SEVEN DAYS without church and Christian fellowship make ONE WEAK!

ONE HUNDRED PERCENT RIGHT!

We have . . . a more sure word of prophecy . . . .
2 Peter 1:19

It's amazing what can be done with statistics. By a clever arrangement of facts, framed in a shrewdly worded context, it is possible to make even a poor situation sound good. For example, a weatherman once boasted, *"I'm 90 percent right — 10 percent of the time!"* His claim sounds quite impresive until it is analyzed. He needed such a manipulation of statistics to cover up his poor record. Such, however, is not necessary with the Bible. Its predictions are *100 percent right.* There's no need for double-talk when it comes to the Scriptures.

The Lord Jesus was born in the city of Bethlehem as prophesied by Micah (Mic. 5:2); of a virgin (Isa. 7:14); at the time specified by Daniel (Dan. 9:25). Infants in Bethlehem were massacred as foretold by Jeremiah (Jer. 31:15); Jesus went down into Egypt and returned as prophesied by Hosea (Hos. 11:1). Isaiah foretold His ministry in Galilee (Isa. 9:1, 2); Zechariah predicted His triumphal entry into Jerusalem riding upon a colt (Zech. 9:9); His betrayal for 30 pieces of silver (Zech. 11:12); and the return of this money for the purchase of a potter's field (Zech. 11:13). David lived 1,000 years before the birth of Christ, and had never seen a Roman crucifixion; yet in Psalm 22, he penned under divine inspiration a graphic portrayal of the death Jesus suffered when He died upon a Roman cross. Isaiah 53 also gives us a detailed picture of our Lord's rejection and death. These few prophecies alone should impress the worst of skeptics with the reliability of the Bible.

Since these predictions have all been fulfilled to the smallest detail, let us also accept with confidence that which the Bible says about the future. Remember, *we have a sure word of prophecy which is 100 percent right — all of the time!*

I'll trust in God's unchanging Word
Till soul and body sever;
For though all things shall pass away,
His Word shall stand forever!   *— Luther*

Through the pages of the Bible, as through a window divinely opened, men can look into the future of earth and the glories of Heaven.   **—T. Carlyle**

THE SOURCE OF POWER

. . . power belongeth unto God. Psalm 62:11

In ourselves we are spiritually impotent and weak as water. Therefore, to live the overcoming life, the Christian must yield himself unreservedly to the power of God (Rom. 6:13-19).

Years ago workmen were building a bridge across a portion of the New York harbor. Seeking a base for one of the buttresses, they struck upon an old scow full of stone that had sunk deeply into the mud and sediment at the bottom of the bay. Divers were sent down to place great chains under the flatboat so that it could be raised, but every device failed. At last a special engineer was called to solve the problem. He ordered two barges brought to the spot and lines were attached to them and secured around the scow. The work was done and the cables fastened tightly when the waters were at low ebb. Then he ordered them to just stand by and wait a few hours. As the incoming tide swept higher and higher, it raised the two barges by its mighty power and the submerged ship first shook, then shivered, and finally responded. *It had been released by the power of the Atlantic Ocean!* So, too, by the Holy Spirit's Heavenward "lift" and irresistible activity, lives are raised from the miry clay of sin. Gripped by His might, they find victory over the pull of inhibiting habits, and the luring enticements of Satan, and so advance to higher ground.

Dr. R. A. Torrey once said, "The whole secret of why D. L. Moody was so significantly used is found in Psalm 62:11. He was energized by God's power. I am encouraged to know that this power did not belong to D. L. Moody; I rejoice that it did not belong to Charles G. Finney, Martin Luther, or to any other Christian whom the Lord has raised up. If these, along with D. L. Moody, have had great influence and impact, it is because they were energized by the Spirit of God."

We too must find our vigor and spiritual vitality not in our weak wills or in our vacillating energies, but in Him who is the source of strength; for truly *"power belongeth unto God!"*

> Spirit, now melt and move
> All of our hearts with love,
> Breathe on us from above
> With old-time pow'r! — Paul Rader

The human spirit FAILS unless the Holy Spirit FILLS!

A MOTHER'S WISE CONDUCT

Whatever he saith unto you, do it. John 2:5

On the special day when our minds are lovingly directed to her who gave us birth, I am reminded of one of the most pleasant duties I perform as a pastor. To visit the hospital and call on mothers of new babies is delightful because of the radiant happiness they display. Sometimes I engage in a bit of levity, telling the girls that motherhood will always be the best profession for women, since it is entirely free from male competition. However, I also impress upon them their responsibility to rear their children in the fear and nurture of the Lord. Parenthood should be one of life's most rewarding experiences. However, it should remind us as well to seek God's help and guidance in the training of our little ones.

Today we call your attention to the blessed example set by Mary, the mother of our Savior. Although she couldn't understand some things Jesus said and did, she trusted Him fully, knowing He never made a mistake. She therefore instructed the servants at the wedding, who were in need of wine, to implicitly obey His every command. Her faith was rewarded, for Jesus immediately performed the miracle necessary to supply that which was lacking.

Mother, let Mary's wise faith be the guideline of your own conduct. Allow Jesus to control your life and aid you in handling the affairs of your household. The needs of your home — like those at the wedding in Cana — will be fully met if you heed Mary's words, "Whatever he saith unto you *do it.*"

Whatsoe'er He bids you, do it,
Fill the vessels to the brim;
But remember, 'tis His battle —
Leave the miracle to Him! — T. H. Allan

I think we can say that the virtues of the mothers shall be visited upon the children as well as the sins of the fathers.
—Charles Dickens

MOODY'S AMBITION

. . . What shall I do, because I have no place to bestow my crops? Luke 12:17

The story of the rich fool can stand frequent reading in this day of abundance and materialism. The misguided man in Jesus' parable had so much wealth he couldn't begin to use it all. His barns were crowded and overflowing; yet his thoughts never turned to charity. Instead, he decided to make new granaries that would be large enough to accommodate his ever-increasing goods, and he thought to spend the rest of his years in luxury. Poor fool, he died that very night, not having laid up treasures in Heaven. To the rich man's question, "What shall I do?" John Wesley said he would have liked to reply, "Are there not those at your door whom God has appointed to receive what you can spare? Give to the poor, feed the hungry, clothe the naked. Freely thou hast received, freely give."

An aged fisherman, rich in faith, was known for his hospitality. Many hungry folk were fed by him during the hard winters. Finally, when he was 73 years of age, he had only $60.00 left in his possession. Yet he insisted on using it all to buy food for the needy children of his neighborhood. Someone said, "You are getting old; you shouldn't give your last money away." The hearty old fisherman wisely replied, "Friend, God will take care of me. It wouldn't do to have those folks go hungry, would it? It would look to them as if I didn't have much faith in my Savior!"

D. L. Moody frequently said, "I have always been ambitious— *ambitious to leave no wealth or possessions.*" His son declared that his father's desire was realized. Though thousands of dollars passed through his hands, Moody gave it away as fast as he received it, and died a poor man.

Which ambition is yours, that of the foolish rich man in Jesus' parable, or that of the spiritual Moody who laid up "treasures in Heaven"?

The gold has come from Thee, Lord,
To Thee belongeth still;
O, may I quickly, faithfully
My stewardship fulfill. —Anon.

Giving is not just a way of raising money, it is God's way of raising men!

PREACHING AND PRACTICING

In all things [show] thyself a pattern of good works.
Titus 2:7

An elderly minister with a doctorate in theology had come to live in the home of his son who was a physician. One day when the telephone rang, the father answered it, saying, "Hello, Doctor Swans speaking." After a slight hesitation, the voice on the other end came through, "Which Doctor Swans are you? The one who *practices* or the one who *preaches?*" This anecdote reminds us of the saying sometimes employed by preachers: "Don't do as I *do,* but as I *say.*" It should be noted, however, that stories which point up the shortcomings of ministers are sometimes told because individuals are trying to make themselves feel more comfortable concerning their personal failures and sins. They have set a low standard for their own Christian devotion and like to think that everyone else is on their level. The apostle Paul excused no one from the obligation of Christlike conduct. He therefore exhorted Titus to instruct all—the aged and the young—to be very careful in the matter of Christian deportment. He had a special word for the young pastor, telling him that he should be a "pattern of good works"; that is, *a model Christian!*

This exhortation applies to everyone who is entrusted with Christian leadership—whether as a parent in the home, a teacher in the Sunday school, a director in the youth program, or an officer in the church. Our influence should be such that we are indeed "a pattern of good works." Precept and example must go hand in hand, so that we "practice what we preach." What a solemn responsibility!

> *Living for Jesus a life that is true,*
> *Striving to please Him in all that I do;*
> *Yielding allegiance, gladhearted and free,*
> *This is the pathway of blessing for me.* — Chisholm

"Good works" is love for Christ made visible!   —Bran

YOUR WONDERFUL BODY

*I will praise thee; for I am fearfully and wonder
fully made.*   Psalm 139:14

The man who heads the medical school of the University of
Mississippi, Dr. A. C. Guyton, says: "The human body is the
most beautifully engineered and the most complicated system
there is. It works by means of several hundred patterns of control, each affecting the other. A complete understanding of it
can hardly be gained without the help of computers with their
ability to handle vast amounts of data." For instance, the brain
has 10 billion nerve cells to record what you learn. The information travels inside you at speeds of up to 300 miles per hour
over a network of nerve fibers 100 thousand miles long! *There
are more interconnections in your nervous system than there are
street corners in the entire world!"* Your brain which weighs less
than four pounds can do certain things that couldn't be matched
by *all* of the world's computers!

Biochemists tell us that utilizing the most up-to-date laboratory
equipment, the typical protein must be boiled for at least twenty-
four hours in a chemical solution to be thoroughly broken down.
However, the chemical plant of your body completes the identi-
cal job in only four hours and without high temperatures. A
portion of skin the size of a postage stamp contains four yards
of nerves. In all, there are millions of these nerve endings fan-
ning through your skin, each of them especially constructed to
deliver only one type of message, heat, cold, pain, or pressure.
In a single day your blood travels about 168 million miles — the
equivalent of 6,720 times around the world! No wonder David
exclaimed, "I will praise thee; for *I am fearfully and wonder-
fully made."*

> *By God's wise designing*
>   *We are wonderfully made,*
> *Every part essential*
>   *And in perfect balance laid.* —Anon.

**Proper praise to God for your marvelous body involves giving
it back to Him for spiritual service (Rom. 12:1, 2).**

THE "DARKROOM"

> . . . *when he hath tested me, I shall come forth*
> *as gold.*   Job 23:10

In his article on *The Discipline of the "Darkroom,"* B. G. Lovelace compares photography to the Christian experience. When a picture is taken, at the very moment the shutter opens, an instantaneous exposure occurs, and an impression is made upon the film. It must, however, pass through a darkroom treatment for the image to become fully developed. So, too, the believer at conversion is exposed to the light of the Savior, and His very own likeness is indelibly impressed upon the sensitized spirit of the new Christian. This "exposure" must then be followed by a developing process. The image of Christ, imprinted inwardly upon our hearts by faith, is brought out for others to see as we are changed into His own likeness. Writing to the church at Corinth, Paul said, "But we all, with unveiled face beholding as in a mirror the glory of the Lord, are *changed into the same image* from glory to glory, even as by the Spirit of the Lord" (2 Cor. 3:18). Knowing full well that this transformation involves a "darkroom," the author of Hebrews encourages us by giving this reminder, "Now no chastening for the present seemeth to be joyous, but grievous; nevertheless, afterward it yieldeth the peaceable fruit of righteousness unto them who are exercised by it."

Are you in the "darkroom" today? If so, don't forget that "all things work together for good" to those destined to be conformed to the image of God's Son. For "whom the Lord loveth he chasteneth . . . that we might be partakers of his holiness" (Heb. 12:6, 10). Thank God for your "darkroom" experiences!

> *There's nothing God permits in grace*
> *That ever comes in vain;*
> *He has a shining "afterward"*
> *For every cloud of rain!*   — G. W.

God sends us to the "darkroom" of trial not to IMPAIR US but to IMPROVE US!
                                                    —H. G. B.

AMAZING LIGHT

> . . . *now are ye light in the Lord; walk as children*
> *of light.*   Ephesians 5:8

Light can do startling things! One single burst from a laser beam can drill a hole through a diamond. Such a ray of concentrated and amplified power can melt steelplate in a fraction of a second. A laser beam aimed at the retro-reflector placed on the moon by the astronauts has given the scientists greater accuracy in measuring the distance between the earth and the lunar surface. Medical science too is broadening its field in the use of light. A tiny laser aimed at cells diseased by cancer will in a split second destroy a great number of them. What amazing energy! I remember seeing (or was it hearing?) music transmitted on a ray of light in one of the "Sermons from Science" conducted by Keith Hargett of the Moody Institute of Science. That was an interesting demonstration — an uninterrupted flow of sharply focused electrons carrying a beautiful melody!

And divine Light — who can tell *its* great effect? Every child of God is not only the possessor but the reflector of it. Jesus said, "Ye are the light of the world."

Light must be concentrated and directed, however, to be most effective. Lives controlled by God's Spirit will shine with a glowing witness, bringing spiritual health and blessing to others. Indeed, heavenly harmonies will be transmitted when the Lord Jesus shines in and through us. As the hymnwriter reminds us: "Out in the highways and byways of life, many are weary and sad; carry the sunshine where darkness is rife, making the sorrowing glad." Jesus said, "Let your light so shine before men, that they may . . . glorify your Father, who is in heaven" (Matt. 5:16).

> *Is your life a shining witness*
> *With a testimony true?*
> *Could the world be won to Jesus*
> *Just by what they see in you?* — Adams

The light that shines farthest shines brightest at home.

ON HAVING PEACE WITH GOD

*Therefore, being justified by faith, we have peace with
God through our Lord Jesus Christ.*   Romans 5:1

Some people think that they can "make peace with God." They
are quite surprised if you tell them they are almost 2,000 years
too late to do that. It was our Lord Jesus Christ who accomplished that tremendous spiritual feat "through the blood of His
cross" — a thing impossible for any sinful man to do. No, we do
not have to make peace with God, all we have to do is *accept it!*

Dr. F. B. Meyer tells of an experience he had with a woman
in England. He had been speaking to her of receiving God's
grace by faith. She could not understand his message, and told
him so. At tea with her a day later, he suddenly turned and
said, "Madam, may I please have a cup of tea?" She looked at
his table and said, "Why, Dr. Meyer, you have a cup of tea."
A little later he said again, "Will you please give me a cup of
tea?" She replied, "Why, Dr. Meyer, don't you see, you have a
cup of tea right there at your plate." In a few moments he said
again, "Please give me a cup of tea! I'm so tired, and I need it."
Utterly bewildered, his hostess started to speak, then caught her
breath. After a moment she said, "Oh, Dr. Meyer, I see it all
now. What you mean is that the Lord's blessing, power, and forgiveness are right here before me, yet I am asking and asking for
it, instead of taking it and finding peace through our Lord Jesus
Christ."

Some people say, "I prayed and prayed that God would receive
me when I came earnestly seeking salvation, but I still do not
know if I have it!" Why, my dear friend, God is much more
eager to save you than you are to be saved. *The very first time
you came, He received you!* For He has promised, "Whosoever
cometh unto me, *I will in no wise cast out."* The devil is making you concentrate on your "feelings" and your own unworthi-
ness, when you should be looking to the Lord Jesus Christ, for
it is His righteousness that you need. You can't make peace,
He has made it — all you have to do to receive it is to *accept Him.*

Peace rules the day when Christ rules the heart!

ONE KING

No man can serve two masters. . . . Ye cannot serve
God and money.   Matthew 6:24

A good commentary on this verse can be found in the words
of L. A. Banks as he writes about the kingdom of the bees.
"There can be but a single queen to a colony. As soon as the
first one is born she goes around to the other queen cells, rips
them open and kills the about-to-be-born queens just as fast as
she can. In this way she disposes of all possible rivals. Her
course meets the entire approval of the other bees; in fact, if
two queens happen to be born at the same time, the bees bring
them together immediately and make them fight until one or
the other is dead. *Two queens would be worse than none at all.*
If they are disposed to tolerate one another, and will not fight,
the other bees force them to it. Surely a man ought to be as
wise as a bee, and when he is, he knows that Christ's word is
true, and that *'no man can serve two masters!'* "

Recognizing this principle, Joshua, standing before his people,
threw out the challenge: "Now, therefore, fear the Lord, and
serve him in sincerity and in truth . . . , *choose you this day*
whom ye will serve" (Josh. 24:14, 15). In other words, "Make
up your mind! Declare yourselves! On whose side will you take
your stand?" Even as in the kingdom of the bees, so in the "kingdom of men," *two sovereigns are worse than none at all!* As
Jesus said, men will either hate the one, and love the other, or
else hold to the one, and despise the other.

Do you have but One to whom you yield dominion? Is He
the King of kings? If you are uncommitted, may you say with
Joshua, "As for me and my house, we will serve the Lord!"

> *"Choose you this day"; time hastens on,*
>   *Thou canst not neutral be;*
> *To serve the world or Christ thy Lord,*
>   *"Choose now, which shall it be?"* —Meyer

One cannot successfully WALK with God while RUNNING
with the devil.   —G. W.

THE CHALLENGE OF THE WOODPECKER

*Many, O Lord, my God, are thy wonderful works
which thou hast done.*   Psalm 40:5

The woodpecker is an amazing bird, especially designed by God for its activity of climbing trees and digging for grubs. It has sharp, curved claws and a powerful, drill-like beak. Its stiff, spiny tail-feathers are also well adapted to propping and bracing the colorful creature as it delivers hundreds of rapid and forceful beak-strokes into the bark of trees in search of beetles and insect eggs. Once a hole is made in the wood, the bird's long, slender, sticky tongue is deftly inserted to remove the desired grubs. How a woodpecker can slam its head so violently against a solid object without destroying itself is still a mystery. Scientists say its skull is reinforced inside with sets of tiny "cross braces" which accounts in part for its ability to withstand such unusual "punishment." Fred J. Meldau in his notable book, *Why We Believe in Creation, Not Evolution,* says, "Surely every woodpecker in the world is a living witness to the fact that God made it as it is. Evolution can in no wise explain how it got its unique tongue, its specially constructed tail, its unusual feet, and above all its marvelous chisel-like beak! That such amazing equipment was perfected through long ages of 'gradual change' is a preposterous assumption. *Any specialized organ* — like the tongue, or beak, or tail, of the woodpecker — *must be perfectly 'adapted' before it serves its intended purpose.* A beak that is only half developed . . . or a tongue only one tenth as long as it needs to be to reach a grub hidden inside the trunk of a tree, would be absolutely useless. If specialized organs came to pass through the process of *gradual* change, due to 'random mutations,' what purpose did they serve while they were in the process of 'developing'? Indeed, where in all nature is there *one* example of a partially developed 'special organ' that is not *now* a useful one?" Evolutionists, let's have your answer to the challenge of the woodpecker!

Nature is but a name for an effect whose cause is God!
                                                    —W. Cowper

SWEET ASSURANCE

*[We] . . . are kept by the power of God through
faith unto salvation.*   1 Peter 1:5

A little Scottish girl had just finished her testimony to a small
group of friends. Joyfully she had told of saving grace and how
the love of God had reached her heart. With appropriate assurance, she had put the capstone upon her poignant testimony by
quoting those beloved verses from the tenth chapter of the gospel of John, the words of the Savior, "And I give unto them
eternal life; and they shall never perish, neither shall any man
pluck them out of my hand. My Father, who gave them to me,
is greater than all, and no man is able to pluck them out of my
Father's hand." Just then a joshing, doubting friend piped up
with a flippant question, "But suppose, Maggie, you slip through
His fingers?" Quick as a flash and evidently guided by the Holy
Spirit, she shot back at the inquirer, "Never, never! You see,
I'm one of the fingers!"

Maggie may not have been well versed in the language of
theology, but a Biblical principle had been lodged in her heart;
namely, that "we are members of his body, of his flesh, and of
his bones" (Eph. 5:30). She knew that she had been joined in-
separably to Jesus Christ, and that the very life of God was hers.

If by faith we have received the Lord Jesus, then we too have
the life of the risen Christ abiding in us, and so "are kept by
the power of God." The Savior's life, the Father's power and
the Spirit's presence are the source from which flows the sweet
and endless assurance guaranteed in the Scriptures.

Friend, rest in this wonderful fact — *God is keeping you!*
Away with doubts and fears! His Word is strong and sure: *"They
shall never perish."*

> *Saved to the uttermost; Jesus is near;*
> *Keeping me safely, He casteth out fear;*
> *Trusting His promises, now I am blest;*
> *Leaning upon Him, how sweet is my rest.*—Kirkpatrick

Eternal life once kindled in the soul glows undimmed forever!

THE WIDOW'S COMFORT

*For thy Maker is thine husband; the Lord of hosts
is his name . . . . The God of the whole earth. . . .*
Isaiah 54:5

The Bible tells us to "honor widows" (1 Tim. 5:3), and highly
condemns those who in any way take advantage of them (Matt.
23:14). In fact, God has a special care which He bestows upon
helpless orphans (Ps. 68:5, 6) and bereaved women (Prov. 15:25;
Exod. 22:22, 23; Deut. 24:19). The Lord, as our Good Shepherd, is not only concerned over weak, helpless lambs, but also
"gently leads" the more matured sheep who need an extra amount
of sympathy and loving assistance.

A Christian who had read the Lord's command in Zechariah,
chapter 7, to "show mercy and compassion every man to his
brother" (Zech. 7:9, 10), decided that as a board member he
should make a special visit at the home of a recently bereaved
widow. He dreaded to go because he had heard that she was on
the verge of despondency. However, he also knew it was through
the loving ministry of His children that "the Lord . . . relieveth
the fatherless and widow" (Ps. 146:9). When he arrived at her
door, he was pleasantly surprised to find her full of peace and
contentment. Greatly amazed he asked the reason for her change
of attitude. "Well," she answered, "in reading my Bible the
other day I found that the Lord has promised to be the *widow's
husband.* Comforted by His grace, I made up my mind that if
I have such a Husband, *I must begin to live up to my income!"*
All who saw that woman's radiant trust in God were impressed
by what the Lord had accomplished in her life through the "comfort of the Scriptures." As a result, the people in her church
rallied to her support not only with their gifts, but also with their
acts of love and attention.

To those who have recently been bereaved of a husband, the
words of Jeremiah 49:11 come with true comfort and a holy
directive: "Let [the] widows trust in Me!"

No cloud comes into our life but God has put a rainbow in it!

ADVERTISING THE GOSPEL

And daily . . . they ceased not to teach and preach
Jesus Christ.   Acts 5:42

According to a recent newspaper article the ten top advertisers in the United States spent more than $1.3 billion in one year alone for the promotion of their products. How much more is spent annually by thousands of other firms I don't know, but the total must reach astronomical proportions.

Webster's New American Dictionary defines the word "advertise" as follows: "To make public by a printed notice, broadcast message, or any means of publicity. *To give warning or information.*" As believers we too have an obligation to "advertise." It is our duty to "make public" the good news of God's Word by every means available. Jesus said, "Go ye into all the world and preach the gospel to every creature."

J. I. Rodale, in his book *The Synonym Finder,* gives the following substitutes for the word "advertise": "To make a public announcement of, to circulate, post, blazon, propagate, disseminate, trumpet, proclaim, or make known." This is what we should do with the message of God's saving grace. To send forth the Gospel is "advertising" in the best sense of the word without any of its distasteful connotations.

When we consider the tremendous effort and huge expenditures being made today to promote the material things of this world, with their temporary worth and shallow satisfaction, how much more diligent we should be in "telling the story of Jesus"! Let's not be stingy in the work of *"advertising" the Gospel!*

Tell it out among the highways and the lanes at home;
Let it ring across the mountains and the ocean's foam!
Like the sound of many waters let our glad shout be,
Till it echoes and re-echoes from the islands of the sea!
                                    — Havergal

It is a solemn responsibility to have in one's possession a reprieve for men under condemnation and then not to deliver it!

"PERPLEXED, BUT NOT IN DESPAIR"

*We are troubled on every side, yet not distressed;
we are perplexed, but not in despair . . . cast down,
but not destroyed.*   2 Corinthians 4:8, 9

There is a great deal we can read between the lines in 2 Corinthians 4 which suggests that the apostle required much grace to endure his struggles with oppressing pain and growing weakness. Due to persecution he was often cast down, yet he never despaired. So, too, when we get into impossible situations, God is seeking to get us to look above the circumstances into His loving face. Many incidents in the Old Testament bear this out. For instance, God brought about the miracle of the Red Sea deliverance by shutting His people Israel in on every side, so that there was no way out but the Divine way. The Egyptians were behind them, the Red Sea in front of them, and the mountains on either side of them. They could only look above. So, too, we can only get out of some of our difficulties *at the top!* They are but God's challenges, and He makes them so hard that we must either sink beneath them or *get above them!* In such an hour we realize the highest possibilities of faith and are pushed by the very emergency into God's best. As a preacher once said to a lady who was near despair, "Beloved, this is God's hour! If you will rise to meet it, you will get such a hold upon Him that *you will find your extremity His opportunity!* Even as the famine in Canaan stripped Jacob of earthly comforts in his old age to bring him to the Goshen of plenty where he saw Joseph in all his glory, so you have been brought to this hour not to make you despair, not to destroy you, but to lead you to the higher ground of victory in Jesus!"

Yes, Christian friend, we may sometimes be "perplexed," but *we are never to be "in despair!"*

> *Never be sad or desponding,*
> *Only have faith to believe;*
> *Grace, for the duties before thee,*
> *Ask of thy God and receive!*—F. Crosby, alt.

The tests of life are sent to make us, not to break us.

SIMPLE AS ABC

Not by works of righteousness which we have done,
but according to his mercy he saved us.   Titus 3:5

One of the greatest difficulties in presenting the Gospel today is the overcoming of the wrong idea that human works play a part in obtaining salvation. The Bible, however, is very clear on this matter. It says, *"Not by works of righteousness which we have done,* but according to his mercy he saved us" (Titus 3:5). "For by grace are ye saved through faith; and that not of yourselves, it is the gift of God — *Not of works,* lest any man should boast" (Eph. 2:8, 9). "Therefore, by the deeds of the law there shall no flesh be justified in his sight" (Rom. 3:20). Salvation is received by faith, and is not earned by man's effort. It is the very simplicity of the Gospel that causes so many people to stumble over it. The plan of salvation is as simple as ABC.

A. *Admit* you are a sinner. "All have sinned, and come short of the glory of God" (Rom 3:23). Accept the picture the Bible gives of the human heart. Assent to God's description of you. Agree with Him that you cannot save yourself. Abdicate the throne of "self."

B. *"Believe* on the Lord Jesus Christ." This is what Paul told the Philippian jailer when he cried out, "What must I do to be saved?" Believe that Jesus Christ — truly God and truly man — died on the cross and shed His blood in your place. Trust in Him alone for your salvation.

C. *Confess* Him before others. Having received Christ as Savior we should then publicly acknowledge Him before others. "Whosoever, therefore, shall confess me before men, him will I confess also before my Father who is in heaven" (Matt. 10:32). An inner possession should result in an outward confession.

Don't make salvation complicated. Although it took the very wisdom of the infinite God to devise such a wondrous plan, and it cost Him dearly, the Lord made salvation as "simple as ABC."

ACCEPT Him today, BELIEVE and be saved;
His joy in your heart then will spring;
God's wonderful grace will loosen your tongue,
Its praise and CONFESSION to bring! — H.G.B.

We are saved by God's mercy, not by our merit — by Christ's dying, not by our doing!

A HAT WHICH CHANGED TWO LIVES

> *. . . the things which happened . . . have fallen out*
> *rather unto the furtherance of the gospel.*
>
> Philippians 1:12

The apostle Paul displays the right attitude toward suffering. To preach the good news of Jesus' love, he made many sacrifices. He gave up his business, left his friends, suffered beatings, stonings, shipwreck, hunger, and imprisonment. He even had a thorn in the flesh. But Paul did not complain about his difficulties; instead he saw the good in them, for he wrote, "I would ye should understand, brethren, that the things which happened unto me have fallen out rather unto the furtherance of the gospel."

Richard Storrs and Gordon Hall were students together at the same theological seminary. One Saturday toward the end of the semester, Hall was preparing to go to Braintree, Massachusetts, to preach, hoping that he might receive the invitation to become their pastor. That afternoon as he was splitting some wood, his hat fell beneath the ax and was destroyed. He didn't have the money to replace it and it was bitter cold, so he asked his friend to take his assignment. Storrs preached and later accepted the call, and he remained the minister of that parish until his dying day — a *period of more than half a century!* Hall, although disappointed, sought other outlets for his talents and became a *renowned foreign missionary.* No one who believes in divine providence will for a moment doubt that God stationed Storrs at Braintree and Hall on the mission field. By means of that ruined hat, the courses of two lives were changed, and it worked out *"unto the furtherance of the gospel."*

> Go thou with God, all things shall work for good,
> E'en all the things that are not understood;
> The seed thou sowest in the Gospel field,
> Mingled with tears, shall bring a glorious yield. —Anon.

There are no accidents in God's dealings; all things have divine purpose!

THE EVERLASTING ARMS

The eternal God is thy refuge, and underneath are the everlasting arms.   Deuteronomy 33:27

In these days of jet travel, when we can cruise at altitudes of over 30,000 feet, flying can be most enjoyable as we wing our way above the storms and the turbulence of lower altitudes. Occasionally, however, some rough air is still experienced, and in those moments how reassuring it is to see the plane's wings outstretched like two huge arms bearing us up. Recently, while flying from Atlanta to Chicago, we passed through some choppy air. As I looked out upon the giant silver wings of the jet, I was reminded of the words of Moses in Deuteronomy 33:27: "The eternal God is thy refuge, and underneath are the everlasting arms." What a comfort it is for the true Christian to have such an assurance in the storms of life! When the bottom seems to fall out of living, how encouraging is the realization that the eternal God is bearing us up and will give sustaining grace for every trial.

When Joseph was sold by his brethren into Egypt, it must have seemed to him the end of everything worthwhile in life; and yet the everlasting arms of God bore him up into a place of prominence and blessing. When Daniel was cast into the den of lions it seemed as though death was certain; yet even in that tragic situation he discovered that "the angel of the Lord encampeth round about them that fear him" (Ps. 34:7). Many Christians can testify from personal experience that those very circumstances of life which seemed to be most threatening were used by God to bring about increased blessing, greater joy, and more effective service.

Are you disturbed today by the trials of life? Is the air a little "choppy"? Are you experiencing some "turbulence"? Then just rest, relax, and trust in the Lord and you too will feel the strengthening resources of His power and know beyond a shadow of doubt that "underneath are the everlasting arms."

> *Oh, how sweet to walk in this pilgrim way,*
> *Leaning on the everlasting arms;*
> *Oh, how bright the path grows from day to day,*
> *Leaning on the everlasting arms.* —E. A. Hoffman

You can't break God's promises by leaning on them!

HONORING THE DEAD

*And devout men carried Stephen to his burial, and
made great lamentation over him.*   Acts 8:2

Memorial Day was unofficially begun by women of the South
during the American Civil War when they strewed flowers over
the graves of the "men in gray." In 1868, General John A.
Logan, Commander in Chief of the Grand Army of the Republic,
issued an order officially setting aside May 30 as Decoration Day.
It has now become an occasion on which we remember not only
those who have fallen in war, but all our dead.

However, we will not honor them in a fitting manner if we
think of them as prisoners in their caskets or if we let grief and
despondency overpower us. Certainly God expects us to shed
tears when we recall vividly those "memories that bless and burn,"
but knowing *our believing loved ones who died are with Christ,
we should not feel any sense of pity for them!* Furthermore, if
they could, they would tell us that *we honor them best by living
wholeheartedly for Jesus Christ.*

Stephen, the first Christian martyr, died at a very young age.
He was a talented and courageous leader, and many felt keenly
the tragedy of his loss, for we read that he was buried by godly
men who greatly lamented his departure. However, they did not
completely give way to numbing grief or paralyzing despair but
kept up their spiritual courage. Even the wave of violent persecution, triggered by Stephen's death, did not silence them. Instead they scattered, and everywhere they went they told the
story of Jesus — the very message for which Stephen had died —
and thus paid a glowing tribute to this first martyr.

Let us also honor our Christian dead this day by renewing
our devotion to Jesus Christ!

> *We sorrow not as others do,*
> *Whose hopes fade like the flowers;*
> *There is a hope that's born of God,*
> *And such a hope is ours!* — E. McNeil

The caverns of sorrow oft contain mines of diamonds.

THE DRAMA OF THE AGES

. . . for the coming of the Lord draweth nigh. James 5:8

As a student in a college English Literature class, I was assigned various portions of Shakespeare's writings for memorization. Although many of those passages have long since been forgotten, there is one that has remained with me until this very day. I have never forgotten the lines: "All the world's a stage, and all the men and women merely players: they have their exits and their entrances." I must admit that when these words were first committed to memory, they did not mean very much to me. The necessary effort to engrave them upon my mind was accepted simply as a disciplinary exercise which had to be endured. As the years have passed, however, I have come to realize that the renowned Shakespeare really knew what he was talking about, and that he has beautifully framed in human language a tremendous truth. All the world *is* a "stage" upon which God's great drama of the ages is being enacted. Ever since the dawn of human history, men and women have been making their individual appearances, fulfilling their special functions. Some play leading parts, while others seem to take only minor roles.

As we look out upon the "stage of the world" today we can see a thickening of the plot and a quickening of the pace. Everything indicates that soon the curtain will rise on the final, climactic act in God's great drama of the ages: the return of the Lord Jesus Christ Himself. Reverently speaking, those who have read the "play" know that "the coming of the Lord draweth nigh" (James 5:8). His return will not take them by surprise. How wonderful it would be if even today we might witness and become a part of that glorious scene when "the Lord himself shall descend from heaven with a shout" and the saved shall all "meet the Lord in the air" (1 Thess. 4:16, 17). For the believer this truly will be the crowning act in God's great drama of the ages!

Oh, joy! oh, delight! should we go without dying,
No sickness, no sadness, no dread and no crying,
Caught up through the clouds with our Lord into glory,
When Jesus receives "His own."   — H. L. Turner

Those who are most ready for the second coming of Christ are those who are most interested in His first coming to save the lost!

JUST "HOLDING" THE SILVER COIN

*For we brought nothing into this world, and it is
certain we can carry nothing out.* 1 Timothy 6:7

Material things are temporary — but the devil would have us
set our hearts on them, lest we begin to live for Christ and "lay
up treasures in Heaven!" We entered this world naked and with
nothing in our hands, and it is obvious that when we leave we
shall carry nothing out. The poet has said: "There are *no pockets
in a shroud!*" Yet we build our nests so strong that one would
think we expected to stay here forever.

In Sweden there was once a poor boy who managed to get a
job watching the cattle which belonged to a very rich man. One
day, tiring of his task and wanting to get away for a while to
play, he asked his younger sister to help him. He promised, "If
you'll watch the cows for me, I will let you *hold* my pretty
silver coin all day." Eagerly his sister agreed. She spent a long,
hard eight hours watching the grazing animals, all the while
holding the bright silver coin in her hand, and spending much
time looking at it. At the end of the day when her brother returned, she handed him the coin, quite content with her "day's
wages" of *just holding* the precious piece of silver! Years passed
and the boy grew up to become the rich owner of a large business. One day he told a friend the story of what had happened.
He laughed derisively as he said, "How simple my sister was!
She was happy to work hard *just to hold that coin for one day.*"
His Christian friend replied, "You think your sister was a fool,
but as a grown man who should be much wiser, aren't you doing
exactly the same thing? You slave and work hard to accumulate
riches, but you can hold them only for 'the day' of your life. At
the end you will have to give up all of your cherished pieces of
silver. Your time on earth will be gone, and *then what?*"

Beware, my friend, death will likewise slacken your hold on
the "silver coin" of materialism. Then what will you say when
the Master demands, "Give account of thy stewardship"?

> *He possessed all the world had to give him,*
> *He reached every coveted goal;*
> *But, alas, his life was a failure,*
> *For he had forgotten his soul!* — M. Denison

The poorest man is he whose only wealth is money!

OUR LIVING HOPE

Blessed be . . . God . . . who . . . hath begotten
us . . . unto a living hope.   1 Peter 1:3

I cannot think of a more pitiable situation than that described by Paul in his letter to the believers at Ephesus. He says that before their conversion they had "no hope" and were "without God in the world." A person in such a state has not much left to live for. One author expressed it this way: "Hope is an essential ingredient of life. A man works in hope, he saves in hope, he dies in hope. Every great religion, every political movement has offered hope. This explains the phenomenal appeal of the communist ideology. It seems to offer a future to the disillusioned and despairing peoples. A communist soldier said, 'We are happy, not because we are rich, but because we know where we are going.' This provides the dynamic!" Such worldly hope upon which men set their hearts, however, does not last. As says Omar Khayyam, "It turns to ashes — or it prospers, and anon, like snow upon the desert's dusty face, lighting a little hour or two — is gone!"

As believers we have a genuine and enduring prospect of glory as "an anchor of the soul, both sure and steadfast . . ." (Heb. 6:19). We *know* where we are going, that Heaven is our home, and that the Lord Jesus and the pleasures of His right hand will be our eternal portion. This certain hope motivates us to faithful service and victorious living. Even when the way seems dark, we move forward with confidence, assured that it's brighter just ahead.

Today may "the God of hope fill you with all joy and peace in believing, that ye may abound in hope, through the power of the Holy Spirit" (Rom. 15:13).

> *Oh, ours is the greatest of riches,*
> *A hope that is lively and sure;*
> *For what the dear Savior has promised,*
> *We know shall forever endure.*   — Bosch

True hope is like the sun, which, as we journey toward it, casts the shadow of our burdens behind us!

THE POOR YOUNG RULER

And he . . . went away . . . .   Mark 10:22

Some years ago an English clergyman went to see a wealthy man who was at the point of death. In giving him spiritual counsel he asked if he might hold his hand while they prayed together. The man declined; instead he put his clenched fist beneath the bedcovers. Shortly afterward the old miser breathed his last, without giving any assurance that his soul was saved. Later when they turned down the blankets, his hand was found clasping the key to his safety deposit box with the rigid grip of death. Once again the truth was emphasized: the love of money will blind a man and warp his soul so that he will prefer the grasp of a bank key to the hand of Christ extended in salvation.

We have a classic and equally tragic example of the evil power of riches in the case recorded for us in Mark 10. This ruler who came to Jesus was a promising young man. He was morally clean, seemed very religious, and possessed many fine qualities. However, *although he was sincere, he was eternally lost!* Someone has pointed out that in spite of his (1) moral earnestness, (2) ethical purity, (3) outward attachment to Christ, and (4) recognition of the Savior's love for him, he went away unsaved. The trouble with this young ruler was that *he loved himself and his money more than he loved God or his neighbor.* Jesus put His finger on this when He asked him to distribute his riches to the poor, renounce his own inclinations and carnal desires, and take the cross-crowned way of God's leading. Faced with this decision, the man failed to realize that his "great possessions" were not his riches, but rather his eternal soul. He went away sad at losing salvation, but satisfied if he might only save his silver.

As the spiritual is much more important than the material, we should put the emphasis where it belongs and call him not the "rich" but the *"poor* young ruler"!

> *Jesus calls us: by Thy mercies,*
> *Savior, may we hear Thy call,*
> *Give our hearts to Thine obedience,*
> *Serve and love Thee best of all!* —C. F. Alexander

To be rich in God is better than to be rich in goods!

POWER IN WEAKNESS

> *I was with you in weakness, and in fear, . . .*
> *[yet] in . . . power.*   1 Corinthians 2:3, 4

The title of this devotional seems to be a contradiction in terms. How can there be *power* in *weakness?* Yet the apostle Paul said, "God hath chosen . . . the weak things . . . to confound the . . . mighty."

"In a gun factory," writes an unknown author, "an elongated bar of steel, which weighed 500 pounds, was suspended by a chain. Beside it an average-sized cork was hanging by a silk thread. It was swung gently against the bar which remained motionless. For ten minutes the cork, with rhythmic regularity, continued to strike. Then the heavy piece of steel began to move slightly. At the end of an hour both objects were swinging together like the pendulum of a clock!" Many of God's children feel that they are not exerting a feather's weight of influence upon others or making a dent upon the bastions of evil. Not so! How powerful is the cumulative influence for good which emanates from even the weakest and most obscure of the Savior's faithful followers! Yes, the Lord takes pleasure in using the weak things to accomplish His purposes. In addition to the impact made by their repeated efforts through a consistent life of service, the power of God himself is imparted to those who look to Him for help. The apostle Paul said, "Most gladly, therefore, will I rather glory in my infirmities, that the power of Christ may rest upon me" (2 Cor. 12:9). As we faithfully serve the Lord and recognize our dependence upon Him, we shall find that our spiritual weapons are "mighty through God to the pulling down of strongholds" (2 Cor. 10:4). In His hands there is *power in weakness!*

> *Inadequate but mighty —*
> *How strange, yet wholly true;*
> *Weak men endued with power*
> *The Lord's blest work shall do!* — G. W.

The weakness and inadequacy of the instrument does not matter as long as the Master's hand uses it!

LIFT THINE EYES!

I will lift up mine eyes . . . .   Psalm 121:1

A woman who did much reading and research, began to have great difficulty with her eyes and so consulted an oculist. After examination he said, "Madam, your eyes are just tired; you need to rest them." "But," she replied, "that is impossible; my engagements and my work demand that I make much use of them." After reflecting for a moment, the doctor said, "Have you any wide views from your home?" "Oh, yes," she answered with enthusiasm, "from the front porch I can see the noble peaks of the Blue Ridge Mountains, and from the rear windows I can look out upon the glorious Allegheny foothills." "Very well," replied the oculist, "that is just what you need. When your eyes feel tired, go look steadily at your mountains for ten minutes — twenty would be better — and *the far look will rest your eyes!*"

What is true in the physical is also true in the spiritual. The eyes of the soul are often tired and weary from gazing at the problems and difficulties that beset us on our pilgrim way. The upward look — the far look — will restore our spiritual perspective.

Often we have to admit with the Psalmist, "Innumerable evils have compassed me about . . . so that I am not able to look up" (Ps. 40:12). If by grace we roll these cares upon the Savior and seek His aid, we shall, with the help of the Holy Spirit, be able to *look above our circumstances.*

If we fail to exercise our will power in the direction of "setting our affections above," God may have to take away from us that present treasure, dear as it may be which is making us so earthbound. In fact, He may well lay us upon a bed of affliction that we may better "look up." Let us say, therefore, with spiritual determination, *I will* "direct my prayer unto thee, and will *look up*" (Ps. 5:3).

> *I lift my eyes unto the hills of God;*
> *And though the shadows move across the space*
> *That is my life, and seasons change their face,*
> *I know, come fear or war, come night or day,*
> *The hills of God shall never pass away!*
> — Ruth Gibbs Zwall

Spiritual blindness sets in when we cease to lift our eyes to Him.

DISSENSION—DIVERSION—DESTRUCTION

For we wrestle . . . against spiritual wickedness in high places.   Ephesians 6:12

While I was enjoying a visit with Mr. H. Hildebrand, of the Briercrest Bible Institute, Caronport, Saskatchewan, he pointed out to me that the book of Acts, chapters 6, 7, and 8, suggests three ways by which the devil tries to hinder the work of the Lord. These three avenues of attack are: (1) dissension, (2) diversion, and (3) destruction.

Satan attempts to frustrate our efforts for the Lord by causing dissension and strife within the church. In verse 1 of Acts 6 we read: "And in those days . . . there arose a murmuring." How often we have seen strong testimonies completely silenced because of dissension, murmuring, complaining, bickering, and backbiting on the part of some within the church. In addition to *dissension,* however, the evil one will also resort to *diversion,* sidetracking us from our main purpose. How he would like to have seen the twelve apostles in Acts 6 "leave the word of God and serve tables." The devil is busy at work using this very same tactic today. It is easy in our busy church programs to become sidetracked, diverted, and engaged in everything else but the ministry of the Word. In addition to dissension and diversion, the devil uses *destruction.* In chapter 7 we see Stephen martyred, and in chapter 8 we are told that Saul "made havoc of the church." But, even as the Psalmist declared: "The wrath of man shall praise thee," so Satan's destructive attack is taken by God Himself and used for the accomplishing of His own program. As a result of the devil's persecution the believers "that were scattered abroad went everywhere preaching the word."

Conscious of these three possible areas of attack, let us be on guard and prepared for the onslaughts of the adversary that the "work of the ministry" be not hindered. Let us put on "the whole armour of God" that we "may be able to withstand in the evil day" (Eph. 6:13). And through it all remember, "the battle is not yours, but God's," and He it is who "goeth before you."

> *I want to live above the world,*
> *Though Satan's darts at me are hurled;*
> *For faith has caught the joyful sound,*
> *The song of saints on higher ground!*—J. Oatman, Jr.

Exercise your graces, or Satan will exercise your corruptions!

THE WORD OF A "GENTLEMAN"

*. . . lo, I am with you always, even unto the end
of the age. Amen.*   Matthew 28:20

That famous preacher G. Campbell Morgan tells of a time he read the words of our text to a fine Christian woman over ninety years of age. He closed the Bible and said, "That is a great promise." With a twinkle in her eye she replied, "Sir, that is not a promise. *It's a fact!*"

We live in a world that is often hostile to the Gospel. Many of God's children have suffered much, and some have even died for Christ as they bore witness to Him and His salvation. However, a large percentage of those who know Christ are not actively bearing witness for Him nor fully enjoying the blessed consciousness of His companionship.

The students of Glasgow University were deeply moved when David Livingstone stood before them after sixteen years of service in Africa. One of his arms had been rendered useless as a result of a lion's attack, and he bore other visible evidence of the suffering he had endured through twenty-seven bouts with various jungle fevers. In a voice charged with emotion he broke the awed silence of the assembly by saying, "Shall I tell you what sustained me amidst the trials and hardships and loneliness of my exiled life? It was the words, 'Lo, I am with you always, even unto the end of the age.'" Later, when he had returned to Africa, they found him one day kneeling by his bed, but his spirit had flown. Near him a small New Testament lay open at that very comforting statement of Jesus, and in the margin he had written, *"The word of a Gentleman."*

Yes, the promises of Jesus can be depended upon as the Word of a Living Savior who will love us forever and compensate for any hardship we may have to endure for Him by His constant companionship.

> *I have a Friend so precious, so very dear to me,*
> *He loves me with a tender love, He loves so faithfully;*
> *I could not live apart from Him, I love to feel Him nigh,*
> *And so we dwell together, my Lord and I!* —Mrs. L. Shorey

God has two dwellings: one in Heaven, and the other in the heart of His trusting child!

SPIRITUAL PSYCHIATRY

For the word of God is living, and powerful, and sharper
than any two-edged sword . . . and is a discerner of
the thoughts and intents of the heart.   Hebrews 4:12

My son Kurt was only four years only when he came running
into the house one afternoon, just after my wife Margaret had
lit some new candles, letting them burn long enough to give
them the correct appearance. As Kurt rushed past the living
room, he stopped in his tracks. His eyes opened wide with ex-
pectancy as he cried out, "Hey Mom, *I smell a birthday!*" You
see, whenever that important day rolled around, he always had
candles on a cake, so the odor of burning wax spoke of just one
thing: Happy Birthday! Although the smell of burning candles
meant this to Kurt, the same stimulus could trip various responses
in the minds of others. We are conditioned to some extent by
prior experience. How we react to a certain situation — what these
things suggest to us — often can be quite revealing. Indeed, they
may be a key to what we really are. A device used by psychia-
trists is based on this very principle. A list of terms is recited
and the patient is instructed to utter the first thing that comes
to his mind. Whether this is a completely reliable means of
analysis may be debatable; but, in spiritual matters, it certainly
might be helpful in determining the state of the "inner man."

Take this spiritual "test." Note the first thought that comes
to your mind at the mention of the following terms: *Sunday.*
(Did it suggest a morning to sleep in, or church?) *Wednesday.*
(Did you think of bowling night, or prayer meeting?) *Your*
pastor's name. (Was there an urge to criticize, or to pray for
him?) *Witnessing.* (Your first thought—did it suggest a burden,
or a privilege?) What did your answers reveal? Regardless of
one's response, the KEY to knowing what a person really is, depends upon his reaction to the following word: JESUS! (What
does that Name suggest to you? Merely a good Man? Or do you
regard Him as truly the Son of God?) Is Christ *your* personal
Savior?

> *Jesus! the very thought of Thee*
> *With sweetness fills my breast;*
> *But sweeter far Thy face to see,*
> *And in Thy presence rest.*—Bernard of Clairvaux

As a man "thinketh in his heart, so is he" (Prov. 23:7).

WHAT CAN I DO FOR YOU?

Lord, what wilt thou have me to do?   Acts 9:6

A prominent individual recently said that his little daughter often supplements her usual evening prayer with many requests for special favors from the Lord. However, one night—as a sweet afterthought — she closed with the words, "And now, God, what can I do for You?"

I am sure the Lord was pleased with this petition. True, He is not helplessly standing by, hoping people will come to His aid, for He is Almighty God, the Creator and Sustainer of the universe. The "cattle upon a thousand hills" are His, and He is entirely self-sufficient. However, in His infinite wisdom and good pleasure He has chosen to carry out His program upon earth through people like you and me — frail and imperfect as we are. Therefore He loves to see us warmly and willingly offer Him our hearts and hands.

When Paul met the risen Christ, the question he asked was basically the same as that voiced by the little girl. He exclaimed, "Lord, what wilt thou have me to do?" From the day of his conversion he never forgot that he had been saved to serve, for he calls himself "Paul, a servant (literally, *bondslave*) of Jesus Christ . . ." (Rom. 1:1).

Christian friend, God wants you to rejoice in the riches of your salvation, and He also invites you to come to Him with your requests. However, He is especially delighted when one of His children looks upward and says, "And now, God, *what can I do for You?*"

> *O let us be loyal to Jesus,*
> *The faith we confessed let's renew;*
> *And ask Him this question each morning,*
> *"Lord, what wilt Thou have me to do?"*
> — Pangborn

The work of the Lord is done by the few; ask God what part He would have you do!

YOUR BURDEN AND YOU

Cast thy burden upon the Lord, and he shall
sustain thee.   Psalm 55:22

The Psalmist David was beset by a host of difficulties. His enemies were hunting him as a wild carnivorous animal stalks its prey. But even worse, the king had been betrayed by his trusted counselor and friend. Fearful and trembling, David wanted so much to escape from it all and "with the wings of a dove" fly away; but this he couldn't do. In great anxiety of spirit and depression of heart he comes to the only happy solution — one which is best for all of us as well: "Cast thy burden upon the Lord, and he shall sustain thee."

Henry Moorhouse, a noble servant of the Lord, was going through very trying circumstances. His little daughter who was paralyzed was sitting in her chair as he entered the house with a package for his wife. Going up to her and kissing her, he said, "Where is mother?" "Upstairs," she replied. "Well, I have something for her." "Let me carry it to mother," said the daughter. "Why Minnie dear, how can you carry this package? You cannot carry yourself." With a smile on her face the child replied, "O no, papa; but if you give it to me, *then* I will carry the package and you can carry me." God spoke softly to his heart that this was his own position. He was carrying his burden, but was not the Lord carrying him?

"Cast *thy burden* upon the Lord, and he shall sustain *thee.*" There is no need for us to carry our burdens alone when the Lord Jesus will carry both them and us. The apostle Peter puts it this way, "Casting all your care upon him; for he careth for you" (1 Pet. 5:7).

> *Christ will not fail me, a child of His care;*
> *All of my burdens He gladly will share.*
> *He's ever beside me, no harm can betide me,*
> *For when I most need Him, my Savior is there!*—Poole

God tells us to burden Him with what burdens us.

TRUE FORGIVENESS

. . . even as Christ forgave you, so also do ye.

Colossians 3:13

Old Joe was dying. Realizing that time was running out, he was concerned about making everything right. One matter especially stood out in his mind. For years he had been at odds with Bill, formerly one of his best friends. He often argued with him over the most trivial matters, and in recent days had been unwilling even to speak with him at all. Wanting to straighten things out, he sent word for Bill to come and see him. Graciously, Bill consented. When he arrived, Joe told him that he was afraid to go into eternity with such a bad feeling between them. Then, very reluctantly and with a great effort, Joe apologized for the things he had said and done. Reaching out to shake Bill's hand, he asked forgiveness. Everything seemed just fine until Bill left. He was just about out of sight, when Joe cried after him, "But, remember, if I get better, this doesn't count!"

We may smile, but what a picture this draws of the way we treat one another. The forgiveness we profess is frequently superficial. It is often given out of fear, to gain some selfish advantage, or to clear our conscience — rather than out of a genuine love for God or the one who may have wronged us. Oh, yes, we say that we forgive, but when the least little friction arises, *how quick we are to resurrect the past grievances and add them to the present charges!* We like to "bury the hatchet" with the handle sticking out. That way it's so easy to pick it up again if we can use it to our own advantage. How much better to follow the admonition to be "kind one to another . . . *forgiving one another,* even as God, for Christ's sake, hath forgiven you" (Eph. 4:32).

If our sinless Lord is willing to forgive us, why shouldn't we, with all our faults, extend pardon to those who trespass against us? To be Christlike, we must have a forgiving spirit. Is there someone you should call right now?

Since the Lord all sin forgave,
When He stooped our soul to save;
We with charity should live —
Ready always to forgive!   — G.W.

"I can forgive, but I can't forget," is just another way of saying, "I cannot forgive!"

—Beech

CONFESSING OUR FAULTS

Confess your faults one to another   James 5:16

One of the most difficult things to do is to admit our mistakes and to say from our hearts that we are sorry about something we have done. Yet this is precisely what James admonishes us to do. This does not mean that we are to engage in indiscriminate public or even private confession of all our sins and shortcomings, for the Bible clearly teaches that the things known to God alone need be confessed only to Him. However, instead of trying to defend the wrong things we do, we should let those who are aware of our sins know that we are truly sorry and will seek to avoid these offenses in the future.

Dr. Alan Redpath, former pastor of Moody Memorial Church, tells of the time his father, after a brief period of tension in the home, looked across the table at his wife and said, "I'm so sorry I spoke to you the way I did. I'm ashamed of myself." Dr. Redpath said that although at that time he was not a Christian, he went to his room after the meal, knelt, and prayed, "O God, I thank You for a father like that. Make me more like him."

Humble confession has a twofold result. Sincere believers will be able to pray for us intelligently; and secondly, our lives will become effectual in their influence upon others. Remember:

> *You are writing each day a letter to men;*
> *Take care that the writing is true.*
> *'Tis the only gospel some men will read,*
> *That gospel according to you.* —Anon.

Is your stubborn pride hindering your spiritual development and impairing your effectiveness by preventing you from making an open confession of your faults to others?

> *While I kept guilty silence, my strength was spent with grief,*
> *Thy hand was heavy on me, my soul found no relief;*
> *But when I owned my trespass, my sin hid not from Thee*
> *When I confessed transgression, then Thou forgavest me.*
> —Psalter

COVERED SIN brews misery — CONFESSED SIN distills forgiveness!
—G. W.

A PATTERN FOR PRAYER

Daniel [told] . . . his companions; that they would de-
sire mercies of the God of heaven. . . . Daniel 2:17, 18

Daniel had many wonderful traits. Evidently he was hand-
some, intelligent, and possessed outstanding abilities. Furthermore, he had deep convictions and great courage, and dared to
stand for the right — even though it would bring disfavor from
the king. One of his finest characteristics was that he was *a man
of prayer!* In the second chapter of his prophecy, we find him
calling his friends to pray in time of an extreme emergency. In
chapter six we see him kneeling three times a day according to
his custom; and in chapter nine we hear him utter one of the
most outstanding petitions of confession in the entire Word of
God.

Note, in chapter two, three facts concerning Daniel's prayer-
life. In verse 16 he is found *doing everything possible to answer
his own requests!* Aware of the crisis he and his friends are
facing, he goes without delay to the king himself, asking for
more time. In verses 17 and 18, we see him *calling for group
supplication!* He tells his companions, Shadrach, Meshach, and
Abednego, to begin praying with him that the God of Heaven
would reveal the king's dream. Then in verse 19, after Daniel's
request has been granted, he is heard *giving thanks and praise
to the Lord for His gracious answers!* Let us put these principles
into practice in our own lives: First, do all we can to answer our
own petitions; then, call for the prayers of others; and, finally,
always remember to give thanks.

Be a 20th century Daniel: a *praying, working, thankful* Christian!

> The heart is a temple when God is there,
> And we place ourselves in His loving care;
> Then the burdens, which seemed too heavy to bear,
> Are lifted away on the wings of prayer!—Helen S. Rice

**Prayer with obedience is POWER; prayer without obedience
is PRESUMPTION!**   —Bosch

"WHICH WAY TO SHORE?"

Is it nothing to you, all ye that pass by? Lamentations 1:12

Many today are so independent and self-centered that the difficulties of others leave them unmoved. Some time ago a young woman was attacked and killed while 15 or 20 onlookers refused to give her aid. Their excuse was, *"We didn't want to get involved!"* Certainly such an attitude cannot be countenanced by anyone who considers himself a Christian. I am my brother's keeper, and must love my neighbor as myself.

In 1952, *The Prairie Overcomer* carried this touching story: " 'Which way to shore?' came an anguished cry. Pawing the water and struggling, a young man in New England frantically appealed for help. As the beach was only 30 feet away, the swimmers paid no attention; and the young fellow, exhausted and bewildered, finally gave up in despair. Suddenly it dawned on someone on shore that he was really desperate. Jumping in to assist, he soon reached the spot from whence the urgent calls had come, but the man had gone under. When he was finally found, he was pronounced dead. But what had he meant with his cry, 'Which way to shore?' The answer became obvious when they discovered that he had been *blind*. In spite of all his frenzied efforts, he actually did not know how to reach safety." So today, men blinded by sin, struggle and die because they do not know the way to the Heavenly Shore. Yes, many are sinking into Christless graves because we have failed to aid them. Therefore, the question found in Lamentations 1:12 comes to each of us with searching earnestness, *"Is it nothing to you, all ye that pass by?"*

> *Perishing, perishing! Thronging our pathway,*
> *Hearts break with burdens too heavy to bear;*
> *Jesus would save, but there's no one to tell them,*
> *No one to lift them from sin and despair!*   —L.R.M.

No matter what good we may be doing, if we are not trying to "rescue the perishing," we are majoring on minors!—F. Webb

NEW DISCOVERIES

I rejoice at thy word, as one that findeth great spoil.
Psalm 119:162

My boys and I have had some wonderful hours together walking along the ocean beaches searching for shells. The endless variety, the limitless number, and the indescribable beauty of God's creation never cease to fascinate. Strolling down the shore with the sound of the surf pounding in our ears, we wondered who would make the greatest discovery. What a thrill it was to happen along just as a big salty breaker gushed out a "treasure" as a personal gift! It need not have been the biggest shell, or even the most beautiful, or the one with the strangest shape; but the fact that the ocean wave had dropped one of the secrets of the deep at my very feet gave me genuine satisfaction. As I picked it up, I imagined this was the first time human eyes had gazed upon this particular object . . . the only occasion on which anyone had reveled in its intricacy of design and breath-taking color. You see, this was my own personal discovery! Then, showing it to my boys — seeing their eyes open wide and hearing their excited exclamations — this was the crowning moment of delight.

Isn't it much the same way with the treasures of God's Word? The Bible is an ocean of truth, limitless in its wealth, and rich with blessings just waiting to be brought to the surface. Even though we revel in having the best of Bible teachers and expositors display their findings, how much more blessed it is to uncover these truths for ourselves. What a joy there is in conducting our own "treasure hunts." And then the greatest satisfaction of all comes in revealing those "spiritual gems" to others!

How long since you have discovered something for yourself in the Bible? When was the last time you shared your find with someone else?

Thy Word is like a deep, deep mine;
And jewels rich and rare
Are hidden in its mighty depths
For every searcher there. — Edwin Hodder

Why be satisfied with "secondhand" goods, when "new treasures" are yours for the searching?   **—R.W.D.**

"IT WORKS!"

*. . . his delight is in the law of the Lord; and in his
law doth he meditate day and night.*   Psalm 1:2

The first Psalm emphasizes that the truly happy man is one
who finds delight and continual refreshment in the Word of God.
In fact, the "law of the Lord" reveals the way of life and victory,
and indicates the direction he must take to find contentment and
spiritual usefulness.

A Christian repairman was once called to service the mechanism of a giant telescope. During the noon hour, the chief astronomer found him reading his New Testament and asked,
"What good do you expect to get out of that? With our scientific
advancements, the Bible is now completely outdated. Why, *you
can't even be sure who wrote it!*" The mechanic was silent for
a moment, then he looked up and said, "Don't you make considerable use of the multiplication tables in your calculations as
an astronomer?" "Yes, I certainly do," replied the other. *"Do
you know who wrote them?"* "Why no, I guess I don't." "Then,"
said the mechanic, "how can you employ them when you're not
even sure of the author?" "We trust them because — well, *because they work,"* the astronomer finished with a note of irritation.
"Well, *I trust the Bible for the same reason!"*

Dwight L. Moody once accepted the challenge to debate an
atheist on the condition that the fruit of the infidel's position
would be evidenced in the lives of ten or more people. Moody
agreed to have at least a hundred on the platform who could tell
how Christ had radically changed their lives from drunkenness,
debauchery, and slothfulness to shining examples of virtue, usefulness, and happiness. Not being able to produce ten worthy
testimonials, the atheist withdrew his offer. Moody had proven
once again that the Gospel is the power of God unto salvation.
Yes, *it works!*

> *Who in God's law takes keen delight,*
> *And meditates both day and night,*
> *Him shall prosperity attend*
> *And bless his work till life shall end.* —Anon.

**Study the Bible to be wise, believe it to be safe, practice it to
be holy!**

"HEAVY EARS AND SHUT EYES"

*Go, and tell this people, Hear ye indeed, but under-
stand not . . . .*   Isaiah 6:9

Isaiah had received the strange commission from the Lord to preach a message which he knew the people would not believe. Their ears were to be made heavy and their spiritual eyes shut, lest they should understand and be converted. Isaiah knew ahead of time that the majority would reject his faithful proclamation. No wonder we hear him ask in verse 11, "Lord, how long?" He wanted to know if he would be expected to continue indefinitely such a difficult task. He is told he should persevere "until the cities be wasted without inhabitant, and the houses without man, and the land be utterly desolate . . . and there be a great forsaking in the midst of the land." In other words, Isaiah was to keep on preaching even though he knew full well that his hearers would not believe him, and that things would go from bad to worse.

You and I are faced with a similar situation today. We are well aware that the world will not be converted through our witnessing — that the majority "hear indeed, but understand not." We know in advance that this age will end in apostasy. We expect no great, worldwide revival (much as we would like to see one). Isaiah was commanded to bring the message with little hope of results; and we also are to "go into all the world and preach the gospel to every creature." While the crowd continues on its downward course, God will call out a small minority as "a people for his name." When the Church is complete, Jesus Christ will come again to take these saved ones unto himself. In the meantime, we are to be faithful to our commission, remembering that our reward will not be based on numbers, but on faithfulness!

> *Go in the strength of the Master,*
> *"Go," 'twas His parting command,*
> *Seeking the lost ones to gather,*
> *Scattered abroad o'er the land!*
> —Mrs. C. H. Morris

Though we cannot bring all the world to Christ, we must bring Christ to all the world.

A FATHER'S LEGACY

And Abraham gave all that he had unto Isaac. Genesis 25:5

Fathers are being honored today, and yet, to have parental responsibility entails awesome obligations. Primarily, our text refers to Abraham's unstinting generosity to his son Isaac, but one can also see the general principle that fathers *are constantly giving to their children by their example!* Most of this is done so gradually and subtly that they do not realize what they are leaving to the next generation. However, little ones quickly notice enmity between a father and a mother, discourtesy to neighbors, unkindness toward the poor, lack of love to God, or evil speaking concerning friends and acquaintances. These acts and attitudes greatly influence children.

A little fellow with bright eyes and brown curly hair was attending Sunday school when the discussion turned to the subject of Heaven. "Dick," said the teacher, "whom do you want to meet first when you get to Glory?" The startling reply was, "Oh, but I'm not going there!" "Not going there?" said the teacher. "No," said the boy calmly and decisively, "Mama and sister are, but *I want to go with Papa!*" Some time later the teacher met Dick's father who was their family physician. He repeated the incident and then added pointedly, "And now, Doctor, *just where* ARE *you going?*" Confirmed unbeliever that he was, the physician nervously paced the floor with tears in his eyes. "It's just like Dick to say that," he sighed remorsefully, "I'll have to change my ways I guess. I have noticed that he always wants to be with me and be like me!"

Father, you are constantly "giving" to your children. Take inventory — what legacy of Christian influence and grace are you leaving your offspring?

> You're setting an example
> Every day in all you do,
> For the little boy who's waiting
> To grow up to be like you! —E. Guest

What they leave IN their children should concern parents more than what they leave TO them.

THE IMPORTANT "ONE"

Now, then, we are ambassadors for Christ . . . .
2 Corinthians 5:20

In this day when we can reach millions with the Gospel by radio, TV, and the printed page, it seems that many Christians have succumbed to the false opinion that their own personal witness to a single individual doesn't count for much. But how significant it is to read in the Gospel that even though Jesus' public ministry was limited to a meager three and one-half years — and He had to make every minute count — many hours were spent in dealing with one person at a time. We thrill when we read of Jesus preaching to the multitudes in Judaea, ministering to the five thousand gathered by the Sea of Galilee, and we behold with glad hearts the crowds that thronged about Him in Capernaum. But how refreshing also to read in the Gospel record that amidst the multitude in Judaea, He was not too busy to heal one leper. Surrounded by the hungry thousands in the desert, He found time to use one young lad to bless the entire multitude; and in the crowded house in Capernaum He stopped to heal one man let down through the opened roof.

No, Jesus Christ, although besieged and mobbed by the multitudes, never lost sight of the value of one soul! How comforting it is to read of His conversation late at night with a single individual, Nicodemus; of His visit with one woman at the well of Samaria; and of His vital, personal interest in that little man, Zacchaeus, sitting up in a sycamore tree. How blessed are His words to this one man singled out of that whole passing multitude: "Zacchaeus, make haste, and come down; for today I must abide at *thy* house"; and again, when true repentance had been indicated, "This day is salvation come to this house" (Luke 19:9).

If you are ever tempted to minimize the value of your personal, individual witness, remember Jesus' words: "There is joy in the presence of the angels of God over one sinner that repenteth!"

Lord, lay some soul upon my heart,
And love that soul through me;
And may I nobly do my part
To win that soul for Thee. —L. Tucker

You can test all your big sentiments about love for humanity by what you are doing for individuals!

THE RESURRECTION PLANT

*And I give unto them eternal life; and they shall
never perish . . . .*   John 10:28

Christians are sure of salvation, but, oh, the dried-up testimonies, the withered lives that are found among God's people because they fail to keep drinking at the Fountain of Living Waters!

In John 15 the Lord Jesus Christ compared those that are His to the branches on a grapevine. I am told by those who keep vineyards that one can prune the branches, let them lie on the ground for a long time, apparently dried up and dead — yet, if one gathers them and puts them into water they will freshen up, blossom forth, and be suitable for planting in the vineyard, where in time they will once again produce fruit.

Some years ago I had the privilege of making a brief visit to the state of Florida. While going through the lush vegetation there, I came upon an amazing growth called the "resurrection plant." Some of these had been dehydrated, placed in cellophane bags, and were offered for sale. I purchased one which was as dry as dust. While I could see the delicate root system and the ball of shriveled foliage, it seemed good for nothing but the trash can. However, a short time in a bowl of water produced wonders. The fronds uncurled into a lovely, fernlike plant. I am told it could be dried again, kept for years, and yet be "resurrected" each time it is placed in water. I thought to myself how like the Christian! While the Lord Jesus began the good work of salvation in him, and will complete it to the day of Christ (Phil. 1:6), yet he can become shriveled spiritually if he fails to partake daily of the "water of the Word." However, if the believer will get back to his prayer and Bible study, it will soon become evident that his "dormancy" was not "death" but suspended animation!

Oh, Christian with the "dried-up" testimony, remember the parable of the "resurrection plant," and immerse yourself once again in the reviving waters of the Word.

*Let me drink the precious water
That alone the soul can fill,
Thrilling all my thirsty being
With the treasures of His will!* —G.W.

These two are wedded, and no man can part: dust on the Bible and drought in the heart!

HEARING GOD

*I will hear what God, the Lord, will speak; for he
will speak peace unto his people . . . . Psalm 85:8*

One of the most beautiful sounds at daybreak is the singing
of birds. What a joy there is in listening to the happy tunes
cheering us on to the duties of the day. However, their beautiful
melodies can become so commonplace that we no longer hear
them.

One day as I awakened, it suddenly dawned on me that, although our regular early morning visitor Mr. Mocking Bird was
outside the bedroom window with his bag full of imitations, I
was no longer appreciating him. The first time I had listened to
him, many months before, I was thrilled by the beauty of his
song. I reveled in recognizing his skillful imitations of other
feathered friends. Gradually, however, I must have begun to
take this songster's dayspring concert for granted, until I no
longer really heard him. Mr. Mocking Bird was there singing
for me every morning! The fact that I did not hear him was my
fault!

How often we experience the same thing when it comes to
"hearing" God speak to us. When first we are saved, how blessed
and satisfying are the Scriptures with their stirring instruction
and spiritual food. As time goes on, however, we begin to read
the same portions over and over again in such a routine manner
that they no longer "speak" to us. They become commonplace,
due to our lack of spiritual attunement. But what a joy when
some passage in the Word of God suddenly bursts forth into
special meaning, and we are appalled that for so long we had
not been "hearing" what God was saying. We need to read with
understanding and to recognize God's voice.

As Thomas a Kempis expressed it: "Blessed are they who are
glad to have time to spare for God, and who shake off all worldly
hindrances. Consider these things, O my soul, and shut up the
door of your sensual desires, that you may hear what the Lord
your God speaks to you (Ps. 85:8)."

**When you READ the Bible, always do so expecting to "HEAR"
God speak.**
—R.W.D.

DON'T BE A "SPIRITUAL VAGRANT"

And Enoch walked with God, and he was not;
for God took him. Genesis 5:24

Efficient leaders of organizations and responsible individuals set specific goals for which they constantly strive. A vagrant, on the other hand, is an extreme example of one who has no such purposes in view. He does not hold a steady job, does not obligate himself for the purchase and maintenance of a home, and often has no loved ones for whose future he is concerned. The utter aimlessness of such a life was strikingly demonstrated by the tramp who declined a ride someone offered him, saying, "No, thank you! I am not going any place, so I am just as well off here as I would be 10 miles farther on."

All who do not believe in God are in a sense "spiritual vagrants" — living without an ultimate aim or goal. The Christian, however, knows where he is going. He also perceives his purpose — "To glorify God, and to enjoy Him forever." Moreover, Hebrews 11:1 says that a believer's faith gives him absolute assurance that he will certainly enjoy the "things hoped for," and that "the things not seen" are definite realities. For this reason he seeks to please the Lord by worshiping in an acceptable manner like Abel, by walking in fellowship like Enoch, and by working faithfully like Noah. These men believed in God and directed their efforts in doing His will. They did not wander aimlessly through life without purpose or goal. Neither should you.

Dear reader, what is your highest ambition? Are you truly seeking to glorify God and do His will, or are you a "spiritual vagrant"? When you pass from this earthly scene may it be said of you as it was of Enoch, he "walked with God."

Such be the tribute of thy pilgrim journey
When life's last mile thy feet have bravely trod —
When thou hast gone to all that there awaits thee,
This simple epitaph — "He walked with God!" —Anon.

Our lives constantly manifest what we truly think about God!

HYPOCRITES IN THE CHURCH

Woe unto you . . . hypocrites.   Matthew 23:27

Webster definies a hypocrite as "one who feigns to be something he is not." According to this, he is a "counterfeit," a mere pretender. Jesus, in speaking to the scribes and Pharisees, called them "blind guides" and "whited sepulchers," and said they were "full of . . . all uncleanness." He added that they appeared outwardly righteous, but were "full of iniquity."

One of the weakest excuses offered by Christ-rejecters today, and yet one of the most common, is this: "I'm not interested because there are too many hypocrites in the church." A born-again believer, presenting the Gospel to a certain man, ran into this objection. Mentioning the name of a prominent person who had been a church member, the unbeliever said, "Look at the awful crime he committed, while parading under the name of religion." The other replied, "Do you suppose that man ever was a true Christian?" "Of course not," said the unbeliever. "Exactly!" answered the saved one. "He was not actually one of us. He was just trying to play along with God's people."

"But," I can hear someone say, "I know of those who really do seem to be what you would call 'born again,' and yet they're quite inconsistent. *They surely don't 'walk' the way they 'talk!'*" Much as I dislike it, I must admit this is true. There are *some* like this in our churches today, but is *that* an excuse for rejecting *Christ?* Was *He* a hypocrite? We are amazed that intelligent people should use such a flimsy argument as this.

Remembering Jesus' words, "Woe unto you, hypocrites," never allow such a one to stand between you and Christ, lest you be included in their condemnation.

> *As many men, their vows fulfilling,*
> *By God's grace are true and willing,*
> *You must not let the false "professors"*
> *Quell your faith in true "possessors"!* —Anon.

Christianity isn't worth a snap of your finger if it doesn't straighten out your character.   —Moody

GOD REMEMBERS TO FORGET

And their sins and iniquities will I remember no more.   Hebrews 10:17

Sometimes it is difficult for man, fallen as he is, to imagine that God would act differently toward us than we do toward each other. Forgiving and forgetting never quite go together in our experience. To clear the record is one thing; to erase the transgression from the memory is yet another.

There is a colorful Celtic allegory which tells of an angel who was sent to a certain saint to tell him that he must start for the Celestial City. The Christian received the messenger and his message with gladness, and at the appointed hour they set off together. As they passed up the shining way beyond the bounds of this world, the saint was suddenly troubled with the thought of his sins. Addressing his angelic guide, he said, "Where did you bury my sins?" "I only know that I buried them," he replied, "but I cannot remember where." Then the angel added, "As for the Father, *He has forgotten that you ever sinned!*" What a wonder is divine forgiveness! How absolutely complete the atoning work wrought by Christ's shed blood!

If God has forgiven you for Christ's sake and forgotten your sins purged by His blood, why should *you* allow an accusing conscience or the wily tempter to plague you with them? That sufficient work of the Savior has separated our sins from us "as far as the east is from the west." The Heavenly Father remembers them no more. Dean Alford has called it the "oblivion of sins" — blotted out, never to show up on the account again. Dear Christian, rejoice that this is true, and as adoring children, let us praise the "Father of mercies."

> *As far as the west is removed from the east,*
> *He banished my sins, both the greatest and least;*
> *And this is the reason I'm pardoned today,*
> *Because with His blood He has washed them away!*
> —Habershon

God does not forget the sinner; He just forgets his sin!

STAIR CLIMBERS

Cast thy burden upon the Lord, and he shall sus-
tain thee . . . .   Psalm 55:22

A young lad took a position as a messenger in a large commercial building. It was his job to deliver communications from
one office to another on the various floors. At the end of the first
day he was so tired and discouraged that he decided to quit. Since
he was a very likable youth and showed much promise, the boss
called him and asked him why he was leaving so quickly. The
young man replied, "I'm sorry, sir, but the duties you have given
me are too tiring. I can't take all this stair climbing. Hiking up
to the tenth floor from the first, and then down to the third and
back up to the ninth — it's just too much!" Patting him on the
shoulder, and with a smile breaking across his face, the boss led
the lad out into the corridor. Pointing to some sliding doors, he
said, "Son, didn't you know there are elevators in this building?
No wonder you're tired and discouraged! You have used all your
energy running up and down under your own power, when you
could have been riding the elevator!" Many Christians, too, become weary and frustrated in their service for Christ *because
they labor "under their own power" rather than "riding the elevator" of God's sustaining grace!*

Recently an outstanding servant of the Lord testified concerning a transforming experience in his life. He had literally worn
himself out in Christian work. He was depressed and perplexed,
and wondering what to do, when he suddenly came to the realization that he was carrying a greater burden than God intended.
While he had been trying to accomplish things in his own
strength, the Lord was more desirous of doing that work—through
him. Yes, as Isaiah testified, ". . . they that wait upon the Lord
shall renew their strength; they shall mount up with wings like
eagles . . ." (Isa. 40:31). Struggling Christian, cast your burden
upon the Lord, and "he shall sustain thee" (Ps. 55:22). Why
climb the stairs when you can ride "the elevator"?

> *Never be sad or desponding,*
> *If thou hast faith to believe;*
> *Grace, for the duties before thee,*
> *Ask of thy God and receive.* — F. J. Crosby

**The call of God to a piece of work is the guarantee that He
will be the resource of all the strength it will require!**

FAITH AND LOVELINESS

. . . Would to God my lord were with the prophet who is in Samaria! For he would cure him of his leprosy.   2 Kings 5:3

The little girl of our story was probably intelligent and attractive. It is doubtful that General Naaman would have selected one to serve as a slave in his home who did not possess these qualities. However, her memory has been immortalized in the Scriptures not because of her intelligence and beauty, but because she displayed a sweet and spiritual sensitivity that is truly outstanding. A marauding band of Syrian soldiers had swooped down upon their home and taken her captive. She was now a slave girl in this wealthy man's home, unable to see her father and mother, or any of the other familiar faces of her girlhood days. If anyone had reason to sulk and be unhappy she did. It would be easy to hate the Syrians who had taken and enslaved her. Many a person in a similar situation might have been secretly glad that her owner was suffering from a dread disease. This Hebrew maiden, however, couldn't rejoice in his misfortune, and one day told her mistress that God's prophet in Israel could cure her husband of his leprosy if only they could be brought together. Her loving concern set in motion a chain of events which culminated in the healing of Naaman.

What accounts for this Hebrew girl's beautiful character? It was her faith. She possessed a simple childlike trust in God, and apparently believed that all things work together for good to those who love God. What a tribute to her parents who must have led her to this vibrant faith in the one true God which enabled her to be sweet even while a slave in Naaman's home.

If you will trust God, even in life's most difficult circumstances, you too can become a lovely person—a shining example of faith—like the little maid who was held captive by the Syrians. Try it and see!

> *If our faith were but more simple,*
> *We should take Him at His Word;*
> *And our lives would be all sunshine*
> *In the sweetness of our Lord.*— F. W. Faber

Faith is never so beautiful as when it has on its working clothes!

DELUSIONS OF GRANDEUR

. . . if a man think himself to be something, when
he is nothing, he deceiveth himself.   Galatians 6:3

There is a story told about a proud woodpecker who was peck-
ing away at an old, dead tree, when the sky blackened, the lightning flashed, and the thunder began to roll. Undaunted, he went
right on working. Suddenly a big bolt of lightning struck the
tree on which he was perched, splintering it into a million pieces.
Startled, but unhurt, the haughty bird flew away screeching to
all his feathered friends, "Hey, everyone, look what *I* did! Look
what *I* did!" This proud, deluded woodpecker reminds me of
some people, the kind described by Paul in his letter to the
Christians at Galatia, the ones who think themselves to be something, when they are nothing (Gal. 6:3). Bragging about their
own achievements, and *how great they are* (in their own eyes),
they fail to recognize that all their ability comes from God. Without Him they can *do nothing!*

A certain braggart, after enumerating what he considered to
be some of his outstanding achievements, exclaimed, "I'll have
you know that *I'm a self-made man!*" One of those who heard
him, remarked, "Well, I'm glad to hear that! It certainly relieves
the Creator of a tremendous responsibility!" Truly, there is nothing quite so disgusting as a proud individual who fails to realize
his complete dependence upon God, and egotistically takes all the
credit for his so-called successes.

Remember, no matter who we may be, whether of low or high
degree, everything we have which is worthy of commendation
is from God. Rather than boasting, and deluding ourselves as
to our own worth, how much better to remember Paul's words
in 1 Corinthians 1 where he says that ". . . God hath chosen the
foolish things of the world to confound the wise; and . . . the
weak things . . . to confound the things which are mighty . . .
that no flesh should glory in his presence . . . according as it is
written, *He that glorieth, let him glory in the Lord*" (1 Cor. 1:
27, 29, 31).

> *Let others have the honors,*
> *The glory and the fame —*
> *Seek thou to follow Jesus*
> *And glory in His name!*   — Lola Horton

The "self-made man" is usually eager to worship his maker!

GOD IS GOOD

Enter into his gates with thanksgiving. . . . For the
Lord is good.   Psalm 100:4, 5

Recently I stopped at the home of a fine Christian who has been confined to his bed for some time because of a severe back ailment. He and his wife have been unusually dedicated in serving the Lord, and their two sons and one daughter are in full-time Christian work. Lying flat on his back and suffering quite a bit of discomfort, he told me the doctors had been unable to clearly diagnose his malady and had given him little encouragement. When I said something about this being a rather disheartening situation, he replied, "I am not going to let this 'get me down' spiritually. I am almost 70 years old and have always enjoyed the best of health. When I think of all the Lord has done for me, I feel I would have nothing to complain about, even if I never walked again. *God has been so good!*" These words of gratitude touched my heart, and I found myself repeating, "Yes, God is good."

Psalm 100, our Scripture reading for today, is a wonderful song of praise and thanksgiving. It was sung by worshipers as they entered the outer court of the temple to bring their thank offerings to the Lord. They expressed their joy in knowing the one true God who is both their great Creator and their loving Shepherd. The last verse of the Psalm sums up their reasons for gladness of heart, "For the Lord is good; his mercy is everlasting, and his truth endureth to all generations."

Yes, God is good! Every believer should daily remind himself of this glorious truth. Those who do so will be enabled to sing praise even in the darkest night.

> *Yet, in the maddening maze of things,*
> *And tossed by storm and flood,*
> *To one fixed trust my spirit clings;*
> *I know that God is good!* —Whittier

Because of His infinite care and kindness, God alone is worthy of the name "Good."
                                                    —Beecher

LEADING THE LAMBS
> *. . . bring . . . [your children] up in the nurture and*
> *admonition of the Lord.*   Ephesians 6:4

In his book, *The Appearances of Jesus After His Resurrection,* J. Vernon McGee wrote an excellent commentary on Jesus' words, "feed my sheep," which our Lord addressed to Peter (John 21:16). Dr. McGee comments, "Today we have it all mixed up— we try to discipline the young Christians and feed the old ones. The Lord said, 'Feed the young ones and discipline the old ones.' An anxious father asked, 'How can I bring up my boy in the way he should go?' and the answer was, 'By going in that way yourself.' You will find great worth in these verses by Charlene Fuller:

> 'Twas a sheep, not a lamb, that strayed away,
> In the parable Jesus told;
> A grown-up sheep that had gone astray
> From the ninety and nine in the fold.
>
> Out on the hillside, out in the cold,
> 'Twas a sheep the Good Shepherd sought;
> And back to the flock, safe into the fold,
> 'Twas a sheep the Good Shepherd brought.
>
> And why for the sheep should we earnestly long,
> And as fervently hope and pray?
> Because there is danger, if they go wrong,
> They will lead the lambs astray.
>
> And so with the sheep we tenderly plead,
> For the sake of the lambs today;
> If the sheep are lost, what terrible price
> Some lambs will have to pay!

It's not junior, it's his father, who needs the discipline."

Say, are you bringing your children up in the "nurture and admonition of the Lord"?

> There's a wide-eyed little youngster
> Who believes you're always right;
> And his ears are always open,
> And he watches day and night;
> You are setting an example
> Every day in all you do,
> For the little one who's watching
> To grow up and be like you!   —Anon.

A close look at the "chips" may reveal flaws in the "block"!

* © 1955, Zondervan Publishing House, by permission.

NOURISHED BY THE WORD

. . . be a good minister of Jesus Christ, nourished up
in the words of faith and of good doctrine . . . .

1 Timothy 4:6

To be a strong Christian, one needs the spiritual nourishment of the Word of God. Paul, who was keenly aware of the sanctifying influence of the Scriptures, instructs young Timothy to feed upon them constantly that his faith might be strengthened and his knowledge of good doctrine be increased. It is well for us to be reminded that the Bible is too important, too deep in its meaning, to be just flippantly read and put aside. One who would grow in grace must meditate upon it carefully, compare spiritual things with spiritual, and prayerfully ask the Holy Spirit to use its precious contents to guide, comfort, and enrich his life.

D. L. Moody was well aware of this for he penned these words on the flyleaf of his Bible: "This Book contains the Word of God, the state of man, the way of salvation, the doom of sinners, and the happiness of believers. Its doctrines are holy, its precepts are binding, its histories are true, and its decisions are immutable. Read it to be wise, believe it to be safe, and practice it to be holy. It contains light to direct you, food to support you, and comfort to cheer you. Christ is its grand object, our good its design, and the glory of God its end. It should fill the memory, rule the heart, and guide the feet. Read it slowly, frequently, prayerfully. It is given you in life, will be opened at the judgment, and be remembered forever!"

In the light of our Lord's warning that in the end-time there would be much deception and false teaching, how especially important it is for us today to be "nourished up in the words of faith and of good doctrine."

Within this wondrous volume lies
The mystery of mysteries.
O happiest of human race
To whom his God affords the grace
To ope, to read, to hope, to pray.
To lift the latch and force the way.
But better ne'er to have been born
Than read to doubt, or read to scorn!

—Sir Walter Scott

Bibles that are coming apart usually belong to people who are not!

SUBMISSION AND RESPECT

Submit yourselves to every ordinance of man for the Lord's sake. Fear God. Honor the king.
1 Peter 2:13, 17

The cruel Diocletian was bitterly persecuting the church. Actors on the stage often included in their routine a parody on baptism, the Lord's supper, and other items of the Christian faith. An entertainer named Genesius, who had been reared in a Christian home, was doing a pantomime on baptism one day when suddenly an arrow of conviction pierced his heart. To the amazement of the crowd and the consternation of the emperor who was seated in a box near the stage, Genesius cried out, "I want to receive the grace of Christ that I may be 'born again' and be set free from the sins which have been my ruin!" Turning fearlessly toward Diocletian, he said, "Illustrious Emperor, and all of you who have laughed loudly at this parody, believe me, Christ is the true King!" The enraged Roman demanded a slow and tortuous death for the actor, and Genesius died a noble witness for Christ. But did you notice how he addressed the temporal ruler? He called him *"Illustrious* Emperor."

Peter, in today's Scripture lesson, declares that believers should respectfully yield to authority, and closes the discussion of this subject with the words, "Fear God. *Honor the king"* (1 Pet. 2:17). We are to hold God in reverential awe, but we are also instructed to honor earthly rulers who have been placed in their positions by His permissive or directive decree. This means we will be submissive even when we cannot obey, and that we will be respectful even when we do not agree with their actions.

> *To every ordinance of man*
> *Be sure that you give heed;*
> *And honor those who bear the rule*
> *By word as well as deed.*   —Bosch

Whatever makes men good Christians also makes them good citizens!
—Daniel Webster

CONSTRAINING LOVE

For the love of Christ constraineth us. 2 Corinthians 5:14

One of the radicals of our day was addressing himself to a group of young people. "In the world as it is," he said, "man moves on the basis of self-interest and not on the basis of mythical ideals. These come later as a justification. Let us try to organize people around things, not issues; around their self-interest, not around what is right or wrong. People do the right thing for the wrong reasons. So one of the things an organizer tries to do is look for the wrong reasons."

This advice is a far cry from the words of the great apostle in today's Scripture reading. Rather than telling us to move "on the basis of self-interest," Paul reminds us that the service of those who have been "born again" should be prompted by "the love of Christ." Christians, therefore, who have come to know what it really means to live, are no longer to "live unto themselves, but unto him who died for them, and rose again." Commenting on this verse, one author says that believers "should live no longer to the psychic; that is, the animal, selfish, egoistic life, but to their Savior."

Perhaps "in the world as it is," as the revolutionary expressed it, "man moves on the basis of self-interest." That, however, should not be the case of the follower of Christ as he lives in the world. The highest motivation for service is *constraining love.* "For the love of Christ," says the apostle Paul, "constraineth us."

Remembering all that God has done for us through Christ, let us serve Him and others with willing, thankful and loving hearts.

> *Does the love of Christ constrain us?*
> *Do we live for Him each day?*
> *Rendering service free and hearty,*
> *Do we walk the "Jesus way"?*   —Anon.

Remember, love that stops at itself breeds only trouble!
                                                        —Bosch

A BIBLICAL FAITH

Christ died for our sins, . . . was buried, and . . .
rose again.   1 Corinthians 15:3, 4

Some time ago I asked an elderly lady in the hospital if she was a Christian. She replied, "O yes, I don't know what I would do if it were not for my faith. I believe in *goodness* and tell myself that things like *evil and sickness are not real!*" Recognizing that she had been confused by the teachings of an erroneous cult, I inquired more pointedly, "What do you believe about *the Lord Jesus?*" She replied, "Well, I don't think it is very important what you believe. Just so you have faith." As gently as possible I told her that true faith must include a knowledge of who Christ is and of what He has done to redeem us. I shared with this dying woman the great truths of today's Scripture lesson, prayed for her, and tried to show her that saving faith must be placed in the Lord Jesus.

Christian friend, aren't you glad your faith is not just a nebulous belief in abstract "goodness"? What a tragic mistake we make if we close our eyes to the grim realities of sin, suffering, and death as they are revealed in the Bible! Thank God, our trust reposes in a living Person and is firmly based upon established historical facts. The New Testament authors wrote from experience. They saw Jesus Christ die on the cross, had the opportunity to talk with Him after His resurrection, and finally watched Him ascend into Heaven. Then, empowered by the Holy Spirit, they proclaimed the living Savior with such zeal and courage that thousands were swept into the kingdom. Praise God, the Christ revealed in the Word is our Savior and Lord. It is vitally important that we have such a Biblical faith.

Yes, 'tis sweet to trust in Jesus,
Just from sin and self to cease;
Just from Jesus simply taking
Life and rest and joy and peace. — Stead

True faith may be defined as the heart's rest in Jesus!—Anon.

THE "FOURTH" AND ITS FOUNDATIONS!

Blessed is the nation whose God is the Lord . . . .
                                        Psalm 33:12

Years ago when the members of the Continental Congress were assembled at Philadelphia to consider the adoption of a Declaration of Independence, King George III of England also met with his Prime Minister, Lord North. The latter urged a policy of "sweet reasonableness" and "conciliation" toward the colonies. The King, however, unwisely rebuffed his Prime Minister with the words: "The American rebels must be subdued. We shall grant these ungrateful people nothing—nothing except what they may ask on their knees with a halter around their necks!" The situation which confronted the Congress was therefore desperate. The armies of Washington had been suffering severe reverses, and if this resulted in defeat, every signer of the proposed Declaration would be hanged as a traitor! Yet, because they considered liberty and justice more important than life, the Congress went ahead and the leaders penned their names to the document which initiated this great American republic.

It was during this time of special danger that a farmer who lived near the battlefront approached Washington's camp unheard. Suddenly his ear caught an earnest voice raised in agonizing prayer. On coming nearer, he saw it was the General, prostrate on his knees in the snow, his cheeks wet with tears! He was asking God for His Almighty assistance and guidance. The man returned home exclaiming, *"George Washington will succeed! The Americans will certainly secure their independence!"* "What makes you think so, Isaac?" asked his wife. "Well, I heard him pray out in the woods today, Hannah, and the Lord will certainly hear such a fervent, earnest petition. Yes, I am sure He will!" And the farmer was right!

To continue to prosper, America today needs more *righteousness* — less *riots;* more *prayer* — less *pride;* more of *God,* and less of *greed!* Indeed, we will remain "independent" as a nation only as long as we recognize our "dependence" upon the Lord's favor and blessing.

Men who will not be governed by God will soon be dominated by demagogs!

WAITING IS NOT WASTED

*Wait on the Lord; be of good courage. . . . Wait,
I say, on the Lord.*   Psalm 27:14

The *Convair 880* had taxied out to the strip approaching the runway. The voice of the captain came over the intercom announcing, "Ladies and gentlemen, we are number 12 in line for takeoff. We may expect a delay of 15 to 20 minutes." His words brought a concerted groan of impatience from the passengers in the plane. This chafing restlessness and desire for action seem to be the trademark of our age. The business of waiting is difficult. Christians sometimes display this same trait in their attitudes toward God in His dealings with them — especially when His providence seems strange or restricting. We never lose time, however, "waiting on the Lord."

Actually, the word "wait" in Psalm 27 means to "trust" or "hope." What better occupation of time could the Christian make than to trust in the Lord? This casts us upon an all-knowing, all-powerful Heavenly Father. We may confidently expect that in His own good time He will bring to fruition His plans for us. The perplexing problems of the present have already been solved in His wise design. Our impatience belies our trust.

Our church secretary inserted the following choice gleaning in the weekly bulletin: "You can make the clock strike before the hour by putting your own hand on it, but it will strike wrong. You can tear the rosebud open before its time, but you will mar its beauty. So we may spoil many a gift of blessing which God is preparing for us by our own eager haste. He is weaving our lives and has a perfect plan for each. *Don't pull at the threads!*"

> *Not so in haste, my heart!*
>   *Have faith in God and wait;*
> *Although He seems to linger long*
>   *He never comes too late.*   —Anon.

Patience may be bitter, but its fruit is sweet!—Rousseau

THE SAVIOR'S SAFE LEADING

. . . so he led them through the depths . . . . And
he saved them . . . .   Psalm 106:9, 10

The story is told of a ship that was grounded in the shallows during a storm. It was night, and fearing the vessel would be broken by the rough seas, it was decided that the passengers should try to make it to land. One who was in this situation writes, "The waves were rolling heavily, and I was frightened at the thought of attempting to make shore, when a man came to me saying, 'Don't be afraid, I'll take care of you.' He bore a peculiarly shaped lantern from which only a single ray of brilliant light was emitted. 'Take my hand,' he said, 'and hold fast. Don't look about you from side to side, but concentrate on the small spot which will be illuminated. Be sure to place your footsteps firmly there.' Following his advice and clinging tightly to his strong hand, the danger was overcome, and we made the beach in safety. The next day the guide asked me, 'Would you like to see how we came last night?' When I replied in the affirmative, he pointed out a perilous path which snaked its way between a maze of jutting rock. I knew then that had I made one misstep, I would have lost my balance and been swallowed up by the dark waters. However, by holding fast to his hand, and treading where the light fell, all danger was averted."

The believer, too, often finds himself beset by storms which are difficult to face, and yet he must go forward. It is at such times that he arrives at a new appreciation of the promises made by the Lord to guide and direct him safely through the depths. If he takes just one step at a time as the Savior lights the way, he will be safe and enjoy true peace and spiritual serenity even in the most adverse circumstances.

> *Just trust me when through paths unknown*
> *I lead — perchance with pain.*
> *Lean hard, my child, take thou my hand;*
> *Someday I'll make it plain.*   — C. K. Wilmoth

Though their pathway may lead through canyons of care and valleys of vexation, those who are guided by the Good Shepherd always find green pastures!
                                                   —G.W.

A DROP OF OIL

Be kindly affectioned one to another with brotherly love, in honor preferring one another. Romans 12:10

In a very old book, its pages yellowed with age, I found this story with a modern application: "Bang! Slam! Every time any one went in or out of the front door, they had to shut it with such force as to disturb the entire household. It made Grandma drop stitches in her knitting, awakened Junior from his nap, and gave Aunt Nellie a headache. Then Uncle Jim came to see us, and after hearing the door bang only twice he sprang to his feet saying, 'Fred, my boy, get your mother's oil can.' He applied a drop of lubrication to the catch and worked the door back and forth a few times. What a change! No longer was it necessary to slam the door; it now closed with ease. 'Always try oil,' my uncle said, 'it makes things work smoothly!' People as well as locks need oiling. And a good way to preserve peace and quietness is to *use the oil of kindness.*"

In our family relationships, in our church life, and at work, how many times situations are handled brusquely and forcibly. As a result, the whole "household" is disturbed. How much better to drop in the "oil of kindness." Many use a "sledge hammer" when they should be using the "oilcan." The next time you are faced with stubbornness in another member of your family, are upset by the inconsiderate action of a fellow worker, or are offended by some brother or sister in the Lord, remember the "oil of kindness." With a warm heart, and a sympathetic and understanding spirit, try the lubrication of Christian love. Thus, "in honor preferring one another," you will eliminate a lot of carnal "friction."

If things are not going smoothly today, why not try "a drop of oil"?

> *God, make me kind!*
> *So many hearts are needing*
> *The balm to stop the bleeding,*
> *That my kind words can bring.*
> *God, make me kind!*   —Duncan McNeil

If you are not very kind, you are not very holy!

HOW A PRINCE LEARNED HUMILITY

> *. . . learn of me; for I am meek and lowly in*
> *heart . . . .*   Matthew 11:29

Many years ago a prince in India—proud of the small munici-
pality he governed and convinced that he was "quite someone"—
exhibited a very rebellious attitude toward England. Eventually
he arranged a visit to that country hoping to pick up new ideas
to spark the smoldering rebellion of his people against the Crown.
Arriving in the great city of London, he entered a cab and ordered, "Drive me to the country!" The coachman drove through
street after street, passing thousands of houses, parks, and business establishments. Finally the sun reached its zenith and began
to set, but there were still more bustling avenues ahead. "Aren't
we near the country, yet?" asked the prince. "No, sir, we still
have a long way to go before you'll see any fields." As night fell
and the lights of the mighty city were lit, the visitor said in
humble amazement, "Drive me back!" He had come to realize
how great was the nation of England, and how small the little
rebellious section of India he represented. From that day forward
there was not a more humble servant of the Queen than that
prince.

As I read that story, I thought of how proud and rebellious
we often are, how impressed with our own importance. However,
if we will but "learn" of Christ and view the unlimited meekness
and lowliness of mind exhibited by Him, we too will see how
small and insignificant we really are. Frequently we think people
owe us more than they render of appreciation, understanding,
and praise; however, when we look at the sinless, compassionate,
self-sacrificing Savior who was spit upon, reviled, and crucified
(despite the fact that He was perfect in all His words, actions,
and attitudes), we fall upon our knees and say, "Lord, forgive
me for my pride and arrogance! Help me to *learn of Thee* that
I too may be 'meek and lowly in heart.' "

> Thou canst not serve the Master
> With stress on "I" and "me."
> Self-centered service never finds
> God's Spirit close to thee.   —Anon.

**Getting rid of the "self-life" is like peeling an onion: layer upon
layer — and a tearful process!**   —A. T. Pierson

CHILDREN OF THE KING

*Hath not God chosen the poor of this world to be rich
in faith and heirs of the kingdom . . . ?*   James 2:5

At prayer meeting last night during "testimony time," one of
the ladies related an experience she had in a supermarket. She
noticed that the woman at the cash register seemed excited and
elated. When she arrived at her station, this clerk blurted out,
"Wouldn't you like to touch me? I just shook hands with a
movie star!" Mentioning his name she continued, "He passed
through this very line a few minutes ago. Wouldn't you like to
touch my hand?" "No, thank you," the other replied, "but
wouldn't *you* like to touch *me?* I'm better than a movie star. *I'm
a child of the King!*" She went on to explain that she was one
of the "heirs of the kingdom of God" through faith in the Lord
Jesus Christ.

The world doesn't pay much attention to Christians. In fact,
those who really believe the Bible and talk about being "born-
again" are often snubbed. Yet, our relationship with God through
Christ sets us apart from all others. By faith in Him, we have
been born into the family of God. We are "heirs of God, and
joint heirs with Christ" (Rom. 8:17). Heaven is our real home.
We are just passing through this world while our mansions are
being prepared for our eternal habitation. "The cattle upon a
thousand hills" belong to our Father. United to Him, the Ruler
of the universe, we become true royalty.

When things look dark and the world mistreats you, take
heart, believer. The day is coming when your true identity will
be revealed at the ". . . manifestation of the sons of God" (Rom.
8:19). We may not amount to much in the eyes of men, but
God views us as His dear children and "heirs of the Kingdom"!

> *A tent or a cottage, why should I care?*
> *They're building a palace for me over There;*
> *Though exiled from Home, yet still I may sing:*
> *All glory to God, I'm a child of the King.* —H. E. Buell

No man is poor who is heir to all the riches of God!

DO A LITTLE "SOUL-STRETCHING"!

> *. . . do good, and lend, hoping for nothing again;*
> *and your reward shall be great.*   Luke 6:35

In the *Alabama Baptist,* R. L. Sharpe related this experience: "When I was just a lad, my father called me to go with him to old Mr. Trussel's blacksmith shop. He had left a rake and a hoe to be repaired, and when we got there they were fixed like new. Father handed him some money for the work, but Mr. Trussel refused to take it. 'No,' he said, 'there's no charge for that little job.' My father kept insisting, but I shall never forget that great man's reply. 'Ed,' he said, 'can't you let a Christian do something now and then — *just to stretch his soul?'* That short but effective sermon from the lips of that humble, lovable blacksmith set me to thinking. I since have found the great joy and quiet happiness which comes from doing little things for Jesus and in the process 'stretching my soul.' "

We live in such a selfish, materialistic world that we seem to expect pay for everything we do. As a result we are in danger of becoming shriveled up with greed and self-centeredness.

If you want to please the Savior, look for an opportunity today to help someone either materially or spiritually who cannot compensate you for your efforts. (See Luke 14:12-14.) It will stretch your soul and make you a bigger person and a better Christian. The Lord delights to have us aid the needy, helpless, and neglected, for He knows that we are not doing it to get something in return, but because we truly love Him and have His heart of compassion for the sick, the destitute, and the lost.

How long since you have "stretched your soul"?

> *Be unselfish, aid the needy,*
>   *Let your light shine for the Lord.*
> *"Stretch your soul" in helping others—*
>   *Heaven will bring you rich reward.*—H.G.B.

Live for thy neighbor if thou wouldst live for God!

LIVING WINSOMELY

Let your light so shine before men, that they may . . .
glorify your Father, who is in heaven.   Matthew 5:16

The early followers of Jesus were charged with breaking up homes, dishonoring their parents, lacking patriotism, practicing cannibalism, and engaging in gross immorality. It was true that Christians rejected the religious rituals of their pagan parents, that some family units were broken when young people chose to be driven from home rather than renounce their faith. Believers also refused to offer a pinch of incense to the Roman emperor and did not purchase images. But it was not accurate to say that they ate human flesh and drank blood at their communion service, or that they were immoral.

What were these Christians to do? Should they issue vehement denials? No! Peter, in our Scripture reading for today, exhorted them instead to look upon themselves as strangers unable to accept the standards of this world. They were to make their conduct among the unsaved so attractive and winsome that their lives would answer every charge made by their enemies. Do you know what happened? The behavior of the early believers was so pure and good that thousands of pagans were saved. Even those who hated the Gospel couldn't help but admire the way Christians lived. And when a period of intense persecution came almost two centuries later, Christians were accused of ignorance, superstition, and a lack of patriotism, but they were no longer denounced as immoral, cruel, or dishonest. If we who know Christ today would be lovely and winsome in our behavior, we too could make a greater impact upon the world about us. Let's try, and watch the Lord work!

Would you shine for Jesus 'mid the careless throng?
Imitate His graces as you pass along?
Make no weak surrender to the coarse and vile;
Keep yourselves from evil and your tongue from guile.—Anon.

In regard to Christian living—one example is worth a thousand arguments!

THE UNFINISHED WORK OF CHRIST

*Wherefore, he [Christ] is able also to save them to the
uttermost that come unto God by him, seeing he ever
liveth to make intercession for them.* Hebrews 7:25

Although we hear much of Christ's redemptive work which
was finished at Calvary, we hear little of His unfinished intercessory work which continues unabated! Yet it is a great and
comforting truth to know that even as Jesus prayed for Peter in
a time when he was experiencing severe temptation (Luke 22:
32), so our Lord now constantly intercedes on our behalf before
the Father's Throne. This work of the Savior will never be completed as long as we creatures of the dust are in need of help,
comfort, and blessing. R. M. McCheyne, much impressed with
this truth, remarked, "If I could hear Christ praying for me in
the next room, I would not fear a million enemies. Yet the distance makes no difference; *He is praying for me!"*

Recently when facing a personal crisis, I realized the truth of
these words in Hebrews 7 in a new and wonderful way. I asked
the dear Lord to pray and intercede in my behalf, for Satan
seemed to be seeking to "sift me" in his sieve (Luke 22:31). I
recognized the impotence of my own weak prayers and the need
of special grace. The very next day the problem of several months
was solved by the Lord's special intervention. Never before had
I so fully appreciated the high-priestly work of our risen Savior.

If there is a great problem in your life, Christian, and your
prayers seem of no avail, tell the Lord Jesus about it and *ask
Him to pray for you!* He will take your request and present it
to the Father — perfumed with the everlasting incense of His own
merits. Because of His wonderful intercessory work on your behalf, you too may experience the remarkable results which only
His all-powerful prayers can obtain.

> *In the hour of trial, Jesus, plead for me,*
> *Lest, by base denial, I depart from Thee;*
> *When Thou seest me waver, with a look recall;*
> *Nor for fear or favor suffer me to fall.*—J. Montgomery

It is the power of Christ's prayer which defeats Satan!

FAITH AND WORKS

. . . faith without works is dead.   James 2:20

In Hebrews 11:7 we are told that "By faith Noah, being warned of God of things not seen as yet . . . prepared an ark to the saving of his house. . . ." God had warned the ancient patriarch that a huge flood was coming, and He also instructed him to build an ark in which he and his family might escape this judgment. The fact that Noah did prepare such a ship in obedience to the Lord's command proved that he really believed God's warning about the coming catastrophe.

What would you have thought of Noah's faith, however, if he had said to the Lord, "I believe all that Thou hast told me about the coming flood. I am convinced that unless I get busy and prepare an ark I will perish with the rest of the ungodly" — but then, after having made such a profession of faith, he did nothing about it? What if he had gone home, sat down in his rocking chair, and from morning until night continued to pray, piously chanting over and over those same glowing words of faith, and yet had never made an attempt to lift so much as a finger to prepare the necessary ark? I say, what would you have thought of Noah's faith then? I think you will agree that it would have been the kind described by James when he writes of a "faith without works" which is *"dead."* It's much the same with us and our attitudes and reactions to the whole matter of salvation. (Now don't get me wrong. I know our works have nothing to do with *obtaining* salvation, but they should, as a matter of course, *follow* a genuine conversion experience.) Noah's preparation of the ark was an *exercise* of his *faith. It was a demonstration that he truly did believe!*

You may have made a *profession,* but do your works prove that you have a genuine *possession* of God's free salvation?

> *Old Noah, trusting in God's Word,*
> *Did build himself an ark,*
> *So when the flood of judgment came,*
> *By faith he did embark!*   —G. Woods

"Good works" is faith made visible!   —K. G. Bran

YOU REAP WHAT YOU SOW!

He that soweth iniquity shall reap vanity . . . .
                                                    Proverbs 22:8

The Bible is full of instruction concerning "sowing and reaping." Both the wicked and the righteous shall be rewarded in kind for their evil or good deeds (Prov. 11:18; 22:8). Not all of the results await God's final judgment, but some fruit will mature in this life, as the following illustrations will show.

In the early days of the settlement of America, a Frenchman persuaded some Indians to exchange fur for gun-powder, saying they would obtain a fine crop by sowing it in the ground. The Indians prepared a field, scattered the powder in furrows, and set a guard to watch it. Discovering that they had been cheated, they took revenge some time afterward when the partner of the deceiver visited the same tribe with a large stock of goods for trade. Each brave helped himself to such things as he pleased until all the items were gone. When the Frenchman demanded payment, the chief shrewdly commented that full justice would be done *as soon as the harvest of gunpowder should be gathered!* Seeing that he had reaped what he and his partner had sown, the man left hastily before the angry Indians might extract an even heavier punishment.

A Communist agitator rode into a city park one day and leaned his bicycle against a tree. Mounting a soapbox he proceeded to address the crowd, "If you want something," he shouted, "raid a shop and take it, and don't care what anybody says. If your wife hasn't got a coat, pick the best fur you see, and ignore the law." After finishing his speech, he was preparing to leave when suddenly he shouted, "Hey, *where's the bum who took my bike!*"

How true the words of Scripture, "They that plow iniquity and sow wickedness, reap the same."

> *When we come to the reaping time in life,*
> *And our harvest is full-grown,*
> *Will our hearts be glad, or spirits sad,*
> *As we view the things we've sown?*—M. V. Harris

The best flings in life aren't free!

PAINFUL PRUNING

> . . . *and every branch that beareth fruit, he*
> *purgeth it.*   John 15:2

The boxwoods in our yard had become large, unsightly, and lifeless-looking. Being totally uninstructed in the science of horticulture, we called the garden center for pointers. *"Prune them, cut them back,"* came the reply. The pruning shears had been used very little, and now too they were not employed in a professional manner. When the job was completed, that border of boxwoods looked as if they had had it! Leafless stubs stared at us. Had the pruning been too severe? Would foliage ever develop again? After some weeks, little green sprouts appeared, and soon full, healthy boxwoods adorned our walk.

Our Lord desires growth and fruitfulness in every believer. He cannot be pleased with unsightly spiritual stagnation and the pallor of arrested circulation. The Father is the "Vinedresser." He needs no instruction in the art of spiritual pruning and cleansing. He knows precisely what is required to bring the Christian to fruit-bearing. The process is not without pain. The "shears of the Word" and the sharp "arrows of affliction" are used skillfully in His hand for our correction. However, while "no chastening for the present seemeth to be joyous, but grievous; nevertheless, afterward it yieldeth the peaceable fruit of righteousness unto them who are exercised by it" (Heb. 12:11).

If perchance the sharp blade of the divine Gardener is being experienced in your life today, it is for your good and His glory. Jesus said, "In this is my Father glorified, that ye bear much fruit." Submit to His pruning; be obedient to His Word. "Afterwards" will come spiritual foliage and fruit.

> *The fruits are growing and flourishing*
> *At last in a lovely way,*
> *Since I through God's holy chastening*
> *Have learned how to watch and pray!* —Bosch

The pruning of sanctified affliction results in spiritual promotions.

"LIFT UP THE FALLEN"

*O Lord, I know that the way of man is not in him-
self; it is not in man that walketh to direct his steps.*
Jeremiah 10:23

Some years ago a Christian family befriended a 19-year-old
lad who had just been released from jail. Warmed by attention,
he soon trusted Christ in one of our church services. Through
him the terrible plight of the thousands of children who grew
up in the slums of our cities was vividly brought to mind. Young
as he was, he had already served time in prison, and his body
showed the physical repercussions of the dissolute life he had
lived. He mistrusted almost everyone. The grace of God, however, soon worked wonders. One day at the home of the family
who had befriended him, the birthday of one of their little girls
was celebrated. As the young man saw the joy and affection
manifested around the table, he burst into tears saying, "I never
knew that people could really love one another like that!" The
poor fellow had never enjoyed such consideration and attention,
for his own mother, a woman of the streets, apparently found
her children a nuisance. Her boys grew up like thousands of
others around them, unwanted and unloved.

Those of us who have been born in better circumstances should
not sit in harsh judgment upon such individuals, but should remind ourselves that there are many things over which we have
little or no control. In humble gratitude we should turn to God,
thank Him for His goodness, and acknowledge that we are in no
way worthy of such special favors. How appropriate the words,
"O Lord, I know that *the way of man is not in himself;* it is not
in man that walketh to direct his steps." Instead of taking pride
in our family, our health, our appearance, our personality, or our
intelligence, we should ask God to enable us to assist the less
fortunate. They need our prayers, our love, and our help!

**We who know the Lord should hold the lamp of happiness so
that its beams will fall upon the shadowed hearts of others
around us!** —E. Petterton

EAGER FOR HEAVEN?

For to me to live is Christ, and to die is gain.
Philippians 1:21

After preaching about Heaven one night, a certain minister put this question to his congregation, "How many want to go to Heaven? If you do, stand right where you are." Without any hesitation, everyone in the auditorium jumped to his feet. The preacher then said, "And how many of you want to go *right* now?" Stunned by the thought of such an immediate departure, they all quickly settled back into their seats. Evidently they were not quite as anxious for Heaven as they thought.

Are not many Christians just like that? They sing the hymn "Jesus May Come Today" with great enthusiasm, but would really prefer that His return were delayed long enough to allow the completion of some cherished plan. They talk about the wondrous and appealing beauty of their "Heavenly Home," while laboring for the things of this world as though they were going to be here forever. They claim to be eager to meet the Savior face to face, but they tremble at the thought of being ushered into His presence empty-handed, with unfinished business, unconfessed sins, and broken fellowship with other believers.

Do *you* want to go to Heaven? *Today?* May we so live that with joy we can daily anticipate that moment when the summons will come, and we shall be transported from time to eternity and into the realms of Glory. If we are truly eager for Heaven, we can with sincerity join the great apostle in saying, "We are . . . willing rather to be absent from the body, and to be present with the Lord" (2 Cor. 5:8).

Father, perfect our trust,
O give us faith to see
That death is now the door to life,
And shall but set us free!   —G.W.

It is impossible to have real joy in the hope of Heaven and still be deeply engrossed in the pleasures of earth.

THE LESSON OF THE JAPANESE DENTIST

. . . exercise thyself . . . unto godliness. 1 Timothy 4:7

A man, selling a new kind of liquid adhesive, displayed his merchandise along with a sign which read: "A box of this glue given free to anyone who can break these items apart." At the base of the poster were spools, pieces of wood, and other articles which had been cemented together. An Oriental gentleman stopped to look, pointed to a peg that had been inserted and glued into a two-inch-deep hole drilled in a small wooden block, and asked what the reward would be if he could pull it out. *"Pull it out!"* cried the man; "why, if you can do that, I'll not only give you a free box of glue, but ten dollars on top of it!" The dowel projected scarcely a quarter of an inch above the surface of the block, but the challenger was undismayed. Placing his left hand on the square of wood, he took the peg between the thumb and forefinger of his other hand, and removed it with apparent ease — although a portion of the wood block came along with it. The salesman gasped. "What kind of a strong man are you?" *"I'm just a Japanese dentist!"* replied the other with a smile. So saying, he pocketed his reward and walked away. The *London Telegraph,* which reported the incident, confirmed the fact that some Japanese dentists do use their fingers for forceps. Part of their dental training in the Orient consists of *strenuous exercises which develop an incredible amount of power in the hands.*

Whether in dentistry in Japan, or in the realm of the Christian life, it is constant application to the task and diligent *exercise* which brings results. The believer must give daily attention to prayer and the study of the Scriptures. He must frequently examine himself in regard to his spiritual walk, and put forth a zealous effort to grow in the grace of witnessing.

Let us heed Paul's admonition to "exercise" ourselves in these necessary endeavors, and we too will soon be doing incredible things for God in the "power of His might."

Exercise your FAITH, before the devil gets you to exercise your FAULTS!   **—H.G.B.**

ADVICE TO THE ANXIOUS

*Those things which ye have both learned, and received,
and heard, and seen in me, do.*   Philippians 4:9

One should never reject the advice and example of a truly
godly person. Paul, though a humble follower of Christ, urged
the Philippian Christians to listen to him and to emulate his conduct. You see, he was in prison when he wrote this letter, and
had experienced the peace of God that results when one casts his
care upon the Lord through "prayer and supplication with thanksgiving." He also knew the blessing that came to his own heart
when he meditated upon things that are true, honest, just, pure,
lovely, and of good report.

Are you a worrier? If you are, let me tell you something that
may add to your list of anxieties. Worry is a major factor in the
breakdown of personal health and may shorten your life! It is
also a sin to brood over your troubles, for you are implying that
the Lord is either unable or unwilling to meet your needs.

When worrisome thoughts cloud your mind, why not take
the tested and proven advice of the apostle Paul? Talk to the
Lord and trust Him to do what He knows is best for you. The
old adage, "The devil trembles when he sees the weakest Christian on his knees," is still true. Then after you have prayed,
proceed to empty your mind of your worries by setting your
thoughts upon "whatever things are true, . . . honest, . . . pure,
. . . lovely, . . . [and] of good report" (Phil. 4:8). This is the
kind of "positive thinking" that pleases the Lord, and He will
give peace, strength, joy, and victory to all who will obey Paul's
inspired injunction.

> *For all His children, God desires*
> *A life of trust, not flurry;*
> *His will for them each day is this:*
> *That they should trust, not worry!* —Anon.

**It is comforting to know that the Lord who guides us sees
tomorrow more clearly than we see yesterday!**

"REFRESHING BUT NOT FILLING"

That he would grant you . . . to be . . . filled with
all the fullness of God.   Ephesians 3:16, 19

I am told that the Pepsi-Cola Company once used a slogan which read, "Refreshing but not filling." This is what many seem to want regarding the things of the Lord. They desire just enough religion to solve their most weighty problems and keep their names on the church rolls, but not enough to actually change them and make a difference in their lives. They don't wish to be "filled with all the fullness of God" because of the demands imposed by such total dedication. They want just enough for-giveness to take away their guilt complex, but not enough to make them swallow their pride and forgive others. They gladly bear His name but not His reproach. They crave His blessings but not His yoke.

A young man seeking counsel said to his pastor, "What is the use of telling me to be filled with the Spirit? It would be futile, for I'm as full of cracks as that old wastebasket in the corner!" Silently praying for God's help in dealing with this distressed soul, the minister replied, "You say you are spiritually full of cracks. Well, brother, what if you are? If that basket were to be lowered into the sea, it would be filled and remain so! It would only lose its contents if it were lifted from the water. Young man, cracks or no cracks, *if you abide in Christ,* you will always be filled with His Spirit." It was a point well taken, and the seeking soul was led to a life of new holiness.

When you want to be *more than* "*refreshed*" and actually "hunger and thirst after righteousness," you will begin to study God's Word with renewed zeal and truly "*be filled.*"

Refining Fire, go through my heart,
 Illuminate my soul;
Scatter Thy life through every part,
 And sanctify the whole!   —Wesley

ATTACHMENT to Christ is the secret of holiness and results in DETACHMENT from the world!

SWIMMING LESSONS OR A SAVIOR?

For the Son of man is come to seek and to save that which was lost. Luke 19:10

If a man unable to swim fell into deep water and was crying out for help, what would you do? Throw him a book on *Five Easy Swimming Lessons*? Shout encouragement? How about jumping into the water and crying out, "Just look at me, brother! Follow my example! I'll teach you how to swim and save yourself!" You would do no such thing! This drowning man doesn't need swimming lessons. It's too late for that! What he needs is a savior, one who will come to him in his desperate state, reach down, lift him up, and deliver him from the clutches of death.

It's the same way with man's spiritual condition. The Bible says that "all have sinned" and that the "wages of sin is death." Everyone born into this world has fallen into sin, and in its clammy embrace is doomed to destruction. The only means of escape must be through a "Savior," one who stoops down in grace and delivers the needy soul from judgment. It is impossible for a man to learn to "save himself." Trying his best won't do, and following the example of others is of no avail. What he needs is a Savior. How thankful we should be then that "the Son of man is come to seek and to save that which was lost" (Luke 19:10). He delivers all who trust Him for their salvation. Even as a drowning person must relax and cease his struggling in the arms of his rescuer, we must do the same with this Savior, the Lord Jesus Christ. Someone has aptly expressed it in this way, "Let go and let God." "Believe on the Lord Jesus Christ, and thou shalt be saved" (Acts 16:31).

I was sinking deep in sin, far from the peaceful shore,
Very deeply stained within, sinking to rise no more;
But the Master of the sea heard my despairing cry,
From the waters lifted me — now safe am I. —Rowe

The God who was wise enough to make a perfect man is loving enough to rescue a fallen one.

July 22

IN DEBT

I am debtor both to the Greeks and to the barbarians.
                                        Romans 1:14

A veteran missionary to the Piro Indians of Peru was being transferred to a new field. We had accompanied her on a final visit and were about to return to our base camp. I recall her wistful look as those Indian believers waved their farewells, and our litle boat headed across the lake. Because she had translated the New Testament into the native language, many Piros had received the Savior. She told me that when she had informed them she was being sent to Colombia, they had replied, "We will permit you to go because *you no longer owe us;* for now we are full, and they are hungry as we used to be." One of God's servants had thus discharged her obligation and paid her debt to some formerly unevangelized people.

The debt which the apostle Paul needed to pay, *to preach the Gospel to others,* was not just his alone. *Every Christian* is a debtor to a world that needs to hear the good news that Jesus saves. As believers we have only to ponder the marvel of God's grace in drawing us to himself to know that it was not alone for *our* sake. There was nothing in us that deserved the opportunity to hear and believe the Word. What did we have to do with choosing our advantageous place of birth where it was possible for us to receive the Gospel? Because we are the recipients of His grace, however, we now owe others the same privilege. In our homes, in our neighborhoods, and around the world are people who are "hungry" for the Bread of Life. We are debtors to them! Let us not be guilty of spiritual dishonesty by failing to fulfill our responsibilities!

> *Out in the highways and byways of life,*
>   *Many are weary and sad;*
> *Carry the sunshine where darkness is rife,*
>   *Making the sorrowing glad.*   — Wilson

What a responsibility to have a reprieve for men under condemnation, and not to deliver it!

O.H.M.S.

*And whatever ye do, do it heartily, as to the Lord,
and not unto men.*
Colossians 3:23

I am told that the letters O.H.M.S. imprinted on the note
paper and envelopes of the British government mean: "On Her
[or His] Majesty's Service!" So, too, every child of the heavenly
Ruler should remember that he likewise bears a similar "seal"
(2 Cor. 1:22; Eph. 4:30) which marks him as a special ambassador of Christ to a needy world (2 Cor. 5:20). All he touches
must therefore summon up his best and most consecrated efforts,
for truly, he too is ever "On His Majesty's Service"! The faithfulness God requires in *whatever we do* allows no exceptions.
The Lord knows that so-called "little things" often lead to mighty
consequences, and so they demand our complete dedication and
unstinted attention. When we thus begin to act — imbuing every
effort with zeal, and doing all as "to the Lord, and not unto
men" — life becomes a meaningful and glorious adventure. Colossians 3:23 then beautifies all our actions and makes each day
a blessed investment in consecration — an investment that will
reap an abundant and eternal reward.

Many years ago the *Moody Monthly* told how a committee
called on Enrico Caruso at the zenith of his operatic fame to ask
if he would sing at a concert for the benefit of the men of the
armed forces. The chairman of the committee hastily added, "Of
course, Mr. Caruso, as this is a charity affair, we would not expect you to do your best. Your name will draw the crowd and
you can merely sing some song requiring little of your strength
or skill." Caruso drew himself up to his full height as he replied
sternly, *"Caruso never does less than his best!"* Regrettably, too
many Christians give God the fag ends of their time and the
dregs of their energy, forgetting that they are marked with the
seal: "O.H.M.S." How shamefaced they will be when they have
to stand someday at the judgment seat of Christ.

Oh, Christian, put your heart and full energy into every activity of life, remembering at all times that *you are "On His
Majesty's Service!"*

**In God's eyes it is a GREAT THING to do a LITTLE THING
well!**

THE HONEST MIRROR

. . . for by the law is the knowledge of sin.
Romans 3:20

A woman was getting ready for church when suddenly she dashed into the living room, gazed at her reflection and said, "I looked just awful in that bedroom mirror, but I look better in this one!" The difference may have been due to the quality of the glass or the availability of light. However, the lady should not have been so concerned about which mirror made her appear better *to herself,* but which one actually gave *an honest picture.*

Many people react this way concerning their true spiritual condition. They don't like what they see in the mirror of God's Word. The image of man's true nature, revealed in Romans 3, is utterly revolting to them. They refuse to believe that verse 10 is true: "There is none righteous, no, not one." So they look about for other "mirrors" which will make them "look" better. They seek churches which never mention man's depravity but emphasize only his dignity. They prefer preachers who say things to make them feel good. What they need, however, is a good look at themselves as God sees them. It may hurt their pride to know they have sinned and "come short of the glory of God," yet, it is this true introspective look which will turn them to the Savior and His righteousness.

On the other hand, the mirror of the Word is flattering for the true believer. For when a person trusts the Lord Jesus, he is justified and clothed in the very righteousness of God Himself (Rom. 5:1). In Christ he is without flaw and accounted blameless.

Be sure you use an honest "mirror" when you judge your spiritual condition — *one which tells you the truth!*

> *Holy Bible, Book Divine,*
> *Precious Treasure, Thou art mine;*
> *Mine to tell me whence I came,*
> *Mine to teach what I am.* — John Burton

The Bible is God's mirror which shows man as he is—not as he thinks he is!

"IRON SAINTS"

. . . Joseph, who was sold for a servant, whose feet they hurt with fetters; he was laid in iron. Psalm 105:17, 18

The last part of Psalm 105:18 might better be rendered, "His soul entered into iron," or, as we would phrase it, *"Iron entered into his soul!"* As a boy, Joseph tended to softness. He was full of dreams concerning his foreshadowed greatness. There may have been even a touch of pride in his makeup, for his attitude often upset his brothers. A "starry-eyed idealist," he seemed to lack the strength and force of character needed to rule. His imprisonment, however, appears to have changed him. From that time forth he exhibited a wisdom, modesty, courage, and manly resolution that never failed him. He began to act like a born ruler of men. He carried Egypt through the stress of a great famine without a symptom of revolt. He held his own with the proudest aristocracy of that time, while promoting the most radical changes. He learned to trust God completely and wait. Surely "iron had entered into his soul."

Friends, this is what adversity, properly received, can also do for us. *God wants "iron saints"* — those who have learned patience because the binding fetters of pain have restrained their too eager feet. The Lord is looking for those who have been betrayed by their dearest friends, and yet have not soured under the experience. Yes, He delights to use those who have grown in the dark prison of trial and the servitude of disappointment and have emerged triumphant by the power of grace! God knows there is no other way of imparting character and saintly attitudes, except by the uncomfortable "mining" process of pain, and the refining furnace of life's "hard knocks."

Bear your burdens triumphantly and patiently, Christian; it is God's chosen way of preparing you for greater usefulness by infusing "iron" into your soul.

> *Afflictions, though they seem severe,*
> *Are oft in kindness sent;*
> *They fit us for God's service here,*
> *And are for blessings meant!* —Anon.

Extraordinary afflictions are not always a corrective for sin, but frequently the testing of extraordinary graces!—Leighton

A LIFTER

Bear ye one another's burdens, and so fulfill the law
of Christ.   Galatians 6:2

A man had just written a very harsh letter to one who had
injured him. The mailbox into which he was going to drop the
letter had the instructions on the trap "Lift up." As he paused
to read it, those words jolted him. The Spirit of God convinced
him that the letter he was depositing certainly would not *"lift
up'"* anybody, but it would have been more appropriate if the
sign had read "Pull down."

No doubt you can think right now of many Christians who
are going through trial and are carrying heavy burdens. Perhaps
someone near and dear to you is weighed down. Are you a
"lifter"? Paul said if we are to fulfill Christ's law, the law of
love, we must get under the load and assist them.

We have a friend who is confined to her bed in a convalescent
home. Much of her day is occupied in "lifting" others. Between
times of prayer for those in need, she uses the telephone to call
someone who would welcome a word of cheer. She also sends
many cards of sympathy, encouragement, and happy greetings.

The Word of God reminds us that the Body of Christ is made
up of particular members; and that these "members should have
. . . *care one for another*" (1 Cor. 12:25) and make it a point
to "lift up." It should not be drudgery but rather a blessed privilege to "bear one another's burdens." Instead of engaging in that
which adds to the load others carry, we must participate in that
spiritual comradeship which lightens and lifts the weight of
trouble and woe. How about it, *will you be a lifter?*

> *Help us to help each other, Lord,*
> *Each other's burden bear;*
> *Let each his friendly aid afford,*
> *And feel his brother's care.* —Lloyd

Your own burdens lighten if you lift others' burdens!

OF SIN AND THE SEA

*. . . thou wilt cast all their sins into the depths of
the sea.*   Micah 7:19

This glorious promise is addressed not only to Israel, but to
all who seek forgiveness through the atoning work and Person
of the Lord Jesus Christ. D. L. Moody used to say, "There are
two ways of covering sin: man's way, and the Lord's way. If *you*
seek to hide them, they will have a resurrection sometime; but
let *God* cover them, and neither the devil nor man will be able
to find them again." Someone has said, "Thank the Lord that
He promises to cast them into the sea, and not a river; for a
river might sometime dry up, but the depths of the sea cannot."

A woman who was much troubled about her sin met her
minister as she was walking along the seashore. After they had
conversed for a few moments, and he saw how troubled she was,
he suggested that they sit down on the beach so that they could
talk about her soul. As they conversed, she began to build a
little fortress of the wet sand. With tears trickling down her face
she finally said to him, "Do you see the innumerable grains that
make up this castle? They are like my sins — too many to be
counted. Oh, how wretched I am! How can one such as I ever
be saved?" Knowing that the tide would soon be coming in, the
preacher suggested, "Leave your building of sand there for a few
more minutes, and let's move back a little." As the waves crept
up the beach, the undertow quickly lapped up her frail tower
of sand and washed it down into its foaming depths. "Look!"
said the minister, "your castle is gone, never to be seen again."
"Oh, I see now what you mean: the blood of Christ will likewise
wash all my sins away, casting them forever out of His sight in
the depths of the sea." From that hour she trusted the Savior
fully.

Have you come to Jesus for the cleansing tide? Then do not
torture yourself any longer by remembering sins which God has
forgiven and *forgotten!*

> *In the deep, silent depths, far away from the shore,*
> *Where they never may rise to trouble thee more,*
> *I have buried them there where no mortal may see:*
> *I have cast all thy sins in the depths of the sea.* —Anon.

**God pardons like a mother who kisses the offense into ever-
lasting forgetfulness!**
                                    —H. W. Beecher

THE LIVING THIEF

. . . ye are not your own.   1 Corinthians 6:19

A minister of the Gospel was trying to impress upon a certain man his obligation to convince him of his responsibility to be obedient to the Word of God. When asked if he had ever been baptized, the man replied, "No sir, I haven't! But why should I? The dying thief was never baptized and he went to Heaven!" When the preacher urged him to be more faithful in church attendance, the other answered, "Why should I? The dying thief didn't go to church, and he was saved!" Finally the man's pastor spoke to him about the matter of giving and his duty to support the work of the local assembly with his financial gifts. To that the man responded, "That's not necessary. The dying thief went to Heaven, and he never gave one cent to missions or anything like that!" Turning away, the man of God said with disgust in his voice, "Mister, the only difference I can see between you and the thief on the cross is this: He was a *dying* thief, and you're a *living* one!"

"Will a man rob God?" writes the prophet Malachi. "Yet ye have robbed me. But ye say, How have we robbed thee? In tithes and offerings. Ye are cursed with a curse; for ye have robbed me . . ." (Mal. 3:8, 9). Not only does a believer rob God when he fails to give financial assistance "as God hath prospered him" (1 Cor. 16:2), but also when he holds back of his time, talents, love, and devotion. Therefore Paul reminds us, ". . . ye are not your own . . . ye are bought with a price; therefore, glorify God in your *body and* in your *spirit,* which are God's" (1 Cor. 6: 19, 20). Let us then withhold nothing. Rather, as the Bible says, we should "present [our] bodies a living sacrifice . . . unto God" (Rom. 12:1). May it be said of us, as it was of the Macedonian Christians, "They first gave themselves to the Lord," so that "the abundance of their joy and their deep poverty abounded unto the riches of their liberality" (2 Cor. 8:2, 5).

> *What do I owe? Nay, Lord—what do I not?*
> *All that I am, all that I've got;*
> *All that I am, and that how small a thing,*
> *Compared with all Thy goodly fostering!*—J. Oxenham

God looks not to the quantity of the gift but to the quality of the giver!

THE CURE FOR ATHEISM

If any man will do his will, he shall know of the doctrine, whether it be of God . . . . John 7:17

Some years ago a very popular teacher at Yale expressed atheistic ideas on some points, and agnostic views on others. During a special series of meeting at the college a visiting preacher engaged the brilliant professor in conversation. "Doctor," he said, "if the things I have been preaching are true, and if Christ really forgives men who trust Him, wouldn't you like to know and experience this reality, seeing the peace and joy it has given to so many?" After a thoughtful pause the professor answered, "Yes, I believe I would." "Well, you can come to a certain knowledge of God if you will be sincere and honest with yourself and the Lord. Simply accept the challenge Christ offered in John 7:17, 'If any man *will do his will*, he shall *know* of the doctrine, whether it be of God.'" "But," said the learned Doctor, "I wouldn't know where to begin. I don't even know if there is such a Being as God." "Start like this, " said the preacher; "pray, 'Oh, God—if there is such a Being—give me light. I promise to follow such light wherever it leads.' If you do that, Professor, you will find God!" Three years later that same man of learning stood in the chapel before all the students of Yale and said, "I have long ridiculed preachers and churches, but I have made a discovery that they were in the light, and I was in the dark. I have put God to the test. I know that Christ is my Savior. By His grace He shall be my Friend, and I will be His disciple forever!"

Doubter, unbeliever, I challenge you to follow this professor's example. Read a portion from the Gospels and a few verses from the Psalms every day for the next few weeks with an open mind and a willing heart, and see if God doesn't likewise speak to your soul!

> Come ye sinners, poor and needy,
>   Weak and wounded, sick and sore;
> Jesus ready stands to save you,
>   Full of pity, love, and power;
> He is able, He is able,
>   He is willing, doubt no more. —J. Hart

Honest doubt, if properly handled, can become the vestibule of faith!

TESTED AND TRUE

> *. . . be it known unto thee, O king, that we will*
> *not serve thy gods . . . .*   Daniel 3:18

When doctors perform surgery, the attending nurse must keep careful tab of the number of hemostats and sponges used, so that an incision is not closed until each item has been removed. A young nurse on her first day with this duty told the surgeon he had used twelve sponges, but she could account for only eleven. The doctor curtly announced that he had removed them all. The young woman insisted that one was missing, but the doctor grimly declared he would proceed with the suturing. The nurse, her eyes blazing, said, "You can't do that! Think of the patient!" The doctor smiled and, lifting his foot, showed the nurse the twelfth sponge which he had deliberately dropped to the floor. "You'll do!" he said. *He had been testing her to see if she had the courage and integrity to carry out the duties of her position!*

Daniel's three friends were also tested by King Nebuchadnezzar's evil edict. They knew that their refusal to worship the image of gold might result in their death. However, they never wavered but proved they were true to God by standing firm in the face of the enemy's threats.

The Lord still permits trials and temptations to enter the lives of his children. The challenge may come as an invitation to gratify the lusts of the flesh, or as a series of disheartening circumstances. Whatever form it assumes, you must not yield, or you will experience spiritual defeat. However, overcoming the temptation will strengthen you and enable you to reach a new plateau in your Christian life.

> *Yield not to temptation, for yielding is sin,*
> *Each vict'ry will help you some other to win;*
> *Fight manfully onward, dark passions subdue,*
> *Look ever to Jesus, He will carry you through.*
>   —H. R. Palmer

A gem cannot be polished without friction, nor a man perfected without trial!

THEY CALLED ME THEIR "CANARY"

Now will I sing . . . a song of my beloved . . . .
                                        Isaiah 5:1

Known in his hometown as "that boy soprano," he began singing hymns at the tender age of two. Because his God-fearing parents filled their home with music, he soon committed to memory scores of sacred songs. Then disease laid its hand upon him and he wasted away to just "skin and bones." At night the pain was excruciating, but during the day it lessened, and so for hours at a time he would cheer himself by singing comforting gospel hymns. He knew that Jesus was his Savior, and early loved the things of the Lord. His devoted parents sought out the best doctors and surgeons in a vain attempt to bring health to their bedfast youngster. At last, with death apparently fast approaching, they had to take their only son to the hospital. Lonely and homesick, the seven-year-old boy began to warble hymns of praise to keep up his courage. He didn't know patients were supposed to be quiet in the wards. Nurses and doctors soon surrounded him, amazed to see this "little fellow who was going to die" singing so cheerily. They didn't have the heart to tell him this was not permitted—besides, *he wouldn't be here long anyway!* One doctor with a tear in his eye exclaimed, "Well, my boy, *you're quite a canary!*" The name stuck, and soon patients, doctors, and nurses from the various floors began to visit his ward, asking him to sing their favorite hymn. A thoughtful person placed a metal coin bank near his bed; as a result, the requests for a song were followed by small contributions. The little "canary" had no idea of the value of money — he just loved to sing — but in three weeks he had collected quite a sum. God stepped in and in a marvelous way restored his health sufficiently to allow him to return to his bed at home. His thankful parents were amazed to find that enough had been contributed to pay overdue medical expenses! A baritone now, and quite husky, no one looking at me today would ever suspect that I, Henry Bosch, was that "canary"!

Through all life's turmoil and its strife,
I hear God's music ringing;
It finds an echo in my soul—
How can I keep from singing?—R. Lowry, alt.

The truest expression of Christianity is not a sigh, but a song!

"LOONS" OR "EAGLES"?

. . . be filled with the Spirit.   Ephesians 5:18

When I was a lad, my father was my "authority" on the world of nature. One day as we were talking about those birds from which we get the expression "crazy as a loon," he mentioned that without any wind blowing it was almost impossible for them to take off and fly. I took his word for it, but it didn't seem to make sense to me until one evening some time later when my brother and I were out fishing. Not a breeze was stirring, and the surface of the small lake was like glass. The quietness of the moment was suddenly broken by the loud flapping of wings. Evidently we had scared "Mr. Loon," and he decided to get out of there. Yet, despite his heroic effort, he just skimmed along the surface of the water unable to gain altitude. Reaching the other side of the lake, he still wasn't high enough to clear the trees, and, executing a fancy turn, he came back toward us still flapping his wings with all his might. We held our breath as he reached the opposite shore, barely missed the treetops, and disappeared from view. He had made it — but what a struggle! Recalling that experience, the thought came to me: what a contrast there is between that struggling loon and the majestic eagle which ascends high in the heavens with wings outstretched, gliding effortlessly to new and thrilling heights. The flapping loon and the soaring eagle portray two kinds of Christians. There are some dear souls who seem to be always "flapping" without making much headway, while others can truthfully and joyfully sing with the hymn writer, "New heights I'm gaining every day." The latter are those who have learned to wait upon the Lord, have renewed their strength, and hence "mount up with wings like eagles" (Isa. 40:31).

Do we have a Spirit-filled life? Do we rest upon the Lord and let Him work *through* us? I wonder, when others see us, are they reminded of flapping loons or soaring eagles?

> *I want to scale the utmost height,*
> *And catch a gleam of Glory bright;*
> *Still praying as I onward bound,*
> *"Lord, lead me on to higher ground!"*
> ——J. Oatman, Jr., alt.

Resting upon the "wind" of the Spirit, one may soar to heights unattainable by "flapping" the "wings of human endeavor."

"FILLED WITH THE SPIRIT"

*. . . we . . . are changed . . . from glory to glory,
even as by the Spirit of the Lord.* 2 Corinthians 3:18

There are many splendid goals which could be reached by
Christians if they would cease their frantic self-efforts and just
let the Holy Spirit fill and control their lives. Only thus can
they go "from glory to glory."

S. L. Brengle once said, "If you ask how the Holy Spirit can
dwell within us and work through us without destroying in the
process our personality, I cannot tell. However, it is true. How
can an electric current transform and fill a dead wire and make
it into a live one, which you dare not touch? How can a mag-
netic current fill a piece of steel and transform it into a mighty
magnet which by its force can raise tons of iron as easily as a
child lifts a feather? How can a flame engulf a piece of iron
until its very appearance is that of fire, and turn it into a fire-
brand? I cannot tell you. Yet, what fire and electricity and mag-
netism do in iron and steel so the Holy Spirit operates in those
who trust in Jesus and follow Him completely. He indwells
. . . them until they are alive with the life of God Himself."

C. I. Scofield once visited an asylum in Staunton, Virginia.
The superintendent pointed out a young man who seemed to be
the picture of health. He had a clear complexion and a powerful frame. Scofield asked, "Wouldn't that man be very difficult
to manage if he became violent?" "Yes," said the superintendent,
"but he never exerts his power. *His delusion is that he has no
strength!* He is always asking for medicine and complaining of
weakness." Scofield thought to himself, "How many in the
Church are like that. Divinely gifted with the indwelling power
of the Holy Spirit, they lack the faith, knowledge, and consecration to use it. People are always praying for power. There is
power enough. What they need is the willingness to be used
in any humble position, and the faith to exercise the strength God
has given."

*Lord, fill us with Thy Spirit's might,
That we may live as in Thy sight,
On all Thy children lay Thy hand,
That they may live as Thou hast planned.*
—A. M. Lloyd

The human spirit FAILS unless the Holy Spirit FILLS!

SEND ME A MAN WHO READS!

*. . . and he shall read therein all the days of his
life, that he may learn to fear the Lord his God . . . .*
Deuteronomy 17:19

Recently the International Paper Company ran an ad which read in part as follows: "We asked 100 company officers, 'How many magazines, books, and newspapers have you read in the past week?' The total of their answers: magazines, 338; books, 53; newspapers, 1,490. Then we asked 100 men in the same age group whose salaries had never reached $7,500 a year: 229 magazines for them, and 28 books — about a quarter of a book each. The conclusion is as clear as print: *Men who read more achieve more!*" Even if their income had failed to rise, their interests had been stretched to new dimensions!

Yes, "send me a man who *reads*" — and especially one who rates the Bible as the most treasured Book in his library. Secular volumes are valuable, but how sadly lacking is the person who neglects the world's greatest Book — the one that helps us in this life and prepares us for the next.

It is said of Charles Haddon Spurgeon that one Sunday when the time for reading Scripture came, he left the Bible closed. "Some have found fault with me," he said, "contending that I'm too old-fashioned. I am always quoting the Bible and do not say enough about science. Well, there's a poor widow here who has lost her only son. She wants to know if she will ever see him again. Let's turn to science for the answer: Will she see him? Where is he? Does death end all?" There was a long pause. "We are waiting for an answer," he said. "This woman is anxious." Another long pause. "Nothing to say? *Then we'll turn to the Book!*" Spurgeon clinched his point by reading the wonderful promises concerning Heaven and eternal life.

Are you a man who reads? Do you include the most important of all Books? I hope so!

Oh, open your heart to His precious Word;
Drink deeply its treasures rare.
Your soul will be cleansed and your life transformed,
By meeting the Savior there!   —G. R.

In all literature there is nothing that compares with the Bible!
—John Milton

PARABLE OF THE DUTCH ROSE

. . . to be conformed to the image of his Son . . . .
Romans 8:29

I was intrigued when I found how the Dutch cultivate new varieties of roses. I am told they will plant an inferior one close to a lovely bloom of superior quality. Then they carefully watch the undesirable plant, and when the anthers on the stamens develop they remove them to prevent any form of self-pollination. The object of placing the poor variety of flower so close to the beautiful rose is to have the golden dust from the stamens of the good one fall upon the deprived buds of the other. Gradually the inferior rose, thus treated, takes on the characteristics of the life, shape, and color of its companion. Dr. A. S. Gumbart saw in all of this a lovely spiritual parable. Said he, "This is indeed a beautiful illustration of the blessing that comes to the soul of him who knows the companionship of Jesus. If our lives are pollinized, as it were, by His righteousness; if His life-transforming truth is received into the heart, and the 'self' is sacrificed to make room for the in-coming of His superior life, gradually the unlovely one loses its own inferior characteristics and develops a likeness to the blest life of Him who is 'altogether lovely.'"

Are you living close to the Savior so that His compassion, His love, and His righteousness are increasingly permeating your life? Is communion with God making you more conformable to the image of His dear Son?

To make room for God's Spirit to work His wonder of grace in your life, the "self-pollinating anthers of your own willful ego" must be pinched off and destroyed. Yes, *the self-life must go if the Christ-life is to prevail!*

> *More like the Master I would live and grow;*
> *More of His love to others I would show;*
> *More self-denial, like His in Galilee,*
> *More like the Master I long to ever be.*
> —Charles Gabriel

If we want an increase of Christ, there must be a decrease of self!

LESSONS FROM THE HEART

*Keep thy heart with all diligence; for out of it are
the issues of life.*   Proverbs 4:23

A good Christian friend in Monrovia, Liberia, recently related
to me some of the unique expressions of certain non-English
speaking tribes in his area. For example, in speaking of *conversion,* they would declare that a person "turned his heart." Instead of saying an individual is *patient,* they express it: "He put his
foot on his heart." It is interesting to note how their picturesque
speech corresponds to the true Scriptural meaning. Acts 15:3,
for instance, mentions "the *conversion* of the Gentiles," and the
term literally means: "to turn to," or "to turn around." That is
also what those who became Christians in Thessalonica did: they
"turned to God from idols" (1 Thess. 1:9). How fitting then
that the Africans should say that conversion is *"a turning of the
heart."* Note, too, that Ecclesiasties 7:8 tells us: ". . . the *patient* in spirit is better than the proud in spirit." The word "patient" is basically the same term as that translated *"slow"* in
Proverbs 14:29, "He that is *slow* to wrath is of great understanding: but he that is hasty of spirit exalteth folly." When aroused
to become angry, he who is wise will be patient, and *slow* to
lose his temper. Once again the African correctly says, "He put
his foot on his heart."

To express the fact that one is *disappointed,* they say: "His
heart fell down." *Satisfaction* is expressed in this way: "His heart
is set on fire."

All of these things are related to the core of man's being, and
rightly so, for as the Bible says, "out of it [the heart] are the
issues of life." The first step in the direction of God is to have
it *"turned around,"* the second is to *wait patiently on Him* for
guidance. If we have done this, our heart will never "fall down"
(be disappointed), but will rather experience blessed and holy
satisfaction — or, as the African says: "It will be *set on fire!"*
Indeed, these four native expressions aptly point out the only
way to peace and true happiness.

Hardening of the heart ages people more quickly than hardening of the arteries!

Read Acts 6:8-15

August 6

GLOWING FACES

*. . . when Moses came down from Mount Sinai . . .
the skin of his face shone . . . .* Exodus 34:29

The late G. Campbell Morgan once told of a factory girl who, after she was saved, simply radiated Christian joy. One day while waiting for a train at York station she slowly walked up and down the platform to pass the time. A highly cultured lady, sitting nearby, observed her closely. Finally, impressed by her sweet face, she called to her, "Excuse me, Miss, but what makes you so happy?" The girl replied, "Was I looking happy? I didn't know it showed, but I certainly am. I'll be glad to tell you why!" She then witnessed to the woman concerning the wonders of salvation and the joy it brings to the heart, and eventually led her to a personal acceptance of Jesus Christ.

This girl wasn't *trying* to look happy. Her face just naturally reflected the joy of her soul. Moses also did not know his skin was shining with a celestial glow when he came down from the Mount. It glistened because he had been in close touch with God. The same was true of Stephen the day he laid down his life to become the first martyr of the Christian church (Acts 6:15). His face lit up with angelic glory because of his close relationship to Jesus Christ.

I am not much impressed when I see someone deliberately turn on a "Pepsodent smile" and assume a "happy" attitude in a Christian meeting. Unsaved people in the entertainment world have the ability "to put on a happy face," even when their hearts are full of pain and sorrow. What we need is such a glorious consciousness of the indwelling presence of the Lord that we will glow with spiritual health like Moses who "wist not that the skin of his face shone." This will give us a song in the darkest night, and joy in the midst of life's deepest trials. It will make us living demonstrations of the transforming power of the Savior.

> You don't have to tell how you live each day,
> You don't have to say if you work or pray,
> A tried, true barometer serves in its place;
> However you live, it will show in your face! —Anon.

The light of God's Son in your heart will put His sunshine on your face!
—Bosch

SHOOTING AT THE MOON!

But the word of the Lord endureth forever . . . .
1 Peter 1:25

Recently someone sent me the story of a lad who was born without all his mental faculties. For some reason he developed a violent dislike for the moon. It became such an obsession with him that he went about muttering: "I'll kill that moon! I'll shoot that moon! See if I don't!" To carry out his threats he got hold of a blunderbuss — a clumsy, old-fashioned gun — which makes plenty of noise and smoke, but does little else, and he hid it until the first night the full moon shone brightly in a cloudless sky. Then, removing the gun from its hiding place, he took aim and fired. Hearing a noise the neighbors rushed out to find the boy dancing with delight and shouting at the top of his voice, "I've killed the moon! I've killed the moon!" Sure enough, at that moment it wasn't visible, for the dense smoke of the blunderbuss hid it. But when the air cleared, the moon was seen shining as calmly and clearly as ever before — far beyond the reach of any fool's blunderbuss. Is not this a picture of what men are doing who try to destroy the Bible? When they have sent a loud report against it, and made smoke sufficient to hide it for a minute, they say, "We've discredited the Bible! We've destroyed the Bible!" But they, like that ignorant boy, soon find that they are mistaken, and that the old Lamp is still shining as brightly as ever to "give light to them that sit in darkness," and to guide men "into the way of peace" (Luke 1:79).

Dr. R. D. Wilson of Princeton Seminary decided years ago to answer the question: "Is the higher criticism scholarly?" After more than four decades of intensive scientific research he declared: "I have come now to the conviction that no man knows enough to assail the truthfulness of the Old Testament. Whenever there is sufficient documentary evidence to make an investigation, the statements of the Bible, in the original text, have stood the test!"

The Bible stands like a mountain tow'ring
Far above the works of men;
Its truth by none ever was refuted,
And destroy it they never can! — H. Lillenas

The Bible is the Word of Life! I beg that you will read it and find this out for yourself!   **—Woodrow Wilson**

"DUMB" CHRISTIANS

*. . . thou shalt be dumb . . . because thou believest
not my words . . .*   Luke 1:20

Zacharias and his wife Elisabeth, having reached a "ripe old
age," had long ago given up hope of being blessed with children.
One day, however, an angel of the Lord appeared to Zacharias as
he was going about his duties in the Temple. Seeing this heavenly messenger, Zacharias was greatly troubled. "But the angel said
unto him, Fear not, Zacharias; for thy prayer is heard; and thy
wife, Elisabeth, shall bear thee a son, and thou shalt call his name
John" (Luke 1:13). This news seemed too good to be true, so
Zacharias went on to ask for further proof. "Whereby shall I
know this?" he inquired. The angel's word should have been
sufficient, yet he wanted a sign. It was given to him, but it involved something for which he had not bargained. The angel
said, ". . . behold, *thou shalt be dumb,* and not able to speak . . .
because thou believest not my words. . . ." And so Zacharias
became speechless because of his unbelief! What a picture of
many Christians today who are often silent because of the weakness of their faith!

Do we *really* believe the Bible when it says that ". . . the
Lord Jesus shall be revealed from heaven with his mighty angels.
In flaming fire taking vengeance on them that know not God . . ."
(2 Thess. 1:7, 8)? Do we *really* believe the Scripture which declares that ". . . whosoever was not found written in the book of
life was cast into the lake of fire" (Rev. 20:15)? If we actually
do, how then can we refrain from warning sinners of the judgment to come? When we fully believe God's Word, it will so
grip our hearts that we will be moved with compassion for those
who are lost in sin. Because of the urgency of the message we
will not be able to remain silent.

How many there are today to whom the Lord might well say,
even as did the angel to Zacharias, ". . . behold, thou shalt be
dumb . . . because thou believest not my words. . . ."

> *White are the fields for the harvest,*
> *Workers are all too few;*
> *Souls are awaiting the message.*
> *Can God depend on you?*   —Anon.

**The "guess-so" Christians are never found among the soul-
winners!**

OPEN YOUR MOUTH!

Then Peter opened his mouth, and said, Of a truth
I perceive that God is no respecter of persons.
Acts 10:34

Have you ever found yourself doing something you thought
you never would? I have. I know people who have said, "I'll
never give up the pleasures of sin and become a Christian." But
they did! Praise God!

Peter never expected to preach the Gospel to the heathen. He
felt that they were outside the scope of God's redemptive love,
and most likely found it difficult to develop a keen love for Roman soldiers who held the Jews in captivity. However, God had
been working. He had prepared both Peter, and Cornelius the
Centurion, for this special occasion recorded in Acts 10; and so
the Apostle "opened his mouth" to present God's message.

As children we used to say, "Sticks and stones may break my
bones, but words will never hurt me." We wanted to give the
impression that unkind expressions or insults did not really give
pain; but down deep in our hearts we knew better. Words can
hurt, harm, yes, actually destroy a person. God speaks to human
hearts through words, and permits our mouth, when controlled
by the Spirit, to become a channel through which He brings the
Gospel to needy hearts. Yes, it is by the witnessing of believers
that souls are brought to the blessings of salvation.

Too many of us seldom open our mouths for Christ. We open
them to eat, to gossip, to criticize, and to cheer for the home
team, but not to present the Gospel. Perhaps we are afraid it
will cost us something. You may suffer a bit of ridicule, or be
the recipient of a look of disdain, but think of the gain if a soul
is saved from eternal death. Notice: *Peter opened his mouth for*
Jesus Christ, and a whole household was led to salvation!

How about your mouth? Are you willing to open it for Jesus?
Your testimony for Christ may make you a partner with God in
working the greatest of all miracles, the miracle of salvation.

Is there anything else that's of more worth
As along life's way we plod,
Than to find some wandering soul of earth,
And bring him home to God?   —Anon.

The torch of Christianity may be lit in the church, but it does
its best burning in the shop and in the street!

THOUGHTS ON LIFE

For the ways of man are before the eyes of the Lord,
and he pondereth all his goings.   Proverbs 5:21

Life at times can be difficult and frustrating. A noted phil-osopher once said downheartedly, "Sometimes I think I have spent my entire existence in laboriously doing nothing." A great emperor declared, "I have tried everything, and nothing seems of any profit." The Indian poet Tagore wrote, "I have spent my days stringing and unstringing my instrument, *while the song I came to sing remains unsung!*" A layman exclaimed recently, "I have always wanted to be something, but now that I am grow-ing older I must confess I haven't done much or been much. I just feel frustrated!"

Frankly, taken by themselves, your life and mine are probably very insignificant affairs. However, if properly viewed as small but vital parts in God's great program of the ages, they become of infinite importance. No one else can fill the particular spot God has assigned to you, nor take on the tasks that He has laid astride your pathway. The Lord's eyes are constantly upon you, and He ponders all your goings to see if you will live for His glory. He wants to know if you will persevere whether you are praised or not, and still keep faithfully going on when the way seems hard and your cherished "air castles" disappear before the winds of adversity.

Do not fret if your neighbor's garden of joy seems bigger than yours. If each day you pick every flower of duty that grows along the way, by nightfall you will have as big a bouquet as you can carry, and fragrance enough to please the One you serve.

To improve your life, and to make the Lord's heart rejoice as He scrutinizes your ways, learn the true value of time, the suc-cess of perseverance, the pleasure of working, the worth of char-acter, the influence of example, the obligation of duty, the wis-dom of economy, the virtue of patience, and the *power of love!*

> *Lord, grant to me the oil of joy for tears,*
> *And faith to conquer crowding doubts and fears;*
> *And when life poses problems most unkind,*
> *Thy beauty for earth's ashes let me find!* —H.G.B.

Happiness is not the goal of life — but rather service in the will of God!

PEACE AND SLEEP

I will both lie down in peace, and sleep; for thou,
Lord, only makest me dwell in safety.　　Psalm 4:8

Recently in one of the nation's leading newspapers, there appeared a report of an interview with a world famous toy designer. This millionaire, after admitting that he was a lonely and frightened man, acknowledged that all his money couldn't buy him love and happiness. He went on to say that although there are times when he feels life has a purpose, and there is a personal Creator behind the universe, yet the contemplation of the end of life here is the thing that shatters all his joy. He sees death as a "disgraceful defeat, a mockery . . . a dirty joke to play on man . . . an insult." He told the reporter that the only way he can get to sleep at night is to lose himself in a fantasy, like a little child building air castles. He imagines himself in a warm, safe and cozy fortress with high walls and barred doors to keep out everything that might harm him. With such thoughts he is finally able to drift off to sleep.

My heart goes out to this poor rich man! Without God he has no hope, no peace, and doesn't know the meaning of real love. The Psalms we suggested you read were written by David while he was banished from his palace. His wicked son Absalom had led a rebellion against him and had succeeded in driving him out of the city. Things didn't look very promising but David could still pray and trust. In the morning he could testify, "I laid down and slept; I awaked; for the Lord sustained me" (Ps. 3:5). In the evening he could declare, "I will both lie down in peace, and sleep; for thou, Lord, only makest me dwell in safety" (Ps. 4:8). I'd rather have this peace than a million dollars! Wouldn't you?

> *In peace I lay me down to sleep,*
> *And pray Thee, Lord, my soul to keep,*
> *With Thee at hand to guard my bed,*
> *Fear takes its flight — there's naught to dread.*—I.H.

They slumber sweetly whom faith rocks to sleep, for no pillow is as soft as God's promises!

VICTORY!

> . . . *thanks be to God, who giveth us the victory*
> *through our Lord Jesus Christ.* 1 Corinthians 15:57

Many years ago a group of clergymen were discussing whether or not they ought to invite the famous Dwight L. Moody to their city. The success of that zealous and warm-hearted evangelist was brought to the attention of the men by a member of the committee who was especially in favor of the move. However, one unimpressed minister commented sharply, "Does Mr. Moody have a monopoly on the Holy Spirit?" Another man quietly replied, "No, but *the Holy Spirit seems to have a monopoly on Mr. Moody!*" Ah, yes, that was the secret of the evangelist's innumerable victories in his personal life as well as in his public endeavors.

If you want to test the quality of your discipleship and the power of God in your life, see how well your actions and attitudes conform to this pattern of victory which Rev. John McDonald has so thoughtfully outlined.

"When you are forgotten, or neglected, or purposely set at naught, and you smile inwardly, glorying in the oversight — *that is victory!* When your good is evil spoken of, your taste offended, your advice disregarded, and your opinions ridiculed, and you take it all in patient and loving silence — *that is victory!* When you are content with any food, any raiment, any climate, and any interruption — *that is victory!* When you find no special thrill in referring to yourself in conversation, or in recording your own good works, or in seeking after men's commendation, when you truly love to be unknown — *that is victory!*"

In our own strength we can never reach such spiritual heights; but as we yield our *life,* our *talents,* yea, our *all* to the Holy Spirit's control, we shall indeed begin to "live unto God" and obtain the *"victory through our Lord Jesus Christ!"*

> *Jesus is victor! without and within,*
> *Saving and cleansing and keeping from sin;*
> *Jesus is victor! the heavenly Dove*
> *Comes to abide and makes perfect in love.*—R. K. Carter

The road to Christian victory is found only by taking the pathway of complete submission to the will of God.

GOD IS IN HEAVEN

. . . the Lord's throne is in heaven . . . . Psalm 11:4

A little child once exclaimed, "Daddy, if God *is* dead, then He must be in Heaven!" It seems that all the nonsensical talk about God's being dead had been confusing and upsetting to this youngster. So, in her own innocent way, she found at least some comfort in the conclusion, "If God IS dead, then *He must be in Heaven!*" Well, she was right about His being in Heaven, but He certainly is not there because He is dead. We know that He "liveth forever and ever" (Rev. 15:7), and is still ruling, controlling and directing the affairs of both men and nations. If I did not have that assurance, life itself would not be worth the struggle. It is comforting to know that the all-righteous, all-powerful God of the Bible is aware of everything that is going on in the world, and even makes the evil deeds of wicked men serve His own righteous purposes. At times His long-suffering silence may disturb those who are weak in faith. His apparent inactivity and lack of intervention in world affairs may cause some to conclude that He is dead or defeated, or has been dethroned by the devil. Yet those who know the Bible and the divine program can see in these very things the proof that God is alive and His Word is true. Through the writers of Scripture, the Lord has predicted "that in the last days perilous times shall come" (2 Tim. 3:1). He also forewarned that "evil men and seducers shall become worse and worse, deceiving, and being deceived" (2 Tim. 3:13). Despite the fact that "the nations rage, and the peoples imagine a vain thing" (Ps. 2:1), the day is coming when our living Lord will actively step into the picture. Then "He who sitteth in the heavens shall laugh; the Lord shall have them in derision" (Ps. 2:4). So take heart; "the Lord is in his holy temple," and someday soon all the earth shall "keep silence before him" (Hab. 2:20).

> The Lord in His temple shall ever abide,
> His throne is eternal, whatever betide,
> The wicked His anger shall drive from their place,
> The upright in rapture shall gaze on His face. —Anon.

Keep calm; God's will shall ever prevail, for His resources are not only adequate, they are infinite!

WHEN A FISH "CAUGHT" A MAN!

Now the Lord had prepared a great fish to swallow
up Jonah . . . .   Jonah 1:17

Some people say there isn't a creature in the sea that is capable of performing such a feat. Scientists know better. For instance, in 1912 Captain Charles Thompson harpooned a huge mammal off the coast of Florida which, when it was brought to land, was found to contain another 1500-pound fish that had been devoured whole. Those who examined Thompson's catch said *it could have swallowed twenty average-size men!* A Baptist minister who came upon the scene stood in the creature's mouth — holding his hands above his head — and still found he was too short to reach the top of the fish's palate. We must not forget, too, that the creature referred to in Jonah 1:17 *was especially "prepared" for its unique assignment by the Lord Himself!*

One day a young man traveling on a train began to discuss the Bible with a Christian seated next to him. "If you can prove to me that Jonah was swallowed by a whale, I'll believe all the rest of the Bible," he said. "What do you think of Christ?" asked his companion. Surprised by the strange rejoinder, the first man exclaimed, "That's beside the point." "Oh no, it's not," replied the other. "Tell me, do you think that Christ was wise?" "Yes," he said, "I think He was the wisest Man who ever lived." "Well, He believed what you call 'a fish story,' for see what He said in Matthew 12:40." The unbeliever was amazed to find that the passage read, "For as Jonah was three days and three nights in the belly of the great fish, so shall the Son of man be three days and three nights in the heart of the earth." "You see," said the Christian, *"Jesus believed the account of Jonah!"* "Thanks, Mister," was the reply. "That's proof enough for me!"

To avoid Jonah's difficulties, stay in the will of God. And always remember that when God has something important He wants done, He can even make a fish catch a man!

> God stopped the man Jonah upon his wrong path,
> Bringing forth a great storm in displeasure and wrath.
> The prophet confessed it was due to his sin,
> So the crew threw him out, but a fish took him in. —Anon.

Out of the will of God there can be no success; in the will of God there can be no failure!

A LOST EXPERIENCE

*Restore unto me the joy of thy salvation, and uphold
me with a willing spirit.*   Psalm 51:12

A pastor in Los Angeles called on a man who had lived in
that city for some time and asked whether he professed to be
a Christian. "Oh, yes, I was a member of a church in Ohio,"
he said, "And when I asked for my 'letter' on coming west, I
sat down and wrote out my Christian experience. I took them
both and put them in a little box. I would like to show them
to you." Upon examination he found that a mouse had gnawed
its way into the container and had destroyed the papers. In great
confusion he said to the pastor, *"I have lost my Christian experience,* and also my church letter."

Well, it was not much to lose I would say, But, dear friend,
there are multitudes like this man who have nothing real or lasting. Many put great stock in a baptismal certificate or a church
letter, but have experienced no genuine work of grace in their
heart. There are those who, if confronted concerning their relationship to God, could only plead that their membership was
inscribed on the register of some assembly. They could not say,
"Yes, my name's written there, on the page white and fair; in
the book of God's kingdom, yes, my name's written there!" Only
faith in the Savior can avail for the sinner.

Some genuine Christians can also take a warning from this
story. Their once vital "experience" may have been "put in a
box" and allowed to deteriorate. They have failed to keep it fresh
and vibrant by daily fellowship with the Lord through prayer
and Bible study. Friend, if you are among this number, cry with
David, "Restore unto me *the joy* of thy salvation."

> *Gracious God, my heart renew,*
> *Make my spirit right and true;*
> *May Thy joy then ne'er depart;*
> *That my lips may praise impart.* —Psalter, alt.

**You cannot effectively witness to those who are WITHOUT
until you know the joy of the Spirit's witness WITHIN!**

THE SHUT-IN

. . . and the Lord shut him in.   Genesis 7:16

God had a wise purpose when He invited Noah into the ark and locked him in. Had He not done so, the powerful giants who lived at that time would certainly have invaded that first craft and forced their way inside when the flood came, with perhaps dire consequences for all concerned. By being shut in the ark — even though it was a place of confinement — Noah and the whole human race were preserved. He became a "shut-in" not through God's disfavor, but rather because *he had "found grace in the eyes of the Lord."* The same is true of many shut-ins today. While they may feel hemmed in by their small environment, God has a wise purpose in it all. If you are one of those Christians who has been temporarily removed from the mainstream of life by sickness or disablement, remember, divine love and grace are especially at work in your life. If you have been "shut in by God," then it is the best and safest place for you. So, stop pouting — *start praising!*

Among the students at a well-known college was a young man who had been confined to his bed for many years but was now able to get around on crutches. A homely sort of fellow, he had a talent for friendliness and optimism. He soon won many scholastic honors and the hearty respect of his classmates. One day he was asked the cause of his deformity. "Polio," was the brief reply. "But tell me," said the friend, "with a misfortune like that and all the years you have had to spend as a shut-in, how can you face the world so confidently?" "Oh," he replied smiling, *"the disease never touched my heart!"* Like Noah, this Christian young man had found that "every cloud wears a *rainbow,* if your heart keeps right!"

Shut-in, if you know the Lord, it is not by accident that you find yourself in your present restricted circumstances. The purposes of God are being served by your confinement. Be patient, therefore, and remember the words of Lamentations 3:26, "It is good that *a man should both hope and quietly wait for the salvation of the Lord."*

God sends us trials not to IMPAIR us but to IMPROVE us!
—Bosch

DEAD MEN IN THE CHURCH

. . . ungodly men . . . denying the . . . Lord . . . .
These are spots in your love feasts, . . . twice dead.
Jude 4, 12

Charles Haddon Spurgeon once asked, "Have you ever read *The Ancient Mariner?* I dare say you thought it one of the strangest legends ever put together, especially that part where the old mariner represents the corpses of all the dead men rising up to man the ship — dead men pulling the ropes, steering the vessel and spreading the sails. I thought what a strange idea that was. But do you know that I have lived to see the time when something similar has come to pass in our day? I have gone into churches, and I have seen a dead man in the pulpit, a dead man as a deacon, and many dead men sitting to hear."

In his epistle, Jude warns that "in the last time" certain men would creep into the organized church "unawares." Denying the "only Lord God, and our Lord Jesus Christ," their mouths will speak "great swelling words, having men's persons in admiration because of advantage." These men, never having been born again, are spiritually dead; in fact, Jude says, "twice dead"! When such are allowed to fill the pulpit, we behold with Spurgeon a modern-day reenactment of the tale of the ancient mariner with dead men rising up to man the ship. We see a church with a dead man in the pulpit, dead deacons, dead ushers, dead men handling the plates, and dead men sitting to hear. If you love your local assembly and recognize it to be a "church of the living God, the pillar and ground of the truth" (1 Tim. 3:15), you will do everything in your power to make sure that the man you call as pastor is "born again," and that those chosen to serve with him are possessors of that new life in Christ.

Beware of dead men in the church!

> *Base error stalks the church today,*
> *While God's own truth goes by the board;*
> *O bend your knees in earnest prayer,*
> *And seek revival from the Lord!* —Anon.

Error in the church is like fire in a hayloft!

LITTLE THINGS — LARGE CONSEQUENCES

Though thy beginning was small, yet thy latter end should greatly increase.   Job 8:7

Benjamin Franklin once said, *"Little strokes fell great oaks!"* It is truly amazing how many large and important things have come from small beginnings. Did you know that a man conceived the idea for making the huge zeppelin after observing a shirt waving on a clothesline; or that a spiderweb strung across a garden path was the inspiration for the suspension bridge? A teakettle singing on the stove suggested the steam engine; a lantern seen swinging in a tower, the pendulum clock; and an apple falling from a tree, the discovery of the law of gravity! Yes, little things often have large consequences!

Some years ago a farmer from southern Illinois, very plainly dressed, came to the Moody Bible Institute in Chicago and casually asked if they would mind if he looked around. A very gracious student was assigned as his escort and he was given an extended tour of the buildings. Everyone was especially kind to him, although he was a total stranger. On returning home, he wrote a letter to the Institute commending them for the excellent Christian spirit he had found displayed there, *and enclosed a check for $20,000!* The gift was completely unexpected, for they had wondered if the man had even sufficient pocket money to buy his dinner. Yet folks at the Institute had been faithful in the "little things" of common courtesy and Christian love, and the end result brought much blessing.

Grasp the small opportunities that will throng your path in this day, make each word and deed count for Jesus, and you will find on that great accounting day that "though thy beginning was small," yet thy latter end shall be greatly increased in reward and blessing!

> *The Master has need of the little things,*
> *There are none too slight or small;*
> *He adds His own blessing and makes them great—*
> *And uses them one and all.*   —Holloway

Despise not small opportunities, they are often the beginnings of great enterprises!

ALL YOUR NEED

. . . my God shall supply all your need . . . .
Philippians 4:19

In our Scripture lesson today we find Ezra the scribe ready to leave Babylon for Jerusalem. Not only did the king allow him to make this journey, but we hear him declaring in verse 21, "And I, even I, Artaxerxes, the king, do make a decree to all the treasurers which are beyond the river, that whatever Ezra . . . shall require of you, it be done speedily." What a beautiful picture of the Heavenly King who also makes gracious provision for the needs of His children! How assuring those words of Philippians 4:19, "But my God shall supply all your need . . . ."

Beecher gives the following illustration relating to Ezra's experience: "Suppose," he said, "I were to go on a pilgrimage to Jerusalem, and before I started would obtain from Brown Brothers & Co., letters of credit for such cities as London and Jericho. I should then proceed with confidence and cheer, saying to myself, 'As soon as I come to London I shall be in funds. I have a letter in my pocket from Brown Brothers & Co., which will give me $500 there, as well as in the other cities to which I am bound!' But suppose that instead of this confidence, I were to sit down and torment myself in this fashion. 'Now, what am I to do when I get to London? I have no money, and how do I know that these bits of paper will amount to anything? I'm afraid I shall starve in the strange city to which I am going.' I should be a fool, you say; but should I be half the fool as that man who, bearing the letters of credit of the eternal God, yet goes fearing all his way, cast down and doubting whether he shall ever get safely through his journey? No fire, no violence, nor any chance can destroy the checks of the Lord. When He says, 'I will never leave thee, nor forsake thee,' and 'My grace is sufficient for thee,' believe it; and no longer dishonor your God by withholding from Him the confidence you would freely accord to Brown Brothers."

His blessed Word reveals His care,
On Him you can depend;
Beyond your ev'ry circumstance
His promises extend! —Georgia B. Adams

True faith is the simple confidence that God will certainly do what He has promised. —L. S. Chafer

"STUDY TO SHOW THYSELF APPROVED"

So they read in the book . . . of God distinctly . . .
and caused them to understand. Nehemiah 8:8

An old professor was addressing his class, "Gentlemen, you do not use your powers of observation the way you should." Pushing forward a beaker containing a chemical of exceedingly offensive smell, he continued, "When I was a student I used my sense of taste much more frequently than you do." So saying, he put a finger into the liquid and then into his mouth. "Taste it, gentlemen, taste it," he exclaimed, "and exercise your perceptive faculties." The container was pushed toward the reluctant class, and one by one the students resolutely dipped into the concoction and, with many a wry face, sucked the abomination from their fingers. "Gentlemen! Gentlemen!" said the professor, "I must repeat that *you do not use your powers of observation!* For had you looked more closely, you would have seen that *the finger which I put into my mouth was not the one I dipped into the liquid.*" We smile, but this incident points up the carelessness that beclouds much of our learning and understanding.

The same inattention to important details often accompanies our reading of the Word of God. We go over it so rapidly that the words blur into each other and the sense of the passage is obscured. This holy Book demands our full attention, and the use of all our mental faculties. Only as we reverently meditate upon it—"comparing spiritual things with spiritual"—will we be able to distill the Bible's full meaning. False teachers will delude us as easily as that professor fooled his inattentive students if we do not *"study"* to show ourselves "approved unto God" (2 Tim. 2:15).

> Be careful how you read God's Book,
> 'Tis filled with treasures rare;
> And those with faith's discernment
> Glean strength and knowledge there. —Anon.

The Bible does not need to be rewritten—it needs to be reread!

"SPARENTS"

> . . . I will judge his house forever for the iniquity
> which he knoweth, because his sons made themselves
> vile, and he restrained them not.   1 Samuel 3:13

Many of today's homes are suffering because of a lack of discipline. There seems to be a feeling that parents show a lack of love when a request is refused or when misconduct is punished. To be sure, a negative reply is not always popular, and our young people are never very pleased when a parent takes punitive action. The fact remains, however, that true love does not eliminate the necessity for discipline.

A little child, who was very unhappy because her parents had refused her something, unwittingly amused her mother that evening when she prayed, "Please, Lord, don't give her any more children, for she doesn't know how to treat the ones she's got now!" We may smile at this little incident, but we do not feel like laughing when we read in the Bible concerning the evil that resulted when parents were lax and did not do their duty. For instance, David's son Adonijah had rebelled against his father and tried to usurp the throne. The reason for his evil actions and attitude is spelled out for us in the words of 1 Kings 1:6, "And his father had not displeased him at any time in saying, Why hast thou done so?" In similar fashion, judgment also fell upon the house of Eli because of his failure to be a strong father in dealing with the sins of his sons (1 Sam. 3:13).

A young person who comes from the background of family discipline, to which he has graciously submitted, will find himself well equipped to face the demands and restrictions that will be placed upon him in life. Loving parents will seek to curb the improper drives of their youngsters. Disciplined children grow up to be better servants of their God and their country.

> "Sparents" are those that "spare the rod"
> When offspring need attention.
> They find their troubles multiplied
> In ways too sad to mention! —Alice M. Graves

If you find your son going down the wrong track, perhaps it's because you didn't "switch" him soon enough!

SAFELY HOME

. . . man goeth to his long home . . . . Ecclesiastes 12:5

"Be sure to call me when you get home. I want to know you arrived safely." Does that sound familiar? I'm sure it does. Having said, "Farewell," to dear ones — committing them to the keeping of the Lord — we eagerly await word from them that will asure us they have arrived at their intended destination. What a welcome thing it is then, when the telephone rings and a re-assuring voice exclaims, "We're home — safe and sound!"

It isn't necessary for our loved ones who have been summoned to their eternal Home to send such word back to us since we *know* from the Scriptures that their journey from earth to Glory was a safe one. Even as Jesus told the dying thief, "Today *shalt* thou be with me in paradise," just so certain is the swift and blissful arrival of every child of God in the Gloryland. With that in mind, listen to these familiar poetic words so expressive of the experience of all who die in Christ: "I am home in Heaven, dear ones; all's so happy and so bright! There is perfect joy and beauty in this everlasting light. All the pain and grief is over, every restless tossing past; I am now at peace forever, safely home in Heaven at last. Did you wonder I so calmly trod the valley of the shade? Ah, but Jesus' love illumined every dark and fearful glade. And He came Himself to meet me in that way so hard to tread; and with Jesus' arm to lean on could I have one doubt or dread? Then you must not grieve so sorely, for I love you dearly still; try to look beyond earth's shadows; pray to trust our Father's will. There is work still waiting for you, so you must not idle stand; do your work while life remaineth, you shall rest in Jesus' land. When your work is all completed, He will gently call you Home. Oh, the rapture of the meeting! Oh, the joy to see you come!"

> *My heavenly Home is bright and fair;*
> *No pain, nor death can enter there;*
> *When life is past my soul shall rise*
> *To dwell with Christ beyond the skies.*
>
> —Wm. Hunter, alt.

Death for the Christian is not bane but blessing, not tragedy but triumph!   —Bosch

COBWEBS

*And how shall they believe in him of whom they
have not heard?*   Romans 10:14

The story is told of an artist who was asked to paint a picture
of a decaying church. To the astonishment of many, instead of
portraying on the canvas an old, tottering ruin, the artist painted
a stately edifice of modern design and grandeur. Through the
open portals could be seen the richly carved pulpit, the magnificent organ, and the beautiful stained glass windows. In the
vestibule was an offering plate of elaborate design for the gifts of
the fashionable worshipers. But here the artist's idea of a decaying church was made known, for above this hung a box bearing
the inscription "For Foreign Missions"; and over the slot through
which contributions ought to have gone he had painted *a huge
cobweb!*

The church, or the individual Christian whose heart and life
is not involved in the worldwide proclamation of the Gospel, is
most certainly decadent. We may be engaged in feverish "Christian" activity, but our energies may be misdirected while the
main thrust of God's program for this age goes unaided or un-
attended by us.

God has so ordered His plan of world evangelization that every
believer may be vitally involved. We all should be *pray-ers* that
the "Lord of the harvest may send forth laborers into his harvest."
Some will also hear His personal call to be *preachers,* else "how
shall they hear?" Still others will be *senders,* for "how shall they
preach, except they be sent?"

May there be no cobwebs over the cause of "world missions"
in our life.

> Far and near the fields are teeming
>   With the waves of ripened grain;
> Far and near their gold is gleaming
>   O'er the sunny slope and plain.
>
> Lord of harvest, send forth reapers!
>   Hear us, Lord, to Thee we cry;
> Send them now the sheaves to gather,
>   Ere the harvest time pass by. —Thompson

Untold millions are perishing — UNTOLD!

WORSHIP AND SERVICE

> . . . his brethren . . . were . . . in . . . the business
> of the Lord, and in the service of the king.
>
> 1 Chronicles 26:30

Some time ago I came across this little poem dealing with the
subject of church attendance:

> Some go to church just for a walk,
> Some go there to laugh and talk;
> Some go there to gain a lover,
> Some go there their faults to cover!
> Some go there for observation,
> Some go there for speculation,
> Some go there to sleep and nod,
> But few go there to worship God!

Although this presents a somewhat exaggerated situation, it
does remind us of our obligation to make sure that our purpose
in attending church is a proper one. It should be for fellowship,
instruction, and worship; and these things in turn should be
stepping stones to service.

The religious section of one of our newspapers carried an article
by a minister who related the following story: "Entering a church
one Sunday morning, a man asked, 'When will the service be
over?' An usher replied, 'The congregation is still at worship,
sir, but the *service* will actually begin when the people *leave*
the church!'"

If our worship is simply a matter of going through some religious motions, if it fails to transform and change our lives, if
it does not thrust us forth as effective and zealous servants of
Christ, then it is failing to achieve one of its major objectives.
Worship of God and service for Him should go hand in hand.
Let us then be ". . . fervent in spirit; serving the Lord" (Rom.
12:11).

I went to church one morning and sat in a comfortable pew,
But the offering I gave to Jesus was far too small I knew.
I bent my knees before Him, and with contrite heart I did pray,
"Lord, I'll not only call You Master, but heed the words You say!"

—Ferreau, alt.

The feast of the sermon results in spiritual indigestion unless
followed by religious exercise.

CIVILIZATION'S "TITANIC MOMENT"

*And . . . the God of heaven [shall] set up a king-
dom, which shall never be destroyed.*   Daniel 2:44

An insurance company recently pictured the *Titanic* sailing
straight for the iceberg which many years ago sank that great
luxury liner. States the advertisement: "They called her the 'Millionaire's Special.' Four city blocks long, eleven stories high,
powered by triple propellers, protected by the latest, most ingenious devices, luxurious and beautiful beyond words, she caught
the fancy of the world. On April 10, 1912, she slipped out of
Southampton on her maiden voyage to New York. Less than
five days later, she went down in 12,000 feet of icy water, 300
feet of her hull ripped open by a massive iceberg. Actually the
Titanic was more than a ship. She was a symbol of man's power.
Majestic! Colossal! Unsinkable! But when the 'unsinkable' sank,
something went down with it. No one would ever again feel the
same confidence in man's strength." What a perfect illustration
this is of all of human society. Proud, modern civilization—heedless of the claims of Christ—is rushing headlong toward destruction.

In Daniel 2 the Bible outlines the succession of world governments under the symbolism of a great image. Majestic, colossal,
and apparently secure and unbreakable, a stone from Heaven
smites the statue and grinds it to powder. The interpretation given
is that the Stone—the Lord Jesus Christ—is coming in power and
glory to destroy all of godless man's vain dreams. Yes, *civilization
is rushing toward its "titanic moment"* when the wicked shall be
punished and the Lord shall establish His perfect kingdom. Are
you ready for that day to come?

Christ shall come in justice,
Evil to redress,
And to judge the nations
In His righteousness.   —Psalter

**The importance of Christ's return may be seen in the fact that
it is mentioned 318 times in the New Testament alone.**

THANK GOD FOR THE "BREAKERS"!

. . . he that hath suffered . . . hath ceased from sin.
1 Peter 4:1

While walking along a beach on the Gulf of Mexico early one morning, I came upon a section which contrasted sharply with what I had seen before. Here was perfect calm, whereas just a few steps back, the waves had been crashing upon the shoreline, gushing their crystal tide upon the swirling sands. "Why is this?" I wondered. Looking out over the surf, I saw the answer. Several hundred yards off shore a string of low-lying islands were taking the beating of the breakers, thus leaving the waters on the shore-ward side quiet and placid. A most tranquil atmosphere prevailed. Observing the situation more closely, I discovered that the sandy bottom was covered with silt, while a very annoying odor filled the air. Here in this protected area, away from the turbulent waves, the waters had become so stagnant that I was glad to move on ahead where the breakers once again pounded against the shoreline.

In thinking upon this experience, it has become a "parable" to me. Even as that "harbored" area of shoreline became a polluted and undesirable place, so it is in life. Without the winds of difficulty, and the purifying action of the waves of adversity breaking in upon us, we tend to stagnate spiritually and become contaminated with the things of this world. So, believer, when the billows of trial would seem to threaten your very life, take heart, remembering that even though "no chastening for the present seemeth to be joyous, but grievous; nevertheless, afterward it yieldeth the peaceable fruit of righteousness unto them who are exercised by it" (Heb. 12:11).

Thank God for the "breakers" in life!

> *His oath, His covenant, His blood,*
> *Support me in the whelming flood;*
> *When all around my soul gives way,*
> *He then is all my hope and stay!* —Mote

God had but one Son on earth without sin, but never one without suffering.
—Augustine

OVERCOMING OUR WEAKNESSES

*He that overcometh . . . shall be clothed in white
raiment.*   Revelation 3:5

The cynical attitude of Judas, described in John 12, stands in
sharp contrast to that scene of surpassing loveliness presented
by the adoring Mary anointing the feet of Jesus with her costly
perfume. Judas had become a thief and a warped personality
who could no longer see beauty even in an act of unselfish love.

I have often asked myself why Jesus made Judas treasurer for
the Twelve. Undoubtedly our Lord had a good and loving purpose in doing so. Knowing that Judas had a tendency toward
dishonesty the Lord Jesus gave him a position where he would
be brought face to face with his weakness. Judas should have
recognized his need of help and turned to the Lord with a humble
petition for the necessary grace to overcome his weakness. Instead, he became increasingly greedy, gradually yielded to the
temptation to steal, and finally betrayed the Lord for a paltry
thirty pieces of silver.

God sometimes permits us to be tested in the very areas where
we are weak, not because He desires us to fall into sin, but because He wants us to recognize our spiritual need and so turn
to Him for aid. Whenever such trying situations arise, remember the truth of 1 Corinthians 10:13, "There hath no temptation taken you but such as is common to man; but God is faithful, who will not permit you to be tempted above that ye are
able, but will, with the temptation, also make *the way to escape.*"
Be honest enough to admit your infirmities, *depend upon God
to help you,* and someday in Glory you will be counted among
the overcomers.

> *Are you halting and struggling, o'erpowered by sin?*
> *Full of evil enticements without and within?*
> *Lo, the Savior stands waiting to strengthen your soul,*
> *He will make you o'ercomer, and "ev'ry whit whole!"*
> —Kirkpatrick, alt.

**Temptation is the abrasive God uses to rub off the rust of our
sinful self-sufficiency!**

"WHERE IS YOUR FAITH?"

And he [Jesus] said unto them, Where is your faith?
Luke 8:25

In the briefing room of an airbase, someone posted these words: "By all the known laws which can be proved on paper or tested in the wind tunnel, the *bumblebee cannot fly*. The size of his wings in relation to his body, according to mathematical and aeronautical science, means that he cannot 'take off.' It is an impossibility! But, of course, the bumblebee doesn't know this, so he goes ahead and flies anyway." In like manner, true faith never counts the difficulties or reckons with impossibilities. Resting on the promises in the Word, it just reaches out and claims God's almighty power in the hour of need, and thus accomplishes the incredible!

Ah, but you say, "My faith is weak." Well, if you want it to grow, there are several rules you must follow. One is to absorb the Scriptures into your soul by constant study, for "faith cometh by hearing, and hearing *by the word of God.*" Next, as F. B. Meyer says, *"You must be willing to have a great faith.* When men say they cannot believe, ask them, 'Are you *willing* to believe?' If the will is toward faith, the Holy Spirit will produce the needed trust. Also *you must use the faith you have!* A child will never be able to wield a sledge hammer unless he begins little by little to use his slender arm muscles. One will not learn to swim great distances until he first wades into the pool and prepares himself for great exploits." Finally, if you will *live a life of daily obedience to God's will* as you discern it from the Word, your faith will continue to grow; and you will go from victory to victory displaying a spiritual maturity that will bring glory to God.

> *O for a faith that will not shrink,*
> *Though pressed by every foe,*
> *That will not tremble on the brink*
> *Of any earthly woe!* —Bathurst

Feed your faith and your doubts will starve to death!

A GREAT WORK

Now therefore, O God, strengthen my hands.
                                        Nehemiah 6:9

The modern missionary movement was begun by William Carey, a man who was called the "shoemaker preacher." For many years his heart was breaking with compassion for the heathen while he worked at his trade. Finally he received an opportunity to present his burden to a group of clergymen. On this occasion he uttered words that have become a slogan for all who are involved in spiritual endeavors: "Expect great things *from* God, attempt great things *for* God!"

Nehemiah was also a man with such courage, determination and faith. Building the walls of Jerusalem to make the city strong and well-fortified, he was engaged in "a great work." He therefore rejected letters from the enemies of Israel requesting that he attend a summit conference. When the fifth messenger came with an open letter accusing him of conspiring against the King of Persia, he did not panic or cease from his important labors. Nor did he listen to the suggestion of Shemaiah that he hide in the temple for safety. Not being a priest, Nehemiah knew he had no right to enter the temple; and recognizing Shemaiah to be a false prophet, he rejected his counsel. He knew he was involved in a "a great work," and would do nothing to hinder his effectiveness.

Every Christian should look upon his service for the Lord as necessary and important. Whether you teach a Sunday school class, serve as a church officer, or function in any other capacity, your contribution is worthwhile if you perform your task zealously and faithfully. As you advance on the pathway of service, pray like Nehemiah, "O God, strengthen my hands"!

Day by day perform thy mission,
With His help keep at thy tasks;
Have no fear that God will chide thee,
Faithfulness is all He asks!   —Bosch

It is a great thing to do a little thing well.

REJOICING CONFIDENCE

. . . the Lord will take me up.   Psalm 27:10

Psalm 27 has been called a song of shade and sunshine. The writer sometimes glows with glorious certainty as he expresses his faith in God, while at other times he declares his deep concern as he faces his trials and pleads with the Lord for mercy. In verse 10 he depicts himself as friendless and forsaken like a deserted child, but is joyous because of his assurance that God has a love for him which is stronger than the nearest and dearest of human relationships. Even though he should be abandoned by both his father and his mother, he declares that the Lord will remain faithful and take him up!

The consciousness of God's presence as a loving Father is ever a source of comfort and strength to the believer. This is graphically illustrated in a story told by Dr. Ellis A. Fuller. Though a busy pastor, he took time from his crowded schedule to be with his son when the lad had his tonsils removed. Dr. Fuller went with him into the operating room, and afterward stayed with him throughout the entire recovery period. It was a hot, humid day, and the boy was very uncomfortable. However, toward the end of the afternoon, he took his father's hand and said, "Dad, *it was worth it just to have you with me all day!"*

Friend, when we reach the end of life's road, we too will be able to tell our Heavenly Father that His constant presence made all of life's suffering worthwhile.

The believer who has truly experienced the reality of God's love and fellowship is able to meet life's burdens and problems with quiet assurance and rejoicing confidence!

What a fellowship, what a joy divine,
Leaning on the everlasting arms;
What a blessedness, what a peace is mine,
Leaning on the everlasting arms.   —Hoffman

The man who walks with God always gets to his destination.

GOD AND THE RAVENS

I [God] have commanded the ravens to feed thee.
                                        1 Kings 17:4

The *Associated Press* carried this story under the heading "Crow Feeds Dog": "For six days a puppy, trapped in an animal snare, was kept alive by a crow. Both animals belong to a couple living at a road construction camp. After the dog disappeared recently, the pet crow stopped eating normally. It would take a bit of food in its beak, fly off and return a short time later to fetch another scrap. One day they followed it and were led to the spot where the dog lay trapped." The article then concluded, "The earliest reference to this type of thing was the feeding of Elijah by the ravens."

The provision of bread and flesh for the prophet Elijah was certainly a marvelous thing. As children of the Heavenly Father we can know something even more wonderful—God's daily supply of all our needs. In 1 Kings 17:4 the Lord said to Elijah, "I have commanded the ravens to feed thee." And the apostle Paul writing to believers at Philippi declares, *"God* shall supply all *your* need." He may not actually use birds for this purpose today, but He does have His "ravens" whereby His bountiful provisions are delivered to us.

The Lord expects us, however, to be diligent in fulfilling our responsibility as well. His Word therefore emphasizes, ". . . work with your hands." And the writer of Proverbs exhorts, "Love not sleep, lest thou come to poverty; open thine eyes, and thou shalt be satisfied with bread." Once we have done our part, we may rest in the assurance of the Lord's gracious supply, for He has His "ravens" in every age!

> Say not, my soul,
>   "From whence shall God relieve my care?"
> Remember, Omnipotence
>   Has servants everywhere!   —Anon.

God ever has His "ravens" for the righteous, but He has no loaves for the loafer!   —Bosch

SAVED OVER TOKYO

*For whosoever shall call upon the name of the Lord
shall be saved.*   Romans 10:13

While on a tour through some of the southern states, I had
the privilege of meeting and fellowshiping with a pastor who told
me the thrilling story of his conversion. He related that he had
been one of those individuals who prided himself in his church
membership and good works, but had never been born again. He
joined the Air Force during World War II and was assigned to
fly with the first group of planes to make a low-level raid over
Japan. Naturally tension was high as they took off on this dangerous mission, and it continued to mount as they approached their
general target area. Taking their places in formation with their
flight patterns established, they zeroed in: no turning back now.
With anti-aircraft fire bursting all around, and with the black-
ness of night enshrouding them — punctured only by the explod-
ing bombs — they flew at such a low level that smoke from the
fires on the ground came up with suffocating intensity to block
their vision. It was then, with his plane convulsing from direct
hits, and when all seemed lost, this man realized that although
he had been religious and a good church member, these things
in themselves had not saved him. He was keenly aware of the
fact that he had never been born again. In that moment of utter
desperation and almost certain doom, he received Jesus Christ.
Knowing he could never save himself, he freely admitted that he
was a sinner. He knew God loved him so much that He gave
His Son to die on the cross to merit his redemption. Therefore,
moved by the Holy Spirit, he asked Christ to save him right there
in the air over Japan. The Lord, who always hears the cry of
the believing penitent, gave him eternal life and flooded his soul
with joy and peace.

Remember, friend, having your name on the church rolls will
not save you. By simple faith you must receive Jesus Christ.
"For whosoever shall call upon the name of the Lord shall be
saved." Believe on the Lord Jesus Christ *today!*

Many a man is ALMOST SAVED yet ENTIRELY LOST!

ONE WHO KNOWS

> . . . *he knoweth what is in the darkness, and the*
> *light dwelleth with him.*   Daniel 2:22

When Daniel had received from the Lord the interpretation of King Nebuchadnezzar's dream, he blessed and praised the God of Heaven. Included in that praise was this phrase, "He knoweth what is in the darkness." What frightful words these are to the workers of iniquity! Nothing is hid from Him. Every wicked word He hears, every sinful thought He knows, every cunning scheme of unrighteousness He detects. *"He knoweth what is in the darkness!"* But what comfort this Scripture brings to the child of God! There is no night of sorrow but that He understands and cares. He is well aware of the disappointments and trials we face. Therefore with Job we may say, "He knoweth the way that I take; when he hath tested me, I shall come forth as gold." The Lord describes Himself in Jeremiah 23:23 as the "God at hand." He is always there to see His child through distressing emergencies.

A long hallway with a turn to the right led to my little bedroom in our old homestead. When I was young it seemed like a considerable distance from my parents' room. The place was especially gloomy and foreboding to my childish mind as my mother would flick off the light and say goodnight. More than once in the darkness they would hear a voice from that room way down the hall. "Mother! Dad! Are you there?" And everything would be all right when I heard the reassuring words, "Yes, Paul!" Dear friend, if you are going through the night of trial or disappointment, remember, "He knoweth what is in the darkness," and He *is* with you!

> *From Thee, O Lord, I am not hid,*
> *Though darkness cover me;*
> *The darkness and the light of day*
> *Are both alike to Thee.*   —Anon.

Though the gloom of trouble may surround you, your future is as bright as the love and promises of God!

COCKLEBURS OR STRAWBERRIES?

*Only take heed to thyself, and keep thy soul diligently,
lest thou forget the things which thine eyes have seen,
and lest they depart from thy heart all the days of thy
life; but teach them to thy sons, and thy sons' sons.*

Deuteronomy 4:9

The Bible is full of instruction about how we should raise our
children in the "fear and admonition of the Lord." God often
reminded His ancient people of Israel that they should not depart
from His Word, but they should diligently teach the younger
generation the things they had learned and experienced by His
grace. This month as we are thinking about our children returning to the grade schools and higher institutions of learning, how
important it is to remind ourselves not to neglect their spiritual
education.

An agnostic who once went to visit the famous poet Coleridge
took strong issue with him. He argued vehemently against any
spiritual indoctrination of youth, and declared his own determination not to "prejudice" his children in favor of any form of
"religion," but to allow them at maturity to choose for themselves.
The defensive answer of Coleridge is worth noting. "If your position is sound," said he, "why then do we prejudice a garden in
favor of flowers and fruits? *Why not let the clods choose for
themselves between cockleburs and strawberries?"* The agnostic
was silenced!

Contrary to popular opinion, children do not naturally tend
in the right direction. Being sinners they must be converted,
trained, and encouraged to develop Christian character and aspire
to noble deeds. Parents, teachers, and preachers all have a contribution to make. Much of the trouble we are experiencing in
the world today is due to the fact that the older generation has
frequently failed our young people in this important area of life.
Beware of developing "cockleburs" when you should be nurturing
"strawberries"!

**If we had paid no more attention to our plants than we have
to our children, we would now be living in a jungle of weeds.**
—Luther Burbank

CHRISTIANS AND LABOR

Not slothful in business. . . .   Romans 12:11

People of the world sometimes criticize Christians by saying of them, "They're *so heavenly minded* that they're *no earthly good!*" Let us pray that such an accusation may ever remain slander and not fact; for the child of God should be the most highly motivated of all to be industrious and "work while it is day." *Never must we be slothful in business!* If you and I are not the best laborers in our office, factory, or other place of employment, we are poor testimonies. True Christians always "redeem the time" and make the moments count, for they realize that they are to do each task "with all their might" and "as unto the Lord."

Thomas A. Edison, the great inventor, is quoted as saying, "I am wondering what would have happened to me if . . . some fluent talker had converted me to the theory of the eight-hour day, and convinced me that it was not fair to my fellow workers to put forth my *best efforts?* I am glad that the eight-hour day had not been invented when I was a young man. If my life had been made up of brief, easy working hours, I do not believe that I would have accomplished a great deal. This country would not have amounted to as much as it now does if the young men of my day ∴ . . had been afraid that they might earn more than they were paid!"

Says A. P. Gibbs: "It is not without significance to the Christian that each member of the divine Trinity is described as '*working.*' Christ said, '*My Father worketh* hitherto . . . .' Then He added, '*and I work*' (John 5:17). Also in 1 Corinthians 12: 11 we read: "*But all these worketh that one and the selfsame Spirit, dividing to every man severally as he will.*' Thus the Father, Son, and Holy Spirit are seen to be ever *active!*" Therefore if God is a worker, and we are His children, we had better not be found among the slothful!

> *They who tread the path of labor*
> *Follow where My feet have trod;*
> *They who work without complaining,*
> *Do the holy will of God!* —Henry Van Dyke

It's not the hours you put in, but what you put in the hours that counts!

THE EXERCISE OF ELOQUENCE

These are murmurers, . . . and their mouth speaketh
great swelling words.   Jude 16

A man was trying to explain the meaning of oratory. He commented, "If you say that black is white, that's foolishness! But," he continued, "if you say that black is white, and you roar like a bull and pound on the table with both fists and race from one end of the platform to the other, that's oratory!" I certainly would not discredit the beauty and the effectiveness of great eloquence when it is properly exercised. There is nothing quite so stirring, so moving, and so persuasive as a silver-tongued orator who, with all the power of the English language at his command, can stimulate the emotions and motivate the will. We are thankful for men of God who have been endowed with the gift of spirited, appealing, and persuasive communication. It is possible, however, to be swept off our feet by the *manner* in which a man expresses himself, rather than by the *truthfulness* of what he has to say. Jude warns us concerning those whose mouths speak "great swelling words." The masses are oftentimes moved by *style* rather than by *content!*

Today many strange voices are making their appeal to those who "heap to themselves teachers, having itching ears." How important it is then that we be not overwhelmed by mere oratory. Analyze, study, and compare everything with the Scriptures — even that which the most brilliant and gifted of men proclaim. One demand we should make of all ministers is that they "speak the truth in Christ and lie not." The exercise of eloquence can never be a substitute for the plain truth!

> *While eloquent voices*
> *May tickle the ear,*
> *'Tis far more important*
> *That truth be made clear!* —Bosch

It is well to remember that honesty is the better part of eloquence!   —Hazlitt

HOW TO BE TRULY SUCCESSFUL

*But seek ye first the kingdom of God, and his righ-
teousness; and all these things shall be added unto
you.*   Matthew 6:33

A very rich man, who had run after the things of the world
and had overtaken them, lay dying. He was visited by the daughter of a friend with whom he had been associated in early youth,
but who had left their profitable business to serve Christ. Now
he too was dying but with great peace of mind and holy confidence. "You may wonder why I cannot be as happy and quiet
as he," said the unsaved millionaire, "but just think of the difference between us. He is going to his treasure and I — I *must
leave mine!"*

One who feels wretched and defeated cannot be considered
successful regardless of how much wealth he may have amassed,
or how many honors may have been heaped upon him. Nor can
any person be termed "successful" if he has lived his life without God. I can think of some very happy people who never
acquired wealth or fame. An elderly couple I know are still
deeply in love with each other and radiate spiritual joy. They
have four children, all married and in full-time Christian service.
They are *truly successful!*

Some men will risk anything, will lie, cheat, and traffic in all
sorts of dishonesty and immorality in order to obtain that illusive
will-o'-the-wisp called fame!

The rich fool — mentioned in Luke 12 — looked upon himself
as a successful man, but God didn't agree. *True success is to
find one's place and to fill it — to seek first the kingdom of God
and his righteousness!* You may be poor, have relatively little
talent, and be quite unable to do anything that looks big; however, if you are faithfully handling the task God has given to
you, in complete yieldedness to His will, you will find true happiness. God eventually will give an accurate estimate of your life;
then "many who are last shall be first; and the first last!'

> "Seek ye first," not earth's aspirings,
> Ceaseless longings, vain desirings
> But your precious soul's requirings,
>   "Seek ye FIRST"!   —Anon.

**Happiness is not having and getting; it consists in giving and
serving!**   —H. Drummond

THE BEST GIFT

. . . they . . . first gave themselves to the Lord . . . .
2 Corinthians 8:5

A missionary friend told me the following true story. At one time when the offering was being taken during a service in a little church in Africa, he noticed from his vantage point on the platform the rather strange actions of a young native girl. Having been passed the collection box, she held it for a few moments with bowed head and closed eyes. Then she passed it on without putting in a single thing. The missionary's eyes filled with tears as he watched that scene. Those to whom he ministered were extremely poor. For that reason money is very seldom placed in the offering plate. Instead it is not at all uncommon to see the folks put in bananas, Kola beans, and eggs (some of the latter are frequently ready to hatch). Evidently this poor little African lass had nothing to give, but, knowing her spirituality, the missionary imagined her praying, "Lord Jesus, I would like to give you something. I love You with all my heart. I have no money; but what I have I'm giving to You right now. *I'm giving myself!"*

I'm sure that in many cases the sizable contributions we make are not as pleasing to the Lord as that "sacrifice of praise" which was offered by that sincere little African child. As much as God desires and uses our gifts of money in the spread of the Gospel, *He would first of all have us present our hearts and lives to Him!* Paul commended the believers in Macedonia that they "first gave themselves to the Lord."

You may have given hundreds, perhaps thousands, of dollars to your church and other worthy Gospel endeavors, but I wonder have you ever presented yourself to God? This is what He wants most of all. And then, whether you can give much or little, it is comforting to know that "if there be first a willing mind, it is accepted according to that which a man hath, and not according to that which he hath not" (2 Cor. 8:12).

> *Give of your best to the Master;*
> *Give Him first place in your heart;*
> *Give Him first place in your service,*
> *Consecrate now ev'ry part.*   —H. B. Grose

An empty heart is a greater misfortune than an empty purse!

THE "MEASURING DAY"

Till we all come . . . unto a perfect man, unto the measure of the stature of the fullness of Christ.
Ephesians 4:13

God wants us to grow in grace and advance in spiritual knowledge. Therefore, along with His Word, He gives us Christian leaders who, because of their maturity, can act as ministers and teachers to edify us (Eph. 4:11), give us a broader insight into the deeper life of consecration, and instill in our hearts a better understanding of the true wisdom which is from above. As we thus mellow and mature through grace we shall grow "unto . . . the measure of the stature . . . of Christ!"

Peloubet's Notes relates in substance the following incident: It is said that those who wished to qualify for positions in the elite guard of King Frederick of Prussia were required to measure up to a certain commanding stature. A Christian lady thought so much about this annual "Measuring Day" ceremony that when she went to bed one evening she had a dream in which she imagined there was a day when everyone's growth in *grace* was similarly computed. An angel stood with a tall, golden rod in his hand over which was fastened a scroll on which appeared these words: "The measure of the stature of the perfect man." The angel inscribed in a large book all the important statistics as the people came up one at a time in response to the calling of their names. The instant anyone touched the rod an astounding thing happened — each shrank or increased in size to his or her true *spiritual dimensions!* Everyone, including the recording angel, could thus miraculously see what otherwise would have been perceived only by the eye of God.

If today were the "Measuring Day" (and it may well be if Jesus suddenly returns), would you be ashamed of your spiritual stature? Take inventory; is your soul shrinking from "malnutrition," or are you feeding on the Living Bread, and thus daily attaining a little more of the "stature of the fullness of Christ"?

More purity give me, more strength to o'ercome;
More freedom from earth-stains, more longing for Home;
More fit for Thy kingdom, more used would I be;
More blessed and holy, more, Saviour, like Thee.—P. P. Bliss

Live now as you shall wish you had lived when you stand at the judgment seat of Christ! —Culbertson

GENTLE GUIDANCE

*I will instruct thee and teach thee in the way which
thou shalt go; I will guide thee with mine eye.*
                                              Psalm 32:8

When I was a boy, men sometimes abused horses. They would
pull hard on the reins, thus yanking the bit in the poor animal's
mouth. It disturbed me to see this done because I knew it was
painful, and actually most horses didn't need this kind of treatment.

In Psalm 32:9 we are admonished to walk in obedience so that
we will not need a "bit and bridle" to hold us in check. Figura-
tively, these pieces of equipment speak of trials and troubles
which come as correctives from God. Sometimes it is necessary
for the Lord to deal in what seems to be a harsh manner with
His disobedient children. In fact, 1 Corinthians 11:30 tells us
that some believers at Corinth became ill and others died because
of their improper conduct in connection with the Lord's table.

God desires that every Christian should rejoice in the fact that
the burden of his sins has been lifted and borne away, its foulness
and its guilt removed. God further promises that He will instruct
us, teach us, and gently guide us in the way that we should
go, ever keeping His watchful eye upon us. If we live in fellowship with Him, many of the trials that come into our lives are
not intended as chastening, but are sent to lead us into a deeper
and more intimate communion with God. In all of these difficult
experiences He will "compass us about with songs of deliverance,"
thus enabling us to rejoice with exuberant gladness.

There are times, however, when we need the "bit and bridle"
treatment. Let us then quickly confess and forsake our sin, accept His gracious forgiveness, and walk once again in close fellowship with the Lord. If you thus put your hand in His, He
will lead you *gently* Home.

> *Precious promise God hath given*
> *To the weary passerby,*
> *On the way from earth to Heaven,*
> *"I will guide thee with Mine eye."*—N. Niles

**The indispensable requisite for a God-directed life is a meek
and quiet spirit that is willing to be led.**   —L. Mitchel

DEATH—THE KEY TO A PALACE

In my Father's house are many mansions . . . .
I go to prepare a place for you.   John 14:2

A mother tells how one evening, when she was tucking her small daughter in bed, the child exclaimed, "Mother, stay with me while I go to sleep." Remembering all the tasks that still awaited her, she hesitated, but seeing the troubled look on the little face and knowing her dread of the creeping darkness, she sat down by the bedside and caressed her daughter's soft hand in her own. Soon the child drifted away to dreamland. As the mother sat there, the Lord brought home to her heart a blessed and comforting thought. Bowing her head she prayed, "Oh, Lord, when life's evening shall come, bring before me all Thy good promises, so that by grace I too may be able to say with a child-like trust, *'Father, take my hand — stay with me while I go to sleep,* guide me safely in the valley, and receive me when I awaken in Glory!'" In the light of John 14:2, this is a prayer every Christian can utter with holy confidence.

Someone has said, "God conceals from us the full happiness that follows death, that we may be able to endure life!" Today you may be sorrowing for a loved one whom God has called home to Heaven, but actually it is for yourself that you weep. Your dear one is so rapturously happy in the place which Jesus especially prepared for him in the Mansions of Light, that it is almost sacrilegious that you should selfishly wish him back in this dismal land of the dying. Apart from the inspired writers of the Scripture, John Milton perhaps said it best when he exclaimed, *"Death for the believer is the golden key that opens for him the palace of eternity!"*

O mourner, meditate on John 14:2. Think of the joy your Christian loved one is now experiencing in Glory, and it will put a rainbow in the cloud of your sorrow.

Weep not because I walk no longer with you,
Remember I am walking streets of gold;
Weep for yourselves that you awhile must tarry,
Before the blessed Lord you may behold.—Barbara C. Ryberg

We think of death as ending, but for the Christian it is a glorious beginning; we think of it as going away, but it is really a wondrous arriving!   **—N. Macleod**

A PAGE FROM THE PAST

Take, my brethren, the prophets . . . for an example
of suffering affliction.   James 5:10

My heart was blessed one morning as I paged through an old
Methodist hymnbook published in 1849. It had no music, just
words. This unusual volume measured about 4½ by 2½ inches
and yet included over 700 pages. As I read the lyrics penned by
saints of old, I was reminded that often we sing our hymns without really thinking of the words. I am sure you will find it profitable sometimes to take a sacred song and carefully read the text.
Your heart will be blessed — you might even feel some tears trickling down your cheeks. Listen to this one:

> Think not that they are blest alone
>   Whose lives a peaceful tenor keep;
> For God, who pities man, has shown
>   A blessing for the eyes that weep.
>
> The light of smiles shall fill again
>   The lids that overflow with tears;
> And weary hours of woe and pain
>   Are promises of happier years.
>
> Nor let the good man's trust depart,
>   Though life its common gifts deny —
> Though with a pierced and broken heart,
>   And spurned of men, he goes to die.
>
> For God has marked each sorrowing day,
>   And numbered every secret tear;
> And Heaven's eternal bliss shall pay
>   For all His children suffer here.

A page from the past. May it bless your heart today and help
keep your eyes on the future glory.

> *There is a day of sunny rest,*
>   *For every dark and troubled night;*
> *Though grief may hide an evening guest;*
>   *Yet joy shall come with early light.* —Anon.

God promises a safe landing, but not a calm passage.

"CHARGE IT!"

*Ho, every one that thirsteth, come to the waters, and
he that hath no money; come, buy and eat; yea, come,
buy wine and milk without money and without price.*
                                                    Isaiah 55:1

It was Sunday and an emergency had arisen at a small country
church. The teacher who was to speak to the young children had
not arrived. A visitor was asked to take charge of the class. He
accepted, but was rather alarmed when he saw that the lesson was
based on the fifty-fifth chapter of Isaiah. The first verse was the
text of the morning. The leader thought this might be easily
explained to senior pupils, but could mere children be made to
understand how to *buy "without money?"* This invitation to
salvation couched in figurative language seemed extremely difficult material to convey to little folk. Yet, he had agreed to teach
the class, so while the singing was going on, he prayed silently
for special guidance and light upon the subject. Immediately the
Lord brought to his remembrance another beautiful verse, namely,
"A little child shall lead them." Believing that perhaps the Lord
meant by this that one of the small scholars could better explain
what the text was intended to teach than he himself, he began
by reading the verse and asking what they thought the prophet
Isaiah meant by inviting people to *"buy . . . without money."* A
sweet young girl raised her hand, and when he acknowledged it
she exclaimed, "Please, sir, he means *'charge it'!"* It was a simple
thing then for the teacher to explain how Jesus had paid the
price of our redemption, and that those who receive Him need
not pay the great debt of their sin. They may freely take of the
water of life and the wine and milk of salvation without money
and without price by virtue of the fact that it has been *charged*
to the Savior's account.

> *Mark the sacrifice appointed!*
> *See who bears the awful load!*
> *'Tis the Word, the Lord's Anointed,*
> *Son of man, and Son of God!*—Thomas Kelly

**SALVATION: God thought it; Christ bought it; the devil
fought it; have you got it?**

A GLORIOUS CERTAINTY

*God is our refuge and strength, a very present help
in trouble.*   Psalm 46:1

Many who experienced firsthand the horrors of Nazism are
still living today. Millions of their fellow citizens were put to
death in the "gas ovens," while thousands who opposed Hitler
or criticized his policies were imprisoned or banished. A young
man, Dr. Herbert Gezork, was one of those forced into exile. The
night before he left for America, he wandered through the dark
streets of Hamburg lonely and deeply discouraged. He kept thinking, "What hope is there in a world where demonic forces are
triumphing?" He heard the tones of an organ as he passed a
church, so he entered and stood in the vestibule to listen. The
organist, completely unaware of Gezork's presence, was playing,
"A Mighty Fortress Is Our God." The words of one verse of
that hymn passed through Gezork's mind as he heard the majestic
music: "And though this world, with devils filled, should threaten
to undo us, we will not fear, for *God hath willed His truth to
triumph through us!*" At first they seemed a hollow mockery.
Gradually, however, the lonely and disheartened young man began to realize that God is indeed on the throne, that He never
changes, and that those who trust Him will surely triumph. Before long, catching the spirit of the song, he lifted his voice and
sang, "Let goods and kindred go, this mortal life also; the body
they may kill: God's truth abideth still, His Kingdom is forever."

We live in a day of change and uncertainty. Everywhere
people are cynical and afraid. But as Christians we can thank
the Lord we have a living, sovereign God who loves us and
never changes!

> *The Lord of hosts is on our side,*
> *Our safety to secure;*
> *The God of Jacob is for us*
> *A refuge strong and sure!*   —Anon.

**Our great matters are little to God's power, and our little
matters are great to His love!**

"THE SHEAVES ARE SURELY SEVEN"

*Cast thy bread upon the waters; for thou shalt find
it after many days.*   Ecclesiastes 11:1

The truths of the Gospel may lie dormant for a long time in
the human heart, until in some way they are once again brought
under the light and warmth of the Holy Spirit's influence. Then
those precious seeds will shoot up and bloom in beauty. The instructions of a pious mother, for instance, may lie in the heart
fruitless from childhood to old age, and yet at last be the means
of saving the soul into which they were planted.

Recently a friend gave me a helpful poem written shortly after
the Civil War by an anonymous author. It speaks of the spiritual
impact made by a Sunday school teacher who many years before
had cast his "bread upon the waters." The poem is entitled:
"The Noisy Seven." "I wonder if he remembers, that teacher,
blest in Heaven, the class in the old red schoolhouse, known as
the 'Noisy Seven'? I wonder if he remembers how restless we
used to be, or thinks we forgot the lessons of Christ and Gethsemane? I wish I could tell the story as he used to tell it then;
for surely with Heaven's blessing I could reach the hearts of men.
That voice so touchingly tender comes down to me through the
years, with pathos which seems to mingle his own with the
Savior's tears. I often wish I could tell him, though we caused
him so much pain, by our thoughtless, boyish frolic, *the lessons
were not in vain!* I'd like to tell him how Harry, the merriest one
of all, from the bloody fields of Shiloh went Home at his Master's
call. I'd like, yes, I'd like to tell him what his lessons did for me,
and how I am trying to follow that Christ of Gethsemane. Perhaps he knows it already, for Harry has told him, may be, that
we are coming — coming, through the Christ of Calvary! How
many besides, I know not, will gather at last in Heaven — the
fruit of his faithful sowing — but *the sheaves are surely seven!"*
Don't be discouraged — keep plowing, planting, and praying!

*Cast thy bread upon the waters;
Why wilt thou still doubting stand?
Bounteous shall God send the harvest,
If thou sow'st with liberal hand.*—J. Hanaford

If enough good seed is sown, some is bound to germinate!

BLESSING FOR CURSING

Bless them who persecute you; bless, and curse not.
                                        Romans 12:14

Many years ago a soldier, hearing General Robert E. Lee speak to the President in complimentary terms about an officer, was greatly astonished. "General," he said, "do you know that this man you speak of so highly is one of your worst enemies and misses no opportunity to malign you?" "Yes," said the general, "but the President asked for my opinion *of him.* He did not ask for his opinion *of me.*"

A friend recently visited one of the large television studios in Hollywood where a leading network program was being taped. By special arrangement he was allowed to view a portion of the production. The thing that impressed him most was the rapport the various performers had with each other, and the genuine appreciation of their fellow artists. What a contrast may be seen as we observe many church members who are prone to criticize other believers and quickly downgrade zealous Christian workers. Too often, instead of encouraging one another, a spirit of jealousy and unholy competition is displayed.

The real test of a genuine Christian spirit is to return blessing for cursing. We are to respond to criticism with praise, meet envy with good will, and subdue a selfish, competitive attitude by offering cooperation. Paul tells us in 1 Corinthians 13 that "love suffereth long, and is kind; love envieth not; love vaunteth not itself, . . . seeketh not its own, is not easily provoked."

Let us be kind one to another, and be ready to bless those who curse us.

> *If wrongs to me from others come,*
> *Lord, teach me what to say;*
> *May I love those who persecute,*
> *And for them ever pray!* —Bosch

I shall allow no man to depress and belittle my soul by making me hate him!
                                        —B. T. Washington

"INTERESTING TROUBLES"

Fret not thyself. . . . Trust in the Lord. Psalm 37:1, 3

One evening at a church dinner, Mr. Simms found himself seated beside a youthful-looking matron with a vivacious personality. After they became acquainted, she told him she was married to an invalid and that they had two sickly children. Their financial means was small, and the heavy expenses entailed by illness, coupled with her husband's inability to practice his profession, had reduced their income to a minimum. "In fact," she said, "sometimes when I go to bed at night, I scarcely know where tomorrow's meals are coming from." Mr. Simms remarked that she seemed to have her full share of troubles and asked if she did not find the anxieties of life almost overwhelming. "Anxiety?" she replied, "Oh no, I never feel that! I've learned by God's grace never to fret, but always to trust. *Troubles seem to me intensely interesting. Every difficulty that comes along is a perpetual source of wonder. I am so eager to see how the Lord will get me out of it!* To stand aside and watch God's ever-varying but never-failing methods of extricating me from each tangle of trial is a thousand times more engrossing than the most thrilling drama ever written. Knowing as I do from past experience that in every difficulty He will somehow land me safely on the other side, I can find no room for anxiety. Why," she added with a fine touch of spiritual enthusiasm, "if life was stripped of what men call its cares and anxieties, it would be robbed of nearly all its interest and worth."

Do you have a faith that never frets, *but finds trouble interesting* because it is so wonderful to see how God will lovingly solve for you life's difficulties?

> *Fierce drives the storm, but wind and waves*
> *Within His hand are held;*
> *And, trusting His omnipotence,*
> *My fears are sweetly quelled.*   —Brown

The trusting Christian finds that most of his comforts grow up between crosses!   —Young

DAILY "REVIVAL"

. . . O Lord . . . I cry unto thee daily. Psalm 86:3

I shall never forget one particular chapel service during my college days. As I entered the auditorium that morning I had no particular sense of expectation, but I shall always remember the deep moving of the Spirit of God in the meeting that followed. An almost unbearable conviction of sin gripped my heart during that hour. It made even simple, so-called trivial matters loom up as huge, mountainous sins against a thrice holy God. *I was in the midst of a great revival!* That day the Holy Spirit wrought a deep conviction of sin upon the student body. It was an experience that defies description. Sin had never seemed more awful, and the Spirit's convicting power never greater. The chapel service extended right on through the lunch period, the dinner hour, and into the evening. Many of the students not only acknowledged their sins and shortcomings to God, but also made public confession. There were outsiders who criticized the events of those days, saying it was a scene overcharged with emotionalism. However, I know the Lord did a special work in my heart which is still bearing fruit in my life at this present time.

We desperately need revival today. But it cannot be forced; there is no magic formula to induce it. The revival in which I was involved came without warning or preparation. *God* sent it! It may be that most of us will never be in the midst of such a great public moving; yet the Lord has revealed in His Word how we as individual believers may experience personal, spiritual refreshing *every day* of our lives. We can have it by facing the fact of our need, confessing our sins, and feasting daily on the three complete foods of the spiritual man: the Word of God, prayer, and witnessing. So don't sit back and wait for a mass revival; *seek that individual, personal refreshing which can be yours every day!*

> *Let the Spirit take possession of your soul;*
> *Let the Savior in His sweetness have control.*
> *Feed upon the Word each day,*
> *Ever witness, work, and pray,*
> *And the waves of heavn'ly joy will o'er you roll!*—I.H.

Revival is the daily experience of a soul which is full of Jesus and running over!

THE PARABLE OF THE TWO DOGS

*For now we see in a mirror, darkly; . . . but then
shall I know even as also I am known.*
1 Corinthians 13:12

The apostle here was not speaking of the kind of glass with which we are familiar. The original language indicates he was referring to a *mirror* made of polished brass. The reflections it produced were dark and distorted. Now, says Paul, that's the way we see God's plans and purposes here — vaguely and imperfectly. However, when we reach Heaven, we will behold all things with the clarity of an "eye-to-eye" meeting!

Recently a lady passed along to me a little incident which well illustrates this truth. She wrote: "This morning I threw a plate of old cookies out into the yard for the birds, because I do not like to waste any God-given food. I have two Dachshunds: a mother dog, Hilda, who is very heavy and fat, and her offspring, Heidi, who is very slim. Both dogs are properly cared for and are in excellent health, but the mother just loves to gorge herself. When I let her out to get exercise, she immediately goes hunting and eats anything she can find. Now this morning both dogs discovered the cookies and started eating them. I was afraid for the mother dog; I don't want her to have a heart attack because of overweight. I therefore went out and put her on a leash so that she could still get some sunshine, but not the extra food. She looked hurt and disappointed, and hung her head because I let her puppy keep on helping herself. Maybe Hilda thought I was more fond of Heidi, but the truth is I love them both equally well. She couldn't understand that the cookies wouldn't hurt her slim puppy, but might harm her. So, too, I thought, Christians cannot always fathom God's wise judgments. He may have to take some things from a believer that he enjoys very much, but which the Lord knows will eventually hurt him."

Why pout when things don't go exactly the way you like? Everything God sends or withholds is done with loving forethought. Someday you will clearly see that all was for your good.

*Well I know His great heart planneth
Naught but good for me;
Joy and sorrow interwoven,
Love in all I see!*   —Anon.

The will of God is not a burden to carry, but a pillow to rest on!
                                        —Hannah W. Smith

"BALDING" CHRISTIANS

. . . let a man examine himself . . . . 1 Corinthians 11:28

Barney, who had always been proud of his thick, black, wavy hair, began to lose it. It kept dropping out until one lone hair remained on top of his shiny pate. One morning Barney awoke, looked at his pillow, and was shocked to see, lying there all alone, that one remaining hair. Jumping out of bed, he ran downstairs crying, "Martha, Martha, *I'm bald!"*

What a picture of the Christian who begins dabbling in the things of this world. He progressively goes downward spiritually, getting deeper and deeper into sin — steadily sliding back farther and farther away from the Lord without even knowing what is happening. It is not until he has had some startling experience, perhaps due to divine chastening, that he is made to realize his true condition before God. You see, the devil would lead the believer so gradually downward that he doesn't perceive what's going on until he has been brought into the very depths of sinful degradation. Then, when suddenly brought under the powerful searchlight of the Word of God, the deluded one is shocked as he realizes how subtly and deceitfully old Satan has stripped away his spiritual power and discernment.

How far some folks have slipped can be seen in their TV habits. Whereas a few years ago, they wouldn't have thought of going to see a movie in the theater, now they invite the so-called "stars" to come right into their very homes where their youngsters with inquisitive, impressionable and open minds are waiting to drink in suggestive and shameful sights and sounds. What makes an "old movie" in the home less offensive spiritually than that "new movie" in the theater? How important that we "examine" ourselves daily and avoid the shock that was Barney's! *Have you been getting "bald" spiritually?* By looking into the mirror of God's Word, you'll see at a glance!

> *If your time is spent for Jesus,*
> *And your soul delights to pray,*
> *You'll retain your Christian witness*
> *As you journey down life's way!* —G.W.

Let Christ conquer within if you would conquer without!

DON'T BE RESIGNED!

As sorrowful, yet always rejoicing. 2 Corinthians 6:10

To rejoice in sorrow, to be happy when we are persecuted, and to give thanks in everything, takes grace. Yet, this is the Lord's command to each of His tested children. If the Savior is leading, and we recognize Him as the tender Good Shepherd who never makes any mistakes, then we should not let distresses unnerve us, or sorrow break our spirit.

Many years ago someone handed me a tract on which were printed these instructive words from an anonymous author: "It is better to rejoice than to be resigned. The word 'resigned' is not found in the Bible, but 'rejoice' runs through the Scriptures like a great carillon of music. There is danger of self-pity in resignation — and self-pity is deadly poison. There is no danger, however, that we will be pitying ourselves while rejoicing 'with joy unspeakable and full of glory.' Resignation often means a certain mock piety — perhaps unconsciously so, but nevertheless real. Joy, however, is 'the fruit of the Spirit'; not a counterfeit, but real with supernatural and divine power. The Lord Jesus Christ told His disciples that hard times were coming for them, and that these difficulties meant blessing (Luke 6:22). And how did the Lord say the disciples should take those experiences when they came? With resignation? God forbid! He said, *'Rejoice ye in that day, and leap for joy; for, behold, your reward is great in heaven'!"*

Yes, we must avoid self-pity and its sorrow-faced counterpart of "mere resignation." Both are unworthy reactions to God's leading. Don't be "resigned"; it is a form of unholy fatalism, and, as such, is never mentioned in the Bible.

> *So bless the travail of gloom-filled hours,*
> *For joy is oft wrought with pain —*
> *And what if the day be dark? Thank God*
> *That the sun will shine again!*   —MacLennan

True victory is to rejoice in what God sends, and never to long for what He sees fit to deny!

IT'S NOT AN EASY ROAD

> *Yea, and all that will live godly in Christ Jesus shall*
> *suffer persecution.*   2 Timothy 3:12

The hymnwriter expresses this same truth as follows:

> Must I be carried to the skies,
>   On flowery beds of ease,
> While others fought to win the prize,
>   And sailed through bloody seas?
> No, I must fight, if I would reign,
>   Increase my courage, Lord;
> I'll bear the toil, endure the pain,
>   Supported by Thy Word.

Christ is the answer to all of life's problems, and He does fully satisfy the thirsty soul; still there is a battle to fight and a victory to win. In this vein, J. L. Stanley writes: "Though Christ was in the vessel, yet there was a storm. Though the twelve were His disciples, they had to face human wolves. Paul was a devoted servant of God, and yet he was in perils continually. The Christian is like a tree: he matures slowly and has to encounter various kinds of weather — sunshine and shade, fair weather and foul. The Christian is a soldier, and like a soldier he has to meet with hardships. The Christian is also a runner; and in contending for the heavenly prize he has to undergo continuous discipline and training. So all the vexations, trials, and difficulties which the believer experiences do not indicate any flaw in the divine arrangements; they are part of God's plan and the working out of His purposes."

Rather than being overwhelmed by the opposition and storms of life, thank God for the strength He imparts and the assurance that "he that overcometh shall inherit all things" (Rev. 21:7).

> *Though round me the storms of adversity roll,*
> *And the waves of destruction encompass my soul,*
> *In vain this frail vessel the tempest shall toss,*
> *My hopes rest secure on the blood of the Cross.* —Anon.

The gem cannot be polished without friction, nor the child of God perfected without adversity.

"GET ON YOUR KNEES"

Let us draw near with a true heart in full assurance
of faith . . . .   Hebrews 10:22

Has your child ever rushed up to you in a moment of fear or panic, nestled in your arms and said, "Daddy (or Mommy), you'll take care of me, won't you?" Well, that's the way God wants His own to "draw near . . . *in full assurance of faith.*" When such warm trust is displayed, the Heavenly Father loves to comfort and reassure His trembling child and give him the protection, blessing, and answers to prayer he seeks.

But I hear some fatalist exclaim, "Hasn't God predestined all things? How then can our prayers have any effect?" Ah, but my friend, you are forgetting that God does more than predestine the *end,* He also predestines the *means* to that *end.* He has decreed that His child shall pray, and, because he does, the things that befall him will turn out for his highest good. The Lord consequently *moves upon the hearts of His own to pray for that which He has already determined to grant them!* In the process, faith is strengthened, and God's name glorified, as men see their petitions bear fruit. Is it any wonder then that James declares: "The effectual, fervent prayer of a righteous man *availeth much*" (James 5:16)!

A band of tourists were once attempting to climb the snow-clad Matterhorn. The way was steep and perilous. On a particularly dangerous and narrow passage, where the snow and ice made the upward journey extremely hazardous, a sudden gust of wind swept down upon the party just as they were rounding a sharp curve in the mountain track. The guide, accustomed to such unexpected blasts but knowing the imminent danger, shouted at the top of his voice, "Get down on your knees! You're safe only when you're on your knees!" What a parable on the Christian life. We often find the upward path difficult and beset with trials. Storms may burst upon us suddenly, but when they do, our Guide is just saying to us, "Get on your knees!" *Get down on your knees!*"

Prayer is not overcoming God's reluctance, it is laying hold of His highest willingness.   —Trench

"A SHAMEFUL WASTE?"

*But I would ye should understand, brethren, that the
things which happened . . . have fallen out rather
unto the furtherance of the gospel.* Philippians 1:12

Some years ago when five trained, talented, and dedicated
young men were massacred by the Auca Indians, the Christian
world was stunned. At the time many of us wondered why
God permitted this seeming tragedy. It appeared that they had
died in a vain effort. Some commentators termed it "a shameful
waste." Today we know that the death of those five missionaries
opened the way for reaching many primitive people with the
Gospel, including some of those who had committed the murders.

During the last part of January, 1968, six Alliance missionaries
died at the hands of Viet Cong soldiers. Again we were deeply
moved when we heard the news; yet, we have faith to believe
that blessing and salvation will also flow from the death of these
martyrs.

Acts 6 and 7 tell us about a talented and dedicated young man
whose promising career was abruptly cut off. His enemies succeeded in killing him, but they did not defeat him. Before they
rushed him out to the place of execution, he stood in their presence radiating the glory of Heaven. Looking up, he actually saw
the resurrected Christ. As they began stoning him, he committed
his spirit into the hands of Jesus, praying, "Lord, lay not this sin
to their charge." In thus asking mercy for his enemies, he followed Christ's example. Victorious even in death, he went to
join the Savior he loved.

The martyrdom of Stephen made a profound impression upon
a young man named Saul, and only eternity will reveal how
much it accomplished. Thus down through the ages of history
the blood of the martyrs has become the seed of the Church!
Indeed, *a life laid down for Christ is never wasted!*

> *The martyr, Stephen, gave his all,*
>   *In standing for the Lord;*
> *Such witness ne'er is wasted here,*
>   *'Tis mightier than the sword.* —Bosch

A grave often speaks louder than a life!   —A. Tyler

"HERE I COME"

Yea, though I walk through the valley of the shadow
of death, I will fear no evil . . . .   Psalm 23:4

When I was about ten years of age I climbed the big pine tree in our front yard. Grabbing the topmost branch, I began pulling myself upward a few more inches to gain the highest vantage point possible. Suddenly the top of the old pine snapped, I came plummeting downward, and hit the ground flat on my back. With the wind knocked out of me, I lay gasping for breath. The sensation was such that I actually thought I was dying; but I wasn't at all alarmed! In fact, I can recall thinking to myself, "I'm going to Heaven." And then, just before lapsing into unconsciousness, I can remember saying with childlike confidence, "Father, here I come."

Dad was studying under a shade tree nearby and heard me come crashing down. Rushing over, he picked me up and carried me into the house. What a surprise was mine when I opened my eyes and found myself on our couch, since I had expected to wake up in Heaven. Although my fall was quite upsetting for Mother and Dad, I'm glad I had the experience because it taught me at a very early age that the Christian can have peace even in the valley of the shadow of death. For believers ". . . to live is Christ, and to die is gain," and ". . . to be absent from the body," is "to be present with the Lord." As children of God, we can live each day with the assurance that come what may, whether we live or die, we are the Lord's.

When Stephen, the first martyr, was being stoned, he called upon God saying, "Lord Jesus, receive my spirit." Stephen had peace even when facing death. His cry, "Lord Jesus, receive my spirit" was simply an adult version of a little boy's cry, "Father, here I come!"

If you know Christ as your Savior, you too can experience a wonderful peace even if you are called to walk through the "valley of the shadow."

Christ has made death just a starlit strip between the companionships of yesterday and the reunions of tomorrow!

THE WELL-SPENT LIFE

*I live; yet not I, but Christ liveth in me . . . and
gave himself for me.*   Galatians 2:20

A messenger came to the home of a minister of the Gospel
with a request that he visit a sick lady. He said she desired to
see him because she had almost reached the end of her journey.
Then he added, "She is very happy in the review of a well-spent
life." Of course, this caused the minister great concern, as he
thought that no doubt here was a soul about to enter eternity
with nothing better to rest on than the memory of her own good
deeds.

Arriving at the house, he questioned the dying one, "Did I
understand correctly that you are very happy just reviewing a
well-spent life?" She gave him a searching, yet contented glance,
as she replied with a smile, "Indeed I am, but it is not MY well-
spent life; it is the *well-spent life of the Lord Jesus* to which I
had reference!" To his joy the minister found that she was resting fully upon the all-sufficient work of the Savior, and was conscious of her identification with Him. She knew that God had
reckoned her as one with the Lord Jesus in His death, burial,
and resurrection, and that any goodness she had manifested in
her life was the result of her union with the Living Christ.

This is the secret of the Christian experience and its undying
vitality — the Lord Jesus Himself. Faced with the impossibility
of performing in a way that would be acceptable to God, we
must receive Him who is *the Life*. Having delivered us from
spiritual death, He now dwells within us in the person of His
Holy Spirit, giving us the continuing and "more abundant" life
that He alone can provide.

As rays of light from yonder sun,
The flowers of earth set free,
So life and light and love come forth
From Christ living in me.   —Whittle

Christianity is not a cloak PUT ON, but a life PUT IN!

"TEAKETTLE RELIGION"

*For by grace are ye saved through faith; . . . not
of works . . . .*   Ephesians 2:8, 9

When my good friend Elmer Strauss, now a missionary in
West Cameroon, Africa, visited in our home, he referred to Mo-
hammedanism as a "teakettle religion," because its adherents carry
these containers filled with water wherever they go. A "good"
Moslem will pray four or five times a day facing east and bowing toward Mecca, but not without first pouring out some water
from his teakettle in a special ritual of cleansing.

A certain Moslem was on a bus one day, and since it was
time for him to pray, he asked the driver to stop so that he
could attend to his devotions. (How unlike Christians who
can pray at any time, any place. Prayer for us is talking with
God, not a matter of going through some external, mechanical
motions or assuming a certain prescribed posture.) At the Mo-
hammedan's urging, the bus driver stopped right in front of the
missionary compound where Mr. Strauss lived. The man who
wanted to pray was in such a hurry to get out that he climbed
right over some of the passengers, spilling all the water out of
his kettle. That didn't stop him, however. He sat down on the
ground beside the bus and went through the outward motions —
lifting up his empty little kettle as though he were pouring the
water on his hands and feet. What a picture of his equally
empty religion!

Right here at home, however, we can also see a form of "teakettle religion." There are those who merely go through the
motions. They attend church, sing hymns, and recite prayers,
but their heart is not in it. We are to serve God "in spirit and
in truth," for the Lord does not want mere perfunctory worship.
No, "the sacrifices of God are a broken spirit . . . and a contrite
heart" — these the Lord will not despise (Ps. 51:1, 17). If you
have not come to know Christ through the new birth, all the
outward acts of your "teakettle religion" will do you no good!

**Religion may REFORM, but only Christ can TRANSFORM a
man!**

LOVE REKINDLED

> . . . *teach the young women . . . to love their*
> *husbands, to love their children.*   Titus 2:4

Some years ago a young lady tearfully told me that she and her husband were having difficulty, and then declared that she no longer loved him and wanted to break up their home. I knew that her husband had some flaws (as all husbands have), but I also felt sure he was a Christian. Further questioning revealed she had no real basis for a divorce. Therefore I told this young wife that she had no choice in the matter, except to obey God's Word and stay with him despite some personality clashes that occasionally marred their relationship. I then read Titus 2, verse 4, to her and told her that *God, in fact, commanded her to love her husband!* You see, love in the home is not an optional matter. It is God's absolute will that love should be present in the relationship that exists between husband and wife, as well as between parents and children (Eph. 6:1, 2). Some of you may object that "you cannot legislate love." In a sense this is true. You cannot solve family problems by passing a law. However, I am sure that if every Christian husband or wife would really take seriously God's command to *"love one another,"* many homes would be transformed.

There is nothing more tragic than to see a family drift apart, and yet this always happens when love has almost died. This does not mean, however, that it cannot be rekindled. If each one concerned would be willing to admit his or her measure of blame, and honestly make confession to God, many homes could be saved.

Today begin to shower special attention upon that partner you have been neglecting; let the sweet winds of grace blow upon the smoldering embers of your "dying marriage" and then watch the flame of love break forth anew!

> *I wonder, if you were to kneel quite low,*
> *And would strive with the tenderest care,*
> *To rescue that spark in the ashes there,*
> *Would it glow again with its beauty rare—*
> *If you were to kneel quite low?*   —Anon.

A Christian home does not happen—it is built, and the building blocks are "LOVE" and "FORGIVENESS."   —Bosch

YOUNG OR NEVER?

Train up a child in the way he should go and, when he is old, he will not depart from it. Proverbs 22:6

A certain preacher asked an audience of born-again believers to write down the age at which they were converted. He tabulated these revealing answers:

Converted before 20 years of age — 548
Converted between 20 and 30 years — 337
Converted between 30 and 40 years — 86
Converted between 50 and 60 years — 13
Converted between 60 and 70 years — 1

These statistics underscore most emphatically the urgency of making sure our children hear the Gospel at an early age. Yet how sad is the lack of emphasis in regard to reaching and influencing them for Christ in our homes and churches. Other things too often seem to take priority. Some time ago I came across an article entitled, "Where Are the Boys?" It related how a pastor in a fashionable city church started a work among the youngsters who lived in a slum area. He succeeded in getting many of them into the church where he taught them the way of salvation. Unfortunately, the lads with their dirty shoes soiled the carpet. The pastor was called before the church officers to discuss the damage. The preacher said, "Suppose that when I am called to give an account to my Lord I say, 'Here, Master, is the church which Thou didst entrust to me; it's in good shape. The carpet is as good as new.' Will He praise me, or will He ask, 'Where are the souls I sent you to win? Where are the boys?'"

While it is extremely important to teach our children the truths of God's Word, it is also essential that we *live the Word before them*. We may spend hours telling them what to do and then ruin it all by not practicing what we preach. That which our little ones hear from our lips and see in our lives in their impressionable years may well determine where they will spend eternity.

Ere a child has reached to seven,
Teach him all the way to Heaven;
Better still the work will thrive
If he learns before he's five. —C. H. Spurgeon

Children brought up in Sunday school are seldom brought up in court!
                                                            —B. Miller

BOMBSHELL ANSWERS TO PRAYER

. . . men ought always to pray, and not to faint.

Luke 18:1

Prayer is more than a privilege—it is a solemn *obligation*. The Scriptures tell us "men OUGHT . . . to pray." More than that, such intercession should not be "hit or miss" and spasmodic, but *fervent* and *constant*. "Men ought ALWAYS to pray." Finally, each petition should be uttered with *faith and hope* so discouragement will not easily seal our lips or dull our interest. We are *"not to faint."*

During World War II a man in Sussex, England, sent some money to the Scripture Gift Mission, mentioning that he wished he could enclose more but that the harvest had been very disappointing on his farm owing to the lack of water. He also mentioned that he was very fearful because so many bombs were being dropped by the Germans, and asked for their prayers that he and his family might be spared in the siege. Mr. Ashley Baker answered on behalf of the mission and said that although they could not ask the Lord that no bombs should be dropped on his land, *they would pray that God's will for their lives in this matter would prevail!* Shortly after the farmer received the communication, a huge German missile crashed down on his place. None of his family or the livestock was injured. However, the bombshell went so deep into the ground that *it liberated a submerged stream!* The spring continued to flow and yielded water not only for his own farm, but also sufficient to solve the irrigation problem of his neighbors. The next year, due to a bountiful harvest, he was able to send a $200 offering to the mission. All were impressed anew with the thought that God is "able to do exceedingly abundantly above all that we ask or think . . ." (Eph. 3:20).

If we ask the Lord for His will for our life with faith, hope, and a good conscience, we may get some "bombshell answers" to our prayers, but they will be infinitely wiser and more blessed than anything we could personally request.

> *God's ways are not like human ways,*
> *He wears such strange disguises.*
> *He tests us with His long delays,*
> *And then our faith surprises!* —Anon.

Keep praying, but be thankful that God's answers are wiser than your prayers!

—Dr. W. Culbertson

THE ICED BELL

. . . the love of many shall grow cold. Matthew 24:12

I once received a letter from Pastor Raymond Biddle in which he related the following incident: "Our church has a good, clear ringing bell, but yesterday we were ashamed of it. The first dull sound sent me looking for the bell ringer, who soon found out what was wrong. Nearly an inch of snow and sleet had blown on it during a night storm, and consequently it was thoroughly encased in ice. What a poor call to worship it gave. And then the Lord impressed the thought upon my heart that Christians, too, often become sheathed in the sound-deadening things of the world. As a result, their witness becomes 'ice encased.'"

It is both our duty and privilege to peal forth with a clear and ringing spiritual testimony; and yet how often our words and deeds are made ineffective by the icy things of this world. They cover up and mute the "joyful sound" of the believer. How the devil rejoices when Christians are drawn away from the Lord and become so cold spiritually that the things of this earth cling to them and "freeze up" their testimony. Some of the "ices" that encase believers are: pride, jealousy, materialism, hatred, lying, gossip, envy, and all the other vices that characterize the "old man." The best way to keep from becoming "iced up" is to *keep "fired up."* This is accomplished through prayer (1 Thess. 5:17), the study of God's Word (Ps. 119:11), and by maintaining fellowship with other believers (Heb. 10:25). Paul tells us in Hebrews 12:1, ". . . let us lay aside every weight, and the sin which doth so easily beset us . . . ." How wonderful the promise that "If we confess our sins, he is faithful and just to forgive us our sins, and to cleanse us from all unrighteousness" (1 John 1:9).

It's time some Christians had a good "thaw," and got rid of all the "ice" in their lives. Their testimony would then sound forth with a clear-cut ring!

> *Make it ring out clear, with a note of cheer,*
> *Keep the bell of your testimony bright;*
> *Let the frosts of sin its sweet tone ne'er dim,*
> *It must echo the Gospel through the night!*—H.G.B.

Spiritual enthusiasm is contagious; remember, more people chase fire engines than ice carts!

UNDENIABLE EVIDENCE

*And all that sat in the council . . . saw his face as
it had been the face of an angel.*   Acts 6:15

Someone gave me a card the other day with this question printed on it, "If you were arrested for being a Christian, would there be enough evidence to convict you?" As I thought of this I couldn't help wondering how many enemies of the Gospel would testify that I was guilty of witnessing to them concerning my Savior? How many wicked people would say that my godly conduct and Christlike spirit put them to shame? Would unsaved individuals charge that the influence of my life constitutes a menace to their cause?

Our suggested Scripture reading (Acts 6) presents Stephen on trial because of his devotion to Jesus Christ, and the evidence was indisputable. In fact, the reason for his arrest was that his adversaries had become infuriated when "they were not able to resist the wisdom and the Spirit by which he spoke." They had been silenced by his arguments and confounded by the Christlike attitude he evidenced. They hated him so much they resorted to bribery and perjury to destroy him. However, as they looked upon him, their faces angry and their eyes flashing, they saw Stephen's countenance glowing as if reflecting the very presence of God. This radiance was too much for his antagonists, and they soon hustled him out to the stoning ground. One of their number, Saul of Tarsus, however, never forgot that scene. The remembrance of it burned in his soul until he accepted Jesus as his Master and, like Stephen, became a Spirit-filled Christian witness.

Ask yourself the solemn question, "If I were arrested for being a Christian, would there be enough evidence to convict me?"

Has someone seen Christ in you today?
Christian, look to your heart, I pray.
The world, with a criticizing view,
Has watched, but did it see Jesus in you?—Hopkins

So live that no man can despise your Savior!   —Miller

WORKS THAT FOLLOW

Every man's work shall be made manifest . . . of
what sort it is.   1 Corinthians 3:13

Walking along the seashore early one morning, I was lost in meditation. Suddenly I became aware of a boat chugging its way out to the ocean. As the sound of the engines faded, I continued to plod along the beach and was again blessed by that feeling of aloneness with God. A few minutes later, however, I was startled to hear the splashing of water behind me, and I swung around quickly, expecting to see someone following me. To my surprise the sound was only that of the boat's wake gushing upon the beach as it reached the shoreline. As I gazed upon the horizon and saw the vessel rapidly disappearing from view, and heard its backwash breaking at my feet, the thought came that we are all like ships at sea, and our "works do follow" us. Everything we do puts something into motion. We leave behind ripples of influence which follow long after we ourselves are gone. The words we speak, the deeds we perform, the kindnesses we show to others — as well as our unloving, inconsiderate, and selfish acts — will all have far-reaching consequences for good or bad. The "wake" of our lives may come rolling in years after our departure for the Heavenly Shore.

John the apostle writes in Revelation 14 concerning those who die in the Lord that they "rest from their labors" and *"their works do follow them."* And Paul reminds us that "every man's work shall be made manifest."

May we all so live that when, like a ship at sea, we have passed out of sight, those who remain behind and see the works that "do follow" may "thank God upon every remembrance" of us.

You never can tell when you do an act
Just what the result will be;
Yet with every deed, you are sowing a seed
And its harvest someday you will see. —Anon.

Which will you leave behind — stepping stones or stumbling blocks?

WORSHIPING WITH THE ACCELERATOR

Submit yourselves to every ordinance of man for the Lord's sake.   1 Peter 2:13

A certain Bible teacher, now gone to be with the Lord, once admitted that for many years he had been careless about speed laws if there was no policeman in sight. Then one day when his wife was at the wheel, she taught him a lesson. Her meticulous observance of every traffic sign and every rule of the road caused him to comment impatiently about her handling of the car. She replied that as a Christian she felt compelled to drive that way. "I look upon it," she said, "as *worshiping the Lord with my accelerator foot!"*

The next time the minister made his 80-miles trip into New York he drove 50 miles per hour if that was the posted limit — not 51. He was determined that he too would "worship the Lord with his accelerator foot," even though it took a lot of self-discipline, especially when going through the 25- and 15-mile-per-hour districts. To his amazement he experienced real spiritual joy. He also noted that he was coming to the lights when they were green, and was finding an opening in the traffic every time he needed one. When he arrived at his destination, he discovered he had made good time, and was relaxed and ready for his appointments.

As Christians we must set a good example before the world, even in the matter of obeying ordinances that may seem trivial. Our conduct should show the unsaved that we are ever conscious of God and His will. Obedience, even in small things, will be enjoyable when we see it as a means through which we may express our love for the Lord.

> *Though some would scarce consider it true,*
> *And some at this thought would balk,*
> *The way you drive your automobile*
> *Is part of your Christian "walk"!* —Bosch

The subjects of the Kingdom should display the manners of the court!

JUST A "DOORKEEPER"

*I had rather be a doorkeeper in the house of my God,
than to dwell in the tents of wickedness.* Psalm 84:10

The *United Press International* reported this interesting story:
"For several years a 14-inch statue was used as a doorstop in the
home of Leo Carey of Green Township, Ohio. It was not until
Carey's estate was appraised recently that it was discovered the
statue was a replica in miniature of Rodin's classic sculpture
'The Thinker' created in the 19th century. Art dealers valued
the find at $16,000! The statue was quickly removed to a bank
vault."

After reading that report, my mind went immediately to
Psalm 84 in which we find our text for today. The lowliest
service in the tabernacle was that of keepers of the gates (2 Kings
25:18). These men, the descendants of Korah, had among their
duties the apparently insignificant job of "holding open the
doors" of God's house. They were sort of "spiritual doorstops"—
little appreciated or esteemed by men. Yet they considered this
small opportunity to be of service to the Lord of greater value
than to dwell at ease and be honored in the "tents of wickedness." They found their life's work a source of spiritual joy
simply because it was where God required their activity. Someday they and other "doorkeepers" will be honored by the Lord
for joyfully carrying on such menial but important tasks for His
glory. Many who are considered "last" here will be "first" in
Heaven when the rewards for faithfulness are presented.

Are you tending some little spot for the Savior, unnoticed and
perhaps unappreciated? Remembering that the Lord giveth "grace
to the humble," make the words of Psalm 84:10 your rejoicing
watchword.

> *Nothing is lost that is done for the Lord,*
>   *Let it be ever so small;*
> *The smile of the Savior approveth the deed,*
>   *As though 'twere greatest of all.*   —A. M.

**Doing little things with a strong desire to please God makes
them really great.**   —DeSoles

THE SURE WORD OF PROPHECY

We have . . . a more sure word of prophecy . . . .
                                                    2 Peter 1:19

Today there is a renewed interest in the claims of certain individuals that they can predict the future. We also hear much about ESP and communication with the dead. Many newspapers feature "horoscopes," and millions of readers consult them. Looking for their "sign" in such columns, they seek advice and counsel for that particular day. It is evident that man not only wants desperately to explain the mysteries of life and the inner workings of the mind, but also has an insatiable curiosity concerning things to come. This increased interest may be due to the complexity of life's situations and the uncertain state of present world affairs. Men desire help from some source outside themselves, from someone greater than they, who can help solve their problems and prepare them for the future.

While many folks talk about these modern-day "prophets" and get excited about what "Seer So-and-So" says will happen, how much better it would be if they got enthusiastic about what *God* says will surely come to pass. Whereas these present-day "prophets" are often disappointing in their predictions (most claim only a certain percentage of accuracy at best), God's Word has never failed. For instance, the 109 prophecies concerning Christ's first coming were all fulfilled to the letter!

One of the Bible's most thrilling prophecies for the future is found in 1 Thessalonians 4:16 and 17: "For the Lord himself shall descend from heaven . . . and the dead in Christ shall rise first. Then we who are alive and remain shall be caught up together with them . . . ." The believer therefore can live each day in the bright prospect of the Savior's soon return. We *know* He is coming, for God's Word is certain. When things look rather dark, and the world situation presents a depressing picture, Christians should not let it get them down. Jesus *is* coming! We have this "*sure* word of prophecy."

> *In this day of much deception,*
> *Prophets false and mystic seers,*
> *God's Word changes not nor varies,*
> *It alone allays our fears.*   —Bosch

The more we read the Sacred Pages, the less we heed the self-styled "sages"!
                                                    —H.G.B.

PROFITABLE CHASTENING

*For whom the Lord loveth he chasteneth, and scourgeth
every son whom he receiveth.*   Hebrews 12:6

We worship a God who is too loving to let us alone in our
unsanctified ways. He therefore carefully disciplines us that we
may grow in grace and holiness. It has been said that parents
who refrain from chastening their children really don't love them
as they ought. In fact, they probably love themselves so much
they can't afford the trouble required to take their youngsters
in hand. Rather than be bothered by the necessary discipline,
they weakly let their children "grow up like Topsy" without ever
using the rod of correction or voicing words of reprimand. Our
Heavenly Father, however, is not so selfishly preoccupied. He
wisely scourges and chastens every wayward child that He may
form in him the character of the Crucified. Yet He weighs every
trial, and tempers the force of each adverse wind. He will not
lay a bit more sorrow or testing upon us than is necessary to
conform us to His purposes and condition us for receiving His
highest blessing.

A woman who had endured much suffering once asked her
pastor, "*When* am I going to get out of these troubles?" He
wisely responded, "You should have asked, '*What* am I going to
get out of these troubles?'" Her attitude showed very definitely
that she still had something in her life which needed purging!
Another dear saint, more clearly recognizing the necessity of
chastening, wisely declared, "I could have done without many
pleasures, but I could not have spared *one sorrow* that God allowed to come into my life!"

Remember, afflicted one, chastening is a *mark of God's love*
and, if rightly received, is extremely *profitable.*

> *We may not fully understand*
> *How underneath God's chastening hand*
> *Pain is fulfilling Love's command,*
> *Till "afterward"!*   —Anon.

**When things get rough, remember — it's rubbing that brings
out the shine!**

TRUE EQUALITY

> *. . . there is neither bond nor free, . . . for ye are*
> *all one in Christ Jesus.*   Galatians 3:28

We hear much about equal opportunities, rights, and privileges for all men. There is, however, a place where everyone is on common ground. When Charles Evans Hughes was received into the membership of Calvary Baptist Church, Washington, D.C., his mother and another man of very humble origin were also welcomed. Extending the hand of fellowship to these three, the pastor commented, "At the foot of the cross *the ground is level!*"

One day when the Duke of Wellington was at the communion table, an old and extremely poor man took his place beside him. An usher was about to ask him to leave, but the Duke, sensing what was going on, grasped the elderly gentleman's hand and whispered, "Do not move, friend, *we are all equal here.*"

Another story which emphasizes this truth is told about Oliver Wendell Holmes. While walking along the water's edge one day, he met a small child. After they had strolled down the beach for a short distance, she announced, "I must go home now." As she was leaving, he remarked, "When your mother asks where you have been, just tell her you have been walking with Oliver Wendell Holmes!" The sweet youngster replied, "And when your folks ask where you have been, just tell them you have been walking with Mary Susanna Brown." The child had caught the spirit of true Christianity. In Christ, there are no "big shots," no "favored" ones. At the foot of the cross, as "one in Christ Jesus," we find the meaning of true equality!

> *There is a fellowship of faith*
> *Where all enjoy communion,*
> *And find within that brotherhood*
> *Equality and union!*   —Bosch

However we may deceive ourselves, the poor peasant is as dear to God as the mighty prince!   —Plato

October 8   Read Psalm 104:16-24

ANTS, ANTIFREEZE, AND ADORATION

*How manifold are thy works! In wisdom hast thou
made them all.*   Psalm 104:24

God speaks to us through His special revelation, the Bible,
but also through His general revelation as it is manifested in
creation.

Some years ago I was sent a clipping which makes some very
interesting observations concerning black carpenter ants. These
little insects have been endowed by God with the ability to in-
stall "antifreeze" in their bodies to preserve their lives during the
cold months of the year. Biochemist Fred Smith, of the University of Minnesota, says they actually manufacture glycerol, a
chemical that closely resembles the substance employed by men
to protect their automobile engines from the frigid blasts of
winter. Since the active summer larvae of these creatures do not
contain this ingredient, Mr. Smith reasons that they must have
a mechanism which reacts to cold to produce this protective "alcohol." Hibernating black carpenter ants proved to have as much
as ten percent of this antifreeze in their bodies, but when they
were gradually warmed up and became active, all of it disappeared.

Incidentally, evolution could not have produced these defenses
in the carpenter ant, for, according to their theory, to develop an
intricate process like that would have taken thousands of years—
by which time the first colony of insects would already have been
frozen to death.

As we delve into the intricate and marvelous designs in nature, which we assuredly believe have been master-minded by
God, we exclaim with the Psalmist, "O Lord, how manifold are
thy works! *In wisdom hast thou made them all!*" Yes, ants,
antifreeze, and adoration are thus subtly interrelated!

> *If God displays His mind and art*
> *In each small creature of the wild,*
> *What intricate design of life*
> *Has He not planned for me, His child?* —Anon.

Nature is an outstretched finger pointing toward God!

THE FOOLISH PARAKEET

It is because of the Lord's mercies that we are not consumed, because his compassions fail not.

Lamentations 3:22

In our home we have a parakeet who loves attention. Sometimes, however, he apparently doesn't want to be disturbed. At such times he strikes a very belligerent pose and launches an attack. This amuses us, because he actually is quite helpless. At any moment that we choose to do so, we could simply encircle him with our large hand and remove him from his cage. He might protest loudly, but it would be all to no avail. All his efforts would be futile. We could close our hand tightly and end his life any time we so desired. Foolish little fellow!

We are entertained by these antics; for, after all, he's only a bird. God is not amused, however, by the rage of men as they focus their fury upon Him and His anointed, Jesus Christ — as it is graphically pictured for us in the second Psalm. Their rebellion is wicked because they, unlike our bird, are intelligent and responsible moral agents. Yet there is something pathetically humorous about this mutiny of puny men who are even less able to harm God than my parakeet is to hurt me. Therefore the Psalmist pictures God laughing in derision. In grace He lets men have their little day while He patiently invites them to repent; but if they will not heed, the time of His wrathful intervention will soon come. Foolish, foolish men!

Are you fighting God? Maybe you are not denying Him, or declaring Him dead, but you are determined to live your life your own way. He could forcibly subdue you, and were it not for His mercies you would immediately be consumed. However, He still seeks to rescue your soul in love. Cease your foolishness, and let God have His blessed way in your life!

> *God lovingly is calling yet,*
> *To men who still rebel:*
> *"O 'kiss the Son,' ere judgment fall,*
> *And thy soul 'wake in Hell!"* —Bosch

To escape God's JUSTICE, flee to His LOVE!

PARTING OR INVESTING?

Lay not up for yourselves treasures upon earth, . . .
but . . . in heaven.   Matthew 6:19, 20

As little Jimmy's uncle was about to leave after a visit, he placed a crisp new dollar bill in his nephew's hand, saying, "Be careful how you spend this, Jimmy. You know the old proverb, 'A fool and his money are soon parted.'" To this the lad replied, "I'll remember what you said, Uncle Bill. But thanks anyway for parting with it!" This youngster may have completely misinterpreted his uncle's generosity, but we would do well to let his experience remind us that there's a world of difference between a fool who thoughtlessly *parts* with his money for the fleeting, selfish pleasures of this life, and the wise man who *invests* it in Heaven. Jesus told the rich young ruler, "Sell all that thou hast, and distribute unto the poor, and thou shalt have treasure in heaven." Such giving is not the "parting" of a fool, but the "investing" of a wise man.

The Sunday school lesson had to do with keeping our minds and bodies clean. As the teacher held up a bar of soap to emphasize the point, one little tyke was heard to comment, "Oh, oh, here comes the commercial!" Isn't that the way many feel about the offering?

After the morning service, dad was knocking the preacher, mother was criticizing the choir, and sister was running down the organist. But they all quieted down in a hurry when little brother piped up, "I thought it was a pretty good show *for a dime!*" This family had never discovered that "it is more blessed to give than to receive."

What are you doing with your possessions? Are you foolishly "parting" with them, or wisely "investing" them in everlasting securities?

> *You may lay up vast riches of silver and gold;*
> *And may hoard precious jewels and treasures untold;*
> *But at last when you come to the end of life's road,*
> *Still your wealth will be just what you've given to the Lord!*
>   —Moncrief, alt.

To be rich in GOD is better than to be rich in GOODS!

WHO'S FIRST?

But seek ye first the kingdom of God, and his righteousness, and all these things shall be added unto you.   Matthew 6:33

When a young man made a public profession of Christ, his worldly father was greatly upset and later complained in a critical tone, "Jim, you should have established yourself in a good trade first. Then, once you had made your way in the world, it would have been time enough to think about religion." "Father," came the spiritual reply, "my Savior advises me very differently. He says, 'Seek ye *first* the kingdom of God!'"

If we put the Lord first, nothing else will get out of order. He should have priority in our thoughts, motives, and deepest desires. *Making a living* is a mere incident, but *making a life* is the reason for which we have been placed in this world. If we put God first, all other good things will be added to us.

Many years ago a package was sent from England to a South African town. The man to whom the box was consigned, however, refused to pay the delivery charges, and for fourteen years it was used as a footstool in the express office. Finally, the consignee died and the box was put up at auction with other unclaimed articles. Out of curiosity a man bid on it and secured it at a very low price. When he opened it, he was greatly surprised to find several thousand pounds in English bank notes. Because the man to whom it had been sent refused to pay the comparatively trifling delivery charges, he had missed a considerable fortune. So, too, he who refuses to meet the requirements of Jesus in regard to discipleship is even more shortsighted. What the Lord asks in regard to complete dedication may seem too much for the non-Christian, but those who heed His call find He gives infinitely more in return than anything they are required to surrender for His sake.

Are you seeking first the gratification of self, men's applause, piled-up wealth — or the approval of the Savior?

> *O the peace of full surrender;*
> *All my joy to do His will!*
> *If I seek His blessed kingdom,*
> *He His promise will fulfill!* —Anon.

He who puts God first will find God with him at the last!

PRAYING AND WATCHING

. . . we made our prayer unto our God, and set a watch
against them day and night . . . .   Nehemiah 4:9

When Nehemiah received word about the remnant of the Jews in Jerusalem, and that the wall was broken down, he wept and mourned and prayed. However, he also decided to do something about it! He asked Artaxerxes for permission to go and rebuild the city. When his request was granted, the prophet made his way to Jerusalem and encouraged the inhabitants to reconstruct its walls. The surrounding nations heard about this, became angry and conspired to come and fight against the city. In the light of this, how significant are Nehemiah's words found in chapter 4, verse 9. He says, "Nevertheless, we made our prayer unto our God, *and* set a watch against them day and night . . . ." Then, down in verse 14, Nehemiah declares, "Be not ye afraid of them. Remember the Lord, who is great and awe-inspiring, *and* fight . . . ." This whole experience teaches us a tremendous lesson about faith and works, about Divine and human responsibility. Nehemiah said, "We made our *prayer* unto our God, *and set a watch* against them." They not only prayed to the Lord and trusted Him to do His part, but also assumed their obligation. Nehemiah told them to remember the Lord and *fight!* While trusting God, they were to engage themselves in battle. Still today, prayer and faith are necessary, but they cannot replace watching and "fighting." The resources of God are not usually intended as a replacement for the responsibility of man. We must trust God, to be sure, but that does not relieve us of the obligation to do our part in the battle for truth. *There are many today who would use prayer as an excuse to be lazy!* They want God to do everything. But, remember, there are some things God would have us *do* while trusting Him. Nehemiah said that the Jews made their prayer unto God *and set a watch.* They were to remember the Lord *and fight.* May we ever be ready to do the same!

"Work and pray!" a slogan blest,
Means: ask His help, but do YOUR best!—G.W.

It's not enough to say a prayer, we have to live one too!

GARBAGE IN THE SALAD

If we live in the Spirit, let us also walk in the Spirit.
                                        Galatians 5:25

Our Christian *walk* should square with our Christian *talk!* Many who know the Lord as Savior are not ready for the life of full surrender and discipleship which is necessary for true joy, victory, and fruitfulness in the Christian life. They love to dabble in the world while still clinging to Christ for salvation. As a result they live defeated lives and their testimony is almost worthless. It was Jesus Himself who declared, "No man can serve *two* masters" (Matt. 6:24). Paul says: "If we *live* in the Spirit, let us also *walk* in the Spirit!" After what Jesus has done to redeem our soul, can we do anything less than obey this admonition if we truly love Him and wish to bring others to His side?

Many years ago the *Home Life Magazine* published the following illustration: One day as a mother was scraping and peeling the vegetables for a salad, her daughter came to ask her permission to go to a worldly center of amusement. On the defensive, the daughter admitted it was a questionable place, but all the other girls were going, and they did not think it would actually hurt them. As the girl talked, suddenly she saw her mother pick up a handful of discarded vegetable scraps and throw them into the salad. In a startled voice she cried, "Mother, *you are putting the garbage in the salad!*" "Yes," her mother replied, "I know; but I thought that if you did not mind garbage in your mind and heart you certainly would not mind a little in your stomach!" Thoughtfully the girl removed the offending material from the salad, and with a brief, "Thank you," to her mother, she went to tell her friends she would not be going with them.

If you have spiritual indigestion, and have a "sick" testimony, maybe it's because you have allowed *too much* "garbage in the salad"!

> *Earthly pleasures vainly call me,*
> *I would be like Jesus;*
> *Nothing worldly shall enthrall me,*
> *I would be like Jesus!*   —J. Rowe

You must separate yourself from the fellowship of the world, or the world will separate you from the fellowship of God!

MONKEY BUSINESS

So God created man in his own image.... Genesis 1:27

A church bulletin carried this humorous poem, "The Monkeys' Jamboree," from the pen of Dr. James McGinlay:

> The monkeys one day had a big jamboree.
> Their leader sat up in the tallest tree
> And said with a chuckle, "My good fellow Monk,
> If you want a good laugh, just give ear to this junk.
> The teachers of men in a place they call 'school'
> Are training each youngster to grow up a fool.
> The kids all run wild and never get spanked.
> If our babies did that, their tails would be yanked.
> No well-mannered monkey dictates to his teacher,
> Beats up the policeman or shoots at the preacher,
> Poisons the baby, or kills with a gun,
> And then laughs and says: 'We are just having fun!'
> Monkeys, my friends, have respect for each other.
> We hand out no sass to our father or mother.
> The picture I've painted you'll agree is quite sad.
> But listen, my brothers, I'm boiling mad.
> For here's what they're taught — that miserable flunky,
> That creature called man, was at one time a monkey!
> An ape just like us, and what's more, if you please,
> He claims that at one time he swung through the trees.
> Fellow monkeys, I think this is going too far.
> We don't envy their home, their wealth, or their car.
> But when they will spread such a horrible rumor,
> It's time for all monkeys to lose their good humor.
> So, come, you must help me prepare a big sign,
> Protesting that man's no descendant of mine.
> If evolution be true, then boys, we are sunk;
> For I'd sooner be father to weasel or skunk."

No, my friend, man was originally created good — in God's image: but because of sin, his history has been that of "devolution" rather than evolution.

The probability of life originating by accident is comparable to the possibility of the unabridged dictionary resulting from an explosion in a print shop!

DON'T LOSE YOUR COOL!

Rest in the Lord, and wait patiently for him; fret not thyself.   Psalm 37:7

Most of us are inclined to think that the pressures upon us are the greatest. The Psalmist would have had ample reason to feel that way. Hunted by his enemies, forsaken by his friends, maligned by his critics, David offers some wise spiritual advice in Psalm 37.

While waiting at the counter to check the delay on a flight home, I overheard a perturbed passenger say to the ticket agent, "If you had told me sooner, I wouldn't have lost my cool." It was rather obvious that whatever he had lost, it was still missing! I confess I thought of regrettable occasions when I too had acted in a similar fashion.

The little trifling things that plague our spirits should not be allowed to irritate us to the point of impatience and fretfulness. Certainly we must not let it be followed by bitter complaint. Three times over, the Psalmist uses the phrase, "Fret not thyself" (vv. 1, 7, 8). There is something we can do about it. We must avoid succumbing to the circumstances and the frustrations, lest we add to this human tendency toward fretfulness.

What is the antidote for this? "Rest in the Lord, and wait patiently for him." *The Berkeley Version* translates this, "Be still before the Lord and resign yourself to him." The hymn-writer says, "Moment by moment I'm kept in His love; moment by moment I've life from above; looking to Jesus till glory doth shine; moment by moment, O Lord, I am Thine." We do not have to lose our "cool." A simple "moment by moment" faith which recognizes that "the steps of a good man are ordered by the Lord" will keep us from fretting.

Not so in haste, my heart!
Have faith in God and wait;
Although He seems to linger long,
He never comes too late.   —Anon.

Patience may sometimes seem bitter, but its fruit is sweet!
—Rousseau

INADEQUATE BUT MIGHTY

*God hath chosen the weak things . . . base things . . .
and things which are despised.* 1 Corinthians 1:27, 28

Looking at the brilliant stars sparkling like precious jewels against a background of black velvet in the nocturnal, oriental sky, the Psalmist is awed as he contemplates the glory of the great Creator. He longs to express how he feels, but thinks his weak words must seem to God as imperfect as the prattle of a baby. Suddenly, however, he remembers that "out of the mouth of babes and sucklings" the Lord accomplishes His purposes and glorifies himself. Encouraged by the realization that God uses the weak, the low, and the despised to win mighty victories over the forces of evil, David completes his Psalm of praise on a note of rapture.

A famous music director tells of a retarded boy who sang in his ensemble. The lad sometimes was a bit of a hindrance and the Christian leader was tempted to ask him to leave the choir. However, one day he met the father of the boy who admitted, "Joey is not quite bright," but said that the lad was responsible for leading his parents, two grandparents, and five brothers and sisters to the Lord. "Not quite bright," but *he won nine to Christ!*

Do you sometimes feel your insignificance and total inadequacy for some task you are called upon to perform? If you do, it indicates that you have seen something of the contrast between God's power and your own imperfection. Be encouraged, however, by the fact that the Lord takes pleasure in those who know themselves to be weak and inadequate, but who seek their strength from Him. Such yielded ones become instruments of His praise and wondrous channels of blessing. God can use you, weak as you are!

> *Inadequate but mighty —*
> *How strange, yet wholly true;*
> *Weak men endued with power*
> *The Lord's blest work shall do!* —Bosch

You can be too big for God to use, but you cannot be too small!

YOUR HAND—A PRAYER REMINDER

*God forbid that I should sin against the Lord in
ceasing to pray for you.*   1 Samuel 12:23

A Christian woman teaching in Africa thought to devise a
good way to remind her young students of the need of praying
daily, not only for self but also for others. Holding up her arm,
the woman explained, "When I am ready to pray, children, I
look at my left hand. I notice that my thumb is the digit closest
to me. This reminds me to pray for those near me — *my family,
my friends, my neighbors.*" Taking hold of her index finger she
added, "My teachers used to point this one at us in school. Sometimes the preacher too will shake this finger in church as a needed
warning. So as I come to this part of my hand I pray for *my
teachers, the preachers, and others who have been my guides.*"
The children waited eagerly for her next comment. "My middle
finger," she continued, "is my largest one. It stands above the
others. This brings to my mind *the rulers of our country, and
others in authority,* and I pray for them. This next finger is
called the weakest," she added. "It makes me think of *the helpless, the sick, and the poor who require my aid.* I ask the Lord
to supply their wants and strengthen them in body and soul."
Coming to her "pinky," she concluded, "This one stands for me,
and so *I finish by praying for myself and all the things that I
need.*" The children never forgot that simple lesson; and it might
be well even for older folk to bear it in mind when they fold
their hands to speak to God.

Our text says that it is a sin to fail to remember others before
the Throne. If you have been guilty of such neglect, go down
the fingers of your hand and let them remind you of your necessary duty of intercession!

> There's no weapon half so mighty
>   As the intercessors bear;
> Nor a broader field of service
>   Than the ministry of prayer! —Anon.

**Pray earnestly; you can't expect a thousand-dollar answer to
a ten-cent prayer!**

BIG CIRCLE OR LITTLE DOT?

I count all things but loss, . . . that I may know him,
and the power of his resurrection. Philippians 3:8, 10

One consuming passion gripped the heart of the apostle Paul. Having met and owned Jesus Christ as Lord, his one desire was that the blessed Savior should be pre-eminent in his life. All else was of little importance. "Things" were counted as "refuse," while the Lord Jesus became everything to him.

The small daughter of General William Booth was invited to spend the day across town in the beautiful home of some rich friends. Upon returning to the small flat in the slums of London where her parents lived, she remarked in childish fancy, "I wish *we* had more *things!*" The father, overhearing her complaint, called the child to come sit on his lap. Taking a piece of paper and pencil, he drew a large circle. In the center of the page, he placed a little dot. Carefully he labeled the circle *"things"* and used the little dot to represent *"Jesus."* Then he said, "Honey, do you want Jesus at the little dot and things at the big circle in your life?" "O no, Daddy," she cried, *"I want Jesus at the big circle* and things at the little dot."

If our Christian experience were to be carefully examined just now, what would be the result of such an appraisal? The apostle Paul had relegated "things" to the dump heap along with all that had previously enamored him. Christ had become the continuing object of his affections and desires. "That I may *know him"* was the motivating force in all that Paul did. He could honestly say, "For to me to live is Christ!"

May the Lord always occupy the big circle of our lives, filling center and circumference!

> *Jesus in sorrow, in joy, or in pain,*
> *Jesus my Treasure in loss or in gain;*
> *Constant Companion, where'er I may be,*
> *Living or dying — Jesus for me!* —Kirkpatrick

Jesus Christ is not rightly valued at all until He is valued above all!
                                                              —Augustine

"ONE OF FIVE HEADING HOME"

For we know that if our earthly house of this taber-
nacle were dissolved, we have . . . an house not
made with hands, eternal in the heavens.

2 Corinthians 5:1

A story in our local newspaper one day during World War II was captioned: "One of Five Heading Home." The account, pertaining to my family, stated that Peter, a Marine (one of five of us who were in the service), was coming home on an extended furlough after years of almost continuous frontline combat duty. My parents were deeply grateful that God had spared his life, for he, more than the rest of us, had been exposed to a great deal of danger. While he was here, however, a tragedy occurred. A telegram came which bore sad tidings. Another son, Cornelius, who was only 20 years old, had died as a result of antiaircraft fire while on a bombing mission! My father and mother received the news calmly because they knew the Savior, and were assured that His will was always best. They were confident that their son had gone to be with the Lord. One member of the family exclaimed, "How true that caption in the newspaper the other day: *'One of Five Heading Home'!"* What a blessing to have the comfort of the Scriptures at a time like that!

As a pastor I have seen many leave this world to be with Jesus without expressing any fear. They too recognize that Heaven is Home! It is our Father's house of many mansions (John 14:2). It is the place where we shall meet our Elder Brother (Heb. 2: 17), and where loved ones who died in Christ will once again be reunited. Tender ties, severed by death, will there be reestablished, never to be broken again. New friendships also will be made, for we shall meet the saints of all the ages. We therefore have a deep and rich comfort in the midst of our grief. Although we mourn, we sorrow not as the worldly man, for we know we shall meet our dear ones again in God's bright and blessed tomorrow!

We are but strangers here, Heaven is our Home;
Earth is a desert drear, Heaven is our Home. —T. R. Taylor

Heaven, the "haven of the happy," is best spelled "H-O-M-E"!
—Bosch

COLD COINS AND MARRED TESTIMONIES

. . . the love of many shall grow cold. Matthew 24:12

A man who visited a great foundry workshop was observing how they struck off a series of metal coins, each of which bore the features of a noble manly face. Picking up one of the medallions that had been put to one side, he noticed that it was marred and spoiled. All the clear, lovely lines of strength and beauty—so obvious in the image engraved on the well-stamped coins—were blurred and indistinct. When asked what had happened to cause this, the man in charge said, "The metal was allowed to grow a little too cool, and so would not properly take the impression that the die in the press should have imparted to it." When I heard that story, I thought to myself, what a parable this is in relation to Christians who have allowed their love for God and His Word to grow cold. As a result, the likeness of the Lord Jesus is scarcely distinguishable in their words and deeds; thus their testimony has become blurred and ineffective.

In these last days, before the return of our Savior, we are seeing a great defection from the faith. There is a "falling away" (2 Thess. 2:3) that is reaching appalling dimensions. Not only is there outright apostasy, but even those who are genuine believers have let their spiritual life decline to the point that they are now "lukewarm" in their attitude toward spiritual things. Consequently, their witness is poor and unacceptable in the eyes of both God and man.

Are you numbered with those who have allowed their zeal and interest to cool to such an extent that they now have "marred testimonies"? Only a return to daily Bible study and prayer, and a full measure of earnest rededication of your life to the Lord's will and service, can effect the changes so desperately needed.

> *Spirit of God, work now upon my heart;*
> *Wean it from earth, through all its pulses move;*
> *Stoop to my weakness, mighty as Thou art,*
> *And make me love Thee as I ought to love.*
> —George Croly, alt.

God makes His ministers "a flame of fire"; am I ignitible? God deliver me from the dread asbestos of "other things."
—Jim Elliot

MISPLACED VALUES

Labor not for the food which perisheth, but for that food which endureth. . . .   John 6:27

A group of boys broke into a hardware store one night, not as thieves or vandals, but as pranksters. They mixed up the price tags on the merchandise in a most ridiculous manner. Nails, for example, were marked at $200 each, lawnmowers at 6 cents a pound, and hammers at 50 cents a dozen. I can imagine the consternation of the owner the next morning when he was faced with the task of re-marking every item in the store.

These completely absurd prices set me to thinking. In a most tragic manner people often display an equally warped sense of values. For instance, how foolish was the multitude Jesus miraculously fed when he multiplied the lad's lunch! They were so taken up with the physical food they had received that they closed their minds to the real meaning of the miracle. In a few hours they would need another meal, but the spiritual food of which Jesus spoke would endure "unto everlasting life."

Every person should give serious thought to his sense of values. Even Christians sometimes put earthly enjoyments ahead of serving the Lord, and will someday be sorry for such wrong priorities. More serious, however, is the mistake people make when they spend their whole lifetime laboring "for the food which perisheth," while rejecting the true Living Bread which alone can "feed their souls" to eternal life. Every person must choose either the fleeting pleasures of this world or the never-ending joys Jesus Christ bestows. Those who have a proper sense of values will accept the salvation He so graciously offers.

O the things of this world are a will-o'-the-wisp,
    Having values that tarnish and fade;
But true treasures of joy with abundant reward,
    Are the ones which in Heaven are laid! —G.W.

He weighs things well, and makes decisions wise, who keeps eternity before his eyes!   —Bosch

SITTING OUT THE CONCERT

And he requested for himself that he might die,
and said, It is enough!   1 Kings 19:4

The concert is in full swing. The conductor is waving his
baton with zeal and enthusiasm. Suddenly a member of the orchestra approaches him. It's the man who plays the triangle.
He bends over and whispers, "Do you mind, sir, if I go home
now? I have come to the end of *my part of the score!*" How
ridiculous, you say; even if he can only function in a minor capacity, he still is a member of the musical group and is expected
to *"sit out the concert!"* Just his presence adds a certain touch
that cannot be missed or the orchestra will not look its best.
It would disturb and disrupt the work of others if some were to
leave the moment they thought their main contribution to the
program had been made.

Some senior citizens feel themselves useless, and some like
Elijah are dwelling under the "juniper tree of self-pity" wishing
that God would say, "It is enough!" They believe they have
already given their performance. Yet, whether they know it or
not, they are still significantly adding to the "orchestra of life"
by just being there. Many people, viewing these dear saints,
have been impressed by their patience, wisdom, and verdant
prayer-life, and consequently have been blessed by their influence.
What the full impact of their spiritual donation will be, only
eternity will reveal. Like Elijah these aged servants of the Lord
still have much to accomplish for God's glory. They are very important, or He would not leave them here on earth.

Elderly Christian, even though your major task here may have
been completed, you are still making a worthwhile contribution
by just *"sitting out the concert"!*

> *Lord, help me be a blessing still*
> *To family and friend;*
> *That I may serve some purpose true*
> *Until my life shall end!*   —Bosch

**You are young and useful at any age if you are still planning
for tomorrow!**

BEAUTIFUL FEET

How beautiful . . . are the feet of him that bringeth
good tidings, that publisheth peace.   Isaiah 52:7

The prophet's words describing the feet of God's messengers as beautiful were strikingly demonstrated in the life of an African believer. He was afflicted with elephantiasis, a disease which causes the lower legs to become greatly enlarged, with the skin thick and fissured like an elephant's hide. Although walking gave him great pain, he visited every hut in two villages, telling the story of Jesus. Then, burdened by the spiritual need of still another settlement, he dragged his leathery legs and huge feet through the jungles ten more miles that he might also give them the message of salvation. That night the missionary doctor was awakened by a noise on his front porch. Investigating, he found the faithful Christian almost unconscious, his stump-like legs bleeding profusely. After placing the man in a clean hospital bed and dressing his mangled feet, the medic wrote, "In all my life I do not know when my heart was more drawn to another believer. All I could think of was that verse in the Word of God, *'How beautiful are the feet of him that bringeth good tidings!'* "

In today's Scripture lesson the prophet first declares the good news that God is going to redeem and restore Israel. Then he portrays the Lord Jesus Christ and shows that through awful humiliation and pain, He would pay the price for human sin and open the door of salvation to all men.

The apostle Paul saw in the beautiful feet of which Isaiah spoke a picture of every believer who proclaims the Gospel (Rom. 10:15). How about your feet? Are you using them to publish "glad tidings of good things?"

Take my feet, and let them be
Swift and beautiful for Thee;
Take my intellect, and use
Every power as Thou shalt choose!—Havergal, alt.

It takes SOLES to win SOULS!

HOPE FOR THE WORLD

We should live soberly . . . looking for that blessed
hope.   Titus 2:12, 13

EARTHQUAKE ROCKS PACIFIC; MOTEL BOMBED BY TERRORISTS; TORNADO RIPS THROUGH TOWN; DELEGATES AT CONFERENCE IN DEADLOCK OVER PEACE ISSUE; THREATENING REMARKS MADE; TENSION RISES. These newspaper headlines selected at random tend to lead us to despair as far as this old world is concerned. There just doesn't seem to be any hope for it. And yet, according to the Scriptures, the dream of abolishing war is not merely wishful thinking. The idea of prosperity for all is more than a political gimmick. The Bible tells us that the eventual taming of nature and the elements is a certain thing.

The hope for this world, however, is not to be found in the efforts of man but in the return of Jesus Christ. He alone can solve the problems that are baffling mankind. The earth will be redeemed, and there will no longer be storms, floods, and tornadoes. The nations will live in peace. No military camp will be in operation. Poverty will be abolished. There will be no religious controversies or divisions. In that day the Lord says, "They shall not hurt nor destroy in all my holy mountain" (Isa. 11:9). This glorious prospect will become a reality when the Lord Jesus Himself returns as "King of Kings and Lord of Lords" to set up His Kingdom of peace and righteousness. Paul encouraged Titus to be "looking for that blessed hope, and the glorious appearing of the great God and our Savior, Jesus Christ." With this hope we can be optimistic even in the deepening gloom of the midnight hour of this age.

Keep looking up!

> *Lift up your heads, pilgrims aweary,*
>   *See day's approach now crimson the sky;*
> *Night shadows flee, and your Beloved,*
>   *Awaited with longing, at last draweth nigh.*—Camp

While sin deformed the world, Christ promises one day to transform it!

MOODY'S BARROOM MEETING

. . . effectual, fervent prayer . . . availeth much.

James 5:16

The power of prayer is most effectively illustrated in the following story concerning D. L. Moody. Entering a tavern in order to ask the bartender if his two little girls might attend his Sunday school, he was told that an infidel club met there every Thursday night, and that the owner of the bar was in no mood to offend them. The tactful soul winner refused to retreat, but looking into the face of the father he pleaded with him earnestly in behalf of his youngsters. Finally the man's heart was touched and he said, "I'll tell you what I'll do, parson; if you'll come down here Thursday night and meet the boys in a joint discussion, and *you win,* you shall have the children; but if not, it is all off." "Agreed," said Moody. Immediately he looked up a crippled newsboy who really knew how to pray and said to him, "Tommy, I need you next Thursday night." When the hour of the meeting arrived, Tommy and the evangelist entered the saloon. It was full of men sitting on whiskey barrels, beer kegs, and even on the counter — all eagerly awaiting the coming debate. Moody began by saying, "Gentlemen, it is our custom to open our meetings with prayer. Tommy, jump up on that barrel and pray!" Tommy turned his little face toward Heaven, and how he did beseech the Lord for the souls of all present. As the tears began to roll down the little fellow's cheeks, the more tenderhearted of the men beat a retreat. Finally even the hardened sinners, subdued by the pathos and spiritual power of the occasion, also slowly retired until there was no one left except the bartender, Moody, and the praying boy. "That will do, Tommy," exclaimed the evangelist. "Now," he said, turning to the father, "I claim your children for my Sunday school!" "They shall come, but it is a queer way to fight," said the bartender. *"It's the way I win many a battle,"* replied Moody. He had instructed the boy not to cease until he had prayed all the men out of the tavern! Such a combination of faith and fervent prayer "availeth much!"

There's no weapon half so mighty
As the intercessors bear,
Nor a broader field of service
Than the ministry of prayer! —Anon.

Where prayers focus, power falls!

THE TEST OF FAITH

Cast not away, therefore, your confidence . . . .
Hebrews 10:35

I read recently about a father and mother who lost three of their children in one week by diphtheria. Only the 3-year-old girl escaped. On Easter morning the father and mother, with the one surviving child, attended Sunday school. Since the father was the superintendent, he led the group in worship and read the Easter message from the Bible without a tear or even a break in his voice. Many were weeping, but the faces of the father and mother remained serene and calm. "How can they do it?" people asked as they left. A 15-year-old boy, walking home with his father said, "Dad, I guess the superintendent and his wife really believe all of it — Easter, you know!" "Of course," answered his father, "all Christians hold to that truth." "Not the way they *believe it!*" said the boy.

Yes, it's easy to talk about what we believe when all goes well. But the reality of faith is shown when we face an actual situation in which it is fully tested. It's how we react under the knife of trial that truly demonstrates the depth of our convictions. This is not to say that a true Christian does not weep at the loss of a loved one. There is pain involved in such separations. However, with the knowledge that those who die in Christ go into His presence, and with the assurance that we shall be reunited at His coming, we "sorrow not, even as others who have no hope" (1 Thess. 4:13).

When everything goes wrong — Mother is ill, Jimmy breaks his arm, and Dad loses his job — that Christian who really takes God at His word can say, "Thank you, Lord," because he believes the Lord means it when He says, "All things work together for good to them that love God . . ." (Rom. 8:28). He can join with the prophet in declaring that "Although the fig tree shall not blossom, neither shall fruit be in the vines . . . yet I will rejoice in the Lord, I will joy in the God of my salvation" (Hab. 3:17, 18).

> *Keep up the song of faith,*
>   *And let your heart be strong,*
> *For God delights when faith can praise*
>   *Though dark the night and long.* —Anon.

True faith is like a kite: a contrary wind raises it higher!

WHAT MAKES JESUS MARVEL?

*When Jesus heard these things, he marveled at
him . . . and said . . . I have not found so great
faith, no, not in Israel.*   Luke 7:9

One morning many eyes were moist with tears during our
Radio Bible Class devotional time. Four little boys who are
cared for and trained in a Christian institution for retarded children were demonstrating that their mental handicap did not hinder them spiritually. They recited the books of the Bible and
answered many questions about the Scriptures and Christian doctrine. We were thrilled and deeply stirred to see what had been
done for these children by their dedicated teachers, but what
moved me the most was their simple faith. When they talked
about Jesus' coming again and spoke of Heaven, their faces
glowed. One of the little fellows sang, "It will be worth it all,
when we see Jesus," and, though he stumbled a bit, I knew
he really believed the words of this precious song. Truly, I marveled at the faith of these unusual lads.

Similarly, it was the centurion's faith — spoken of in Luke 7 —
that caused Jesus to marvel. This soldier was an exceptional man
for he had shown much kindness to the Jews. Moreover, it was
quite unusual for Romans to have love for a slave as this man
did. However, it was his *faith* that impressed Jesus most of all.
This man who had been reared in paganism had heard about
Jesus and believed in Him. Knowing that our Lord according
to Jewish law would defile Himself by entering a Gentile home,
he felt himself unworthy of a visit. He therefore declared that
Jesus needed only to speak a word, and his servant would be
healed. He believed that Jesus Christ was not only the Master
of *disease,* but also of *distance.* As Jesus considered the wondrous, majestic sweep of this man's faith, He marveled. God
delights in nothing more than to see us trust in Him wholly.

> *Fear not to call on Him, O soul distressed!*
> *Thy sorrow's whisper woos thee to His breast;*
> *He who is oftenest there is often blest;*
>   *Have faith in God!*   —Anon.

**When true faith goes to "market" it always takes a "basket,"
for it never doubts of its reward!**

WAIT!

. . . let every man be swift to hear, slow to speak,
slow to wrath.   James 1:19

A clipping with a pointed message recently came to my attention. In it one of God's aged and disciplined servants gave the following golden advice: "When trouble is brewing, keep still. When slander is getting on his legs, keep still. When your feelings are hurt, keep still — at least until you recover from your agitation. Things look different when seen through grace-anointed eyes. In a state of anger and commotion I once wrote a letter. Afterward I wished I had not sent it. The passing of years, with their soul-refining and character-ennobling experiences, taught me some needed lessons. Later, I had another period of emotional stress. Again I wrote a long letter, but this time I put it in my pocket. How glad I was that I did! With the passing of the days, it seemed less and less necessary to send the message. I was not sure it would do any hurt, but in my doubtfulness, I leaned to reticence, and eventually destroyed the letter. Time works wonders. *Wait till you can speak calmly,* and perhaps you will not need to speak at all. Remember, silence is the most massive thing conceivable! It is strength shown in grandeur!"

This is good advice! How many of us have learned its value through sad and bitter experiences. A wise man in a trying situation may be tempted to flare up and speak his mind; yet he knows enough to hold his peace, to consider all the facts, and weigh each word, and then to speak with assurance and calmness.

It is said that a very talkative youth came to Socrates to study oratory. The philosopher charged him double price, stating that he must teach the youth two sciences: first, how to hold his tongue, and secondly, how to speak.

Many quarrels at home, at work, and especially in the church would be avoided if we would learn to heed James' words, "Let every man be swift to hear, *slow to speak,* slow to wrath."

If wisdom's ways you really seek,
Five things observe with care:
Of whom you speak, to whom you speak,
And how, and when, and where!   —Anon.

Think before you speak; remember, silent sense is better than fluent folly!

HOW TO HANDLE A LACK OF FAITH

. . . Lord, I believe; help thou mine unbelief.

Mark 9:24

Coming down from the mountain where He had been transfigured, the Lord Jesus found that His disciples had been unable to cure a demon-possessed boy. The distraught father, who had witnessed their failure, now turned to the Savior. When the Master told him the miracle was possible "if thou canst believe," the man with tears exclaimed, "Lord, I believe; help thou mine *unbelief.*" While he did have a measure of faith, he was acutely aware that doubt was still present in his mind; therefore he felt he honestly needed to acknowledge this weakness. The Lord responded by healing his son.

I often counsel with Christians who come to me deeply discouraged because they feel their faith is weak, or because they are still having difficulty overcoming some besetting sin. They confess to me that this makes them feel as if they are hypocrites, and sometimes they even tell me that they wish to resign from their position as Sunday school teacher, youth leader, or deacon. Now, these people are not hypocrites, for they would not be so concerned if they were. They are sincere Christians. Therefore I refer them to this man's earnest prayer, and ask them if they have told the Lord about their lack of faith and spiritual victory. I remind them that God knows our weaknesses, that He never forgets we are frail creatures of flesh. Jesus Christ understands because He Himself, though sinless, shared in our humanity.

Above everything else be honest with God. Bring to Him your burdens and cares, but also speak to Him about your lack of faith. Hebrews 4:16 exhorts us to "come boldly unto the throne of grace." This means, openly, freely, and truthfully telling Him all that is on your heart. Are you discouraged because you are far from what you wish to be? Try telling Jesus all about it.

> *Only believe, ne'er doubt His love,*
> *Nor place an "if" before His power;*
> *He can, He will, thy faith reward,*
> *And strengthen thee this very hour.* —G.W.

Reach up as far as you can by faith, and trust God to do the rest!

WITH A SHOUT!

> *. . . the Lord himself shall descend from heaven*
> *with a shout . . . .*   1 Thessalonians 4:16

The Bible tells us that when Jesus comes He will do so with a *shout*. In that moment we who are saved shall hear the voice of that same One who, way back in the beginning, spoke the creating word, and this world, surrounded by the stars and the constellations, sprang into being out of nothingness. Yes, we will hear Him call who, as He was tossed about in that little ship on the troubled Sea of Galilee, said, "Peace, be still," and the raging wind and the angry waves lay down in complete submission at the feet of their Master. It will be the same One who, while hanging upon the cross for our sins, declared in the darkness of that dread hour, "It is finished!" The same loving, all powerful Jesus who stood at the tomb of his friend and cried out, "Lazarus, come forth," will also summon us to resurrection life! Yes, the Lord Himself shall descend from Heaven with a *shout,* and when He does, not just one tomb will be opened, but *all "the dead in Christ shall rise!"* What a sight that will be when thousands upon thousands of graves will burst open as Jesus the mighty Conqueror of death calls forth His own with that triumphant *shout* of victory!

Friend, it could be today that the Lord will come to summon the dead in Christ and all living believers to be with Him! Caught up in a moment, together with them whom we have "loved long since and lost awhile," we shall know the full blessing of Heavenly joy, and experience the unhindered fellowship of being with God!

World conditions may wax worse and worse, and the outlook grow increasingly ominous; but we who know Christ have the blessed hope that as the darkness of this midnight age becomes more black, the coming of Christ, as the Bright and Morning Star shines even brighter!

> *The Lord is coming! And with eager eyes*
> *We watch to see the Morning Star arise!*
> *The Lord is coming! Let our hearts rejoice,*
> *We soon shall hear the accents of His voice!* —Anon.

In regard to Christ's second coming, I've stopped looking for SIGNS, I've started listening for SOUNDS! —W. P. Loveless

STANDARD EQUIPMENT

*These . . . received the word with all readiness of
mind, and searched the scriptures daily.* Acts 17:11

The pony express was a thrilling part of early American history. It ran from St. Joseph, Missouri, to Scranton, California — a distance of 1,900 miles. The trip was made in ten days. Forty men, each riding 50 miles a day, dashed along the trail on 500 of the best horses the West could provide. To conserve weight, clothing was very light, saddles were extremely small and thin, and no weapons were carried. The horses themselves wore small shoes or none at all. The mail pouches were flat and very conservative in size. Letters had to be written on thin paper, and postage was $5.00 an ounce (a tremendous sum in those days). *Yet, each rider carried a full-sized Bible!* It was presented to him when he joined the pony express, and he took it with him despite all the scrupulous weight precautions. Why? Because the Scriptures were deemed *standard equipment!* God was important to people in those frontier days, and they recognized the need of daily searching the Word, and giving heed to it with all readiness of mind!

Our life is much like the "pony express." We hurry through it on our way to a distant destination called eternity. God has determined that He will not leave us without compass or guide, so He has provided us with "the standard equipment" of His precious revelation called the Bible. Like the noble Bereans of old, may we receive this important "love-letter" with a readiness of mind that will cause its truths to bear fruit in our lives.

Is the Bible precious to you? Is it *standard equipment* as you go along the journey of life? Do you search its pages daily? I hope so!

> *The Bible, the Bible! more precious than gold;*
> *Glad hopes and bright glories its pages unfold;*
> *It speaks of the Father and tells of His love,*
> *And shows us the way to the Mansions above.* —Anon.

**One evidence of the value of the Bible is the character of those
who oppose it!**

UNSPEAKABLE GLORY

And the city had no need of the sun . . . for the
glory of God did light it . . . .   Revelation 21:23

The Gospel Folio Press of Grand Rapids carried this article in
one of their calendars: "Blind from birth, but having undergone
delicate surgery, and seeing for the first time, Elsie rushed into
her mother's arms and screamed with excitement, 'Oh, Mama,
why didn't you tell me it was so beautiful!' The mother, through
tears of joy, answered, 'My precious child, I tried to tell you,
but I couldn't put it into words.' One can think of that mother
getting her first glimpse of the Heavenly City and rushing to
John the apostle and saying, 'Why didn't you tell us it was so
beautiful!' only to hear John answer, 'I tried to tell you in the
last part of the book of the Revelation of Jesus Christ, but I
couldn't find words to express it.'"

When Paul was caught up into the third Heaven, he heard
"unspeakable words, which it is not lawful for a man to utter"
(2 Cor. 12:4). "Ellicott's Commentary" has this to say of his
experience: "The hymns which the apostle John records in Revelation 4:8,9; 5:12-14; 7:12, and 15:3, may give us some faint
approach to what dwelt in Paul's memory and yet could not be
reproduced. Sounds of ineffable sweetness, bursts of praise and
adoration, hallelujahs like the sound of many waters, voices low
and sweet as those of children, whispers which were scarcely
distinguishable from silence and yet thrilled the soul with a rap-
turous joy — this we may, perhaps, think of as underlying Paul's
language."

We are sometimes accused of preaching a "pie in the sky"
message. Well, I don't care what you may call it — *we do have
a glorious future!* Rather than apologizing for our anticipation
of the joys of Heaven, we should be zealous in telling the whole
world about it. So, believer, whether the way be dark and difficult, or flooded by the sunlight of God's richest blessings, remember there is something even better ahead. There is "unspeakable" glory!

> *The Harvest-Home of God will come,*
>   *And after toil and care,*
> *With joys untold, our sheaves of gold*
>   *Will all be gathered there.*   —Jessie Brown

Heaven is the day of which grace is the dawn!

THE CHRISTIAN'S "INDIAN SUMMER"

*. . . even to your old age I am he; and even to gray
hairs will I carry you . . . and will deliver you.*

Isaiah 46:4

Of all the seasons of the year, to me there is none so beautiful,
so fascinating, and so rewarding as the bright, nippy Fall. After
the heat of summer is past, and the forests are mantled in amber
and crimson, "God weaves around the weather-beaten brow of the
year the golden crown of *Indian Summer!*" So, too, the Lord has
designed old age to be the "Indian Summer" of life—the gentlest,
the tenderest, the most lovely of all the days of our sojourn here
on earth.

Once an elderly man and his aged wife were very ill. Neither
of them could expect to get well. One was upstairs, while the
other was in a downstairs bedroom. Their children thoughtfully
decided to take their mother up to call on their father before both
of them were obliged to say their final good-bys here on earth.
Making a chair of their hands, two of the stronger ones managed
to bring her to his room. Then they left them alone. You can
imagine how they felt — their father and mother together for perhaps the last time on earth! After the two had visited for a while,
the children came back again. Stepping into the room they saw
their father sitting there in his old armchair, as he had done so
many times before, while their mother leaned over him, stroking
his hair and smiling down upon him. The faces of the two were
transfigured. The mother was speaking in a low, musical tone,
saying, "It's getting brighter and brighter, John! Why, it will not
be long and you and I will both be in the sunlight of Glory!"
The children thought it would be a hard time for them, and that
they would be talking about their sickness and death; instead they
were rejoicing in the happy prospect of soon being with Jesus!
If we live for the Savior, the "Indian Summer" time of life can
be a thing of beauty and upward-looking faith!

> *O keep me sweet, and let me look*
> *Beyond the threats that life may hold,*
> *To see the glad eternal joys;*
> *Yes, keep me sweet, in growing old!*
>
> —Mrs. J. P. Hazard

**A graceful and honorable old age is the childhood of immor-
tality.**   —Pindar

TIME

Walk in wisdom . . . redeeming the time. Colossians 4:5

Time is one of life's most precious commodities. Yet I'm afraid we do not give ample consideration to its importance. The value of even each minute and second is emphasized in the following article: "During a New England trial some years ago, a witness appearing in defense of the accused, testified that he had been out of the sight of people for only two or three minutes and thus could not possibly have committed the murder. Commenting on this testimony, the attorney for the prosecution turned to the jury and said, 'Gentlemen, here is my watch. We shall all pause, not for three minutes, but for two minutes, and you may judge what could have been done by the defendant during that space of time.' The wait seemed interminable as the jury sat until 120 seconds had been ticked off. They later returned a verdict of 'Guilty!'"

Yes, much harm can be done in even a few seconds. But remember, much good can also be accomplished. A father took his son to the carnival and waited impatiently while the boy rode the merry-go-round until his last dime was spent. Then he said: "Well, my boy, you've spent all your money traveling, but where did you go?" The merry-go-round is an apt symbol for the existence of many of us. We are not concerned about where the journey of life is taking us, but only in spending the time pleasantly.

How fitting this little bit of verse published by the "Faith, Prayer and Tract League" of Grand Rapids: "No time for God? What fools we are to clutter up our lives with common things, and leave outside heart's gate the Lord of life, and life itself. No time for God? As soon to say, no time to eat or sleep or love or die. Take time for God, or you shall dwarf your soul, and when the angel Death comes knocking at your door, a poor misshapen thing you'll be to step into eternity. No time for God? That day when sickness comes, or troubles find you out, and you cry out for God, will He have time for you? — No time for God?"

> *Life at its best is short;*
> *Time flies so very fast.*
> *Lord, help me not to waste this day,*
> *Lest it should be my last!*   —Anon.

If you want to "kill time," work it to death in serving the Lord!

"BUT GOD . . ."

They [the wicked] encourage themselves in an evil matter; they speak of laying snares secretly . . . . But God . . . .   Psalm 64:5, 7

The arresting phrase "But God" occurs frequently in the Scriptures. There is the "But God" of salvation (Rom. 5:8), the "But God" of the spiritual harvest (1 Cor. 3:7), the "But God" of marital peace (1 Cor. 7:15), and the "But God" of the victory over temptation (1 Cor. 10:13). One could cite many more such references in the Word, but today we shall call your attention to the *"But God" of divine protection!*

It is good for us to realize that we may be hindered, delayed, and sometimes greatly tried by the enemy of our soul, but then, just at the right time our blessed Defender steps in and frustrates the foul plans of the adversary. David experienced such divine intervention when his enemies had encouraged themselves in an evil matter and had plotted against his soul. They laid snares for his feet, *"But God"* in His well-timed providence put a halt to their diabolical schemes.

Bishop Gobat, while laboring among the wild tribes of the Druses, was one day invited by a chief to visit him. Desiring to gain some influence over that wicked man, he eagerly accepted. Regrettably (or so he thought), he became ill, and could not go. When the invitation was repeated, circumstances again interfered. A third summons came and this time he set out with a guide. First the native lost his way, and then when a hyena crossed their path the superstitious guide, in line with certain tribal taboos, would go no farther. As a result the Bishop was obliged to forgo the visit. Later he learned that by these means he had been hindered from falling into the hands of those who had determined to murder him. The treacherous chief exclaimed, "That man must be the servant of God; for though I sent messenger after messenger to bring him, he was always hindered."

When you are frustrated, Christian, remember it may be due to the "But God" of our Lord's providential leading and protection.

If God permitted no trials, we should enjoy no triumphs!

THE ONE YOU CAN TRUST

*Believe on the Lord Jesus Christ, and thou shalt
be saved.*   Acts 16:31

While driving along the highway, I found myself behind a
car bearing a bumper sticker which said, "Vote for Robert Chase—
THE MAN YOU CAN TRUST." In this day of "gaps," and especially the "credibility gap," I can see why this politician chose
that particular slogan. His hope was that the voters in his dis-
trict would think of him as a man they could believe, one who
would make good on every promise he gave. I know nothing
about this Mr. Chase, but I am acquainted with Someone who
can be trusted — a Man with a perfect record and who has the
praise and endorsement of God Himself — One who keeps His
Word. It is the Lord Jesus Christ. After examining the Savior,
Pilate declared, "I find no fault in him." And Judas, following
his dastardly deed, cried out in remorse, "I have betrayed innocent blood." God the Father expressed His approval of Him, for
at His baptism a voice came from Heaven, saying, "This is my
beloved Son, in whom I am well pleased."

We should also believe what He said, for He predicted that
He would die and rise again the third day — and *He did!* His
resurrection was proof that He was everything He claimed to be—
truly the Son of Man, and truly the Son of God. It was a declaration that He had fully paid for the sins of the whole world.
Forgiveness of sin and life everlasting is now offered to all who
put their faith in Him. John tells us in his gospel, "But these
[things] are written, that ye might believe that Jesus is the
Christ, the Son of God; and that believing ye might have life
through his name" (John 20:31). Yes, the Lord Jesus is *"the
One you can trust."*

> *Trusting as the moments fly,*
> *Trusting as the days go by;*
> *Trusting Him whate'er befall,*
> *Trusting Jesus, that is all!* —Page

He pleases God best who trusts Christ most!

THE FROST BELL

Keep thy heart with all diligence; for out of it are the issues of life.   Proverbs 4:23

Awaiting death by execution, Paul wrote his second letter to Timothy from Rome while confined in a chilly, dank dungeon. He was so cold that he asked for his cloak, and so lonely that he begged Timothy to come as soon as possible. He was also keenly disappointed in Demas — a former companion in the work of God. How pathetic his plaintive words, which may be paraphrased as follows, "Do your best to come to me quickly, for Demas has deserted me, having fallen in love with this present world." It is hard to understand how Demas could so cruelly abandon the imprisoned apostle. However, knowing that a grave sin of this nature is always preceded by a backsliding in heart, we can be sure that Demas had been cooling off spiritually for some time before he forsook Paul to seek the pleasures of the world.

Prior to the development of thermostatically controlled heat, many greenhouses were equipped with a "frost bell." This was an electrical device connected to the thermometer which warned the owner when the mercury fell to the danger point. At the signal, he would hurry out to stoke his fires, thus saving his crop of fruit or flowers.

It isn't necessary to attach a frost bell to determine when a Christian is growing spiritually cold. If prayer, Bible reading, and Christian service *begin* to become burdensome and the allurements of the world *begin* to make their appeal, it's time to rekindle the fires of one's spiritual life. This can be done only through humble confession of sin and a renewal of dedication to Christ.

Vain world, I turn away, tho' thou seem fair and good;
That friendly, outstretched hand of thine is stained with Jesus'
*   blood.*
If in thy least device, I stoop to take a part,
All unaware, thine influence steals God's presence from my
*   heart!*   —Mauro

While the Christian must live in the world, he must not allow the world to live in him.   —Bosch

"MORE NOBLE"

These were more noble . . . in that they . . .
searched the scriptures daily.   Acts 17:11

One of the most prevalent causes for spiritual anemia is the neglect of God's Word. How many people day after day never open the Bible to feast upon God's bountiful provisions! Some go to church; they may hear a Gospel broadcast or watch a telecast, and may even hurriedly scan through the stories in this book, *but fail to study the Word of God itself!* By the way, did you read today's suggested passage? If not, please do so now. (Should time allow only one or the other, the Scripture or the rest of this devotional, make the wise choice!)

An unknown author tells the following story: "Some Christian women had gathered in a home for Bible study. The leader, much to her dismay, discovered that she had come away without her Bible. So the hostess hurried to get hers. She looked where she usually kept it, but it wasn't there! She searched for it everywhere but still couldn't find it. 'What will those ladies think of me?' she thought. Running downstairs, she said to the newly employed cleaning woman, 'Pearl, have you seen my Bible?' The maid exclaimed, 'Praise the Lord! Praise the Lord!' 'What do you mean, Pearl?' Beaming with joy, she said, 'The first thing I do when I go to work at a new place is hide the Bible.' 'But why?' the other asked in astonishment. Pearl replied, *'Just to find out how long it takes the people to miss it!* I put yours in the linen closet under the sheets!'"

Dr. Luke tells us that the Christians in Berea "searched the scriptures daily." For this they were commended and called "more noble." Does that describe you?

> *Search the Scriptures, thou wilt find*
> *Guidance there for heart and mind;*
> *Test each doctrine by its light,*
> *Stand "more noble" in His sight.* —Bosch

The truths of Scripture are like flowers; meditation, like the bee, draws the honey out of them!

GIVING OUT A "CERTAIN SOUND"!

> . . . *if the trumpet give an uncertain sound, who shall*
> *prepare himself to the battle?*   1 Corinthians 14:8

If a song is played "off key" or if the time signature is completely disregarded by the musician, the melody will be scarcely recognizable, and the impact on the audience will be negative.

Our lives should be the "Lord's trumpets," ever sending out with unwavering tone the notes of a vibrant faith. In the clear, martial rhythm of holy zeal we must sound the clarion call of grace to stir others to spiritual action! If our lives and witness do not ring true, or if we are in step with the undisciplined beat of the world, we shall miss our calling as "ambassadors for Christ."

One day John Philip Sousa heard a man with a hand organ playing his favorite march "The Stars and Stripes Forever." Irritated at the way the tune dragged, the bandmaster said to the sleepy, lazy organ grinder, "Pardon me, sir, but that's no way to play that march." Seizing the handle of the instrument, he began whirling it vigorously. The old martial flavor surged back into the music. The man who owned the instrument bowed low and smiled. The next night Sousa heard the tune again, but this time it was played in the right tempo. Looking out the window, he saw to his amusement that the operator had printed his own name on a large card, and beneath it in equally bold letters: *"Pupil of John Philip Sousa!"*

This carries a valuable lesson for all Christians. The sound of our witness must be so clear, and in step with Him who called us to be His disciples, that our testimony will let others know we have been with Christ and have learned of Him!

> *Living for Jesus a life that is true,*
> *Striving to please Him in all that I do;*
> *Yielding allegiance, glad-hearted and free,*
> *This is the pathway of blessing for me.*—Chisholm

Every Christian occupies some kind of pulpit and preaches some kind of sermon every day.

DO SOMETHING ABOUT IT!

But be ye doers of the word and not hearers only,
deceiving your own selves.   James 1:22

There is much talk in church circles about the plight of the
world and the need for reaching the multitudes with the Gospel.
Yet what is being done to remedy the situation? The book *Point
and Purpose in Story and Saying* relates this incident concerning
the late Thomas Corwin, former Governor of Ohio. "One evening he dropped into a church where a meeting of the local Bible
society was being held. The order of business was handled in
a very lifeless way. After the secretary reported that 200 families
in the county were without the Word of God, only one man
arose to deplore the shameful fact. Deeply disturbed, Governor
Corwin stood and said, 'I'm afraid you folks are not sincere. Two
hundred families in this county would not be without a Bible
if you were in earnest about your spiritual duty. In the great
presidential contest just past, many of us in government gave
our entire salaries to carry the election. We felt the salvation of
the country depended upon it. If you really believe that each
home should have a Bible, you should go to work and give one
to every man!' The meeting was electrified. Thomas Corwin was
named president of the group, and he responded by saying, 'If
I accept the office, it will be on one condition, that *you get busy
and that no such report as this ever be made again!* When we
meet three months from today, every home in Warren County
must have a copy of the Scriptures.'" Suiting action to the word,
the work was done!

What about your church? Is there some similar "unfinished
business" that sorely needs such practical attention? If so, *why
not do something about it!*

> *Lord Christ, we humbly ask*
> *Of Thee the power and will,*
> *With zeal and readiness of mind,*
> *Each duty to fulfill.*   —Montgomery, alt.

**If a man really believes the Gospel, it will soon give him a
"GO-spell"!**   —Burress

A CRY FOR STRENGTH

In the day when I cried, thou answeredst me, and
strengthenedst me with strength in my soul.
Psalm 138:3

Answered prayer is a great boon to the believer, for it bolsters his faith immeasurably to know that the Lord has heard his pleading cry for help and grace. The Psalmist had enjoyed such a thrilling experience for he exaltingly testified, "In the day when I cried, thou answeredst me, and strengthenedst me . . . in my soul!"

A young man, a student at the Missionary Training Institute, was much discouraged. Bound by carnal appetites and sick at heart because of his many spiritual failures, he decided to forfeit his lunch hour and to spend the time in supplication and prayer. Climbing the mountain behind the main dormitory and kneeling at a natural-rock altar, he lifted his heart heavenward and cried out in desperation of soul, "What can I do to find deliverance?" Bending his head downward and opening his eyes a little, he observed through a blur of tears a spider web in the grass directly in front of him. At that moment a tiny fly settled down and entangled one foot in the gossamer snare. A violent struggle ensued. The more the fly attempted to escape, the more enmeshed he became. At last the weary creature attracted the attention of the spider, who rushed out and proceeded to wrap strand after strand of sticky thread about his victim — preserving him alive but helpless. That little insect for all his excited activity could not free himself. However, the young man put down his little finger, and with the slightest effort freed the struggling captive. Through that experience God spoke to his heart. He saw that the Lord's little finger was worth more than all his vain struggles, and that if he would only trust Him, he would be set free from the habits and difficulties that bound him. Rising from his knees with joy, he was strengthened in his soul by the realization that it was God's power alone which could supply his want. Encouraged and relieved, he went on to new victories of grace!

> *To thy Redeemer take thy care,*
> *And change anxiety to prayer;*
> *His answers sweet will come at length,*
> *And to thy soul impart new strength!* —Anon.

When the OUTLOOK is bad, try the UPLOOK!

AFRAID TO TRUST

And . . . Jesus . . . caught him, and said . . . O thou
of little faith, why didst thou doubt? Matthew 14:31

One of the great American naval vessels destroyed in World
War II was the *Wasp*. Not until it became apparent that the
flames had spread beyond hope of control was the order finally
given to abandon ship. A surviving officer, Lieutenant Bodell,
later said, "I climbed down the cargo net and dropped off into
the water. Then I saw my first sign of panic, because some of
those 'green kids' had no trust in their lifejackets, and instead
of getting clear of the ship, were clinging to its plates by their
fingertips — the worst thing you can do."

It would be easy to criticize the boys who held on to the side
of the boat instead of pushing off into the water and trusting
their well-tested lifejackets; but we "armchair" sailors who have
not lived through such a holocaust would be heartless if we did.
Rather, we should admit that in spiritual matters we conduct
ourselves much like those sailors. Though we believe on the
Lord Jesus Christ for our eternal salvation, we are reluctant to
"let go and let God" take complete charge of our lives. Like
Peter when walking on the waves, if we take our eyes off the
Savior and look at the circumstances about us, we become fearful. Just as the frightened sailors still tried to help themselves by
hanging on to the sinking, burning ship, we have a tendency
to rely partially on our own strength, and to also look for some
help from this wicked world.

Friend, keep your eyes on Jesus Christ and He will meet your
every need. Trust Him completely and you will never be subjected to those words of rebuke reserved for wavering saints, "O
thou of little faith, why didst thou doubt?"

> *'Twas not that Christ had moved or changed,*
> *When Peter's faith grew dim;*
> *But just that Peter saw the* WAVES,
> *Instead of seeing* HIM!   —Maxwell

Faith is God's antidote for fear!

"GOD LOOKED AT THAT!"

*The eyes of the Lord are in every place, beholding
the evil and the good.*   Proverbs 15:3

The fact of God's omnipresence is not only a real comfort but
also an arresting thought. It is wonderful to say with Hagar
in times of distress, "Thou God seest me." No matter where we
might go, we are never lost to the loving eye of our Heavenly
Father. This truth should also cause us to govern carefully
the things we say and do. Some time ago I came across a
story which underscores this. It seems that a little boy of low
mentality was treated most unkindly by other lads and often
ridiculed by adults. They would laugh at his comments and
mimic his odd behavior. Although tending to be imbecilic, he
did at times sense their derision. Lacking the ability to properly
defend himself, he would simply say to his offenders, "Ah! God
looked at that." He would then repeat it with added emphasis,
"Ah, God looked at that!" This made a deep impression on a
young lady who saw the unkind deeds and heard the helpless
child's simple retort. She mentioned that later whenever she
witnessed any injustice, there would come to her mind this lad
and his graphic sermon: "God looked at that!" Although mentally
deficient, that small boy knew how to preach! He got the point
across. The Scripture agrees with his observations; for we read,
"Neither is there any creature that is not manifest in his sight"
(Heb. 4:13). The writer of Proverbs exclaims, "Sheol and destruction are before the Lord; how much more, then, the hearts
of . . . men" (Prov. 15:11).

What a difference it would make if before acting we would
always stop to consider that the Lord is observing us. Whenever
a thing is done, we too must face the fact—*"God looked at that!"*

> There is an Eye that never sleeps
>   Beneath the wings of night;
> Soul, guard thy ways and words today,
>   For thou art in His sight!   —Anon.

Live innocently, God is watching!   —Linnaeus

SINNERS BY NATURE

*For we ourselves also were once foolish, disobedient,
deceived . . . hating one another . . . but according
to his mercy he saved us . . . .*   Titus 3:3, 5

An elderly Gospel preacher told how he and his wife once
went to worship at a certain church, only to discover that the
Bible was not believed and taught there. In the Sunday school
class the teacher declared that no intelligent person today holds
to the obsolete doctrine that people are sinners. He stated that
we must not seek the salvation of lost souls, but rather try to
improve conditions in general. He asked if any of his audience
disagreed. The Bible-believing pastor stood up and announced
that he was one of those old-fashioned individuals who still looked
upon all human beings as sinners in need of salvation by grace.
Turning to the class, he asked, "How many of you had to teach
your children to be bad?" Not a hand was raised. Then he
inquired, "How many of you had to instruct your children to be
good?" Every hand went up. "I have proved my point," he said.
"If children were basically good, they would become evil only
if you had trained them in wrongdoing. It is because they are
sinners that we must first put so much emphasis upon their need
of Christ, and then, even after they are saved, continue diligently to teach them, discipline them, and sometimes chasten
them so that they will avoid the evil and do that which is good."

This faithful servant of God was right. The Bible teaches us
that we are born with a sinful nature which we inherit from
our parents, and which can be traced back to Adam and Eve.
Paul tells believers that before their conversion they were *"by
nature* the children of *wrath,* even as others" (Eph. 2:3).

Even for Christians it is easy to fall into sinful ways, for they
still possess the old Adamic nature. Recognizing this, Paul urged
Titus to instruct the believers to whom he ministered concerning
Christian conduct. A godly life is not an easy achievement. It
is attained only by those who nourish their souls constantly
through prayer and the reading of God's Word.

Would you be free from the burden of sin?
There's pow'r in the blood, pow'r in the blood;
Would you o'er evil a victory win?
There's wonderful pow'r in the blood. —L. E. Jones

**God formed us, sin deformed us, but only Christ can trans-
form us!**

ANYTHING LEFT?

Upon the first day of the week let every one of you
lay by him in store, as God hath prospered him . . . .
                                                1 Corinthians 16:2

As a visitor paid his bill at a very exclusive hotel, he saw a posted reminder near the door which read, "Have you left anything?" Going to the manager he remarked, "That sign is wrong, sir. It should read: 'Have you *anything left?*' "

What a vivid portrayal this is of life itself, when a person expends his talents, energies, and financial resources wholly for the fleeting pleasures and passing things of this present world. Coming to the end of life's journey, he suddenly has that "empty-handed" feeling. Having "spent" everything on himself, and recognizing the reality of eternity, he must face the sobering question, "Have you anything left?" Sad to say, the answer is "No," since the only way to have lasting "treasures" is to send them on ahead through wise, spiritual investments in the things of the Lord. That's why Jesus said, "Lay not up for yourselves treasures upon earth, where moth and rust doth corrupt, and where thieves break through and steal, but lay up for yourselves treasures in heaven . . ." (Matt. 6:19-20).

What a difference it would make if every true Christian really believed this. This matter of "investing" in Heaven would then occupy a much more important place in our prayers. Daily we would ask the Lord what we should do, how much we should give, and where we might wisely expend that which has been committed to our trust. Only in so doing can we be assured of an "abundant entrance." The apostle Paul tells us, "He who soweth sparingly shall reap also sparingly; and he who soweth bountifully shall reap also bountifully. Every man according as he purposeth in his heart, so let him give, not grudgingly, or of necessity; for God loveth a cheerful giver" (2 Cor. 9:6, 7).

How are you investing? When you leave for the eternal Home will there be "anything left"?

O the plaudits of men may be sweet to your ears;
  But the Master's "well done" will be more,
If you lay up your treasure in Heaven above
  Where the Savior has gone on before!   —Anon.

Treasures in Heaven are laid up as treasures on earth are laid down.

LOOKING UPWARD

They looked unto him, and were radiant, and their
faces were not ashamed.   Psalm 34:5

The well-known mission worker Sam Hadley once said, "The night I was converted I went out and looked up at the stars, and thanked God for their beauty. I had not seen them for ten years. A drunkard never looks up." Those who never lift their eyes to scan the sky miss a great deal, but a far more tragic fact is that multitudes never look up in faith to God. In these days of worldwide tension and confusion the only hopeful look is upward. Gazing upon the "things of earth" will only confuse and dishearten us. We are surrounded by unrest, lawlessness, violence, and suffering. Man's wisdom is not sufficient to solve these vexing problems. The American soldier dying from burns put it well when he said to his chaplain, "This is the result of too much chemistry and not enough Christ."

David wrote Psalm 34 as an expression of joyous praise because he had sought the Lord, and God had graciously come to his aid. He calls upon others to join him in worship, and in verse 5 declares that the experience God had given him has been the portion of all who have sincerely looked to their Maker for help. They are bright with joy, and have not been put to shame.

Those who take the upward look of faith find peace of soul in believing. Faith enables them to see things from the viewpoint of eternity. True Christians come to look upon this life as a time of schooling and training for Heaven.

If you are experiencing deep trials or disappointments take the heavenward look, believing that God has a loving purpose in permitting these difficulties. Looking upward helps you to see that even though there are many problems you cannot answer, God is still on the throne, and your eternal welfare is sure.

Through the darkness Christ will lead,
Well He knoweth all your need;
Soon your face with joy will glow
If you "look up" as on you go!   —Anon.

Even as flowers thrive when they bend to the light, so an inner radiance illumines those who constantly turn to the Lord!

A BLESSED PROMISE

And they shall see his face . . . . Revelation 22:4

The words of this precious promise were brought to my remembrance recently in connection with the delightful song, "The End of the Road," which was mailed to me by a friend. I first learned that hymn from my dear father who is now with the Savior. I recall one time after he had become unconscious from a heart attack and I had been giving him first aid, that when he finally came to, he stared at me almost sightlessly for a moment. Then, with a tear trickling down his cheek, he testified with feeling, "Someday I'll have a spell like this and when I open my eyes I won't see you, *but I'll look in my dear Savior's face!*" I knew he was thinking of the last stanza of this sacred song which he often sang around the house:

"When I come to the end of the long, long, road,
      And trials will all be past,
   I'll look in the face of my dearest Friend,
      Safe Home in His Heav'n at last."

What comfort and assurance it gave him to know the reality of that truth!

Yes, one of the crowning joys of the Better Land will be this intimate association with the Savior. Oh, that we might more clearly recognize and appreciate the fact that Jesus is *truly alive*—that He is a *real Man* in the Glory, and that we shall someday actually see His lovely face! It will be the same face that was bathed in tears of sympathy and compassion for a lost world, that those He rescued might avoid the land of eternal weeping! The same face that was marred and pinched with the agony of our sin at Calvary, that we might forever enjoy the loving smile of God's holy approval! The same dear face—but glorified and radiant with victory! Were it not that He shall first wipe all tears from our eyes (Rev. 21:4), we would weep for joy at seeing His lovely countenance! Truly we can sing with the hymnwriter, "When by His grace I shall look on His face; that will be glory for me!"

   When I shall gaze upon the face of Him
   Who for me died, with eye no longer dim,
   And praise Him in the everlasting hymn,
   I shall be satisfied!   —H. Bonar

We must know His GRACE here, to see His FACE over There!

HE COULDN'T GET AWAY

> *. . . if they had been of us, they would no doubt*
> *have continued with us.*   1 John 2:19

The five-year-old boy became angry with his mother and decided to run away from home. He walked out of his house with
a small suitcase and trudged around the block again and again.
Finally, when it was beginning to grow dark, the policeman
stopped him, "What's the idea?" The little boy answered, "I'm
runnin' away." The officer smiled as he said, "Look, I've had
my eye on you, and you've been doing nothing but walking
around the block. You call that running away?" The little fellow burst into tears, "Well, what do you want me to do? I ain't
allowed to cross the street." The youngster obviously respected
his parents and knew that they loved him. He couldn't really
run away.

Sometimes God's children become discouraged and even rebellious. They may disobey the Lord and seek their own way for
a while. But if they truly belong to Christ, they will find they
are held by a power beyond themselves. Like the little fellow
who could not carry out his threat to run away, the child of God
cannot absolutely and finally depart from God.

The apostle John tells us that those who completely and irre-
vocably leave the Christian faith never really knew the Lord.
Their departing is proof that they did not truly receive Christ—
were never actually born again.

Child of God, you need not live in continual fear that you
may deny the Lord and be finally lost. The Lord who saved you
will keep you (Jude 1:24) and someday usher you into Glory.

> *Now I would abide in His shadow,*
>   *Ne'er restless nor fearful would be;*
> *But should I e'er stray from the pathway*
>   *He'll never forget to keep me!*—Graves, alt.

**When a man is truly in Christ, he is safe; all the devil can do
is worry him!**   —Loveless

"GLOOMY CAESAR AND HAPPY JESUS"

*This people have I formed for myself; they shall
show forth my praise.*   Isaiah 43:21

Says Dr. Paul S. Rees, "Some time ago I saw an intriguing
title, 'Gloomy Caesar and Happy Jesus.' In the short article that
followed, the author contrasted what we know of Tiberius Caesar,
who ruled Rome in A.D. 30, with what we know of the Savior.
Of Tiberius with all his power, pomp, and possessions, the historian Pliny wrote, *'He is the gloomiest of mankind.'* But of
Jesus we read that sitting in the shadow of His cross, He 'took
bread, and *gave thanks,* and broke it, and gave unto them' (Luke
22:19), and when the holy supper was over, *they sang a 'hymn'*
and 'went out' (Mark 14:26)." Dr. Rees concludes by saying,
"You and I are not to be dispensers of Caesar's gloom, but rather
transmitters of Jesus' joy!"

The Lord formed us for His glory and *with the express purpose that we should show forth His praise* (Ps. 50:23). There
are enough "gloomy Caesars" around today. What the world
needs, therefore, is thankful Christians who are filled with the
Holy Spirit and Jesus' love. They should be so content with
what has been granted them in grace that they will stimulate
sad and weary men to seek Him who is the "fount of every
blessing."

There is enough in this life to complain about if we are inclined to be sour and discontent. As followers of Him who has
admonished us to "rejoice evermore" and "in everything give
thanks," we should be happy ambassadors of Heaven, spreading
the sunshine of His love to a dark and needy world. To attract
others to your Savior, stop being a "gloomy Caesar" and start
radiating "the joy of the Lord"!

*When all Thy mercies, O my God,
    My rising soul surveys,
Transported with the view, I'm lost
    In wonder, love, and praise!* —Watts

**Praise being the fairest blossom of the soul, we should ever
cultivate the "bloom of thanksgiving"!**

BELIEVING WITHOUT UNDERSTANDING

. . . some things [are] hard to be understood . . . .
                                        2 Peter 3:16

Some people refuse to believe the Bible because they cannot understand it. "Why should we suffer for Adam's sin?" they ask. "How could God create a universe out of nothing?" Now, while there may be many things we do not understand, this should not upset us. *It isn't necessary to comprehend them;* all we need to do is to *believe* what God says. After all, there are many things we do not understand; yet we accept them. Few know exactly how these bodies of ours operate from day to day. I can't explain how in a few brief hours the meat, potatoes, bread, lettuce, and pie which I ate for dinner can all be mysteriously changed into muscle, nerves, bones, blood, hair, and nails. However, this doesn't *prevent me from eating!* If it did, I would soon starve to death. Nor do I understand electricity; however, I do know what it does, and so I make it work for me. Who can completely and accurately define sight, taste, or feeling? We could go on to prove that we really do not understand many things, and yet we accept their reality and appreciate their benefits. How foolish man can be! He rejects the truth of God because he can't understand it, while at the same time he accepts the word of man which he also fails to comprehend. He accepts man's word concerning material matters, but doubts God's Word about eternal things. Mysteries of physiology, science and astronomy do not stagger him, but when it comes to spiritual realities, he must know the exact reason for everything, and insists on calling the eternal God into account concerning His sovereign Word. What folly!

Remember, God doesn't expect you to understand everything He says, but He does want you to believe His Word. "If we receive the witness of men, the witness of God is greater" (1 John 5:9). How strange it is that many can traverse the rocky road to perdition without difficulty; yet they stumble over a feather if it happens to lie on the pathway to Heaven!

> *Through faith we understand*
> *What to our sight is dim,*
> *And still Love's sweet, all-knowing Hand*
> *Leads those who trust in Him!*   —Anon.

Unless you believe, you will not understand!   —Augustine

TWO SOLEMN QUESTIONS

Lord, what wilt thou have me to do?   Acts 9:6

Two portraits by the German artist Sternberg — his "Dancing Gypsy Girl" and the "Crucifixion" — are linked to one another by an unusual set of circumstances. The pretty maiden who served as the model for the first portrait took an unusual interest in the unfinished painting of our Lord's final suffering. One day she commented, "He must have been a very bad man to have been nailed to a cross like that." Sternberg replied, "No, He was a good man, the best that ever lived! Indeed, He died for all men." "Did He die *for you?*" asked the puzzled girl. This question made a profound impression upon the artist. He did not know the Lord as his personal Savior, and didn't understand that salvation is received by faith alone. Some time later, however, he attended a meeting of humble believers who led him to Christ. Sternberg, his technical skill now coupled with a heart full of love and gratitude, completed his painting of the crucifixion and under it wrote the words: "This I did for thee; what hast thou done for Me?" It was placed in a famous gallery where a young aristocratic count named Zinzendorf saw it and was touched by the words written under it. He was a Christian but was convicted of his failure to serve the Lord. He later became the organizer of a missionary brotherhood known as the Moravians.

If you read today's Scripture lesson, John 19:16-22, you were brought face to face with the voluntary death of Jesus Christ. I urge you to answer the gypsy girl's question, *"Did He die for you?"* If He did, *"What are you doing for Him?"*

> I gave My life for thee,
>   My precious blood I shed,
> That thou might'st ransomed be,
>   And quickened from the dead;
> I gave, I gave My life for thee,
> What hast thou given for Me? —Havergal

The only sermon that never wearies us is that of an eloquent life!

M. O. H.

*Let every one of us please his neighbor . . . for even
Christ pleased not himself.*   Romans 15:2, 3

The following poem by an anonymous author has a bearing
on this text. I think you will find it both pleasing and instructive: "When rain beats down and all is drear, as often is the
way, with happy smile I will recall what Grandma used to say:
'Why bless your heart, it doesn't help to let the tears drip too;
just wipe your eyes and look around for some good deed to do.'
With glee three letters she'd repeat, just *M.O.H.* were they; yet
what their meaning we knew not, for did we ask, she'd say:
'Why that's my motto and I've learned the very wisest plan is to
find out what others need, and help them if you can!' With each
success, as we would seek some helpful act to do, we found that
cheering others' lives would brighten our lives too. I told her
this one day and pled, 'This *M.O.H.* make clear.' Then smiling
sweetly, she replied, *'Make Others Happy,* dear. When stormy
days give you the blues, just help to set things right; kind acts
will fill the darkest day with sweetness and with light. Look up
the real unfortunates, and ease their aches and pains; as you
make others happy, dear, you just forget it rains.'"

Those who write their names in kindness upon the hearts of
the many with whom they come in contact each day will never
be forgotten. They will find that in pouring the perfume of
love upon others they inadvertently spill the blessing upon themselves as well. Yes, *"Make Others Happy"* is a motto worth
living. Not only is it Christlike (Rom 15:3) and satisfying, but
also will bring a rich reward.

> *There is a destiny that makes us brothers;*
> *None goes his way alone;*
> *All that we send into the lives of others,*
> *Comes back into our own!*   —Markham

Joy and Heaven's sunshine will requite the kind!   —Byron

EQUAL BEFORE GOD

. . . there is no respect of persons with God.
Romans 2:11

The preamble of the Constitution of the United States declares that God has created all men equal. This statement, however, has sometimes been challenged. Obviously people are not equal in attractiveness, physical strength, intelligence, background, or opportunity. Nor are people equally inclined toward evil, even if they have the same hereditary and environmental factors. (Because of this, the efforts of the communists to produce a society of equal people are doomed to failure.)

The writers of our Constitution were not wrong, however, for they did not intend to say that all men are equally talented, industrious, or trustworthy, but only that every person is entitled to be regarded with respect, that all possess the same rights, and that every effort should be made to give each an equal opportunity. This truth is also taught in the Bible. God is just as concerned with the poorest family in the slums as He is with millionaires and their offspring; and He will deal in absolute justice with all, "For there is no respect of persons with God."

The story of Ahab and Naboth in our reading for today reveals both God's concern with the individual and His justice in punishing wrongdoers. Naboth was a poor man, but God was interested in him and his rights. Ahab was a king, but he could not get by with his sin. This is a wonderful message of comfort for the downtrodden, and it constitutes a grim warning to the strong who oppress the weak or dishonor the name of God.

> *There is no respect of persons with our God,*
> *All are equal and so precious in His sight.*
> *King and peasant He doth weigh before His eye,*
> *And His judgment of them shall be ever right!*—Anon.

Rulers and their subjects find a common level before the law and the foot of the cross.   —Colton, alt.

REASONS FOR PRAISE

Praise ye the Lord. Oh, give thanks unto the Lord,
for he is good.   Psalm 106:1

Years ago a believer with an unusual spirit of gratitude regularly attended the services of a mission in Chicago. Being a black man, he was often the victim of discrimination by the world; yet he radiated Christian joy. One day entering the mission with a bandage on his thumb, he explained that he had smashed it with a hammer. Then he added, "But praise the Lord. *I have my thumb yet!*" On another occasion he purchased a steak with his meager earnings and was on his way home with it when a shoelace became untied. As he laid the package on the sidewalk to tie his shoe, a large dog suddenly grabbed the choice piece of meat and made off with it. Later, as this humble believer recounted his exasperating experience, he said with characteristic cheerfulness, "Praise the Lord. *I still have my appetite left!*" He always found reasons to be grateful.

People who themselves have never discovered the inner joy this dear Christian brother possessed may find it hard to believe these accounts, nevertheless they are true. No matter how skeptical they may be, however, all Christians must agree that the inspired writer of Psalm 92 was right when he declared, "It is a good thing to give thanks unto the Lord." The unsaved man does not understand God, and is often unaware of reasons for thanksgiving. But the devout believer, assured of His goodness, ever rejoices in the knowledge that righteousness will triumph, and those who love the Lord will be vindicated.

On this special day, we should find many reasons to say with the Psalmist, "Oh, give thanks unto the Lord, for he is good; for his mercy endureth forever.

> *Ten thousand thousand precious gifts*
> *My daily thanks employ;*
> *Nor is the least a cheerful heart*
> *To taste those gifts with joy.* —Watts

Hem your blessings with praise lest they unravel!

THE INEVITABLE

. . . it is appointed unto men once to die . . . .
Hebrews 9:27

One of America's well-known poets had the idea that the year of his death would be one which was divisible by 11. For that reason, when he reached 77 years of age, he believed he would live to be at least 88 — and he did! However, he then felt that he would live to be 99 — but he didn't! He died the next year at 89. When I read about his passing, I remembered a statement his wife had made concerning her husband. She declared, "He hasn't failed in anything he started out to do yet!" That may have been the case in most things, but he did fail in his intention to live to be 99. We don't mention this to be critical of him, but simply to underscore the fact that death is something over which we do not have the final say. While a well-balanced diet, ample rest, reasonable exercise, and wholesome recreation might help to better our health, there comes that time when we can do nothing to forestall the grim hand of the reaper. This is simply because ". . . it is appointed unto men once to die." Not in vain do the Scriptures warn, "Come now, ye that say, Today or tomorrow we will go into such a city, and continue there a year . . . whereas ye know not what shall be on the next day. For what is your life? It is even a vapor that . . . vanisheth away" (James 4:13, 14). And again, "Boast not thyself of tomorrow; for thou knowest not what a day may bring forth" (Prov. 27:1).

In view of the uncertainty of life and the certainty of death, how essential it is so to live that when God says, "This is *your* hour," we may pass into eternity with joy and confidence. For us who know Christ as Savior the "inevitable thing" (should the Lord tarry) has lost its real dread and power; therefore we can cry out with Paul, "O death, where is thy sting? O grave, where is thy victory?" (1 Cor. 15:55).

If life be long, I will be glad
That I may long obey;
If short — death hath no venomed sting,
I'll soar to endless day! —R. Baxter, alt.

Epitaph on tombstone: Reader, stop and think, I'm in eternity, you're on the brink!

SHELTERED AND SAFE

There is, therefore, now no condemnation to them
who are in Christ Jesus.   Romans 8:1

Judgment can never touch a believing sinner who is sheltered in Jesus Christ. To be in Him is the guarantee of immunity from the penalty of a broken law, a guilty conscience, and impending doom.

Spurgeon tells of a man who had been condemned to be shot by a Spanish court. Because he was an American citizen and also of English birth, the consuls of the two countries decided to intervene. They declared that the Spanish authorities had no power to put him to death. Their protest went unheeded. How would they protect the life of the man? Finally they deliberately wrapped him up in their flags — the Stars and Stripes and the Union Jack — and defied the executioners. "Fire a shot if you dare! If you do so, you will bring the powers of those two great empires upon you." There he stood. One bullet could have ended his life, but protected by those flags and the governments they represented, he was invulnerable.

So, too, the Lord Jesus takes the soul of the sinner who believes in Him and covers the guilty one with His blood. Thus wrapped and sheltered by the Savior, he is safe. As the hymn-writer points out, "In the Lord we've found redemption — grace and glory in God's Son. O the height and depth of mercy! Christ and His redeemed are one."

Those who have received the Savior are free from condemnation — not only in the future when we will be with the Lord — but right *now!* God has no judgment against us. He views us in Christ and declares us "not guilty"! Therefore we are both sheltered and safe!

> *My God is reconciled,*
> *His pardoning voice I hear;*
> *Because He owns me for His child*
> *I need no longer fear!*   —Anon.

Lives rooted in God's unchanging grace can never be uprooted!

OF BIRDS AND STARS

> . . . *the beasts . . . shall teach thee; and the fowls*
> *of the air . . . shall tell thee.*   Job 12:7

Nature teaches us much about God. For one thing, it shows His kindness in providing animals and birds with inborn impulses and patterns which aid them greatly in adjusting to what is often a hostile environment. Their lives are thus guided and preserved despite their limited native intelligence. For instance, some birds would perish if they had to stay all year in areas which have far-ranging climate and temperature changes. Therefore the Lord has graciously given them migrating instincts. It has been discovered that the small indigo bunting (a member of the finch family) apparently steers his way 2,000 miles south every year just by *looking over his shoulder at the northern sky!* This night-flying bird does not seem to rely on any one star or constellation for his direction, says Steven T. Emlen of the University of Michigan. Rather *he recognizes the whole geometrical pattern of them* within 35 degrees of the North Star, and can be confused only when that part of the sky is entirely blocked off by clouds. He then wisely discontinues his flight until he can once again get a clear view of the configuration made by the Milky Way, the Big Dipper, and other northern star groups. The prophet Jeremiah says the Lord gave these "ordinances . . . of the stars for a light by night" (Jer. 31:35). Apparently they not only aid *man* in navigation, but also assist his feathered friends— *the birds.*

Observing nature, so crammed with beauty, wonder, and design, we should be taught by the beasts and the "fowls of the air" that *there is a gracious Heavenly Father who provides for His creatures in wisdom.* This in turn should call forth our adoration and praise!

> *The Lord's hand has painted the rainbow,*
> *You can see His design in all things.*
> *When looking for wisdom, you'll find it*
> *In stars, birds, and butterfly wings.* —Hein, alt.

God's signature of wisdom and power is clearly impressed on the world of nature!

A BASKET OF THANKSGIVINGS

*Bless the Lord, O my soul, and forget not all his
benefits . . . .*   Psalm 103:2

No story in the Bible more movingly pictures human ingratitude than this one about the ten lepers. In desperation they had
cried out to Jesus for healing. The Lord had cured them, but
only one returned to render praise for his deliverance. It often
happens that when a person gets what he wants he never remembers to say, "Thank you!"

Some years ago a certain radio personality had a program called
"Job Center of the Air" which helped 2500 people find employment. He reported that only ten of that large number took time
to thank him.

A man, remembering a school teacher who had been very
helpful to him when a child, sent her a letter expressing his gratitude. She was now in her eighties and living alone. Upon receiving his communication, she wrote him, "I can't tell you how
much your letter meant to me. You will be interested to know
that I taught school for 50 years, and yours is the first note of
appreciation I have ever received. It came on a blue, cold morning, and it filled me with cheer."

It disturbs us to realize that we are so ungrateful to our fellow-
men, but the base ingratitude to God, exhibited by so many, is
even more distressing. An old legend tells of two angels named
"Prayer" and "Thanksgiving" whom God sent to earth—each with
a basket. The container which carried the prayers to Heaven was
large, for it held many requests. However, the basket for the
notes of thanksgiving was small, since only three expressions of
gratitude were sent to Heaven by the hundreds who had been
blessed.

Today, as we are reminded of our selfishness and sinful ingratitude, let us fill a large basket with "thanksgivings." Then
tomorrow, and the days that follow, let us echo the words of the
Psalmist: "Bless the Lord, O my soul, *and forget not all his
benefits.*"

**Many people act as if the day is ThanksHAVING—instead of
ThanksGIVING!**   —Ralph Mueller

ONE THING LACKING

Jesus . . . said . . . Yet lackest thou one thing.

Luke 18:22

The Lord Jesus was once approached by a certain young ruler who asked what he should do to inherit eternal life. Although he claimed to have kept all the commandments, Jesus told him that one thing was lacking. After Christ explained this lack, the young man "went away sorrowful." (See Matthew 19:22.)

Today, too, no matter how good a person may think he is, he always comes short of meeting God's holy and righteous demands. In fact, the Bible says that *all our "righteousnesses* are as *filthy rags!"* No matter how hard we try, there is something missing. An unknown author has written: "The garden is beautifully laid out; the straight lines and the curves are exact; the terraces are arranged with artistic taste; but no seed is sown,—and the summer says, 'One thing thou lackest.' The watch has a golden case; the dial is exquisitely traced and figured; the hands are delicate and well fixed; everything is there but the mainspring and he who inquires the time says, 'One thing thou lackest'." The very same thing is true when it comes to salvation. "For all have sinned, and come short of the glory of God" (Rom. 3:23). That's why Jesus said, "Ye must be born again." We need a new start. We need a new life. We need that perfect righteousness which God alone can give. "For by grace are ye saved *through faith;* and that not of yourselves, it is the gift of God — not of works, lest any man should boast" (Eph. 2:8, 9). "Believe on the Lord Jesus Christ, and thou shalt be saved" (Acts 16:31). Remember, friend, it is "not by works of righteousness which we have done, but according to his mercy" that God saves us (Titus 3:5). In ourselves we are lacking; but in Christ we stand complete!

> *Complete in Thee! no work of mine*
> *May take, dear Lord, the place of Thine;*
> *Thy blood hath pardon bought for me,*
> *And I am now complete in Thee.* —Wolfe

Every man has a need that only Christ can satisfy!

WILL IT HAPPEN AGAIN?

*. . . ye turned to God from idols, . . . and to wait
for his Son from heaven.*   1 Thessalonians 1:9, 10

In this day as scientists gloomily predict the end of human existence, it is well to remember that man's basic need is still spiritual. If mankind would only turn to Christ, God would enable our leaders to solve many of the vexing problems they face.

About 250 years ago moral and spiritual conditions in England were so deplorable that serious-minded men were afraid the empire would soon collapse. But God raised up Whitefield and the Wesleys, and through their preaching a spiritual transformation of the nation was effected. A prominent historian wrote, "A religious revival burst forth, which changed in a few years the whole temper of English society. The church was restored to life and activity. Religion carried to the hearts of the poor a fresh spirit of moral zeal, and purified our literature and our manners. A new philanthropy reformed our prisons, infused humane treatment into our penal laws, abolished the slave trade, and gave the first impulse of popular education."

Today we are in desperate need of a similar Divine visitation. True, we are looking for Christ's return, but so were the early believers who "turned the world upside down" (Acts 17:6). Although they were waiting "for his Son from heaven," they still "served the living and true God" with enthusiasm. We should watch for the Savior's return with lives that are marked by prayer, purity, and zeal. If we do, the Lord will be glorified, and the world will feel the impact of our consecrated living! Let us hope that a revival will yet arise to restrain the powers of evil and bring renewed consciousness of God and His laws!

*Send revival sweet and precious,
Though the outlook oft is dim;
Help us live the truth we cherish
As we steadfast look for Him!* —Bosch

The virility of a nation, like the moral fiber of its people, is found in the strength of its spiritual convictions!

THE LENTIL-PATCH SOLDIER

*Finally, my brethren, be strong in the Lord, and in
the power of his might.*   Ephesians 6:10

The valiant warrior Shammah, mentioned in 2 Samuel 23, is
not among the familiar names of the Bible. You may not have
known anything about him until you read the Scripture for today. There are just two verses devoted to his life. He was one
of a triumvirate of David's mighty men, who receives special
praise. There was also Adino who lifted up "his spear against
eight hundred, whom he slew at one time," as well as Eleazar,
who fought and fought until his hand was so bent to the sword
that it would not open.

Shammah would never have received the "Christian states-
man of the year" award. In fact, many would not even have
noticed him. But David did! In 2 Samuel 23:12 we read, "But
he stood in the center of the plot, and defended it, and slew the
Philistines, and the Lord wrought a great victory." Guarding a
lentil patch and driving off Philistines is not as dramatic as lifting up a spear and slaying 800, but it was a service to the king
and required no less heroism and faithfulness. *Shammah stood
in a common place, but was steadfast and courageous!*

The Lord asks many of His children to work and serve in
small, inauspicious places where no eye beholds and no voice
praises but His. In fact, it may be that He has called *you* to
just such a task. Christian friend, *are you willing to stay by a
lentil patch and let others stand in the limelight?* If this is
God's appointment for you, rejoice in it! The King will reward
your faithfulness.

*And when the war is over and the vict'ry won,
When the true and faithful gather one by one,
He will crown with glory all who serve Him here,
Will you be enlisted as a volunteer?*   —Brown, alt.

**It is the STRENGTH, not the LENGTH of a man's life that
counts with God!**   —Van Gorder

FADED ROSES

*Remember now thy Creator in the days of thy
youth.*   Ecclesiastes 12:1

An attractive young lady was surprised one day when she received a gift of roses from a wealthy woman named Mrs. Mack. Upon opening the box, her amazement turned to sheer bewilderment, for she saw that the roses were wilted and the petals were falling off. Perhaps the flowers had been packed for delivery a few days earlier and then neglected. Later that day she met Mrs. Mack on the street and thanked her for the roses. The older woman smiled and said, "I'm glad you like them. I cut them last Monday and enjoyed them all week, but this morning when I noticed they were beginning to get old and faded, I thought of you and had them delivered to your door." Seeing the puzzled and hurt look in the girl's face, she continued, "The other evening I was sitting in the car while my husband went into the drugstore. As you walked by I heard you telling someone that you wanted to become a Christian later, but not now while you are still young. You said you wanted to have a good time first. In other words, you wish to give the Lord your life after the beauty, charm, and vigor have faded and you have become old and wrinkled. I thought these roses would be an illustration of what you are doing in relation to the Lord."

The writer of Ecclesiastes wrote this book after he had wasted much of his life in pursuit of empty pleasure. He had found that this world does not satisfy the deepest longings of the heart, and urged the youth to avoid the mistakes he had made. The young person who gives the Lord his best will never regret this decision.

> *"Choose you this day"; time hastens on,*
> *Thou canst not neutral be;*
> *To serve the world or Christ, thy Lord,*
> *"Choose now, which shall it be?"* —Meyer

Waiting until old age to give yourself to Christ is making a sacrifice to God of the devil's leavings.

"IN THE WAY"

And he said, . . . I being in the way, the Lord led me.

Genesis 24:27

At the first meeting of a group of Girl Scouts, they were asked what they had done at home to help their mothers since joining the Brownies. One by one they proudly answered. Some had made beds, others had washed dishes, while still others had dusted their rooms. "And you, Penny?" asked the troop leader. "How did you help your mother?" Came the solemn answer, *"I kept out of her way!"* Keeping "out of the way" can sometimes be helpful; but when it comes to service for the Lord, He wants us to be *"in the way,"* not in the sense of being obstructive, but rather with the object of obediently walking in the pathway of His choosing. When we are thus fully surrendered, God delights to use and lead us.

In Genesis 24 we are told about Eliezer, Abraham's servant, who was sent to secure a bride for Isaac. After meeting Rebekah and receiving the assurance that she was the one "appointed" for his master's son, he blesses the Lord and says, "I being in the way, the Lord led me." Because he was treading the pathway of obedience, Eliezer was divinely *directed* and *used*. As a submissive servant he was an instrument in God's hands in the accomplishment of His purposes.

Are *you* "out of the way" or "in the way" today? Are you hiding out, shirking your duty, or are you in the place of obedience, available for service? Regardless of what your past experiences may have been, determine this day that your response to the Lord's plea, "Whom shall I send, and who will go for us?" will be the ready answer, "Here am I, send me! *I want to be 'in the way'!"*

> *Ready to go, ready to stay,*
> *Ready my place to fill;*
> *Ready for service, lowly or great,*
> *Ready to do His will!* —Tillman

What God wants from us most is not so much our ABILITY as our AVAILABILITY!

NO CREDIBILITY GAP

Take heed unto thyself and unto the doctrine;
continue in them.   1 Timothy 4:16*

There is to be no "credibility gap" in the believer's testimony and life. "He that saith he abideth in him ought himself also so to walk, even as he walked." Do our lives line up with what we *say* we believe?

In one of the letters of John Newton, reference is made to "the remarkable and humbling difference between a believer's acquired and experimental knowledge, or in other words, between *his opinion* and *his practice.*" This is precisely what Paul was saying to Timothy. Right doctrine and wrong practice add up to a minus on the spiritual score sheet.

To increase the copies of Bibles upon the bookshelf is an easy matter; but to multiply the truth of that Book in our lives is something else. In a picture painted in the Middle Ages, a friar is seen dressed in the robes of his order and apparently engrossed in his religious devotions. Looking more closely, however, one can see that what appeared to be a book is really a punchbowl and the friar's clasped hands are squeezing a lemon.

Too often a disparity exists between doctrine and life, preaching and practice, belief and behavior. The apostle's plea was for the balance of the two. Never can there be the sacrifice of doctrine, for right living is possible only when there is right believing. But as others look on, is our life as credible as our creed? Someone has written, "I am my neighbor's Bible, he reads me when we meet. Today he reads me in my home, tomorrow in the street. He may be relative or friend, or slight acquaintance be. He may not even know my name, yet *he is reading me.*" May there be *no credibility gap!*

> *Be like Jesus, this my song,*
> *In the home and in the throng;*
> *Be like Jesus, all day long!*
> *I would be like Jesus.*   —Rowe

Don't pray and talk cream and live skimmed milk!

HE FIRST LOVED US

We love him, because he first loved us. 1 John 4:19

It's easy to be fond of nice people. It's natural to see virtue in one's own flesh and blood. However, to love an outsider who is rebellious and obnoxious is neither easy nor natural. The ability to possess genuine, unselfish regard for completely unlovely people is rare in this world. In fact, it is an impossibility apart from the grace of the Lord Jesus Christ. In the light of this, God's love for mankind is certainly amazing beyond degree. Knowing exactly how wicked human beings would become — how they would lie, steal, be immoral, and manifest hateful and unkind attitudes— He still loved us so much He gave His only Son for our salvation. He loved us from before the foundation of the world, and He loves us still — even though there is nothing in us to draw forth His favor.

Let me tell you a story which made a deep impression upon me when I first heard it in my boyhood days. A mother was sewing while her little girl was busily occupied with her dolls and toys. After some time the little lass came to her busy parent and wanted to be loved and caressed. "Why do you want me to hold you?" asked the mother. The little girl lisped, "'cause I love you." "What about your dolls and your toys, don't you love them too?" said her mother teasingly. The little girl gave this amazing reply, "Yes, but I love you more. I guess it's 'cause *you loved me when I was too small to love you back!*" Tears welled up in the mother's eyes as she contemplated God's great compassion for us, His children. The apostle John summarized this truth in that brief but wonderful sentence: *"We love him, because he first loved us!"* Yes, if God had not taken the initiative, we would have had no inclination to seek Him, and so would have perished eternally. Let each one of us who knows the Lord, meditate on that thought with heartfelt gratitude.

> *I sought the Lord, and afterward I knew,*
> *He moved my soul to seek Him, seeking me;*
> *It was not I that found, O Savior true;*
> *No, I was found of Thee!*   —Anon.

God "repented" that He had made man, but He never repented that He redeemed him!

December 5   Read Psalm 18:28-36

NOT BY ACCIDENT

*The steps of a good man are ordered by the Lord,
and he delighteth in his way.*   Psalm 37:23

It is good when the child of God can recognize that the varying circumstances of life are by divine order. To survey the paths
over which the Lord has brought us and say, "As for God, his
way is perfect," indicates spiritual maturity.

We were driving slowly through a strange city. In an area
of used-car lots and repair shops my attention was attracted to
one large body shop surrounded by wrecked cars. Business was
flourishing. But what really caught my eye was a caption just
under the owner's name. It read, *"We meet by accident!"* For
the Christian, however, there are no "accidents." Sometimes the
Lord leads His children in restricted and lonely paths, but even
in these His way is perfect. What for the moment may appear
to us a "tragedy" is the unerring hand of the Father training and
fitting us for another step in His plan. There may be starless
nights as well as sun-filled days; yet our Heavenly Father is working out His purpose in both.

David could look back upon the way in which God had led
him. First his life on the hills of Bethlehem was a rather secluded,
uneventful one. Perhaps this was the experience of "still waters."
Then he went to the king's court where his life was miraculously
spared. Many times he was delivered from the pursuing Saul.
In all this David could say, "God's way is perfect." At last he
reached the throne. None of this was by accident.

Some may talk of meeting "by accident," but not the child of
God. A loving Heavenly Father has planned and is constantly
ordering our steps.

> *While passing through the wilderness*
> *Full of temptations and distress,*
> *What comfort doth this thought afford:*
> *Our steps are ordered by the Lord!* —Anon.

**There are no "accidents" in God's purposes; the STOPS of a
good man are ordered as well as his STEPS!**   —Mueller

THIEVES AND INFLATION

*Lay not up . . . treasures upon earth, . . . where
thieves break through and steal.*   Matthew 6:19

Thieves and inflation have much in common! In fact, when it
comes to their effect upon a person's "nest egg," they are almost
synonymous. Both rob and deprive the unsuspecting victim of his
resources.

A few days ago, while thumbing through an old 1922 almanac,
I came across this suggestion for becoming financially independent: "If a person, at 20 years of age, would religiously put aside
one dollar per week and invest it every 6 months at 6 percent
compound interest, by the time he reached 60 he would have
established a fund that would make him independent of help
from others for the balance of his life. His bank book would
show the tidy sum of approximately $10,000." How times have
changed! Today, although a lot of money, this amount can no
longer be considered sufficient to make a person financially independent.

Jesus said, "Lay not up . . . treasures upon earth." If spoken
in 1970 I can well imagine our Lord adding the words "where
thieves [and inflation] break through and steal." We certainly
have an obligation to prepare in a sensible way for the future,
and to do what we can to avoid becoming a burden to others in
our declining years. Yet, in every person's savings program, provision should be made for deposits in the Bank of Heaven. It
offers security. It provides a foolproof hedge against inflation.
It guarantees the best returns.

If the insecurity of earthly investments troubles you, "lay up
. . . treasures *in heaven*," where neither thieves nor inflation
"break through and steal."

It has been said with wisdom true,
"The heart will e'er follow the hoard."
Remember this, and then make sure
Your treasure is found in the Lord! —G.W.

**The real measure of a man's wealth is what he shall own in
eternity!**

PAY ATTENTION TO LITTLE THINGS!

For who hath despised the day of small things?
Zechariah 4:10

That well-known Christian, Horatius Bonar, once aptly remarked: "It is well to remember that *a holy life is made up of a number of small things*: little words, not eloquent speeches and sermons; little deeds, not miracles and battles. These, not one great heroic act of mighty martyrdom, make up most Christian lives. So, too, the avoidance of little evils, little sins, little follies, and small indiscretions and indulgences of the flesh, will go far to make up at least the negative side of a holy life."

I have read somewhere that the merchants of Panama, to be secure from fire, build their houses on wooden piles driven deep into the sand beneath the water of rivers and lakes. Soon, however, a minute species of the madrepore, which are miscroscopic in size, begin to do their destructive work unseen by human eyes. They bore, saw, and eat away until the strong posts undergirding the homes become completely honeycombed. Then on some windy day when the sea dashes against such dwellings, they crumple and fall because the weakened pilings cannot stand the strain. In a similar fashion sin honeycombs a man's character, and when the testing days come, he may fall before the onslaughts of temptation.

It is important for us to keep in mind that it was the one act of eating of the forbidden fruit which led to the fall of the entire human race. Only one moment of weakness lost Esau his birthright. One wrong decision landed Lot in Sodom, where he first lost his testimony, then his wife, and finally almost all of his possessions. A kiss, too, is a very small thing, but it betrayed the Son of God into the hands of His enemies.

This day pay attention to little things; they often are of tremendous importance!

> *God often uses foolish things,*
> *The base things and the small,*
> *To bring to naught the mighty ones,*
> *So men can't boast at all.* —Roberta Beck

From a little spark may burst a mighty flame!   —Dante

CHRISTIANS AND THE FBI

> . . . *[they] have their senses exercised to discern*
> *both good and evil.*   Hebrews 5:14

When a man is accepted by the FBI, he is given intensive training to prepare him for his responsible position. As part of the program he is taught to watch for counterfeit currency. He is commissioned to make a thorough study, *not of the "phonies,"* but of the *genuine bills!* This is done so that a fake will be recognized at once because of its contrast with the real thing.

We, as Christians, can learn a lesson from the FBI. While it is helpful to study the cults and to be fully aware of their false and dangerous dogmas, we should also be so well versed in the *truth* of God's Word that when we encounter that which is not genuine, we can immediately detect it. We must study the Bible and be so familiar with the "real article" that anything which is counterfeit will be perceived almost instinctively.

We are living in a day when many are being led astray into cults and isms because they are not actually aware of what they are getting into. The only way to prevent this is to indoctrinate believers with the *truth* so that they will discern the false automatically. For example, if a person is really taught the *truth of grace,* he won't fall for the line of the legalists who inject human works into the matter of obtaining salvation. If an individual is well instructed concerning the *truth about the Person of Christ,* he won't be led astray by those who proclaim Him to be less than God. If one knows the *truth about the second coming of Christ,* he won't be swayed by those who distort this blessed hope, and make it mean something other than the personal, bodily return of the Lord Jesus Himself. Let's be like good FBI agents — *so familiar with the truth that at a glance we will detect the counterfeit!*

The letters FBI, when used in reference to that respected agency of our government, stand for "Federal Bureau of Investigation." We also need FBI Christians — that is, those who have Full Bible Intelligence!

> *"Try the spirits," Christian,*
> *Test them by the Word,*
> *See if they acknowledge*
> *Christ as living Lord!*   —M.E.

Beware! Error often rides to its deadly work on the back of truth!
                              —C. H. Spurgeon

PRECIOUS NAME!

Whatever ye shall ask the Father in my name,
he will give it you.   John 16:23

While visting in the home of a Christian friend, I learned
that some thirty years earlier he had secured a job in the bank
of which he is now an officer. Quite a young man and inex-
perienced in business, he started for the bank one cold morning
to make application. He carried with him a letter which he was
to present to the president of the financial institution. It said
simply, "I desire to obtain a position for the bearer of this letter."
That note bore the signature of the brother of the bank's president; and *that* made the difference! He secured a position in the
name of one who was honored and beloved by the presiding
officer of the business.

Through the Lord Jesus the believer has special access to God
the Father, for we are *"accepted in the Beloved"* (Eph. 1:6). By
Him and through Him our requests are made known to God.
The Father can spell out the meaning of every petition sent up
in the name of Jesus. Just as "for Christ's sake" God has forgiven
us, so for that reason He also hears our prayers as they ascend
in the all-powerful name of His beloved Son. With the poet we
say, "No longer far from Him, but now by 'precious blood' made
nigh; accepted in the 'Well-beloved,' near to God's heart we lie."

Absolutely no one dares approach God in his own name, either
for salvation or sustaining grace. There is One who has perfectly
satisfied the Father in both character and work — the Lord Jesus
Christ, God's Son. If we would be heard, we must plead the
Savior's name before the Throne, and claim the merits of His
work alone.

> *"In the Beloved" accepted am I,*
> *Risen, ascended, and seated on high;*
> *Saved from all sin thro' His infinite grace,*
> *With the redeemed ones accorded a place!*—Martin

**The name of Jesus is a BYWORD to the sinner but Heaven's
PASSWORD to the saint!**   —Bosch

"WE WOULD SEE JESUS!"

. . . Sir, we would see Jesus.   John 12:21

The story is told about a brilliant young minister with several degrees behind his name, who accepted a call to pastor a rather large congregation. The people were pleased with his oratory and learning, but something seemed to be lacking in his sermons. One day when entering the pulpit, his mind crammed with reason and logic, he saw a note addressed to him bearing the words, *"Sir, we would see Jesus!"* The Holy Spirit spoke to his heart. Throwing aside his superficiality and assumed scholarly poses, he became that day an ambassador for Christ, pleading with men to become reconciled to God through the merits of the Savior. It is said that those who came to be thrilled, remained to pray and confess. A tremendous change came over his life and preaching. On a later Sunday the young minister found another note pinned to the pulpit which Scripturally summarized the feelings of his congregation. It read: "Then were the disciples glad when they saw the Lord."

Oh, that we as believers, in our contact with the world, might always show forth and glorify the Lord Jesus Christ in all that we do and say. While it is true that we should seek the best methods of reaching the lost with a winning and intelligent approach, it is well to remember that what men and women need today is *Christ!* This should be our primary objective and concern. *He* is the One whom we should present. *He* is the One who should be seen in our lives. *He* is the one who should be the theme of our song. *He* is the one who should be the subject of our conversation. It was Paul who said, "For we preach not ourselves, but Christ Jesus the Lord . . ." (2 Cor. 4:5). Christianity is more than a religion — it is a *Person!* We are not commissioned to preach a set of religious rules, nor to influence others to submit to a code of ethics, nor to further a philosophic system. Our duty is to point men to the Savior. Let us ever remember that we are "ambassadors for Christ!"

> *O will you give heed to this message today,*
> *And to your commission be true?*
> *Are you representing the Savior aright,*
> *Can others see Jesus in you?* —L. C. Voke

Debate Him and they'll hate Him; live Him and they'll love Him!

TRIUMPH THROUGH TRIALS

. . . affliction, which is but for a moment, worketh for
us . . . [an] eternal weight of glory. 2 Corinthians 4:17

One day I chatted on the phone for nearly thirty minutes
with a discouraged lady as she told me of her trials. She warned
me not to tell her that God has a loving purpose in permitting
afflictions, for she said the promises of the Bible were of small
comfort to her. As we talked I discovered why she was despon-
dent. She had been wronged by certain people and had allowed
her grievances to make her bitter.

If you have been similarly injured by someone and you feel
hateful, remember that the Christians to whom Peter wrote his
epistles were also being treated shamefully. But this was no
reason for them to hate their persecutors. Knowing full well the
trials they were undergoing, Peter begins, "Blessed be the God
and Father of our Lord Jesus Christ." In effect he is saying, "Before we begin talking of our troubles, let us unitedly praise God
for the riches we have as His children. A heart filled with gratitude has no room for bitterness."

This woman with whom I spoke was unable to look at her
problems in the proper perspective. She did not see them as
temporary and purposeful. Do your difficulties appear as a mountain you can never scale? Remember that they are only "for a
season" and will soon end. Furthermore, God permits these hardships in order that through them He may refine your character
even as fire removes the dross from gold. But you must believe
Him and submit to His ways. A spirit of thankfulness and a
daily exercise of faith in times of trial will bring spiritual enrich-
ment to your life.

> *All God's testings have a purpose—*
> *Someday you will see the light.*
> *All He asks is that you trust Him,*
> *Walk by faith and not by sight.* —Zoller

**Troubles are often tools by which God fashions us for better
things.**   —Beecher

"BLUE RIBBON" CHRISTIANS

> . . . *when he hath tested me, I shall come forth*
> *as gold.*   Job 23:10

In New England some time ago, I was presented with a tin of pure Vermont maple syrup. It was given to me by a man who consistently wins blue ribbons for his product. When I was told about these "first place" awards, I revealed my ignorance by asking, "Isn't all maple syrup pretty much the same?" I thought that any variation in it was simply a matter of how much it was diluted. I was sorely mistaken. The *quality, flavor,* and *color* depends upon many factors, including the tree from which the sap is drawn, when it is collected, the existing weather conditions, and the proficiency of the one who controls the boiling process in the sugar bush. There is much involved in the production of good maple syrup. A blue ribbon award is the result of a carefully controlled process from start to finish.

This all reminded me of the way the Lord refines the lives of His children. Someone has said, "God loved His Son so much that He wanted a whole Heaven full just like Him." For that reason He gathers believers to Himself in grace, and has predestinated them to be "conformed to the image of his Son." And even now, He is working on us. As the fires of affliction and trial are applied to us, it may be disturbing at the moment, but afterwards it results in great blessing and reward (Heb. 12:11), for thus the diluting elements of the world are removed from our lives.

I remember well how as boys we collected some sap from our maple trees in the backyard. We put it in a big tub on a burner in the basement, and then promptly forgot all about it. Many hours later mother almost fainted when she opened the basement door and was greeted by billowing clouds of smoke. How thankful we should be that God never forgets us in that way. He knows just the right amount of heat necessary to make us "blue ribbon" Christians!

> *When through fiery trials thy pathway shall lie,*
> *My grace all-sufficient shall be thy supply;*
> *The flame shall not hurt thee; I only design*
> *Thy dross to consume, and thy gold to refine.*—G.K.

God sends trials not to IMPAIR us, but to IMPROVE us!—G.W.

GOD'S WAY IS BEST!

*And Mary said . . . be it unto me according to thy
word . . . .*   Luke 1:38

When I was a fourth grader, one of my classmates suddenly
died due to a ruptured appendix. All of us were shocked when
we heard the news. We knew that adults died, and that sometimes children also were taken, but the death of Donald, a boy
our own age whom we knew so well, had a sobering effect upon
us all. Naturally, the question was in everybody's mind why
God had permitted him to die.

The day came for the funeral, and the whole class was to
attend. Before leaving the school, however, our teacher, a fine
Christian, told us a true story designed to help each of us ad-
just to the tragedy. She knew that we were deeply concerned
about why the Lord had allowed this thing to happen. She related an incident concerning a young woman whose husband had
died many years before, leaving her alone with her precious
little boy. One day this child became extremely ill, and it appeared that he too would pass away. The mother pleaded with
the Lord for healing, and then, when about to close her prayer
with the familiar words, "Not my will, but Thine be done,"
found herself exclaiming instead, "Lord, I can't say that. *I want
my little boy! I won't give him up!*" God listened to her plead-
ings, and her son was spared. However, she lived to see him
become an outlaw, and finally he was sentenced to the execution
chamber. Her son broke her heart with his wicked life, and
she often regretted the day she refused to say, "Not my will, but
Thine be done."

We went to our classmate's funeral service, and I remember
that my heart was touched when a man sang, "Safe in the Arms
of Jesus." I knew that all was well with Donald. But most of
all I remembered from that day to this that I must always live
before God with a humble and yielded spirit, no matter what He
sends in life.

May we ever be able to say with Mary of old, "Be it unto me
according to *thy word!*"

> *Have Thy way, Lord, have Thy way,*
> *This with all my heart I say:*
> *I'll obey Thee, come what may,*
> *Dear Lord, have Thy way!*   —G. Bennard

Don't ever put a question mark where God puts a period!

THRING'S THING

Now, then, we are ambassadors for Christ . . . .
2 Corinthians 5:20

I once read the following article in one of our local newspapers: "It is said that Professor Thring is developing the craziest things — such as a robot that will revolutionize housekeeping by doing every odious chore from ironing clothes to cleaning the oven. 'Within ten years,' says the distinguished engineer, 'we could produce a robot that would completely eliminate all routine operations around the house and remove the drudgery from human life.'"

Now whether or not this "thing of Thring's" will ever become a reality, we do not know. (I doubt it.) However, should such a dream materialize, there is one thing I am sure the "Thring" could never do. It could never take the place of a wife who truly loves the one for whom she labors. Professor Thring himself said, "Man has three brains — emotional, intellectual, and physical. The robot of the future will have a very good logical brain, but it can never have the *emotional* brain." Thring's thing then lacks the one basic element which only a human being can exhibit. As I pondered this further, I knew that Thring's creation could certainly never take the place of a Christian individual, for love to him is even more important. Without it, for instance, he would never effectively witness for Christ. A robot would lack love, compassion, and concern for lost souls. Paul declared in 1 Corinthians 13:1, "Though I speak with the tongues of men and of angels, and have not love, I am become as sounding bronze or a tinkling cymbal." It might well be possible to construct a mechanical man which could talk, but it would only be "as sounding brass" — there would be no love motivating it. Yes, redeemed men and women will always have to witness. As our testimony for Christ is not only a responsibility but a blessed privilege, I'm glad that nothing can replace us in carrying on that activity, aren't you?

> *Lord, speak to me, that I may speak*
> *In living echoes of Thy tone;*
> *As Thou hast sought, so let me seek*
> *Thy erring children lost and lone!*—F. Havergal

Love and kindness have converted more sinners than zeal, eloquence, or learning!

December 15

MY SAVIOR FIRST OF ALL

And they shall see his face; and his name shall be in their foreheads. Revelation 22:4

During a recent flight from Chicago to Tampa, I noticed a family on board who apparently had never been to Florida. The excitement of the two children was especially evident. That day the land surface was obscured by clouds most of the way, but as we began our descent, the plane finally broke through the overcast. At the first glimpse of the ground below, the mother of the family exclaimed to the two little tykes seated beside her, "Bobby, Mary, quick, look, that must be Florida!" The following moments of silence were broken by the young lad's voice as he piped up, "But Mamma, where are the palm trees? Where are the coconuts? I can't see them!" The small boy's conception of Florida immediately brought to mind those typical items, and he wanted to see them first of all.

Christian, as you anticipate your arrival in the Heavenly City, what do you want to see first of all? The hymnwriter puts it this way: "O the dear ones in Glory, how they beckon me to come, and our parting at the river I recall; to the sweet vales of Eden they will sing my welcome Home, but *I long to meet my Savior first of all.*" Yes, it will certainly be wonderful to greet our loved ones who have gone on before. My, what a thrill to visit with the saints of old and how exciting to see the "many mansions" in the Father's House. And yet, as delightful as all of this will be, our first thought of Heaven and our greatest desire should concern the Lord Jesus Himself; for He is the One who made it possible for us to go there. Yes, *"I long to meet my Savior first of all!"*

When my lifework is ended, and I cross the swelling tide,
When the bright and glorious morning I shall see;
I shall know my Redeemer when I reach the other side,
And His smile will be the first to welcome me.—Crosby

Death for the Christian is gain because it means: holiness, happiness, HIM! Hallelujah! —Leona Hertel

THE CRITICS

And there were some that had indignation within
themselves, and said, Why was this waste of the
ointment made?   Mark 14:4

Sooner or later everyone travels the road of criticism. The greater the life, the nobler the endeavor, the more certain is this consequence. The apostle Paul was often unjustly condemned; the disciples were sinfully described as "drunk" at Pentecost; and men even accused our perfect Lord of being demon possessed. In the story related in Mark 14, a woman graciously lavished a very precious box of ointment upon the Savior; yet some were offended and found fault with her. Jesus, however, defended the action, saying, "Let her alone. Why trouble ye her? *She hath wrought a good work on me!*"

Few people criticize in love, most are vindictive and cruel and act very superior. In fact, it is not very wide of the mark to say, *"Criticism is frequently pride in action!"* The acid test of Christian character is this: *can you take it?* can you labor without reward and receive unjust censure without bitterness? If so, God will be pleased, and will bless your life with His joy!

To guarantee flawlessness in his publication, a printer hired two proofreaders. However, they did not get along, and were constantly criticizing each other's efforts. In the course of time, one came across some words in a manuscript which spoke of "Tabasco sauce." Never having heard of Tabasco, he supposed the author must have meant *tobacco;* so he changed the first word. When the second proofreader came to the same phrase and saw *"tobacco sauce,"* he immediately reasoned that such was utterly unthinkable. He therefore proceeded to make a seemingly rational correction by changing the second word. Imagine the consternation of the author and the publisher when the story appeared referring to the use of *"tobacco juice"* on food—instead of "Tabasco sauce." It goes to show that we do not always know what the other fellow is thinking, and it behooves us not to be over-critical, lest we ourselves be misunderstood.

> *I find it is a splendid thing,*
> *Just try it and you'll see,*
> *To keep from criticizing folks,*
> *Let each "I" look at "ME"!* —Anon.

Remember, you can't raise yourself by lowering somebody else!

"THE TRUTH AND NOTHING BUT . . ."

He that speaketh truth showeth forth righteousness,
but a false witness, deceit.   Proverbs 12:17

We have heard much in recent days about a "credibility gap." The cry is raised everywhere, *"Tell it like it is!"* In this day of sham and pretense, folks want to hear the truth, and are looking for integrity.

"One of the striking traits in the character of General Grant," writes an unknown author, "was his absolute truthfulness. He seemed to have an actual dread of deception. One day while sitting in his bedroom in the White House where he had retired to write a message to Congress, word of an unscheduled visitor was brought in by a servant. An officer, seeing that the Chief of State did not want to be disturbed, said to the attendant, 'Just tell him the President is not in.' Overhearing the remark, General Grant swung around in his chair and cried out, 'Tell him no such thing. I don't lie myself, and I don't want anyone else to do so for me.'"

This matter of honesty involves our *hands* as well as our *lips.* Parents who would merit the confidence of their children must both speak and do that which is honorable. Ministers who lead their congregations upward to heights of spiritual maturity are those who not only "speak the truth in Christ, and lie not" (1 Tim. 2:7), but who also set good examples by their lives. Employers too should be truthful in their promises and conscientious in "delivering the goods." If the world is to believe a Christian's testimony, he must be found trustworthy in all things. Therefore let us not only *speak the truth,* and nothing but the truth, but also *provide for honest things* "in the sight of the Lord" and "in the sight of men" (2 Cor. 8:21).

> *"Provide things that are honest"—*
> *Let this now be thy creed;*
> *Then shall thy words be truthful*
> *And love mark every deed.* —Bosch

In regard to honesty—what you DO speaks so loud people can't hear what you SAY!

Read Matthew 6:25-34 December 18

THE SIN OF ANXIETY

*. . . For your heavenly Father knoweth that ye have
need of all these things.* Matthew 6:32

Of all God's creatures, only people are full of worry concerning
the future. Animals show no indication of this inner tension. A
few years ago in one of its bulletins, the United States Public
Health Service declared: "No fox ever fretted because he had
only one hole in which to hide. No squirrel ever died of anxiety
over the possibility that he should have laid up more food for
winter. And no dog ever lost any sleep over the fact that he had
not enough bones laid aside for his declining years." In a way
it isn't fair to use this argument to praise animal behavior, because such creatures do not have the intelligence it takes to be
a worrier. However, the fact remains that to engage our more
fertile brains with such anxious care is both foolish and sinful.
It is foolish for the Christian because it doesn't help the situation, and it is sinful because all anxiety is practical atheism, a
lack of genuine trust in God. Jesus pointed out that we have
a Heavenly Father who provides for birds and lilies, and that He
places a far greater value upon us than upon them. Therefore,
the antidote to anxiety is *a childlike trust in God* which enables
us to live one day at a time. We are not to be heedless about
tomorrow, but we are to be free from undue concern over it.

Unfortunately, the more a person possesses of material blessings, the more prone he is to worry. I have seen emaciated Hai-
tian Christians smile with genuine gratitude when given only a
small portion of grain. Even when supplies are meager, they do
not faithlessly worry about tomorrow's food. However, their
American brothers and sisters in Christ are frequently overanxious
and concerned about whether they will be able to live on a pen-
sion they expect to receive *forty years hence!*

Are you a "worrier"? Confess it as sin — as unbelief — and start
trusting. Remember, ". . . your heavenly Father knoweth that ye
have need of all these things."

> *For all His children, God desires*
> *A life of trust, not flurry!*
> *His will for them each day is this:*
> *That they should trust, not worry!* —Anon.

**Have you ever noticed that "I" is always found in the center
of anx-I-ety?**

THE WORK THAT ABIDES

Then I looked on all the works . . . my hands had wrought, and . . . all was vanity. . . . Ecclesiastes 2:11

No atheist has expressed the utter emptiness of life from the view of naturalism better than Bertrand Russell. He wrote: ". . . Man is the product of causes which had no prevision of the end they were achieving. His origin, his growth . . . are but the outcome of accidental collocations of atoms. No heroism, no intensity of thought and feeling, can preserve an individual life beyond the grave. All the labors of the ages, all the devotion, . . . all the noonday brightness of human genius, are destined to extinction in the vast death of the solar system. . . ."*

In view of such a philosophy of life, we are not surprised that the following news release appeared in one of our dailies: "Just before his 97th birthday, Bertrand Russell made a public confession, and penned this sad conclusion in the third volume of his autobiography, 'My work is near its end, and the time has come when I can survey the whole of it.' Then he said — somewhat out of character for a man who has seldom conceded anything — that *much of what he had done had been useless!"* Contrast those words with the testimony of the apostle Paul. Writing to Timothy, he exclaims, "The time of my departure is at hand. *I have fought a good fight,* I have finished my course, *I have kept the faith;* henceforth there is laid up for me *a crown of righteousness . . ."* (2 Tim. 4:6-8). Note these two careers — a famed philosopher who glumly views much of what he has done as useless, and the persecuted apostle Paul who triumphantly anticipates a "crown of righteousness!"

The lesson is clear: labor not for the food which perisheth (John 6:27); *do the work that abides!*

> He does not pay as others pay,
> In goods that perish and decay;
> But this is sure, let come what may,
> Who does God's work—will get God's pay! —Anon.

Unless we sow good seed, our fruit will be "sour grapes."

* **Mysticism and Logic,** New York, p. 45.

IN MY SHOES

. . . we have . . . an high priest who . . . [is] touched
with the feeling of our infirmities.   Hebrews 4:15

Some contemporary lyrics go like this, "Before you abuse, criticize, or accuse, *walk a mile in my shoes!*" Now that puts it rather straight, doesn't it? Our sympathy with the suffering and the downtrodden is usually limited by the absence of similar experiences of our own. There are times when we cannot enter into the peculiarities of another's sorrow, nor they into ours; but there is One who can! "For we have not an high priest who cannot be touched with the feeling of our infirmities, but was in all points tempted like as we are, yet without sin." He knew what it was to be hungry, tired, penniless, misunderstood, slandered, and hated without a cause. It was He who said, "Foxes have holes, and birds of the air have nests, but the Son of man hath not where to lay his head."

"[He] was *in all points* tempted." What soothing balm for the troubled spirit! What strength for the failing heart! The hymnwriter J. B. Mackay wrote, "Is there anyone can help us— one who understands our hearts when the thorns of life have pierced them till they bleed; one who sympathizes with us, who in wondrous love imparts just the very, very blessing that we need? Yes, there's One, only One! The blessed, blessed Jesus, He's the One! When afflictions press the soul, when waves of trouble roll; and you need a Friend to help you, He's the One!" Yes, He has "walked a mile in our shoes." With complete confidence we may come to His throne of grace. There is not the faintest possibility that He would not understand. He does! *He has walked this road before us!*

Can we find a friend so faithful
  Who will all our sorrows share?
Jesus knows our every weakness—
  Take it to the Lord in prayer.—Scriven

Jesus knows and He alone can supply the grace each trial needs!

THE REAL PERIL

For the love of money is the root of all evil.
                    1 Timothy 6:10

I have often heard people say, *"Money* is the root of all evil."
They think it is a Scriptural quotation, but they are leaving out
an important word. The Bible emphasizes that it is the *love* of
money that is the real peril, and both rich and poor are in
danger of falling into this sin. However, the tendency to this evil
is more prevalent in areas of affluence. Most Christians in Haiti,
for example, live in abject poverty. It is common to see children
with swollen abdomens and spindly legs — the result of a protein
deficiency. Many emaciated adults are slowly dying from various
diseases acquired because of malnutrition. Yet the believers there
have smiling faces, and are content if they can secure one meal
a day. They appear to be far more happy than many rich Americans who are being destroyed because of their love of money.
Sandy Turnbull, a 15-year-old son of missionary parents, upon
visiting the United States was impressed by the material riches
of our country, and on the other hand by the prevailing discontent. He said, "To me, everyone in America seemed rich and
fat — yet unhappy."

Thousands in Haiti are turning to the Lord. Having been
there, I can testify that I have never seen Christians who radiate
more joy. They do not look for earthly riches. In fact, many of
them do not know if they will have even one meal tomorrow,
but they are assured of God's love and of their eternal destiny.

What is your attitude toward "things of earth"? Remember,
money and earthly possessions in themselves are not good or bad.
It is your attachment to them that really counts. An undue affection for them is sure to bring spiritual loss.

> *Lord, I care not for riches,*
> *Neither silver or gold;*
> *I would make sure of Heaven,*
> *I would enter the fold.*   —Davis

The poorest man is he whose only wealth is money!

SOMEBODY FORGETS

. . . do good and . . . forget not . . . . Hebrews 13:16

The following story emphasizes a much-neglected and yet need-ful truth. "A little boy, living in the most poverty-stricken section of a great city, found his way into a gospel meeting and was soundly converted. Not long afterward, someone tried to shake his faith by asking him some puzzling questions. 'If God really loves you, why doesn't someone take better care of you? Why doesn't He tell somebody to send you a better pair of shoes?' The boy thought for a moment, and then said, as the tears rushed to his eyes, 'I guess He does tell somebody, and somebody forgets!'"

While it is true that the believer's primary obligation is to "preach the Gospel" and see people saved, I'm afraid that some-times we use that as an excuse to escape our responsibility to do good and to communicate or share (Heb. 13:16). We need to keep our spiritual balance and not forget to ". . . do good unto *all men* . . . " (Gal. 6:10), thus demonstrating our faith by *our works* (James 2:18). If unbelievers, who know not the Lord, are so conscious of the needs of their fellow men, how much more should we who bask in the love of God desire to supply the wants of others. Of all men, we who have experienced the Lord's saving grace and the bountiful provisions of His faithfulness should have loving compassion, seeking to relieve the suffering and lift the burdens of those who are less fortunate.

Proverbs 3:27, 28 admonishes, "Withhold not good from them to whom it is due, when it is in the power of thine hand to do it. Say not unto thy neighbor, Go, and come again, and tomorrow I will give, when thou hast it by thee."

When God lays a needy person upon your heart, and there is something you should do for him, may he never say concerning you, "somebody forgot!"

> *Somebody did a golden deed,*
> *Proving himself a friend in need;*
> *Somebody sang a cheerful song,*
> *Brightening the sky the whole day long.*
> *Was that somebody you?* —John R. Clements

Good received blesses much—good imparted blesses more.

INDESTRUCTIBLE BOOK

Forever, O Lord, thy word is settled in heaven.
Psalm 119:89

Wycliffe's version of the Bible is prefaced by a very significant illustration of a fire that is rapidly spreading. A number of individuals, including the devil and one named "Infidelity," are trying to devise methods of extinguishing it. False ecclesiastical leaders in their red jackets are also active. Try as they will, they are not succeeding in their efforts to put out the fire. Finally one suggests that they make a united effort to blow it out. There they are with inflated cheeks and extended lips, blowing at the flames with all their might. The only result is that they run out of breath. The fire cannot be extinguished. This vividly illustrates the vitality and enduring nature of the Scriptures!

Believers may put great confidence in the Bible which over the centuries has not succumbed to the attacks of Satan or the changing philosophies of the age. Men cannot destroy the *Word* of God any more than they can destroy the *God* of the Word.

A man may make a will, but it can be broken by unscrupulous legal maneuvers and greedy relatives. However, the Bible, which is the revelation of the *Divine Will* to man, is forever settled in Heaven. To destroy that Word, man would have to storm the ramparts of Glory and drive the omnipotent God from His throne. The Psalmist said, ". . . thou hast magnified thy word above all thy name" (Ps. 138:2). If others prove false and their promises fade with the passing day, you may look with confidence to the faithful Word. It forever stands sure!

> *The Bible stands though the hills may tumble,*
> *It will firmly stand when the earth shall crumble;*
> *I will plant my feet on its firm foundation,*
> *For the Bible stands!*   —Lillenas

The Bible is the only visible object that is eternal! (See Mark 13:31.)

THE REJECTED SAVIOR

> . . . *the world knew him not. He came unto his*
> *own, and his own received him not.* John 1:10, 11

I have often watched the faces of children waiting to be selected in a "choose-up" game, and observed the inner torment of
those picked last or nearly so. Sensing how they must feel, I
always tried to go out of my way to show a bit of special attention to them, realizing their need of encouragement. As a
pastor, too, I often seek to help people who are deeply pained
because they believe no one really cares for them. It hurts to
be rejected!

The Lord Jesus understands perfectly what it means to be
thus humiliated. Although the Creator and Sustainer of the universe, He entered the human race by being born in a stable, for
men found no room for Him in the inn. He grew up in a humble home and in a despised village where His own brothers misunderstood Him. The religious leaders too hated Him; and
finally when He was arrested and placed on trial, His own disciples forsook Him and the multitude loudly clamored for His
death by crucifixion.

The words, "He came unto his own" (John 1:11) really mean,
"He came home." The Lord Jesus entered the world He had
created to rescue fallen men; yet those with whom He was most
intimately associated cruelly refused to accept Him. Their hatred
was closely connected with our Savior's grief, for the prophet
Isaiah said, "He is despised and rejected of men, a man of sorrows, and acquainted with grief . . ." (Isa. 53:3).

Christian, do you feel unwanted and set aside by others? Take
comfort in the knowledge that Jesus loves you and understands
how you feel. He knows and is sympathetic because *He too experienced rejection!*

> *He was despised and His own did reject Him,*
> *Weighted with sorrow, acquainted with grief;*
> *Now His heart bleeds for the sorely afflicted,*
> *And in His grace He gives wondrous relief.* —O.B.

**He who rejects Christ invites his own doom, but he who re-
ceives Him embraces eternal life!**

GOD MANIFESTED IN THE FLESH

For God, who commanded the light to shine out of darkness, hath shone in our hearts, to give the light of the knowledge of the glory of God in the face of Jesus Christ.   2 Corinthians 4:6

A little boy, who was frightened because of the lengthening shadows in his room, called for his mother. She told him he should never be afraid in the dark because "God is here with you." "Yes, I know," responded the child, "but I want some-one with a face!" The little fellow did not intend to be sacrilegious, but was simply expressing a deep longing of the human heart. It is hard to conceive of God as infinite Spirit, but it is easy to picture the Lord Jesus Christ when we pray or reflect upon Him. Even Plato, the pagan philosopher, had declared that he hoped one day to see God walk down the streets of Athens. The desire of the youngster who wanted "someone with a face," and of the Greek philosopher who wished God to reveal Himself in *human form,* was realized when the Baby Jesus was born in Bethlehem's manger.

Some people were privileged to behold the glory of God in the face of the little Babe at Bethlehem. For instance, the shepherds returned from visiting Him "glorifying and praising God for all the things that they had heard and *seen* . . ." (Luke 2:20). The aged Simeon held the forty-day-old Infant in his arms and said, "Lord, now lettest thou thy servant depart in peace . . . for mine eyes have *seen* thy salvation" (Luke 2:29, 30).

Although we can no longer behold Him physically, for He is now in Heaven, down through the centuries thousands have received Christ by faith. God has become real to them because they know He is like Jesus, who is so aptly described for us in the Gospels. Many others, however, have refused to believe the wonderful Christmas story. Blinded by Satan, they have rejected the Savior. We who know Him should earnestly pray that during this season of the year many sin-blinded eyes may be opened by the Holy Spirit to see that Jesus is indeed God manifested in human form!

The FOOL said in his heart, "There is no God," but the WISE MEN found Him in a house!

CHRISTMAS IS FOR EVERYONE!

. . . she . . . gave thanks . . . unto the Lord, and spoke of him to all . . . who looked for redemption. Luke 2:38

The tragic commercialization of Christmas has caused some adults to become so overwhelmed with activity that they feel it is a time of happiness only for children. While this may be true in the secular sense, it does not apply to the real meaning of the season. The birth of Jesus should fill the hearts of everyone with joy; for the aged and the young, the wealthy and the poor, the strong and the weak all need the salvation He came to provide.

One of those most thrilled by the promised Messiah's arrival was an aged widow. She had lost her husband and the physical bloom of youth; yet she kept on believing, continued to worship, and never ceased to pray. Entering the temple one day, she saw the Baby Jesus in the arms of Simeon. She instantly knew that He was the Christ and immediately gave fervent thanks to God.

Certainly the coming of Jesus Christ into the world is good news for children. It tells them that God has provided for their redemption from sin, and promises them that the Lord will be with them throughout their lives and forever. But it is also a wonderful event for adults. It assures them that they need not fear death, because our Savior came, paid the price for sin, and destroyed the power of the grave. The young should therefore take their eyes off the tinsel and toys of Christmas to praise God for the gift of His Son, and the aged should likewise give "thanks . . . unto the Lord." Let us all become less occupied with the gifts, the activities, and the expenses of the Christmas season, and pause to reflect upon the One who came to save us.

> *Jesus my Savior to Bethlehem came,*
> *Born in a stable to sorrow and shame;*
> *O it was wonderful—blest be His name!*
> *Coming for me, for me!*   —A.N.

Though Christ a thousand times in Bethlehem be born, it will avail you nothing unless He is born in you!

SEPARATED—NOT ISOLATED

*I pray not that thou shouldest take them out of
the world.*   John 17:15

Having spent considerable time on a deserted island, a ma-
rooned sailor was overjoyed one day to see a ship drop anchor in
the bay. A small boat came ashore and an officer handed him
a bunch of newspapers. "The captain suggests," said the officer,
"that you read what's going on in the world, and *then let us
know if you want to be rescued!*" The Christian has no such
choice. We have been placed by divine decree in the midst of
this world of trouble, sin, and distress. When God saved our
souls by His grace, He could have transported us immediately
into Heaven. At times we push the "panic button" as Elijah
did and cry, "It is enough! Now, O Lord, take away my life."
However, it is God's purpose that we should remain in the
world — not to be partakers of its evil deeds or to compromise
with its iniquity, but to be display cases of His grace. Where
we have *sinned against Him,* we are now left to *serve Him.*

God does not push us hurriedly into some Christian "compound" the moment we are saved any more than He removes us
from the world itself. We are to be a separated people, but not
an isolated one. Jesus prayed, "Keep them from evil." The Christian is to "keep [himself] unspotted from the world" (James 1:
27) and be an example of holiness. Sanctified by His Word we
are to be both a "salt" and a "light" here where there is so much
corruption and darkness.

Isolation would mean losing contact for witness; but *separation*
from evil will result in a pure and powerful testimony.

O to keep unspotted from the world today,
This is now my goal, to walk the "Jesus" way.
On I go not fearing, heeding His command,
Witnessing and "shining"—doing all to "stand"!—Bosch

**God put the church in the world, but it is Satan who seeks to
put the world in the church.**

"ROADS TO NOWHERE"

Thou wilt show me the path of life. Psalm 16:11

In the middle of the nineteenth century, Ireland experienced a terrible famine. The government put thousands of men to work to pay for the food that was apportioned to them. The projects were not carefully planned, and therefore many were kept busy digging roads which seemed to have no destination. A playwright, depicting this, tells of a little boy who came home one day and said to his father, "Dad, they're makin' roads that lead to nowhere!"

Isn't this exactly what the non-Christian world is doing? It is constructing humanistic concepts of life — viewing man as merely an animal with no purpose and no eternal goal. As a result, many live without considering God and their moral responsibilities to Him. They squeeze a few fleeting moments of pleasure out of a life that has little meaning or design, but find no true satisfaction.

Of course, no person is actually on a road "that leads nowhere." The man who hates the Gospel may deny the reality of Hell, telling himself he is on a pathway that will end in complete oblivion. One day, however, when he must meet God unprepared, he will realize his tragic mistake. But then it will be too late! Believers know their Maker placed them on earth for a reason, and that He has a glorious future planned for them. Therefore, seeking to grow in grace and in the Lord Jesus Christ, they look forward to the new heavens and the new earth (2 Pet. 3:13, 18).

Friend, there is "a path of life" to Glory! Are you on that upward way, or are you treading the downward road that leads to destruction?

> Then I bid farewell to the way of the world,
>   To walk in it nevermore;
> For my Lord says "Come," and I seek my home,
>   Where He waits at the open door.   —Pounds

Living without God means dying without hope.

MISREPRESENTATION OF FACTS

Why art thou cast down, O my soul? . . . Hope
thou in God.   Psalm 42:5

Martin Luther said that at one time he was sorely vexed by his own sinfulness, by the wickedness of the world, and by the dangers that beset the church. One day he saw his wife come to breakfast dressed in mourning clothes. Surprised, he asked her who had died. "Don't you know?" she replied. *"God in Heaven is dead."* "How can you talk such nonsense, Katie?" Luther said. "How can God die? He is immortal, and will live through all eternity." "If you do not doubt that," she said, "why are you still so helpless and discouraged?" Luther must have been brought up short by his wife's remark, just as the Psalmist scolds himself for his discouragement. Enemies had pressed in upon him. They had said tauntingly, "Where is thy God?" Under their cruel oppression he had started to act as if the Lord had left him. He remembered wistfully a bygone day of blessing in "the land of Jordan" (v. 6). The dread disease of melancholy then began to take its toll upon his behavior. His life became a misrepresentation of the facts; for in truth the Almighty had *not forsaken* His servant.

Circumstances may alter our feelings, but they should never be allowed to cause us to act contrary to what we *know* is true from reading the Scriptures. How dare we give the impression that God is dead! *Gloomy Christians are a misrepresentation of the facts!* His promise is true, "I will never leave thee nor forsake thee." As you walk through the temporary shadow, do not doubt your Lord; but with the Psalmist say, "Hope thou in God; for I shall yet praise him, who is the health of my countenance!"

> *O my soul, why art thou grieving;*
> *Why disquieted in me?*
> *Hope in God, thy faith retrieving;*
> *He will still thy refuge be!* —Psalter

Man was not made to DOUBT, but to ADORE!   —Young

JEWELS FOR THE KING'S CROWN

*And they shall be mine . . . in that day when I
make up my jewels.*   Malachi 3:17

Many years ago there was found in an African mine the most
magnificent diamond in the world's history. It was presented to
the King of England that it might blaze in his royal crown.
Because it was still in a rough uncut state, it had to be sent to
an expert lapidary in Amsterdam. He took the gem of priceless
worth, studied it for weeks under a microscope, made drawings
and models of it, and discerned its lines of cleavage in the mi-
nutest detail. Then cutting a notch into it, he struck it sharply
several times with a special instrument; and lo, two lovely jewels
lay in his hands. These were put upon the grinding wheels and
further prepared until two perfect, radiant gems emerged, far
more precious than the original uncut stone. These were fit now
for the king's diadem. The hard blows and the buffing process
were all planned and skillfully executed to make them superbly
beautiful.

Someday our Lord will return from Heaven to joyously col-
lect His "jewels" that they may shine with undimmed luster in
the kingdom of His Father (Dan. 12:3; Matt. 13:43). In this
life, therefore, God in wisdom often puts us upon the grinding
wheel of sorrow that He may begin the necessary "shining up"
process that His "rough gems" require. If we will just remember
that the blows of trial and the rasping irritations of disappointment and frustration are adding to our "preciousness," we will
take such adversity with holy joy and unwavering faithfulness.

Are you one of God's "precious jewels"? Then do not be surprised if you are experiencing trials, for only thus can God polish
you so that you will better reflect the light of His glory.

> *Like the stars of the morning,*
> *His bright crown adorning,*
> *They shall shine in their beauty,*
> *Bright gems for His crown!* —Cushing

**God's jewels, gathered in grace and polished by pain, are des-
tined for His diadem!**   —Bosch

"EBENEZER"

> . . . *[he] called [it]* . . . *Ebenezer, saying, Hitherto*
> *hath the Lord helped us.*   1 Samuel 7:12

As we come to the close of another year, we must confess that
we have often failed to live up to our high calling in Christ Jesus.
The one thing that cheers our heart, however, is that *God has
never gone back on His promises or deserted us!* With Samuel of
old we can exclaim, "Ebenezer . . . Hitherto hath the Lord helped
us!" His mercies, they fail not; they are "new every morning."
God's loving presence, His providential hand, His certain promises, and His eternal Word have accompanied us on the pilgrim
journey; therefore we fear not the unknown morrow. Comforted
and warmed by His Holy Spirit, encamped round about by angel
bands of protection, we walk the desertland of this world confidently; for we know that by grace we shall eventually reach the
blessed "Canaan" of His promise. We do not fear to enter the
new year, for we shall remain under the watchful eye of Him
who has helped us hitherto!

Well has the poet written: "I know not whether dark or bright
this year shall be; I only know He giveth light, and I can trust
His love and might who leadeth me. I know not what this year
may bring to those I love; but I can sweetly rest and sing beneath
the shadow of His wing, here or Above. I know not whether
short or long my life may be, but naught He chooses can be
wrong; and He shall be my strength and song now and eternally!"

Knowing that God is "the same yesterday, today, and forever,"
we can carry His "Ebenezer blessing" into the future as a comforting staff on which to lean as we face the uncertainties of a
new year!

> *Hitherto the Lord hath blessed us, guiding all the way;*
> *Henceforth let us trust Him fully, trust Him all the day.*
> *Hitherto the Lord hath loved us, caring for His own;*
> *Henceforth let us love Him better, live for Him alone!*
> —F. R. Havergal

**We do not know WHAT the future holds, but we go forth con-
fidently knowing WHO holds the future!**

SCRIPTURAL INDEX